Kay Levinson

MARC LEVINSON

The Great A&P and the Struggle for Small Business in America

Marc Levinson is a former finance and economics editor of *The Economist* in London. He spent a decade as an economist at a New York bank and served as senior fellow for international business at the Council on Foreign Relations. His articles have appeared in *The Wall Street Journal*, *Newsweek*, *Foreign Affairs*, and *Harvard Business Review*, among many other publications. His book *The Box: How the Shipping Container Made the World Smaller and the World Economy Bigger* was short-listed for the 2006 Financial Times and Goldman Sachs Business Book of the Year Award.

ALSO BY MARC LEVINSON

The Box: How the Shipping Container Made the World Smaller and the World Economy Bigger

Guide to Financial Markets (*Economist* Series)

Beyond Free Markets: The Revival of Activist Economics

After Reagan: Confronting the Changed World Economy (with C. Michael Aho)

The Great A&P and the Struggle for Small Business in America

MARC LEVINSON

Hill and Wang
A division of Farrar, Straus and Giroux
New York

The GREAT A&P *and the* STRUGGLE *for* SMALL BUSINESS *in* AMERICA

Hill and Wang
A division of Farrar, Straus and Giroux
18 West 18th Street, New York 10011

Distributed in Canada by D&M Publishers, Inc.
Printed in the United States of America
Published in 2011 by Hill and Wang
First paperback edition, 2012

The Library of Congress has cataloged the hardcover edition as follows:
Levinson, Marc.
The great A&P and the struggle for small business in America / Marc Levinson.
p. cm.
Includes bibliographical references and index.
ISBN 978-0-8090-9543-8 (hardcover : alk. paper)
1. Great Atlantic & Pacific Tea Company. 2. Supermarkets—East (U.S.)—History. 3. Grocery trade—United States—History. I. Title. II. Title: Great A and P and the struggle for small business in America.

HD9321.9.G7L48 2011
381'.45641300973—dc22

2011003811

Paperback ISBN: 978-0-8090-5143-4

Designed by Jonathan D. Lippincott

www.fsgbooks.com

1 3 5 7 9 10 8 6 4 2

This is an independent work of scholarship and is not endorsed by The Great Atlantic & Pacific Tea Company.

To my father

CONTENTS

The Great A&P and the Struggle for Small Business in America

1
THE VERDICT

Judge Walter C. Lindley was no one's idea of a flaming radical. Born in 1880 in the village of Neoga, deep in the corn and soybean country of south-central Illinois, Lindley had a reputation as a scholar: at a time when many learned the law as apprentices rather than as students, he earned not only a law degree but also a doctorate in laws from the University of Illinois. In Danville, a commercial hub 150 miles south of Chicago, he became a man of prominence. He built a law practice, won a seat on the city council, and became an attorney for Joseph Cannon, who served eight years as the ironfisted Speaker of the U.S. House of Representatives and represented Danville in Congress for almost half a century.

Lindley was a Republican, and shortly after Warren G. Harding, the great friend of business, became president in 1921, he named Lindley to the federal bench. As a judge, he drew more than his share of high-profile cases. In a 1929 jury trial that held Chicago rapt, Lindley's court convicted sixteen candy wholesalers of terrorizing storekeepers who refused to buy their candy. Two years later, he upheld the near-dictatorial powers of the commissioner of major-league baseball, Kenesaw Mountain Landis. In the early 1930s, he oversaw the restructuring of the collapsed utilities empire of the Chicago entrepreneur Samuel Insull and survived an attempt by Insull's henchmen to have him impeached by Congress. Suggested as a possible nominee to the U.S. Supreme Court in 1929, during Herbert Hoover's presidency, Lindley was not beyond criticizing that court and, by implication, the Democratic administration of Franklin Roosevelt. In 1939, he commented acidly that for some new Supreme Court justices, "precedents may be of little avail and their lack no bar."[1]

On a sunny Saturday in September 1946—the federal courts worked six days a week back then—Lindley issued what would be the most controversial decision of his long judicial career. Before a crowded courtroom on the second floor of Danville's post office, he declared that George L. Hartford, eighty-one; John A. Hartford, seventy-four; their company, the Great Atlantic & Pacific Tea Company; and other company executives had conspired to violate the Sherman Antitrust Act. The fact that the secretive Hartford brothers, two of the wealthiest men in America, were deemed criminals was startling, but their crime was truly remarkable. Rather than being accused of acting like monopolists to keep prices artificially high, the Hartfords were found to have done the opposite. They and their company, Lindley declared, had acted illegally in restraint of trade by using A&P's size and market power to keep prices artificially low.[2]

The victims of this unorthodox conspiracy were not families that purchased groceries. The evidence before Lindley's court made clear that prices at A&P were below those at the competition; as John A. Hartford himself had testified nearly a year earlier, "We would rather sell 200 pounds of butter at 1 cent profit than 100 pounds at 2 cents profit." While selling food cheaply was good for consumers, it was bad for the hundreds of thousands of retailers, wholesalers, and manufacturers who needed high food prices in order to make a living. *U.S. v. A&P* was the climax of decades of effort to cripple chain stores in order to protect mom-and-pop retailers and the companies that supplied them. The Hartfords' real crime was to have endangered mom and pop.[3]

But it was the participants, not the legal issues, that made the Danville trial so notorious. The Great Atlantic & Pacific Tea Company was not just another grocery chain. It was, by a wide margin, the largest retailer in the world. Its footprint stretched from coast to coast, covering thirty-nine of the forty-eight states and parts of Canada as well. It collected more than ten cents of every dollar Americans spent at grocery stores. It was an enterprise so familiar that millions of Americans knew it as "Grandma," so ubiquitous that when John Updike penned a short story about the eternal boredom of teenage life a few years later, he called it simply "A&P." Its influence over America's lunch boxes and dinner tables was so overwhelming that when an ambitious young Florida grocer decided to lower prices at his tiny store, he received one piece of advice: "Don't make A&P mad."[4]

A&P was at the center of a bitter political struggle that lasted for nearly half a century—a struggle that went far beyond economics. At its root were competing visions of society. One vision could be described with such words as "modern" and "scientific," favoring the rationalism of cold corporate efficiency as a way to increase wealth and raise living standards. The other vision could fairly be termed "traditional." Dating to Thomas Jefferson and his contemporaries, the traditional vision harked back to a society of autonomous farmers, craftsmen, and merchants in which personal independence was the source of individual opportunity and collective prosperity. The words of Judge Lindley's ruling against the Hartfords and A&P embodied the conflict between those two visions. "To buy, sell and distribute . . . one and three-quarter billion dollars worth of food annually, at a profit of one and one-half cents on each dollar, is an achievement one may well be proud of," he acknowledged, in a nod to the modern vision. Yet this achievement, he decided, ran afoul of the Sherman Antitrust Act by making it hard for smaller firms to compete with A&P. "The Sherman Act," he ruled, "was intended to secure equality of opportunity." Equality of opportunity could not be secured if big firms were allowed to pummel the small.[5]

There may never have been a more improbable pair of convicts than the Hartfords. The elder of the brothers, George L. Hartford, was as predictable as they come. He lived in the same house for half a century and took rooms at the same New Jersey shore resort every summer. He left home at 9:05 every morning, wore a black suit with stiff collar to work every day, and made a point of tasting the company's coffees at 2:00 each afternoon. His hobbies, when he was a younger man, were repairing cars and building crystal radios, activities that required him to utter hardly a word to anyone; in later years he did jigsaw puzzles. Few employees ever laid eyes on the man known throughout the company as Mr. George. The minutes of meetings of A&P's top executives rarely cite his words. One of the few journalists to meet him said he could be taken "for a retired Polish general—bulky, stolid, rumpled, with a foreign air that his American drawl immediately belies." No one who encountered him on the street would have imagined that he headed one of the largest, most powerful enterprises in the world.[6]

John A. Hartford, his younger brother, had an entirely different personality. A dapper dresser who favored custom-tailored gray suits, Sulka bow ties, and pocket squares, he enjoyed traveling, visiting stores, and pressing the flesh. In his thirties and forties he had raised horses that won prizes at the National Horse Show, a premier event of New York society. He lived in an eight-room suite at the Plaza Hotel and lunched alone on milk and crackers at the Biltmore. On weekends he commuted to his suburban estate, a Tudor mansion with a nine-hole golf course, stable, and polo field, and in the winter he went to The Breakers in Palm Beach. He was married three times, twice to the same woman and, in between, to a woman who came into his life modeling clothes for his wife. It was Mr. John's job to motivate employees, spreading the company's paternalistic management gospel through philosophical missives that often referred to "my brother and I." In the 1930s, when A&P's political troubles became life-threatening, John A. Hartford reluctantly became the company's public face, sporadically meeting with the press, putting his name to the occasional folksy article, and making end-of-year pronouncements about the outlook for food prices in the months ahead.[7]

The brothers' distinct personalities were displayed in the way they ran their company. Mr. George was cautious, favoring a rock-solid balance sheet, wanting each store and each product to pay its own way, distrusting new ideas. Mr. John was more aggressive, more open to new ideas, but always insisting that lower prices would make more money by bringing more customers in the door. The brothers met each morning to discuss the smallest details of their business, from the price of canned tomatoes to the profitability of the stores in Pittsburgh. They made a formidable team. It was Mr. John who engineered the company's remarkable expansion in the 1910s, its climb to be the first retailer to sell $1 billion of merchandise in a single year in the 1920s, and its quick conversion from grocery stores to supermarkets in the 1930s. It was Mr. George who kept A&P solvent.

The Great Atlantic & Pacific lay at the center of both men's lives. Neither ever worked anywhere else. Neither attended a day of college; in fact, neither finished high school. They learned business on the job, from their father, who ran the company before them and gave them meaningful responsibilities when they were still in their teens. They treated the company as their family, almost never dismissing employees, creating one of the first company pension plans, and shortening working hours simply because they could afford to do so. All managers had moved up the ranks, and almost every executive had worked at A&P for decades. Because they completely controlled the company, with no shareholders to please and no creditors to satisfy, they could run A&P however they wished, and they sometimes ran it in ways that drove their more short-term-oriented managers to despair.

George and John Hartford were in the grocery trade at a time when selling food was an activity of enormous economic importance. There were literally grocery stores on every corner: in 1926, Kansas City, by no means the most densely populated of American cities, had 30 food markets per square mile. The first national survey, in 1929, found 585,980 food stores—one for every fifty-one American families. Richard Nixon, a future president, grew up working in his family's grocery in Whittier, California, in the 1920s, and the family of Lady Bird Johnson, a future first lady, sold groceries from a general store in Karnack, Texas. These mom-and-pop stores were serviced by a thick web of suppliers. The United States boasted 13,618 wholesale distributors of groceries in 1929, or one wholesaler for every forty-three food retailers. This wholesale network, in turn, distributed the products of nearly sixty thousand canneries, sugar-beet mills, slaughterhouses, soap factories, and other plants making everything from brooms to baking powder. Mom and pop ran many of these operations, too. The typical food plant had fewer than fifteen workers.[8]

In 1920s America, every town of any consequence had its grocers, its food brokers and wholesalers, its bottling plants and flour mills. These enterprises provided a tax base for their communities, a cadre of owners and managers to serve as civic leaders, and a major source of jobs. Just the retail side of the food business provided livelihoods for 1.2 million workers on the eve of the Great Depression, many of them self-employed proprietors. Food retailers, wholesalers, and processors together engaged one out of every eighteen nonfarm workers in the entire country—more than apparel and textile factories, iron and steel plants, coal mines, or even railroads.[9]

Americans paid a high price to support this balkanized system for conveying food from farm to table. Food was hugely expensive, relative to wages. The average working-class family in the 1920s devoted one-third of its budget to groceries, the average farm family even more. Most households spent more to put dinner on the table than for their rent or their mortgage. And for the average housewife, shopping for food consumed a large part of the day. This money, time, and effort bought plenty of calories, but only moderate amounts of nutrition. With neither display space nor refrigeration, many neighborhood stores carried only token stocks of fresh fruits and vegetables. Fresh fish and poultry were rarities. The poorest third of American households consumed a sorely inadequate daily intake of vitamins and minerals, because there was little of either in the food that their neighborhood shops had for sale.[10]

The Great Atlantic & Pacific did much to destroy this world. The Hartfords were among the most rigorous managers of their day. At a time when many grocers consulted self-help books to figure out how to price their goods, the brothers pored over data to fine-tune operations, closing this store, relocating that one, dropping a product whose sales languished, adding another that promised better margins. They totally reshaped their business at least four times. At its peak, their company owned nearly sixteen thousand grocery stores, seventy factories, and more than a hundred warehouses. It was the country's largest coffee importer, the largest wholesale produce dealer and butter buyer, the second-largest baker. Its sales were more than twice those of any other retailer. Their basic strategy was so extraordinarily simple it could be captured in a single word: volume. If the company kept its costs down and its prices low, more shoppers would come through its doors, producing more profit than if it kept prices high.

The Great A&P transformed the humble, archaic grocery trade into a modern industry, but its relentless expansion posed a mortal threat to a sector of the economy upon which so many families and communities depended. Those mom-and-pop grocers, local wholesalers, and small manufacturers understood the threat full well, and they fought back with a vengeance. The Hartfords were in no sense robber barons, yet they became the most controversial, and most reviled, American businessmen of the first half of the twentieth century. Had Mr. George tuned his crystal radio to America's most widely heard station in the 1920s, he would have heard diatribes against the "childless brothers" who monopolized food retailing. When Senator Huey Long warned in 1934 that "about ten men" have "chained the country from one end to the other," he was talking about Mr. George and Mr. John. When a lawyer working for the administration of Franklin Roosevelt called the country's largest retailer "a gigantic blood sucker," there was no question he had the Hartfords in mind: it was he who convinced Judge Lindley to convict them.

A contemporary of the Hartfords, the economist Joseph Schumpeter, coined the phrase "creative destruction" in 1942 to describe the painful process by which innovation and technological advance make an industry more efficient while leaving older, less adaptable businesses by the wayside. For the economy as a whole, creative destruction is enormously beneficial, permitting a shift of labor and capital from sectors where less is required into areas where new products and services are in demand. It is precisely such shifts that make economies grow. For many individuals and many communities, on the other hand, creative destruction is painful, entailing business restructuring, job elimination, and the disappearance of companies and industries that have provided the economic base for a particular town or an entire region. Whatever its advantages, economic change inevitably leaves major losses in its wake.[11]

When creative destruction brings layoffs to autoworkers or closes coal mines across an entire region, the world pays close attention. When it means the closure of a family-run grocery store or the replacement of a failing supermarket by another store down the street, though, creative destruction does its work unremarked. This invisibility reflects the sheer lack of drama in the retail trade: a shuttered store leaves no gargantuan machinery standing idle, no angry workers milling around outside a padlocked gate. The building, torn down for parking or converted to some other use, will quickly fade from memory. The workers will be expected to find other jobs wherever they can. Displaced industrial workers, tough, rugged, and usually male, are presumed to have had important dreams and plans tragically destroyed by the vagaries of economic change and to merit public sympathy. Displaced grocery clerks rarely get such respect.

That neglect speaks to the prejudices of social thinkers of many ideologies. Thomas Jefferson, along with his contemporaries in the Enlightenment, saw special merit in the toil of the farmer, but very little in the work of the merchants who dealt in the farmer's produce. Karl Marx and Friedrich Engels judged that the course of history would be shaped in vast factories by workers engaged in physical production; the labor of the merchant, they wrote, "is not labor that creates value." Their near contemporary William Graham Sumner, one of the most influential American social thinkers of the late nineteenth century but decidedly no Marxist, fully agreed with their point. "Wealth comes only from production, and all that the wrangling grabbers, loafers, and jobbers get to deal with comes from somebody's toil and sacrifice," Sumner wrote.[12]

The effect of economic change on store owners occasions particular ideological confusion. After all, the independent grocers displaced by the growth of the Great Atlantic & Pacific were capitalists, even if their capital was only a few hundred dollars. Their wives, by extension, were capitalists, too, even if being capitalists did not absolve them from twelve-hour days totting up purchases and keeping the books. When larger competitors undercut their prices and decimated their businesses, these small-time capitalists received neither sympathy nor a mention in the unemployment statistics. They simply vanished.

In the first half of the twentieth century, the Hartfords turned their company into one of the greatest agents of creative destruction in the United States. Although shifts in the way the world buys food are far less heralded than innovations such as cars and computers, few economic changes have mattered more to the average family. Thanks to the management techniques the Great A&P brought into widespread use, food shopping, once a heavy burden, became a minor concern for all but the poorest households as grocery operators increased productivity and squeezed out costs. The proportion of workers involved in selling groceries plummeted, freeing up labor to help the economy grow. And the company's innovations are still evident in the supply chains that link the business world together. Although the Hartfords died decades before the invention of supercenters and hypermarkets, they employed many of the strategies—fighting unions, demanding lower prices from suppliers, cutting out middlemen, slashing inventories, lowering prices to build volume, using volume to gain yet more economies of scale—that Walmart's founder, Sam Walton, would later make famous.

The bitter political and legal battles surrounding the Great Atlantic & Pacific Tea Company were limited to North America, but they presaged similar conflicts around the globe. Under Japan's "big store law," in force from the 1970s, anyone seeking to open even a modest supermarket had to gain local competitors' approval by paying them compensation. West Germany protected mom-and-pop retailers in 1956 by allowing stores to open only from 7:00 a.m. to 6:30 p.m. Monday through Friday and until 2:00 p.m. on Saturday; a worker with a daytime job was essentially forced to patronize grocery stores and butcher shops near home or workplace because there was no time to shop elsewhere. In France, a 1973 law to aid artisans and small merchants restricted the opening of large stores and prohibited manufacturers from selling more cheaply to big merchants than to small ones. Everywhere, the complaint was the same as it had been in America: the unchecked growth of large retailers threatened the traditional role of local merchants and destroyed opportunities for economic independence.[13]

Such restraints faded toward the end of the twentieth century, in part because consumers demanded lower prices, in part because as working hours grew more diverse, more people needed to shop at nontraditional times. Yet the century-old battle between independent merchants and large retailers was by no means over. In the United States and Western Europe, critics of "industrial food" advised consumers to avoid the processed goods at the supermarket and purchase locally grown foods from farmers and independent retailers; the Hartfords' great achievement, making food affordable, was now looked upon with disdain. Merchants' protests led Thailand's government to halt expansion by grocery chains in 2006. In 2010, the Czech Republic required minimum price markups in order to keep chains from undercutting mom-and-pop stores—precisely the same obstacle A&P confronted in the United States in the 1930s.[14]

The Hartfords' enterprise did not prosper without its founders. Within a few years of their deaths, the once-mighty A&P was a basket case, staggering from one failed strategy to another as better-run companies passed it by. Soon enough, the company that had decimated independent stores by the thousands became a victim of the creative destruction it had once meted out. But while A&P's fortunes waned, the economic forces it helped unleash only grew stronger. It made the process of moving goods from producer to consumer impersonal and industrial, but also cheap and efficient, a job for the big, not for the small.

2
THE FOUNDER

In their later years, after they became immensely wealthy and exceedingly controversial, George L. and John A. Hartford allowed certain legends to grow up around the family business. "Back in the year 1859, a little store opened its doors on Vesey Street, New York," the official company history recounted. "This was the first store of the great chain of grocery stores now operated by the Great Atlantic & Pacific Tea Co. George H. Hartford, the Founder, had a vision—the hope of a great national business." In some tellings, George H., the visionary entrepreneur and father of George L. and John A., was claimed to have been the company's first president, the creator of the first of the great chains that would soon dominate American retailing. An even more elaborate version credited George H. with starting the great enterprise by acquiring an entire shipload of tea in 1859 and selling it to the deserving public at 70 percent off the going price.[1]

Those legends, and much else that has been written about the Hartfords and their powerful company, are at best misleading, if not simply false. The story of how an obscure tea-store clerk and two of his sons would come to run the most admired, and reviled, business in America is more improbable, if less heroic, than the myths.[2]

The founder was not George H. Hartford but George Francis Gilman, a man destined to become one of the more bizarre characters in American business history. Gilman, born in Maine in 1826, could trace his ancestry back to the *Mayflower.* His father, Nathaniel Gilman, had become wealthy as a privateer and embargo runner during the War of 1812, and became involved in New York's booming leather industry in 1834, when he came to sell a cargo of African hides and formed a partnership with a young tanner and leather merchant named Thomas

Smull. New York was the center of U.S. leather manufacturing, and the fetid alleyways of the neighborhood known as the Swamp, just two blocks east of City Hall, were lined with tanneries soaking and pounding imported hides into leather. Gilman, Smull & Company was soon among the largest hide and leather dealers in New York. Nathaniel Gilman, a newspaper wrote later, "was a queer individual, a daring speculator, a taciturn, secretive trader."[3]

Over time, much of the tanning process, with its noxious fumes and poisonous runoff, was moved upstate, near supplies of hemlock or oak bark used to make the tannic acid that rendered hides soft and flexible. New York City's erstwhile tanners turned themselves into merchants, buying hides at the docks, storing them, sending them off to be made into leather, and marketing the finished leather to boot and shoe manufacturers. Dozens of leather merchants were located cheek by jowl along Beekman, Spruce, Gold, and Frankfort streets and two alleys, known as Ferry and Jacobs streets, that had been cut to provide access to tanneries built on interior lots. Gilman's partnership with Smull ended around 1845, but by the early 1850s Nathaniel Gilman and three of his sons had three leather warehouses in the Swamp and owned tanneries northwest of the city.[4]

Their father's dynastic dreams abruptly came undone when Nathaniel Gilman Jr., the heir apparent, died in 1853 at the age of thirty-eight. Nathaniel Gilman & Son was dissolved, finally allowing George Gilman, then twenty-seven, to strike out on his own. In 1858, he erected a five-story brick building at 98 Gold Street for his own leather firm, Gilman & Company. His father died in December 1859, leaving an estate worth a million dollars and a tangle of claims and counterclaims that would take nearly half a century to resolve.[5]

George Gilman entered the tea trade sometime in late 1859 or early 1860. Evidence suggests that by then he was working with not one Hartford but two: George Huntington Hartford and George's younger brother, John S.[6]

George H. and John S. Hartford grew up in modest circumstances in Augusta, Maine, just twenty miles from George Gilman's birthplace in Waterville. George Huntington Hartford was born in 1833, seven years after George Gilman. John Soren Hartford was born around 1836. Their parents kept a boardinghouse and ran a livery stable, among other ventures. The 1850 census found the brothers boarding together in Boston, working as shop clerks. After further travels, the young men surfaced in St. Louis in 1859, working for the local office of George F. Gilman's hides and leather business at 31 South Main Street.[7]

The official corporate version of the Great Atlantic & Pacific's founding has George Hartford spending two years in the leather trade in St. Louis, then moving to New York to become a clerk in Gilman's business. Several aspects of this rendition are noteworthy. First, it places George H. Hartford alongside George Gilman at the birth of the tea company that would grow to become the world's largest retailer. Second, it mentions John S. Hartford not at all; the younger brother does not register in any history ever published by the company. Third, the official company history has George H. Hartford moving from St. Louis to New York to work with George Gilman in 1859. The historical record confirms none of these points. The first published reference to George Gilman's tea business, in June 1860, mentioned John S. Hartford but not George. Census takers counted both Hartford brothers at the family home in Augusta in June 1860, but John S. was listed as a "merchant" with a personal estate worth $500, whereas George H. gave his profession as "Box Maker" and claimed no assets—a hint that John, although younger, was the more established. And even if George H. Hartford did move to New York to work with Gilman in 1859, Gilman had no tea shop or other business on Vesey Street in that year. In 1860, Gilman & Company, "Importers of Tea," was operating at the same address, 98 Gold Street, at which Gilman had dealt hides. For a year or two, Gilman may have run the tea business and the hide business simultaneously.[8]

Why did George Gilman start dealing teas and coffees alongside hides? The simplest answer is the most likely. Trading hides could not have been a particularly pleasant vocation. His father's death left Gilman wealthy, and there is no question that he aspired to a higher status in New York's increasingly stratified society; he would shortly be the owner of three carriages, two watches, one piano, and a house on Lexington Avenue in the newly fashionable Murray Hill neighborhood. Working around piles of filthy cattle and goat skins would not have suited his pretensions at a time when New York's capitalists were distancing themselves from the physical labor performed in their firms. The tea trade, which usually involved dealing in coffee as well, was altogether more pleasant and prestigious, and offered opportunities to interact with some of the city's most influential merchants.[9]

Dealing in tea and coffee drew on many of the skills and connections Gilman would have developed as a hide dealer. Like hides, tea and coffee arrived by ship; in New York, hides were second only to coffee in terms of import value in 1860. Gilman would have known his way around the docks, and would have had experience with the commission merchants who received and distributed imports. He would have been familiar with the biweekly *Shipping and Commercial List* and the daily *Journal of Commerce*, both of which were filled with intelligence about shipping and commodity trading; indeed, it was not unusual for seven or eight merchants to offer calfskins, salted goatskins, and buffalo hides on the *Journal of Commerce*'s dense front page. Undoubtedly, he would have known that tea consumption had soared since 1843, when China opened additional ports to U.S. trade. By 1860, an average of one vessel a week was arriving in New York from China. Clipper ships frequently made the run in less than three months, assuring that the tea, packed in lead-lined chests, arrived fresh. And Gilman would have been quite aware of the great public fascination with tea that began in the late 1850s, when leading magazines devoted long articles to tea plantations in distant China, the raucous tea markets of India, and the elaborate Asian rituals of tea drinking. George Gilman was certainly not the only merchant to notice these things: New York, which received 90 percent of U.S. tea imports, had some seventy-five tea dealers in 1860.[10]

Some New York tea merchants were willing to sell in small quantities to individual consumers. Among them was J. Stiner & Company, America's first known chain retailer, which operated several tea shops. The main business of most tea merchants, though, was wholesaling. In some cases, an arriving tea cargo would be offered privately to a merchant, who would inspect individual leaves, taste the tea, and make an offer for hundreds of chests. In other cases, the cargo would be offered for auction one chest at a time. The merchants who bought the imports, in turn, sent samples to representatives in other cities, who would show the teas to retailers or to wholesalers serving smaller towns nearby.[11]

The business was arduous at a time when communications between cities were still poor; the New York dealer might have sold out of a proffered tea by the time an order arrived by post from Buffalo or Cincinnati, or local market conditions might have made the New Yorker's price expectations unrealistic, requiring a further exchange of correspondence before a sale could be arranged. Tea merchants typically extended thirty to ninety days' credit to their customers, and when payment finally arrived, it usually took the form of a draft on a distant bank that the New York merchant would have to sell at a discount to bankers on Wall Street. Customers faced risks, too. Merchants were known to ship tea that was not identical to their samples, that was adulterated with sawdust, or that was not the variety it was claimed to be. Consider this proposition from a sales representative in Boston to a tea merchant in New York: "I fear the Souchong will not sell @22¢ at present or as long as good Congo or Souchong is selling at 18¢. If you will have it labelled Ningyung, I think I could sell it better."[12]

By the time George Gilman entered the tea and coffee business, the established merchants were facing competition from a new type of wholesale distributor, the jobber. Although the distinction was not precise, jobbers generally had less capital and operated on a smaller scale than the better-established wholesalers, filling one-off orders from retailers rather than cultivating long-term relationships with wholesalers in other cities. Gilman may have begun as a jobber. He undoubtedly had the necessary capital, and he would have been very comfortable with the requisite wholesale wheeling and dealing. In 1861, he decided to concentrate entirely on tea and coffee, apparently turning his remaining leather interests over to his brother Winthrop. The substantial building George Gilman had erected at 98 Gold Street in 1858 was not appropriate for a tea company: polite New Yorkers would not have wanted to shop for teas and coffees amid the tanneries and stables of the Swamp. At some point between June 1860 and May 1861, Gilman & Company relocated to rented quarters at 129 Front Street. George H. Hartford later claimed to have joined Gilman around this time. As for John S. Hartford, we know only that he is said to have returned to Maine and died there in 1863. No extant records mention him in connection with the business after 1860.[13]

Front Street, where Gilman & Company made its new home, ran parallel to the East River waterfront. South Street, along the water, was lined with four-story brick buildings occupied by shipping companies, importers, and exporters. Sailing ships docked so close that their prows reached almost into second-story windows, and the street was choked with horses, handcarts, passengers buying steamship tickets, and barrels and bags of cargo. Front Street, just a block away, had an entirely different atmosphere. Almost every one of the brick structures from Whitehall Street, at the south end, to the Fulton Market, at the north end, was occupied by the counting room and warehouse of a provisions merchant. These men dealt in the tea and coffee, whiskey and sugar, salt pork and lard arriving on the piers, storing the goods in their warehouses before sending them by ship to customers in other cities or, in the case of grains and cotton, to buyers in Europe. Sturges, Bennett & Company, one of the city's biggest tea and coffee dealers, was at 125 Front Street, two doors down from Gilman & Company, and John Scrymser, another tea and coffee dealer, was across the street at number 126. The Front Street merchants did business with one another on a daily basis and also traded flour and grains at the rooms of the New York Corn Exchange, on South Street, so having their establishments in close proximity was a great convenience.[14]

Gilman & Company would not have stood out among the hundreds of food merchants on Front Street in 1861. It was far too small to merit much attention from the five largest provision dealers, who were said to "run the works," manipulating prices. Neither Gilman nor anyone from his firm was involved in 1860 when important produce merchants formed the New York Commercial Association to construct a proper exchange building. Gilman was not among the 204 merchants and shipping executives who subscribed to the stock offering used to acquire a square block at Water and Whitehall streets and erect an impressive brick edifice. Some twelve hundred people paid the $20 fee to become members when the New York Produce Exchange opened for business on April 22, 1861, including men from at least sixty-five firms with addresses on Front Street, but there was no one from Gilman & Company. The exchange, where trading opened at 10:00 a.m., six days a week, and closed with the sounding of a gong at 1:00 p.m., did not trade coffee or tea, and Gilman apparently had no interest, yet, in sugar or other commodities.[15]

Nothing, beyond the Front Street location, is known of Gilman's business in 1861 and 1862. The imposition of steep import duties in 1862 to finance the Civil War, fifteen cents per pound of tea and four cents per pound of coffee, probably hurt profits; coffee imports collapsed, and much of the available supply was purchased by the U.S. government, which is unlikely to have patronized dealers as small as Gilman & Company. Even if the firm was prospering, it was doing so on an extremely small scale. George H.'s role during those years is as mysterious as the firm's performance. The New York postmaster Abram Wakeman, who claimed to have known Gilman well at the time, recalled that the Front Street store was run by one Alex. Davidson. Hartford did not earn a mention in Wakeman's memoir.[16]

Whatever the case, being a tiny tea dealer did not satisfy George Gilman's ambitions. After taking a couple of years to learn the business, he struck out on a radical course, establishing himself as a marketer of no small genius. First came a new name. At some point between June 1861 and early 1863, Gilman & Company became the Great American Tea Company—a startling departure from the universal practice of merchants putting their names on their businesses. The Great American banner was soon attached to five different storefronts selling tea and coffee, and Gilman identified himself as both a "retail dealer" and a "wholesale dealer" when paying his federal income tax. By 1863, the company office and warehouse had moved to the five-story brick building at 51 Vesey Street that would later become part of the foundation myth. The Vesey Street location, on the Hudson River side of the island, was just steps from Washington Market, a large produce market, in an area crowded with housewives and servants making their daily purchases of food.[17]

In the most nontraditional departure of all, Gilman began to advertise massively. The company's first known advertisement appeared on May 27, 1863, in *The New York Herald*, announcing, "The Great American Tea Company's New Wholesale Tea House no 51 Vesey street, N.Y." That initial foray into marketing promised that Great American would sell to wholesale customers at a profit of two cents per pound. Three days later, Gilman took out three separate advertisements in a single column of the *Herald*. "The organization of the Great American Tea Company of New York, created a new era in the history of retailing tea," one proclaimed, as if Great American were a brand-new undertaking rather than an ongoing concern. The advertisements promised teas at "old prices, without the duty," and repeated a phrase that was to become a staple of Great American's advertising for years to come: "ALL TEAS sold at TWO CENTS PER POUND PROFIT."[18]

Unbranded tea, sold loose by the pound as "black tea" or "imperial tea," was one of the most profitable items sold by grocers all over the country. Gilman's new strategy was to go directly after that market. By July 1863, Great American was advertising in newspapers outside New York, soliciting both wholesale and retail purchases and—in a frontal assault on the established distribution system—publishing the prices at which it would sell various grades of teas and coffees. The days when the sales representatives of New York merchants could hope to extract an extra cent or two per pound from customers ignorant of market conditions were numbered; Great American touted roasted coffee for thirty-five cents per pound and best-quality young hyson tea for a dollar. "The Company are determined to undersell the whole TEA trade," one advertisement declared.[19]

George H. Hartford had the good fortune to have signed on with a man who possessed not only big ambitions and ample capital but also a remarkable flair for marketing. Gilman was a promoter in the mold of P. T. Barnum, the showman whose famed American Museum, located in lower Manhattan from 1841 to 1865, was a veritable laboratory for testing methods of persuading Americans to part with their money. Drinking tea and coffee was a long-established custom, but no one had ever promoted it quite as aggressively as Great American did. Teams of coal-black horses with white harnesses crisscrossed New York, pulling delivery wagons bearing the sign "An organization of capitalists for the distribution of teas and coffees at one small profit." Even as the Civil War was at its height, Great American advertisements proclaimed, "SIGNS OF PEACE! THE WAR SOON WILL BE OVER!" and shamelessly thanked the police for maintaining order in the company's crowded stores.[20]

Exaggeration was fundamental to Great American's promotion from the beginning. A September 1863 advertisement casually ended with the line "Great American Tea Company, Importers and Jobbers," as if the company were bringing its own teas directly from China; in reality, Great American almost certainly had no agents abroad and imported nothing. The company "will open a large assortment of Teas by the *Benefactress* (the latest arrival from China)," another 1863 advertisement stated, implying that Great American had access to unique products when in fact it was buying the same varieties and qualities of tea and coffee its competitors did. As George Gilman discerned, what distinguished one dealer from another was not the merchandise but the way in which its products were promoted and sold. In April 1864, Great American announced its relocation from 51 Vesey Street to the "larger and more commodious Marble Stores" at 35 and 37 Vesey Street, a move, it explained, that was necessary to handle its large trade.[21]

The marketing task was to persuade consumers in New York and around the country that this tiny tea company was "Great," and Gilman never missed an opportunity to do so. On March 6, 1865, one month before Robert E. Lee surrendered at Appomattox, Gilman secured a prominent place in New York City's Civil War victory parade. Tens of thousands marched down Broadway, past City Hall, then up the Bowery and Lexington Avenue to Thirty-fourth Street before circling back to Union Square. The business division included a float sponsored by the Great American Tea Company. Ten white horses pulled a wagon decorated with the symbols of the thirty-six states of the soon-to-be-restored union. From atop the float, thirty-six tea-store clerks waved to the crowd, while men on horseback rode back and forth alongside. Shortly thereafter, Gilman took retail showmanship to a new level by locating his coffee roaster at Broadway and Bleecker Street in a frenzied shopping and entertainment district. The cost of renting space at this prime location left others wondering about Gilman's sanity. They need not have worried. As Abram Wakeman recalled, "Thousands of dollars could have been spent on advertising and would not have been nearly as productive as the aroma from the fresh roasted coffee at so prominent a locality."[22]

Another stroke of marketing genius followed quickly: the buying club. Advertising heavily in religious weeklies such as *The Methodist*, farm journals like *American Agriculturist*, and professional publications such as *New York Teacher*, Great American urged readers to form "clubs" and submit bulk orders by mail. Prices were one-third cheaper than competitors offered, the ads promised, and the organizer of the order would receive a free gift of tea. Great American sent a club's entire order in a single express shipment, so even after customers paid shipping costs, they could expect a fresher product at a lower cost than their local stores could offer. The ads even illustrated just how orders might be written out, easing timid consumers into the novel task of ordering their tea and coffee all the way from New York City. The company sometimes reproduced these club orders in its advertisements, both to serve as examples and to demonstrate the breadth of its customer base.[23]

George H. Hartford's role in these unusual developments will never be known for certain. The version of history long promoted by his sons credited him as the marketing genius behind the Great American Tea Company's early success, but this was likely not the case at all. Hartford described his profession successively as "clerk," then "book-keeper," then "cashier," then "treasurer," strongly suggesting that he focused on collecting money and paying bills, not on promotion. He was described later as "a quiet, dignified, gentleman, somewhat reserved in manner," "progressive, but never aggressive," "kindly, courteous, and affable"—in short, as a sober businessman, not as a close student of P. T. Barnum's.[24]

The credit for turning an obscure tea dealership into a company people noticed thus rests solidly with the founder, George F. Gilman. Gilman's drive, imagination, and flamboyance distinguished Great American from the dozens of other tea companies in New York. His unique approach to marketing made the company grow very fast. But as it expanded, with new locations, new products, and a growing volume of mail-order sales, Great American would soon outrun its founder's abilities. George H. Hartford's managerial and financial skills would become critical.

3

THE BIRTH OF THE GREAT A&P

By the end of the Civil War, the Great American Tea Company was flourishing. Sales and profit figures have not survived, but tax records show that George Gilman paid 1866 federal excise tax on an enterprise valued at more than $1 million—a considerable valuation for the time. Great American had five retail stores in New York in 1865 and had expanded to fill three buildings on Vesey Street with offices, shops, warehouses, and a plant for grinding coffee.[1]

The Vesey Street location indicates Gilman's aspiration to market to the great, and rapidly growing, middle class. In this he followed his competitors. Rather than pursuing the carriage trade, which tended to concentrate in more fashionable precincts farther uptown, he was going after the largest, most sought-after market. "Vesey street is almost filled from end to end with tea, coffee and grocery houses," the New York *World* told readers. "The competition is so brisk that some of the stores employ solicitors, who stand on the sidewalk and urge passers-by to step in and purchase, pretty much as the retail clothiers do in Chatham street. For the same reason, goods are generally sold cheaper in Vesey street than in other parts of the city." The prices were good, but the deals often were not: a professor hired by the newspaper found that Great American sold short weights of tea, adulterated its tea with willow leaves, and mixed chicory into its ground coffee—practices followed by most of the other merchants on the street as well.[2]

Gilman was a believer in what modern executives would call "image." His ceaseless promotion aimed at portraying Great American as a substantial company worthy of the consumer's trust. In April 1865, to celebrate the opening of its first shop in Brooklyn, Great American filled the entire front page of *The Brooklyn Daily Eagle* with advertisements, a practice unheard of at the time. In May 1867, the *Shipping and Commercial List*, the bible of New York importers, reported, "The recent large purchases of the GREAT AMERICAN TEA COMPANY have taken the trade by surprise." According to the paper, Great American had, in a single week, purchased two cargoes of tea worth $1.5 million, which "indicates the extensive nature of the company's business." The article shows every sign of being a plant: the name Great American appeared in uppercase letters; the newspaper's own reports showed no arriving tea cargoes corresponding to the ones Great American supposedly bought; and the purported value of the purchase was improbably large for a firm with only half a dozen stores. Those details were meant to persuade potential suppliers and customers that Great American had an "extensive" business. Gilman then reprinted the *Shipping and Commercial List* article in a fake newspaper, *The Commercial Enterprise*, which Great American handed out to customers. The front page of *The Commercial Enterprise* carried the prominent line "Entered according to an Act of Congress, in the year 1867," crafted to make the publication seem as if it enjoyed government approval. The front-page article discussed Chinese matchmaking, but the remaining three pages were pure advertising, promising "Customers can save from 50¢ to $1 per pound by purchasing their Teas of THE GREAT AMERICAN TEA COMPANY."[3]

George H. Hartford prospered along with the company. He married in July 1861, shortly after his arrival in New York. Hartford and his new wife, Josephine, moved to 52 Powers Street in Brooklyn, a short ferry commute from Manhattan. Their first daughter, Maria Josephine, called Minnie, was born a year later, their son George Ludlum in 1865. When he was called for military service in February 1865, the thirty-one-year-old Hartford, like almost all Union conscripts, avoided service by paying one of the many intermediaries that arranged substitutes; Peter Bruin, a Scottish-born merchant seaman with a "florid" complexion, joined the U.S. Navy in Hartford's stead. Hartford stayed with Great American, winning a promotion from clerk to bookkeeper and then, in 1866, to cashier, a position of responsibility. His promotions brought pay raises. Hartford reported annual income of $688 in May 1864 and $800 one year later, wages well above what a simple clerk would make, but far short of a manager's pay. In 1866, Hartford moved his family to Orange,

New Jersey, nestled at the foot of the Orange Mountains eighteen miles due west of New York City.[4]

Orange was then a bustling and diverse suburb of Newark, New Jersey's largest city. It suited Hartford because, riding the Morris & Essex Railroad to Hoboken and then catching a ferry across the Hudson River, he could reach his office on Vesey Street in under an hour. In addition to convenience, Orange had glamour and gentility. The women's rights advocate Lucy Stone had made it famous in 1857 when she declined to pay her property tax bill because women had no representation in government; the tax collector promptly sold two of her chairs, four tables, one stand, and two pictures at a widely publicized auction. Orange's leading citizen, Samuel Colgate, owner of the fast-growing New York soap and starch company started by his father, occupied a redbrick mansion called Seven Oaks on twenty-nine acres on the south side of town, and many other New York bankers and merchants called Orange home. In the summer, there was a modest resort business as families from the city came to enjoy the cool heights of nearby Eagle Rock. Yet Orange was not simply an elite suburb. It was becoming an important manufacturing town, its hat factories providing work for thousands of Irish and German immigrants. The town had a small African-American population as well. This ethnic mix would be the dominant factor in the town's political life for decades to come.[5]

The Hartfords soon moved into a sprawling house with stained-glass windows on Ridge Street, directly across from the new St. John's Roman Catholic Church. Ridge Street was on the unfashionable northwest side of town, in between the south-side estates occupied by local aristocrats like Colgate and the suburban villas going up in the carefully planned development of Llewellyn Park, a few blocks west. Shortly after moving there, George H. converted to Catholicism in the first baptism at St. John's. The Hartfords were affluent enough to have an Irish-born live-in servant, Mary Hughes. An eighteen-year-old named Mary Ludlam—perhaps Josephine's sister—also was living with the Hartfords at the time Edward, George and Josephine's third child, was born in 1870.[6]

As the cashier of one of New York's many tea companies, Hartford was not counted a particularly distinguished personage during his first decade in Orange. He does not seem to have been involved in any local civic organization. His time apparently was devoted almost entirely to the tea business, which was expanding by leaps and bounds. By the end of the 1860s, Great American had eleven shops in addition to its thriving mail-order operation. No photographs survive, but it may have been at this time that Gilman's Barnumesque showmanship was introduced into the retail stores. *The Brooklyn Daily Times*, perhaps with financial inducement, described the store at 133 Grand Street in Brooklyn as "new and magnificent," reporting that it "was literally run down with customers, and thronged until the hour of closing." The company now had more than 175 employees, and George H. Hartford, one of the earliest employees, had taken on an important role in its management.[7]

On May 10, 1869, the ceremonial placement of a "golden spike" in Promontory, Utah, completed one of the most difficult engineering feats of the age, the transcontinental railroad. America went mad with enthusiasm. Previously, the trip from the East to California meant months of uncomfortable travel by wagon train from Missouri or by sea around the tip of South America. Now the journey took only a few days by rail. George Gilman, never one to miss a marketing opportunity, figured out how to profit from the nationwide celebration of the new link between the Atlantic and the Pacific. In 1869, he launched a new business, the Great Atlantic & Pacific Tea Company. It was destined to become the biggest retailer in the world.[8]

The Great Atlantic & Pacific Tea Company was a most unusual sort of venture. It presented itself in its first advertisements, in the autumn of 1869, as an entirely new business, "an organization of capitalists for the purpose of Importing Teas and distributing them to Merchants throughout the country at Importer's prices." Its connection to the Great American Tea Company was a closely guarded secret. Great American solicited mail orders at 31–33 Vesey Street, Great Atlantic & Pacific at 8 Church Street—and it took a bit of detective work for the historian Roy Bullock to ascertain that these were two different addresses for a single corner building. George H. Hartford maintained the charade for decades, contending that he became associated with the Great Atlantic & Pacific when it began in 1869, when in fact Great Atlantic & Pacific was simply a front for an enterprise with which he had worked much longer. Someone in Hartford's household told a census taker in 1870 that he was "with Great American Tea Company," one more indication that Great Atlantic & Pacific was not a distinct company. Nor is it true, as A&P later claimed, that the Great American Tea Company was renamed the Great Atlantic & Pacific Tea Company in 1869. Coffee and tea drinkers continued to order by mail from Great American until well into the twentieth century.[9]

The Great Atlantic & Pacific Tea Company was what was later called a "banner," not a company. Gilman's motivation for starting it is uncertain. One reason may have been to fend off imitators. The Great United States Tea Warehouse at 30 Vesey Street, directly across the street from Great American, initiated advertisements much like Great American's, promising low prices to customers who formed buying clubs and ordered by mail. Bertram, Bradford & Company at 26 Vesey Street advertised the fixed prices at which it would sell tea to small-town wholesalers, just as Great American did. Gilman's marketing strategy, which had been distinctive in the early 1860s, was routine by the end of the decade, and he needed to find a way to stand out in a crowded marketplace. He also seems to have believed that his firm could generate more sales by appearing in various guises. Two further Gilman fronts, Consumers' Importing Tea Company and Centennial Tea Company, were soon soliciting mail orders. None of the four Gilman tea dealerships ever disclosed its link with any of the others.[10]

The widely advertised creation of the Great Atlantic & Pacific Tea Company threatened established interests in the tea trade, and they reacted strongly. On September 15, 1869, within a few weeks of the new entity's birth, one Professor John Darby launched *American Grocer* as a newspaper for the grocery business. Almost immediately, the publication went on the attack against George F. Gilman's supposed dominance of the tea business. "One man in particular, with a dash of intellect, has broken through the conventionalisms of contracted ideas which fast bind others in the line, and has far outdistanced all competitors," *American Grocer* wrote. This individual, who was not named by the newspaper but was almost certainly George Gilman, "has purchased in one morning no less than thirty-six thousand chests of tea for his parcel agencies and retail counter trade." This claim is highly improbable, implying that Gilman acquired 9 percent of all U.S. tea imports for 1869 in a single day, but exaggeration served the purpose of raising alarm. The newspaper declared itself on the side of "the masses of the trade," and promised to teach readers how to do a better job of selling tea so families will not "send to monster establishments in order to suit their requirements."[11]

American Grocer, of course, was not a disinterested party. Great American's advertising consistently attacked the importers, tea merchants, and wholesale grocers who extracted profits from the tea trade while delaying the delivery of fresh tea to the consumer. Those middlemen were *American Grocer*'s advertisers, whose business was being undercut by mail-order sales.

The Great Atlantic & Pacific Tea Company developed into an entirely different sort of business from its precursor. Great American's mail-order business and its eleven tea shops in New York dealt entirely in bulk teas and coffees, indistinguishable from those of its competitors. Great Atlantic & Pacific, in contrast, startled the tea trade in 1870, a few months after its creation, by launching a radically different product, a branded tea. Thea-Nectar was said to contain a unique mixture of teas that were dried on porcelain, with no coloring or impurities. Unlike other teas, which came loose, Thea-Nectar was sold prepackaged, in half-pound or pound boxes. It was supported by an unusual marketing campaign, with newspaper advertisements far larger than the standard few lines of agate type. "Thea-Nectar is a pure black tea with the Green Tea flavor," the ads proclaimed. Unlike any other tea on the market, Thea-Nectar was exclusive, available only from the Great Atlantic & Pacific Tea Company.[12]

A brand-name tea was an extraordinary product to bring to market in 1870. At the time, consumers had access to few branded products of any sort, save patent medicines. Almost everything offered in grocery stores, from flour to pickles, was purchased by the shopkeeper in bulk and sold from barrels or canisters, with the store clerk measuring out the quantity the customer desired. The widespread sale of brand-name foods in sealed packages was still two decades in the future. It was only in 1870 that Congress enacted a law allowing businesses to register and protect trademarks such as Thea-Nectar—and when it did so, advertisements announced that "the Great Atlantic & Pacific Tea Company have secured by congress the exclusive right to sell in this country, Thea-Nectar," distinctly implying that its product enjoyed some special imprimatur. With his branded tea, George Gilman was once again on the leading edge of a revolution in marketing.[13]

And once again, the reaction from those threatened by Gilman's marketing prowess was swift. In the autumn of 1870, *American Grocer* published a four-part article purporting to reveal the truth about the "unprincipled monopolists" seeking "to control the vast retail business throughout the country." Without naming names, *American Grocer* dissected a Great Atlantic & Pacific advertisement claiming that company representatives visited the tea-growing districts of China and Japan to oversee the selection and curing of the choicest teas. In fact, said the newspaper, it had found no record of this company ever importing a single cargo of tea. "By diligent inquiry, we have ascertained that this Company never personally visited any tea district except that in the immediate vicinity of Wall and Water streets of this city, and the auction sales where damaged teas are disposed of." Fewer damaged teas are coming to auction than in the past, *American Grocer* claimed; instead, these "wet and damaged teas" are bought directly from importers for as little as seven cents a pound, "and afterward dried, colored and repacked, and sold to the consumer for ninety cents." The result, the newspaper claimed, was "to draw away the trade which rightfully belongs to the retail merchant in the different towns where these teas are sold."[14]

Some of those allegations almost certainly were true. There is no evidence that Great American and Great Atlantic & Pacific imported anything during this period, much less that they had "correspondents in China and Japan," as their advertisements stated. As Abram Wakeman recalled later, Gilman bought most of his teas through the New York house where Wakeman worked. The claim that Gilman sold adulterated teas is credible because adulteration was extremely common, but there is no reason to think Gilman's teas were notably less pure than those offered by the wholesalers advertising in *American Grocer.* If the teas were inferior, customers seem not to have noticed. Yet if its complaints about the quality of Gilman's products were exaggerated, *American Grocer*'s grasp of the implications of his business strategy was insightful. "If this can be done so successfully with teas . . . it can be done in other lines of goods of universal demand," the newspaper warned. On that score, the newspaper would soon be proved right.[15]

Around 1871, Gilman unveiled yet another innovation in marketing: the premium. Chromolithographs—mass-produced colored pictures—had been invented in the 1830s, and after the Civil War they became wildly popular in America, decorating many kitchens and parlors. Great American and Great Atlantic & Pacific began offering chromos as gifts with every purchase of tea or coffee. When other tea companies followed suit, the competition escalated from individual chromos to series on themes such as sporting events and U.S. presidents. The wealthy sometimes framed them, the poor simply tacked them to the walls. But collecting chromos soon lost its novelty. "People do not go there [to the tea store] so much any more, and I think that probably one reason why is, that the pictures are becoming too common," wrote a Pennsylvania schoolgirl in an 1877 essay. Gilman upped the ante again, offering coupons that could be collected and redeemed for china or glassware. The coupons, soon to be known as trading stamps, would be a staple of food-store marketing for a century.[16]

George H. Hartford was almost certainly not the inspired genius behind his company's novel approach to marketing. It is likely that the new tea company, the brand-name tea, and the premium with every purchase all emanated from the mind of George F. Gilman. But in 1871, Hartford's own managerial talents finally came into public view. On October 8, fire devastated the fast-growing city of Chicago. Hundreds of people died, seventeen thousand buildings were destroyed, and food supplies were laid waste. Great Atlantic & Pacific immediately sent staff and food supplies to Chicago. Hartford, in New York, located a map of Chicago, selected a site for a store, and directed the purchase of a property at 114–116 West Washington Street. Within days, the still-hot bricks were removed and the Great Atlantic & Pacific Tea Company opened its first store outside the New York area, accompanied by the usual flamboyant marketing. The Russian grand duke Alexis was touring the United States at the time, attended by great publicity. Ahead of Alexis's arrival in Chicago on December 30, the Great Atlantic & Pacific advertised, "Go where you can see Alexis" and "The Grand Duke will be most happy to receive his friends at no. 114 West Washington street." According to company lore, so many customers flooded in that the rear wall had to be knocked out to make more room. Those who managed to squeeze inside and purchase tea received a "splendid tinted lithograph" of the grand duke.[17]

The Chicago store was so successful that Gilman and Hartford decided to expand aggressively. By 1875, the Great Atlantic & Pacific had tea and coffee stores in sixteen cities as far-flung as Boston and St. Louis. Each was inaugurated with flair. To celebrate the opening of a "magnificent" store in Boston, aglitter with crystal chandeliers, eight "richly harnessed" black horses pulled a wagon laden with 125 chests of tea through the city's snow-clogged streets. The team and wagon traveled to store openings in seven other New England cities; in each, onlookers were invited to guess the ensemble's weight in hopes of winning $500 in gold. By May 15, when the official weighing determined that the horses, cart, and tea chests weighed 11,122 pounds, some fifty thousand people had entered the competition. Great Atlantic & Pacific was not the first retail chain, but it was the first retailer with a presence across much of the country. No other retailer of the time went to such efforts to make its presence widely known. But while promotional gimmickry remained important, running a company spanning much of the country required exceptional organizational skills. Now George H. Hartford's talents as a manager came to the fore.[18]

The year 1878 was to be a turning point in the fortunes of the Hartford family. Within the span of a frenetic six weeks, George H. Hartford was catapulted into an improbable political career and then took full control of the tea company where he had worked for nearly two decades.

Orange, where the Hartford family had lived since 1866, was known for rough-and-tumble politics dominated by a fractious Democratic Party. In 1876, when cities throughout the land celebrated one hundred years of U.S. independence, affairs in Orange were so contentious that the mayor and the city commissioners were excluded from the local centennial parade. A few months later, in the disputed presidential election that saw the Republican Rutherford B. Hayes awarded the White House in return for promising an end to Reconstruction in the South, the Democrats allegedly swept Orange by paying paupers from the poorhouse to vote Democratic. The town's elections were usually tumultuous affairs, marked by intimidation, drunkenness, and brawling.[19]

The burning issue of the day was temperance. No issue more sharply divided Orange by class, religion, and national origin. Frances Willard, a prominent educator and a founder of the Woman's Christian Temperance Union (WCTU), a powerful nationwide organization, spoke at the First Methodist Church in 1876, and the local WCTU chapter convened frequently at Methodist and Baptist churches. Men found their own roles to play. In early 1878, some of Orange's finest citizens met at the First Baptist Church to form the Society for the Prevention of Crime, with sixty-seven people paying a steep $1 membership fee and electing Samuel Colgate, probably the town's wealthiest property owner, as chairman. Both groups campaigned relentlessly against saloons and—implicitly—against the behavior of the Irish and German immigrants, largely Roman Catholic, who saw nothing wrong with having a drink. "We cannot . . . hope to do anything toward closing the one hundred fifty liquor saloons that open upon the streets of Orange," but at least they should close on Sunday as required by state law, the WCTU wrote in its "Appeal to the Citizens of Orange." The Society for the Prevention of Crime backed a law to allow wives to forbid barkeepers to sell liquor to their husbands and, with more success, demanded that hat manufacturers sign a public pledge to keep their two thousand workers from drinking on the job. The temperance forces were closely aligned with the Republican Party, which represented the city's elite plus its small number of African-American citizens, whereas working-class white men and local shopkeepers tended to vote Democratic.[20]

In 1878, local politics took a bizarre turn. Mayor Henry Egner, a Democrat, declined to run for a fourth one-year term after the state legislature refused to allow the mayor to receive a salary. When the city's Democratic convention met on March 9, three days ahead of the March 12 election, it could find no candidate for the unpaid job. The local Republicans had no better success; their convention's choice rejected the nomination, and four other men then turned it down. Both parties scrambled to find candidates. A group of Democratic leaders called on Hartford and asked him to run. The reason for the choice is unknown, but Hartford would have bridged the town's factions: as an officer of a sizable company he would have appealed to Orange's business elite, while as a Catholic he would have drawn support from the Irish and German immigrants who strongly opposed Prohibition. After initially declining, he accepted the nomination on Monday, March 11. The following day, he was elected mayor by a vote of 932–766.[21]

The new mayor was a mystery to almost everyone. His name had not been mentioned in the preelection speculation about candidates. In fact, the name of George H. Hartford is not to be found in any of the surviving records of Orange's four newspapers prior to the date of his election as mayor. "We believe he has never before been a candidate for office, and was therefore unknown to a large portion of the community," reported the *Orange Journal*. Nonetheless, the rabidly Republican weekly lavished praise on the new Democratic mayor. "There is every reason to believe that the new Mayor will prove an excellent and popular officer. He is a quiet and dignified gentleman, somewhat reserved in manner, and has the reputation of a competent, careful and trustworthy man." Concurred *The Orange Chronicle*, "We have a man who although untried, and heretofore not having taken an active part in the affairs of the city, is, we have every reason to believe, a gentleman of excellent business talent and much more than average executive ability."[22]

Hartford took office two weeks later. His first task was to address the nine-member city commission. "I have been very unexpectedly called to this office," he apologized, before calling for the city to improve its schools, strengthen its police department, and establish a water supply, a goal city leaders had discussed, but failed to accomplish, for several years. The mayor's remarks, the *Orange Journal* declared, "will be satisfactory, we think, to our citizens generally, without distinction of party." Hartford's announcement that he would serve only a single one-year term, though, was not to be fulfilled. He was to serve as mayor continuously until 1890, and was repeatedly reelected without opposition.[23]

On April 15, 1878, three weeks after becoming the mayor, George H. Hartford became a partner in the Great Atlantic & Pacific Tea Company. The founder, George Gilman, had personal reasons for wishing to leave the business. In February 1877 he had retired to his estate along the Connecticut shore. Since that time Hartford had run the business day to day, meeting Gilman occasionally in New York or Connecticut.

The partnership agreement gave Hartford ownership of the partnership's assets and full management responsibilities, with the concern's bank account to stay in Gilman's name. At age forty-four, George H. Hartford assumed control of a company with $1 million in annual sales from the seventy stores of the Great Atlantic & Pacific Tea Company and the mail-order business of Great American. The partnership agreement was not put in writing, an omission that would come to cause considerable difficulty.[24]

4
THE GROCER

In 1880, at the age of fourteen, George Ludlum Hartford entered the employ of the Great Atlantic & Pacific Tea Company. He would work there for the next seventy-seven years.

George L., the eldest son and second-eldest child of George H. and Josephine Hartford, grew up in the rambling house on Ridge Street in Orange. There were now five Hartford children, including John, born in 1872, and Marie Louise, born in 1875. George H. Hartford's parents, Joshua and Martha Hartford, lived with the family for several years, as did Josephine Hartford's ailing brother, Louis, and two young servant girls. The 1880 census found the Hartfords hosting a "boarder," the English-born "salesman" John E. Clews, aged twenty-four, who would marry Minnie, the eldest Hartford child, in 1881. And from 1878, a steady stream of visitors swept through the Hartfords' parlors to confer with the mayor, providing the children with a taste of politics. One wonders whether it was his observation of his father's experience in public life that led George L. to become such a very private man.[1]

Orange had no public library and only limited educational facilities in the 1870s. School construction would become Mayor Hartford's chief accomplishment, but when George L. reached high-school age, the choices were few. Rather than sending their twelve-year-old son off to boarding school, George H. and Josephine enrolled George L. as a day student at St. Benedict's College, a recently established preparatory school just down the railroad line in Newark, in 1878. St. Benedict's offered a commercial course, but George L. attended the final two years of the school's three-year classical program. In his brief time at St. Benedict's, George demonstrated that he had a head for numbers, winning a prize in algebra. Although students in the classical program normally pursued further education, George's schooling ended with the ninth grade, in 1880, when he went to work with his father. According to one version of his poorly documented life, he started by stoking the boiler in the store on Vesey Street but was soon made cashier at a store in Newark. From then on, he would spend almost his entire career tending the financial side of the business.[2]

The company young George L. Hartford joined was no longer a small enterprise. Great Atlantic & Pacific claimed to have 150 stores in 1880, in addition to Great American, which had become entirely a mail-order business. Guided by George Gilman's flair for the extravagant, Great Atlantic & Pacific stores had developed into elaborate temples of tea and coffee, lavishly outfitted to appeal to increasingly status-conscious customers. Each store had a large red *T*, lit with gas jets, hanging over the sidewalk. Atop the door and the show windows stretched a wood panel announcing the Great Atlantic & Pacific Tea Company. Inside, beneath a pressed-tin ceiling, the walls were painted in vermilion and gold leaf, supposedly imported from China, and decorated with Chinese-style hangings. Gas chandeliers with sparkling cut-glass pendants provided bright illumination. Bins holding the many varieties of tea and coffee lined the selling floor, and packages of Thea-Nectar and ground coffee were stacked neatly behind the dark wood sales counter. Some stores even had a cockatoo, the company's early mascot, on a perch in the center of the floor. To complete the theme of exotic Asia, the cashier's station, located near the door, was shaped like a Chinese pagoda.[3]

George H. Hartford held complete managerial control over the business. There was, so far as is known, no successor to Gilman as marketer in chief, but his unorthodox marketing ideas may have been less important than in earlier times. By now, Great Atlantic & Pacific was a large-scale business, and promotional antics mattered less than conventional business skills like cost control and inventory management. This was George H.'s strength, but he had to make decisions with only rudimentary information. A store manager kept a simple ledger with two facing pages for each week. The left side listed each day's sales and the weekly total, which was also broken down into "tea" (presumably including coffee) and "sugar." The right side listed outlays, from twenty-five cents for resetting a horseshoe to the weekly salaries of $14.00 for the store manager, $10.00 for the clerk, and $3.50, probably for a boy who helped after school. The difference between receipts and expenditures, usually around $140, was remitted to the company each week. This accounting left store-level profitability unclear, as the store's reported expenses did not include the cost of goods sold.[4]

Hartford hewed firmly to Gilman's strategy of aggressive growth. By 1884, Great Atlantic & Pacific stores could be found as far west as Kansas City and as far south as Atlanta, in small towns as well as major cities. For rural customers, a network of wagon routes radiated from the stores, serving farms and villages across the eastern half of the country. A four-by-six-inch trade card of the sort widely used for advertising in the 1880s attests to the company's geographic reach. It shows a straw-hatted black man, driving his family down a dirt road in a rickety mule cart, pulling the mule up short to read a signboard proclaiming, "The Great Atlantic and Pacific Tea Co's Teas & Coffees are the best"—an indication that the company was marketing its wares even in remote corners of the South. That image, and others featuring bicyclists, baseball players, and inebriates who should have stuck to tea and coffee, may well have been selected by young George L. Hartford, who seems to have taken on such responsibility during a brief stint as a marketer in the early 1880s.[5]

Beneath the surface, though, a problem loomed. Great American and Great Atlantic & Pacific depended almost entirely on two commodities, coffee and tea. Sales of both had mushroomed after the Civil War, aided by repeal of the high tariffs enacted to finance the war. In 1864, Congress, desperate to raise revenue, had raised the duty on tea to twenty-five cents per pound—a tax roughly equal to the value of the tea itself—and the duty on coffee to five cents per pound. The tariffs were finally slashed in 1870 and eliminated in 1872, providing an enormous stimulus to consumption. In the 1870s, the average American drank one-third more tea each year than at war's end, and coffee imports set new records. This tea and coffee boom must have been highly positive for A&P, helping the company reach $1 million in sales in 1878. But in the early 1880s, prices collapsed. The value of U.S. tea imports fell 40 percent in three years as import volume dropped by one-fourth. The average price of imported coffee plummeted from thirteen cents per pound in 1880 to eight cents in 1883. Although the company tried to promote its coffee with the claim that "by their new process of roasting, cooling, etc., the flavor is retained as it is by no other process," it must still have faced the same uncomfortable economic facts as its competitors. Falling prices must have devastated all tea companies' sales and profits, including those of the Great Atlantic & Pacific.[6]

George H. Hartford seems to have responded to the tea and coffee crisis in the only sensible way: by broadening the product line.[7]

The 1880s may have been terrible years for selling coffee and tea, but they were fabulous years for selling sugar. Previously, Americans had consumed little white sugar. Its high price had made refined sugar a luxury, so most people had used brown sugar, molasses, or sorghum syrup to sweeten their drinks and preserve their foods. As tariffs fell and new technology drove down refining costs after the Civil War, refined white sugar became all the rage. U.S. imports doubled between 1865 and 1869, and then, as tariffs fell away, rose by half during the 1870s. But it was only in the 1880s that Americans fully developed a sweet tooth. Through the decade, the federal government paid growers a bounty of two cents for every pound of sugar they produced in an ultimately unsuccessful effort to create a domestic industry that could meet the soaring demand for white sugar. Average consumption went from thirty-six pounds per person in 1877 to fifty-seven pounds in 1886.[8]

Great American and Great Atlantic & Pacific began selling sugar around 1880 and had an immediate hit. Sugar would have been an easy product for store clerks to sell; they would have handled it much like coffee or tea, pouring the bulk product from large bags into shop-floor bins and then serving customers by measuring out the desired quantity on a scale. It is likely that sugar helped the company survive the downturn in tea and coffee sales that killed off some of its competitors. At the Port Chester, New York, store, sugar accounted for about one-fourth of sales in 1882.[9]

Yet George H. Hartford would have been fully cognizant of sugar's limitations. Like coffee and tea, sugar was just a commodity. Great Atlantic & Pacific's fancy red stores were selling precisely the same product as every other grocery or general store. Gaining protection from changes in commodity prices would require something special, an exclusive brand similar to Thea-Nectar. That special product seems to have been baking powder. According to company tradition, George L., still a teenager, asked a chemist why baking powder was so expensive. Young Hartford had assumed the ingredients must be rare, but when the chemist explained otherwise, George suggested to his father that the company make its own. The back of one of the buildings on Vesey Street was soon curtained off, and a chemist was hired to mix the ingredients.[10]

Baking powder was a very controversial product in the 1880s. Invented in the 1850s, it allowed bakers to produce lighter cakes and faster-rising breads. This was an important innovation in a world in which most households did their own baking, and by the 1880s Americans were using an estimated fifty to seventy-five million pounds per year. All baking powders worked by inducing a chemical reaction between common baking soda and an acid to release carbon dioxide gas into batter, but they used different types of acids. The costliest powders contained acid tartrate of potassium, known as cream of tartar, a substance derived from grape juice. Cheaper powders used phosphoric acid or alum salts containing sulfuric acid, and usually produced less carbon dioxide per tablespoon of powder. The cream of tartar interests and the alum interests waged open warfare for four decades, with each side accusing the other of making impure or unsafe products.[11]

As food safety became a prominent issue, chemists started testing the composition of baking powders and found none that were what they claimed to be. Almost all powders contained starch as filler, and many contained a variety of salts as well. Consumers were justifiably frightened. "There appears to be ample ground for requiring that the makers of baking-powders should publish the ingredients," New Jersey's dairy commissioner opined in 1888. "At present, the only guaranty of an undoubtedly wholesome and efficient article appears to be the name of the brand." George H. Hartford had reached the same conclusion several years earlier. Although the Great American Tea Company had started selling unbranded baking powder by mail as early as 1883, it was in 1885 that one-pound tins of baking powder, bearing red labels, became the first product sold under what would soon become a powerful brand name: A&P. To promote the new brand, the company printed cards carrying the endorsement of Professor R. Ogden Doremus of Bellevue Hospital Medical College. "I find on chemical analysis that your Baking Powder is composed of pure materials," the famed chemist attested.[12]

A&P Baking Powder was an important product in the history of retailing. With it, the Great Atlantic & Pacific Tea Company, and many of its competitors, began a transition from being tea merchants to being grocers. It was a transition that would dramatically change Americans' daily lives.

George H. Hartford did not race into the grocery business, because the grocery business held little prospect of profit in the early 1880s. Most Americans, even in cities, still raised at least some of their own food, growing vegetables or keeping animals. The shops where families bought what they could not raise "contained a bewildering assortment of anonymous goods," the historian H. Allen Smith wrote later. "The pickle and molasses barrels stood side by side in sullen antipathy, while the open shelves and bins were an Elysian playground for mice." The inventory was typically heavy on bulk products, such as crackers sold from a barrel, slabs of bacon hanging on hooks, a wheel of cheese beneath a glass bell, a barrel of washing powder. The produce was mainly vegetables that would stay fresh without refrigeration, such as potatoes and cabbages, along with whatever fruits and vegetables were in season locally. Each week, *American Grocer* preached to its readers, "Count, Measure, Weigh or Gauge Everything You Buy," and the same advice was applicable to shoppers: almost every item had to be sliced, poured, or spooned, then measured and wrapped in paper by the store clerk.[13]

The most important feature of grocery stores in the 1880s, from the perspective of a chain-store merchant considering the pros and cons of selling groceries, was the near-total absence of brands. Without brands, stores were limited to selling generic products indistinguishable from what was for sale down the street. Competition was based almost entirely on price: a store's advertising circular might tout molasses at sixty-five cents per gallon, leaving shoppers no way to know whether the store was offering a better deal or just a lower-quality product than a competitor with a higher price. Brands would eventually offer consumers at least the promise (often unmet) of consistency and quality. They would allow market segmentation, enabling grocers to offer higher-priced products targeted at more affluent consumers alongside lower-priced versions aimed at the mass market. Over time, brands would permit major economies of scale in food processing as national companies manufacturing millions of units of well-known products supplanted small firms making small quantities for purely local markets.

In the early 1880s, though, name-brand groceries still lay in the future. Their arrival, and the spread of retail food chains that would follow in their wake, awaited two inventions so prosaic they were quickly taken for granted: the cardboard box and the tin can.

The cardboard box was the result of an accident at the Metropolitan Paper-Bag Manufactory in New York. The paper bag had been invented to replace cotton bags unavailable during the Civil War, and Metropolitan's founder, the inventor Robert Gair, developed the earliest method of mass-producing bags printed with the name of a retailer or manufacturer. By 1878, Metropolitan's eighteen-page catalog included such offerings as oyster-fry boxes and candy boxes, all of which were meticulously folded by hand and were far too costly for general use. Early the following year, one of Gair's workers ruined a print run of paper bags by placing a rule too high above the plane of his printing form, so that instead of printing a line it cut clear through the paper. The mishap led to an inspiration: Gair realized that if he arranged blades at different heights, some could slice through cardboard to create the template for a box while others could simultaneously score the cardboard, without cutting through, where folds were required. In addition to providing a cheap, convenient form of packaging, Gair's boxes offered surfaces that could be decorated with pictures, logos, and brand names. Instead of asking the grocer for a pound of soap powder, the shopper could now request a particular variety by name.[14]

Canned goods, like cardboard boxes, were an old idea that became economical only in the 1880s. Canned goods were first used to feed Napoleon's army in 1795, and the first U.S. canning plant was established in 1819. But cans were expensive: each was made of tin pieces individually cut with shears and then soldered together, with a skilled can maker turning out a hundred cans per day. The industry got a boost from military orders during the Civil War and the start of salmon canning on the Pacific coast in 1864, and by 1870 the United States had over a hundred plants canning fruits, vegetables, fish, and oysters. The key inventions came in 1874, when two Baltimore men, A. K. Shriver and John Fisher, found alternative ways of controlling temperature to avoid explosions during the canning process. A new machine to cap cans was introduced in the mid-1880s, reducing the need for skilled cappers, and the first successful labeling machine was invented in 1893. Automation made canning cheap: one man could cook five thousand cans of tomatoes a day in 1865 but four times that many in 1894, at a lower daily wage. More than a thousand canneries were operating in 1890, and expansion was so rapid that by 1900 food processing accounted for one-fifth of all manufacturing in the United States. Cheap canning provided grocers a wide assortment of branded merchandise to sell.[15]

Cardboard boxes and tin cans appealed to a public increasingly concerned with hygiene and sanitation. The use of sealed containers alleviated at least some of the worry that the flies constantly buzzing about grocery stores would contaminate food and spread disease. Canned goods were often insalubrious—"the consumers thereof are exposed to greater or less dangers from poisoning from copper, zinc, tin and lead," a government study warned in 1893—but for many consumers the risks of metal poisoning from poorly made cans were minor compared with the advantages of being able to buy peaches or tomatoes any time of year. And as George H. Hartford quickly recognized, the new packaging made it possible for the Great Atlantic & Pacific Tea Company to carry branded products that were on sale nowhere else. The A&P brand was soon applied to condensed milk, then to spices and flavorings, then to butter. By the early 1890s, Great Atlantic & Pacific was making the shift from tea company to grocery chain.[16]

As the business changed, two things remained constant: the reliance on extensive marketing and the lavish use of premiums. Just as it was in the days of George Gilman, a store opening was the occasion for a visit by a wagon such as *City of Tokyo,* pulled by a team of eight horses in gold-plated harnesses hung with gold-plated bells, with the driver seated beneath an ersatz pagoda. Now, though, those who came into the store were as likely to be awed by the rewards on open display as by the merchandise for sale. "Greatest inducements ever offered to tea and coffee drinkers," the advertisements touted. Glassware, vases, crockery, lamps: all could be had by purchasing coffee and tea at the Great Atlantic & Pacific. Such offers were especially enticing to women who may have controlled little of their family's spending except the food budget. By collecting coupons or stamps each time they bought groceries, they could hope to acquire goods that their husbands would refuse to purchase with cash.[17]

The firm, though still half owned by Gilman, was George H. Hartford's to run, and the senior Hartford clearly meant to keep it in the family. George L. had been gaining experience on the financial side of the business since 1880, serving as cashier in a Newark store in the late 1880s. Edward, the middle son, chose college instead of the grocery trade, but the youngest Hartford son, John, joined when he turned sixteen, in 1888. John had already shown a flair for earning money, making an impression at Orange's St. Patrick's Day parade in 1887 by parking his father's dray at a strategic location and charging parade goers to clamber up for a better view. He began at Great Atlantic & Pacific in the stockroom at the Vesey Street warehouse, sweeping floors and cleaning inkwells for $5 per week. To teach her son the value of money, his mother took $1 of each week's pay for board.[18]

All three sons still lived in the family home in Orange, where George H. Hartford repeatedly won reelection as mayor. A Democrat, he enjoyed support from both Democrats and Republicans from 1879 through 1888. By all accounts, he was a progressive mayor, building schools, installing electric streetlights, and starting construction of a municipal water system. But there was one issue on which he could make no headway: temperance. In 1888, Hartford bowed to the complaints of temperance advocates and shut down saloons operating illegally on Sunday, drawing outrage from Democratic Party leaders who backed the saloon keepers. "A strong opposition to the reelection of Mayor Hartford has during the past year developed in his own party," *The Orange Chronicle* reported early in 1890. Hartford initially declined to run for reelection, then was renominated by a raucous party convention over heavy opposition. Local Republicans promised to support him, then changed their minds. On Election Day, March 15, anti-Hartford Democrats joined their partisan opponents to oust the twelve-term mayor and give the heavily Democratic city a Republican leader. The election, said the newspaper, "will go down in local history as one of the most remarkable ever held in this city."[19]

The tumultuous mayoral election of 1890 gave the entire Hartford family an understandable aversion to politics. For the next four decades, they would avoid it like the plague. Only the threatened destruction of their company would force George L. and John Hartford to become involved in political life once again.

5
THE DEATH OF GEORGE F. GILMAN

It was not boredom with the retail trade that caused George F. Gilman to hand management of his tea companies to George H. Hartford in 1878. His concern was rather more pressing: he was afraid for his life.

In December 1859, upon the death of his father, George Gilman became one of several executors of the estate of Nathaniel Gilman. This was not a simple assignment. Nathaniel left a widow, Joanna, whom he had married in 1836, and two adult and two minor children, plus George and five other surviving children by his first wife. Nathaniel's children did not get along, and he left his affairs in a state that was bound to add to the rancor among them. Among other things, he avoided declaring a legal residence in order to evade state taxes; as the Maine Supreme Court observed in 1863, "He evidently belonged to that class of men, fortunately small in number, who have no stronger desire than to avoid the payment of taxes anywhere."[1]

When he died at the family homestead in Waterville, Maine, the children of his first marriage claimed the body, brought it to Brooklyn, buried it in Green-Wood Cemetery, declared that Nathaniel had been a New York state resident, and filed the will with a New York court. Joanna and her children, Brooklyn residents all, objected that he had been a Maine resident and filed a purported copy of the will in Maine—not least because Maine law allowed a probate judge to increase the stingy inheritance Nathaniel had left Joanna. Courts in each state appointed executors, competing for control of a sizable estate. Decades of legal battle ensued. George Gilman and the other New York executors took control of Nathaniel's properties in New York, including the buildings in the Swamp that housed the leather business. When the Maine legislature enacted a law allowing a probate judge to increase Joanna's inheritance from $15,000 to $75,000, George Gilman unwisely asked the Maine Supreme Court to block the award; that court, recalling that Joanna was a descendant of the state's first chief justice, instead increased the payment to $85,000, whereupon Joanna and her daughter, Anna, seized George Gilman's property in Maine to satisfy their claim. Anna, acting on behalf of her mother, filed suit after suit against her half brothers and her half sisters' husbands: Maine's supreme court was called upon to hear four different cases styled *Gilman v. Gilman* between 1863 and 1867. The temporary disappearance of one of the husbands in 1870, after he embezzled $300,000 from the estate, did not make relations any better.[2]

On February 3, 1877, two of his half brothers stopped George Gilman as he left his lawyer's office in New York. Their demand that he settle the estate immediately escalated into a fistfight before the police intervened. The incident left George Gilman terrified. Convinced that his relatives were out to murder him, he abandoned New York for his mansion at Black Rock in Bridgeport, Connecticut, the city that was also the home of P. T. Barnum. Gilman turned the tea business over to George H. Hartford.[3]

Gilman's life at Black Rock was far removed from business. He paid his New York taxes scrupulously—George H. Hartford made sure of that—but came to the city only for the occasional social event or horse show, never again entering the office of the Great Atlantic & Pacific Tea Company. When his first home at Black Rock, built in 1762, burned to the ground in 1894, he replaced it with a twenty-room house that had a bathroom between every two bedrooms, a drawing room with dark oak paneling on the walls and painted cupids on the ceiling, and paintings by young artists covering every available bit of wall space. As time passed, Gilman became increasingly eccentric, especially after the death of his wife in 1895. He kept no fewer than thirty-nine horses at Black Rock, along with thirty-five carriages and traps for them to pull. He stocked the house with elaborate furniture and pianos and entertained lavishly. He "adopted" at least two women, one the wife of a publisher, the other the daughter of his barber, whom he provided with everything from art classes to dental care in return for keeping him company. He grew obsessed with death. There were no clocks in the house to mark the passage of time, no mirrors, no doorbells or knockers. When he came upon a funeral procession, he would turn his carriage around so as not to pass it. He would not ride on a train on which there was a corpse. When he took ill, he would not see a physician. Medication was administered surreptitiously, because if asked, he would refuse to take it.[4]

Gilman died at Black Rock on March 3, 1901. Despite his ample firsthand experience with the difficulties of settling estates, he left no will.

Even in death, Gilman was surrounded by a circus. The bank named as administrator of his property, Bridgeport Trust Company, was unable to take possession of Black Rock until it sneaked two officials into the mansion at night. Hundreds of people came for the auction of Gilman's horses and carriages, and the auction of household goods drew more than five hundred people, who rode out to Black Rock on extra trolley cars laid on for the occasion. Some just picnicked on the lawn, while others wandered about eyeing the furniture as they consumed sandwiches and lemonade sold by vendors roaming from room to room. The two "adopted daughters," both much younger than Gilman, each came forward to claim he had promised her his entire estate. As the newspapers filled article after article with family gossip, Frazier Gilman, one of the two half brothers who attacked him in 1877, asked a court to declare his sister, Anna Gilman, incompetent. Anna, who was committed to an insane asylum in England, had spent four decades fighting with and suing her brothers, half brothers, and brothers-in-law to get more money from the estate of Nathaniel Gilman, but she was too ill to join in the battle that followed the death of George F. Gilman.[5]

Many others did join in. George Gilman had no children, but at least sixteen nieces and nephews and two surviving half brothers sought part of an inheritance that was rumored to be worth $40 million. The children of Gilman's full brothers and sisters wanted the case heard in Connecticut, where the law entitled only whole-blood relatives to inherit from a person who died without a will. The descendants of Nathaniel Gilman's second wife, including Frazier Gilman, wanted the matter heard in New York, where the law recognized the rights of half-blood heirs. The wife of a newspaper publisher, Helen Hall, one of Gilman's "adopted daughters," sued to claim all of Gilman's assets. Then, unexpectedly, the estate was served with another lawsuit. The plaintiff was George H. Hartford.[6]

In papers filed with a Connecticut court, Hartford revealed a previously unknown secret: on April 15, 1878, he and Gilman had formed a partnership to own the Great Atlantic & Pacific Tea Company and the Great American Tea Company. The agreement was unwritten, but Hartford asserted it had been made in the presence of Henry E. Knox, Gilman's attorney, in New York City. The agreement purportedly gave Hartford full management control of the tea business and ownership of its assets. The two partners supposedly agreed to share profits and losses equally. The bank account was to remain in the name of George F. Gilman, to avoid alerting the claimants to Nathaniel Gilman's estate that George Gilman had given up a stake in his business, and Hartford agreed to use Great Atlantic & Pacific's profits to help Gilman satisfy those outstanding claims. Hartford won an injunction to keep the Gilman executors from interfering in Great American and Great Atlantic & Pacific while a court heard his claims to a half interest in the unincorporated businesses.[7]

The executors and some Gilman relatives had fancied that Hartford was merely the hired manager of Gilman's business. Hartford, though, presented strong evidence to the contrary. On March 4, 1901, the day following Gilman's death, he had incorporated the Great Atlantic & Pacific Tea Company in Jersey City, New Jersey. The timing suggests that even before Gilman's death, Hartford had been in discussions with some of the Gilman heirs about the future of the business. No one could dispute that he had worked with Gilman for more than forty years and had exercised management control since 1878. All of the store leases were in Hartford's name, indicating that he had personally been at financial risk in the business. With Hartford's assistance, Gilman had in fact bought out some of the competing claims to his father's estate. Hartford had also achieved a greater stature in the business world than one would expect of a mere employee. The Home Insurance Company of New York and the Second National Bank of Orange had named him a director. A carefully groomed man with a well-trimmed beard, he had the demeanor of an executive.[8]

As the accountants plowed through Gilman's records, they discovered that his $40 million estate was a mirage. Aside from the mansion at Black Rock, all of Gilman's wealth was tied up in the tea companies. The heirs realized that a struggle over ownership, as often occurred in businesses upon the death of a partner, could destroy the value of their inheritance. They were dependent upon George H. Hartford.[9]

On February 20, 1902, less than a year after Gilman's death, a deal was struck. The New Jersey corporation Hartford had set up in 1901 would buy the assets of the Gilman-Hartford partnership. The company's capital would be raised to $2.1 million, including $700,000 of common stock and $1.4 million of preferred. The Gilman heirs would receive $1.25 million of the preferred shares paying a 6 percent annual dividend, giving them a priority claim on roughly half the company's annual profits at the time. George H. Hartford would control some of the preferred shares and all of the common stock. The preferred shareholders had the right to vote on any change in capital stock, mortgages, pledges of assets, and purchases of other businesses, but otherwise Hartford had uncontested authority to manage the business. He also agreed to buy back as much of the preferred stock as the heirs wished to sell. Despite judicial skepticism about Helen Hall's assertion that Gilman had promised her everything, she was awarded four hundred shares of preferred stock in return for dropping all claims to the Gilman estate.[10]

In June 1903, a federal court approved the transaction. George H. Hartford, after more than four decades of collaboration with George Gilman, became president and sole owner of the Great Atlantic & Pacific Tea Company. George L. Hartford, still single and living in his parents' house at age thirty-seven, was named treasurer. The middle brother, Edward Hartford, thirty-three, was named secretary, despite his college degree in engineering and his avowed disinterest in the retail trade. John A. Hartford, the youngest of the brothers, did not immediately become a corporate officer, but that was of little significance. More outgoing than his brothers and the only one to have married, John was frequently on the road, visiting stores, meeting store managers, talking with suppliers. George H. Hartford was sixty-nine years old by the time he assumed full control, and George L. and John—one the numbers man who shied away from people, the other the extrovert who was always looking for new opportunities—were preparing themselves to take on much of their father's responsibility.[11]

6

GEARING FOR BATTLE

The Great Atlantic & Pacific Tea Company was already a substantial business when the Hartfords took ownership in 1903. The messy litigation over George Gilman's estate lifted the lid on the company's secrets, revealing that in 1900 it turned a profit of $125,000 on sales of $5 million, a none-too-shabby rate of 2.5 percent. Its capitalization of $2.1 million was puny by the standards of heavy industry—United States Steel Corporation, formed in 1901, was capitalized at $1.4 billion—but among grocery retailers the Great Atlantic & Pacific was one of the largest in America.[1]

Being among the country's biggest grocers was not much of a claim to fame. Food retailing at the start of the twentieth century was a very primitive industry, conducted on a very small scale. The Great Atlantic & Pacific Tea Company's $5 million of revenue came from 198 stores, thousands of wagon routes, and a mail-order tea business. The Hartfords' success depended upon collecting small sums from a large number of widely dispersed sources. The same was true of their competitors. Even the country's largest food stores were tiny by later standards; the floor area of the new wood-paneled emporium of Goldberg, Bowen & Company, heralded as "San Francisco's Finest Grocery," was not much larger than a basketball court. Almost all food shops offered a very limited selection of merchandise, rarely more than a couple hundred items, most of them purchased from wholesalers in hundred pound sacks and wooden barrels and then doled out to individual customers. As it had for three decades, the front page of the leading trade newspaper advised grocers: "Count, Measure, Weigh or Gauge Everything You Buy."[2]

For consumers, the daily trip to the grocery store could be a risky venture. Many independent grocers did not post prices, forcing the housewife to haggle over the cost of each item. And shoppers rarely received what they paid for. When investigators visited 549 grocery stores in New Jersey, they discovered that 63 percent of the weights and measures were incorrect, with only one store in twenty employing strictly honest weights. Sanitary conditions were often unhygienic at a time when electricity and refrigeration were uncommon. Produce was sold from open bins or bushel baskets exposed to dust and flies. In 1903, *American Grocer* found it necessary to remind readers to cover the bungholes of barrels to keep mice and rats from falling in. The social reformer Albion Fellows Bacon encountered a grocery in Evansville, Indiana, around 1906 that lacked even a sewer connection. "It was a wonder to me then, and is still, how a good housekeeper could buy groceries in that filthy place, and in scores of others, little better, scattered over our town and other towns," she wrote. The brand-name packaged goods stacked behind the counter were no safer than the bulk products. Lemon extract often contained no lemon. Bottled soft drinks used coal tar, a carcinogen, as a colorant. Some ketchups used saccharine, even then suspected as a hazardous adulterant, as a preservative. The "tin" in tin cans contained as much as 12 percent lead, which leached into the fruits and vegetables. Zinc chloride, used to prepare the tops for soldering, often ran into the cans during the soldering process, poisoning the food inside.[3]

Scandals involving short-weighting, adulteration, and contamination were frequently in the headlines around the turn of the century. In an environment rife with mistrust, the Hartfords understood how to extract advantage from the Great Atlantic & Pacific brand. "Teas and coffees bought at any of our stores are warranted *strictly pure*," the company advertised. The numerous federal and state investigations into food purity appear not to have snared any Great Atlantic & Pacific products. Even *American Grocer*, which already regarded it as the great enemy of independent merchants, never accused Great Atlantic & Pacific of adulterating any of its products during this period. On the contrary: while criticizing its "supreme selfishness" for stealing business by underpricing competitors, the publication had to admit that the company's low prices were attributable to its ability to buy in volume without middlemen, not to inferior products. "They retail some goods sometimes at less than most small storekeepers pay; and worst of all, they advertise the fact far and near," *American Grocer* complained.[4]

It is not clear how George H. Hartford and his two sons divided up their responsibilities in this period. George H. was still involved in the company on a daily basis. Statements by John, years later, suggest that the three men spent much time discussing business and that important decisions would be taken only if they all agreed. But as the Hartfords came into full control, the grocery trade was changing rapidly. A decade earlier, as its tea stores had begun to develop into grocery stores stocked with canned goods, butter, and soap, the Great Atlantic & Pacific had been the only grocery chain of note. The other chains around the United States all had been tiny enterprises, operating a handful of stores that sold little but coffee, tea, and baking powder. By the early years of the twentieth century, the competitive situation was much tougher. The government would not collect data on retail stores until the 1920s, but the economist Harold Barger estimated that grocery chains accounted for 4.5 percent of food sales in 1899. Admittedly, "chains" was a generous term, encompassing many firms that owned only two or three stores. Even so, Barger's estimate was noteworthy, because his estimate of grocery chains' market share a decade earlier, in 1889, was zero.[5]

Great Atlantic & Pacific was no longer the only player in the chain grocery business. It had opened only four or five stores per year over the course of the 1890s, while other companies had expanded in a big way. In New York, the Grand Union Tea Company, formerly the Jones Brothers Tea Company, owned 140 stores and two thousand delivery wagons by 1901, served by a huge warehouse in Brooklyn, and in 1905 the Irish-born grocer James Butler opened 40 stores in just four months. In Philadelphia, where Great Atlantic & Pacific had been the only chain in 1889, Thomas P. Hunter's Acme Tea Company was opening a store every few weeks and would have 169 by 1908, while William Butler, James Butler's brother, would have 117 by mid-decade. In Chicago, Great Atlantic & Pacific had been the biggest chain in 1895, but it ranked fifth a decade later. In Boston, three local chains surpassed it. In Cincinnati, the Great Western Tea Company was renamed B. H. Kroger's Tea and Grocery Stores and had thirty shops by 1902.[6]

Some of these aggressive chains even outdid the Hartfords when it came to advertising. A few years earlier, Great Atlantic & Pacific had been unusual in calling attention to its prices at a time when grocers, if they bought newspaper space at all, tended merely to list their new goods. By the early twentieth century, advertising had become far livelier. Price promotions were standard, and in some cities shoppers were learning the new custom of cutting coupons from the newspaper to receive special bargains. Great Atlantic & Pacific's newspaper ads, one column wide and filled with dense text, looked old-fashioned at a time when other retailers were running half-page ads with fancy graphics. Although Great Atlantic & Pacific still staged the occasional stunt, such as putting "the Champion Whittler of the World" to work in the show window of a new store in New York, George Gilman's marketing flair was sorely missed. The company did not even have a standard way of presenting itself to the public. In some places, it used an Art Deco logo with the letters *A*, *P*, *T*, and *C* intertwined. In others, the streamlined words "Atlantic & Pacific" were superimposed in bold sans-serif type on a globe turned to the Western Hemisphere, with the words "Tea Co." tucked beneath. A third variant presented the name in varying type sizes set in a single row: Great Atlantic & Pacific Tea Co.[7]

Great Atlantic & Pacific was losing its edge in the tea and coffee business as well. It was still the nation's largest tea dealer and still used the Great American Tea Company name to sell teas by mail. But Thea-Nectar, an unusual product when offered in the 1870s as the first packaged tea, was by now a tired brand. The English tea merchants Lipton and Tetley had set up shop in America, and their branded teas were widely available. In any event, tea drinking was not the fashion it once had been. Consumption was stagnant amid falling prices, and the imposition of a ten-cent-per-pound tariff in 1898 to finance the Spanish-American War did not help matters. In 1902, the United States imported less tea than it had two decades earlier at less than half the average price per pound. The Hartfords, who usually stood aloof from trade associations and lobbying groups, were so worried about the situation that Great Atlantic & Pacific helped form the National Tea Association, a group to promote tea consumption, in 1903.[8]

Coffee had become America's beverage of choice by the early twentieth century, and when it came to coffee, Great Atlantic & Pacific was far from the market leader. The company claimed to be a "direct importer," but the earliest evidence that it imported its own coffee dates to 1909. Between 1896 and 1904, Great Atlantic & Pacific did not rank among the dozens of firms importing more than ten thousand bags per year through the Port of New York, indicating that it bought coffee from importers rather than bringing in its own. The most important importer was Arbuckle Bros., which was established by Charles and John Arbuckle of Pittsburgh in the 1860s and became the world's largest coffee dealer in the 1880s. Arbuckle's Ariosa brand, glazed with sugar to keep it fresh, was America's bestselling ground coffee. In 1896, Arbuckle Bros. announced plans to start refining sugar, and the powerful Havemeyer family, whose American Sugar Refining Company had a near monopoly in sugar production, struck back by purchasing and promoting the Lion coffee brand. In the ensuing battle, coffee consumption soared as prices tumbled. This five-year retail price war could not have been good for Great Atlantic & Pacific's bottom line.[9]

In these mounting competitive battles, Great Atlantic & Pacific faced a serious disadvantage: it was poorly structured to be a grocery chain. Its 198 stores were strewn over twenty-eight states. In many towns it operated only one or two fixed locations, along with wagon routes. This was fine for a tea and coffee retailer, as tea stores did not require frequent resupply. The food business was different. Grocery stores needed new merchandise every day or two. A company with many stores in a single city could gain a big advantage by operating its own warehouse and using its own wagons to supply its stores. Having a warehouse allowed the retailer to obtain quantity discounts on the goods and to buy directly from suppliers to avoid the normal wholesaler markups.

Great Atlantic & Pacific, with few stores in any one city outside New York, would not have been able to supply its stores easily, so its costs were probably higher than those of large local grocers. Its stores carried inventory equal to two months' sales, roughly twice as much as the most efficient grocery chains. Great Atlantic & Pacific's widely dispersed stores also made local newspaper advertising more expensive on a per-store basis. And even if its prices were the lowest in town, Great Atlantic & Pacific might have had difficulty attracting customers to buy its groceries as they did its coffee and tea. Coffee and tea were infrequent purchases, and housewives thought nothing of buying a pound downtown and carrying it home on the trolley. Food shopping, on the other hand, was a daily chore and was almost always done within a few blocks of home.[10]

The historical record of this period is scant, but the available evidence suggests that once the Great Atlantic & Pacific was reorganized, in the summer of 1903, the Hartfords moved aggressively to rebuild a foundering enterprise. Over the next nine years, they opened an average of one store every two weeks, six times the pace of the 1890s. The network of wagon routes was expanded to over five thousand, and commissioned salespeople driving Great Atlantic & Pacific horse carts were to be seen all over the East, Midwest, and South. The Hartfords revamped the company's advertising, too. In 1904, it began using full-page newspaper advertisements with large graphics, giving itself a distinctly modern cast.[11]

In 1907, the Hartfords boldly announced their ambitions by starting construction of a nine-story office and warehouse building on Bay Street in Jersey City, within walking distance of the new underground railroad to Manhattan. The office-warehouse building was the centerpiece of a complex designed to support a very large company. The site had room for several buildings, and over the next decade it sprouted four additional structures linked by tunnels. One was a power plant capable of bearing office floors above. Nearby was the coffee roasting and grinding plant. The bakery building included a plant to make chocolate and cocoa and another to manufacture macaroni. All of these imposing structures were built of reinforced concrete, then considered an advanced material for large-scale construction, and had sprinklers throughout to reduce the risk of fire—and fire-insurance premiums. The complex conveyed the unmistakable message that Great Atlantic & Pacific was a significant business, able to afford the best in modern construction and in need of room to grow.[12]

The year 1907, though, was a most inauspicious time to launch such a bold project. On October 14, an attempt to corner the copper market triggered a series of bank collapses, a sequence of events that would become known as the Panic of 1907. The company's cash was deposited in a bank rumored to be failing. John A. Hartford, then thirty-five, was assigned the task of extricating the money. After spending the night queuing outside the bank's doors, John walked up to the man who had spent the night at the head of the line. "How much have you got in here?" John asked.

"Four hundred and forty-seven dollars and ninety cents," the man replied. "All I got in the world."

"I'll give you four fifty for your place," Hartford said. "You get back in line and maybe you'll get your deposit, too." Hartford was first inside when the bank opened its doors and collected Great Atlantic & Pacific's money in full, saving the company.[13]

At some point around 1907 or 1908, with their father now in his seventies, George L. and John Hartford appear to have divided up their responsibilities. George L. took charge of the financial affairs that had long been run by George H. It would have been his job to figure out how to generate enough cash to fund expansion without selling bonds or mortgaging assets, as either of these moves would have required approval by the Gilman heirs who controlled the preferred stock. John, the more outgoing of the pair, took responsibility for marketing and for relations with employees and suppliers, tasks that would have made his introverted brother uncomfortable. George L. and John would share management responsibilities in this way for the rest of their lives.

John started making major changes in the stores. The first was to create what would become one of the best-known retail names in America: A&P. While George Gilman had been alive, the firm had referred to itself uniformly as the Great Atlantic & Pacific Tea Company, a name evoking grandeur. To the extent that Great Atlantic & Pacific promoted its own brands, it sometimes used the company's initials, as in A&P gelatin powder, but more often relied on distinct names such as Elgin Creamery Butter and Eight O'Clock Breakfast Coffee. A drawing of an old woman sipping tea made its appearance in advertisements and on some product labels in the 1880s, with the phony endorsement "The Great Atlantic & Pacific Tea Co.'s celebrated teas, coffees, baking powder, spices, condensed milk & extracts have been my solace throughout my life. Grandmother." Most goods, however, were sold either in bulk or under manufacturers' brand names, many of which did not resonate with consumers.[14]

John Hartford set about a systematic rebranding. Dozens of products, from canned corn to stove polish, were repackaged under the brand name "A&P." The logo was displayed in a standard way for the first time, with the letters in gold within a solid red circle. With rebranding came market segmentation, drastically increasing the number of items available behind the counters of Great Atlantic & Pacific stores. Shoppers could choose between A&P lima beans for twelve and a half cents per can, Sultana lima beans for ten cents, and Iona lima beans at three cans for twenty-five cents. All three brands were exclusive to Great Atlantic & Pacific, but each catered to a different economic stratum. Canners and manufacturers, who wanted to use branding to increase their own profits rather than the retailer's, were notably unenthusiastic about the expansion of store brands, and some tried to organize a boycott. For most, however, the prospect of selling full carloads of canned goods to a single retailer was too tempting to pass up.[15]

Thanks to rising incomes and more exposure to advertising, grocery shoppers had higher expectations than a few years earlier, and hundreds of new products were available to soak up workers' increased purchasing power. Canned salmon, once a delicacy, became a routine purchase; U.S. production rose 123 percent from 1895 to 1905. Prepackaged cereals battled for shelf space, with several companies promoting their methods of toasting cornflakes as superior to the competition's. The National Biscuit Company's revolutionary Uneeda Biscuit, introduced in 1898, displaced the grocer's ubiquitous barrel of stale, broken crackers; one awed admirer described it as "only a lot of perfectly made, perfectly baked biscuit, enclosed in a package that excludes all air, dust and moisture." Even the coffee department, one of the most profitable parts of the average grocery store, underwent a remarkable change. Great Atlantic & Pacific customers could choose among El Ryad, the "most scientifically blended coffee in the market," at thirty-five cents a pound; Plaza coffee, "No better value on the market," for thirty cents; Sultana, the "Best 25¢ coffee in the city"; and the old standby, Eight O'Clock Breakfast Coffee.[16]

Shoppers also were demanding ever more lucrative premiums. In 1900, Great Atlantic & Pacific's outlay for gifts to customers was $450,000, more than three times the year's profits. The premiums not only were costly but also took up shelf space that could have displayed merchandise for sale. Many stores of the period looked more like gift shops than groceries. Photographs show deep, narrow spaces, lacking the crystal chandeliers and oriental elegance of an earlier day. A wooden counter stretched along one side of the room, the shelves of food behind it tended by store managers in dark vests, male store clerks in white aprons, and female clerks wearing long skirts and white blouses. Along the opposite wall were shelves groaning under displays of clocks, plates, pitchers, and cuspidors, available only in exchange for coupons. Each time she made a purchase, the customer would receive a red-printed coupon bearing the number of points she had earned. The clerk would validate the coupon with the store's stamp. When she had collected the requisite number of points, the customer would bring her coupons to the store, where the clerk would hand her the desired prize and punch holes in the redeemed coupons.[17]

Doing away with premiums was impossible. Customers expected them, and they gave chains a big advantage over independent grocers, who could not afford to tie up money in glassware and crockery. Instead of ending premiums, the Hartfords tried to cut the cost by publishing a premium catalog, with drawings or photographs of the available merchandise; when a family had collected the 150 points needed for an oak clock or the 67 for a Daisy air rifle, it would send its coupons to a central office and receive the gift by return freight. This approach freed up selling space and had the added virtue of creating a promotional publication that customers would consult frequently as they considered what to acquire next. The premium business was gradually turned over to Sperry & Hutchinson (S&H), a company founded in 1896 that popularized the idea of pasting trading stamps into books. Great Atlantic & Pacific gave customers one S&H stamp for every ten cents of purchases. It paid S&H two-tenths of a cent per stamp, and S&H agreed to provide merchandise worth $0.0011 for each stamp redeemed, leaving it with a healthy profit. A customer who bought $99 of groceries would receive 990 stamps worth $1.18 in merchandise—assuming, of course, that the merchandise was worth as much as S&H claimed.[18]

The stamps were easily used for special promotions. Buyers of Silver Key tea could get ten extra stamps with a ten-cent package. A fifty-cent tin of baking powder might come with eighty stamps, for one week only. Newspaper advertisements were crowded with special offers. "The reader of the ad. might infer they were also selling groceries. But giving the stamps is the main thing," *American Grocer*'s advertising columnist commented. Hard as they might try to equal Great Atlantic & Pacific's prices, independent grocers were rarely able to match it stamp for stamp.[19]

Great Atlantic & Pacific's revival, and the growth of competing chains, had political consequences. Independent grocers were being trampled in the price and premium wars. In the first decade of the twentieth century, they began to fight back.

Independent merchants were a notoriously difficult group to organize. They typically tended their stores from seven in the morning until eight or nine at night, often with no help, leaving little time for social life, much less politics. Given the industry's high turnover, many stores were in business for only a year or two, and their owners had no commitment to political action. Money was always scarce, and in the cities many storekeepers spoke little English. The extent of most grocers' collective activity was a local grocers' association, whose main project was to arrange for all stores to close on the same summer day for the merchants' annual outing.

It was the nationwide movement for a pure-food law that led to the formation of the National Association of Retail Grocers in 1898. Few grocers actually belonged: in 1905, at the peak of activity leading to the passage of the Pure Food and Drug Act of 1906, the association claimed 11,382 members, roughly 3 percent of the nation's grocers, and most of those would resign their memberships once the long-sought law was enacted. The costs of the national association and its state affiliates were largely paid by the Sugar Trust and by wholesaler groups, such as the Southern Wholesale Grocers' Association, whose well-being depended upon the survival of independent grocers.[20]

Aside from pure food, the National Association of Retail Grocers' main concern at the turn of the century had been the parcel post. Congress was considering whether the U.S. Post Office should deliver packages weighing more than four pounds. Small grocers were dead set against the plan, fearing that the parcel post would be a low-cost alternative to rail or wagon delivery, making it cheaper for catalog merchants such as Sears, Roebuck and Montgomery Ward to sell staples by mail. Chain stores were not controversial, because there were few chain stores in most parts of the country and almost none outside the cities.[21]

Political views changed as the expanding chains began to squeeze independent grocers' profits. In 1903, the National Association of Retail Grocers debated whether manufacturers should be allowed to give volume discounts to large retailers just as they did to wholesalers. The following year, Massachusetts became the first state to impose a tax on coupons or trading stamps, which were deemed to give chain stores an unfair advantage. By 1905, wholesalers were threatening boycotts of manufacturers that sold directly to large grocers, and Missouri grocers backed a state law to curb competition by requiring prospective grocers to pass a licensing exam, like plumbers or electricians. *American Grocer* led the attack on price discrimination by manufacturers that sold more cheaply to chains than to independent grocers, declaring, "It is the bounden duty of the manufacturers to protect the retailers' profits." In Iowa and Minnesota, engaging in a "gift enterprise" by giving trading stamps with a purchase was made a misdemeanor. The campaign against price-cutting spread to the point that a federal judge in Colorado had to restrain a retailers' association from fixing local grocery prices.[22]

Despite a few successes, independent grocers and their wholesale backers were unable to shackle the chains. At the end of the century's first decade, the chain phenomenon was still modest in size and existed mainly in the Northeast and Midwest. Most Americans had never entered a chain grocery store and had no reason to care, and some appreciated that the large operators' "scientific methods" were holding down handling costs. In 1908, grocery wholesalers in Boston petitioned Congress to permit manufacturers to fix retail prices to help grocers "preserve their commercial existence in the face of the efforts of powerful and selfish monopolies to gradually eliminate the individual dealer," but no legislation followed. The public was far from convinced that chain stores were a problem.[23]

7
THE ECONOMY STORE

The Hartfords were an instinctively conservative family. George Huntington Hartford, whose caution had moderated George Gilman's flamboyance in the tea company's early days and cooled the warfare among Orange's political factions in the 1880s, was not seduced by the conspicuous consumption of the Gilded Age; he lived unpretentiously in the house on Ridge Street until his death in 1917. Minnie, the eldest child, married in 1881, but moved no farther than the house next door to her parents; her son and son-in-law both worked for the Great Atlantic & Pacific. Marie Louise, the youngest child, remained in her parents' home even after marrying the company executive Arthur Hoffman in 1907. George Ludlum Hartford, the treasurer of a sizable business, lived with his parents until 1908, when he was forty-two years old. Upon marrying Josephine Burnet, a forty-four-year-old widow with a teenage daughter, George L. relocated only to the adjacent town of Montclair, into a house he would occupy for half a century.[1]

While such familial closeness has its virtues, a keen sense of changing societal trends is unlikely to be among them. The Hartfords were fortunate that two of George H. and Josephine's sons were cut from very different cloth. Edward, the middle son, avoided his father's efforts to bring him into Great Atlantic & Pacific. Instead, he moved into New York City and entered the leading-edge industry of his day, automobiles. Traveling in France in 1899, Edward attended a bicycle race and observed that a spring attached to the front fork helped stabilize the winning cycle. He and his father bought the patent rights, and Edward developed the concept into the shock absorber, soon to become standard on every car. Edward went on to invent brakes, jacks, and other auto components, all of which were produced at the Hartford Suspension Company's plant in Jersey City, adjacent to Great Atlantic & Pacific's headquarters. Although Edward never worked for the grocery chain, he served as corporate secretary, participating in the direction of a company in which he, as an heir of George H. Hartford's, had a significant financial interest. He would have brought a very different perspective to the Hartfords' family councils.[2]

John was by far the most convivial of the Hartford offspring, and unlike his brother George he had no aversion to enjoying the family's wealth. In 1893, when he was twenty-one, John married Pauline Corwin of Goshen, New York, whom he likely had met while visiting his mother's family. In his mother's eyes, he was a loving and obedient son. "I can say in all sincerity that John has never caused his father or myself an hour's anxiety," Josephine Hartford wrote to his intended bride. "I can assure you that John is guiltless of an evil habit." But John had a strong streak of independence. He and Pauline chose to live in New York, not Orange, eventually taking an apartment at the elegant Hotel Marie Antoinette at Sixty-sixth Street and Broadway. He developed a taste for horses, becoming a fixture at the National Horse Show, New York's most important society event. He and Pauline earned a listing in *Dau's Blue Book*, indicating that they hobnobbed with the city's elite, even if they were not listed in the *Social Register*. Most important of all, John spent time on the road, meeting with store managers, grocery manufacturers, and executives at other companies. He was exposed to new ideas in a way that his father and his brother were not. Had it been up to George H. and George L., the Great Atlantic & Pacific would likely have remained but one of many grocery chains, expanding deliberately into new markets. John had a different vision.[3]

In 1912, John Hartford decided that Great Atlantic & Pacific needed a new approach to running grocery stores. Company lore has it that he was fed up with the high cost of premiums and trading stamps, but there was more to the story than that.

Food was a much-debated subject in 1912. Rising food prices were a major issue in that year's presidential campaign, and were tracked closely by the newspapers and the government's Bureau of Labor Statistics. Sanitary concerns were widespread even after the Pure Food and Drug Act of 1906 authorized the government to ban unsafe ingredients; in

1911, New York City inspectors condemned one hundred tons of poultry and nearly two hundred tons of fish on sale in public markets. The discovery of "vitamins"—a name first applied in 1912 to the substances that became known as vitamin A, vitamin B_1, and vitamin C—helped fuel a new public consciousness about nutrition, and the typical American diet, heavy on fats and carbohydrates, was found wanting.[4]

Most of all, the food distribution system itself was seen as an embarrassment. Scientific management was taking firm hold in manufacturing and in the popular imagination; in 1911, *American Magazine*, one of the most widely circulated publications of the time, serialized "The Principles of Scientific Management" by the famed industrial engineer Frederick Winslow Taylor for a popular audience. By contrast with industry, the process of getting food from farm to table seemed hugely inefficient. Tens of thousands of peddlers eked out precarious livings selling eggs and melons door-to-door. Large quantities of produce and milk simply went to waste. Local prices of fruits, vegetables, and eggs could fluctuate wildly, collapsing as a trainload of new merchandise glutted the market and then soaring as producers responded to the low prices by sending their goods elsewhere. By one estimate, wholesaling and retailing costs accounted for nearly half of New Yorkers' food outlays, with food that sold for $350 million a year at New York rail terminals costing consumers $645 million at the city's grocery stores. The issues were so widely debated that the august American Academy of Political and Social Science devoted an entire issue of its *Annals* to "reducing the cost of food distribution," and the new Harvard Business School, established in 1908, began a series of studies of retail efficiency.[5]

Other grocery chains had taken the lead in applying scientific management by standardizing stores and abandoning costly practices such as credit and delivery. John convinced his reluctant father and brother to try something similar. In 1912, they opened an unmarked store in an unprepossessing, two-story structure at 797 West Side Avenue in Jersey City, two miles from the company's headquarters. At a time when most grocery stores were small, the new store was even smaller, just twenty feet wide and thirty feet deep. The furnishings were simple, only a few shelves and counters and a small ice refrigerator for butter, lard, and eggs; George Gilman's glittering chandeliers, red-painted pagodas, and Chinese wall hangings were banished. Unlike Great Atlantic & Pacific's other stores, the experimental store offered no credit, no premiums, and no trading stamps. There was no telephone, so customers could not call in orders for delivery. The manager, the sole employee, locked the door when he went to lunch. The company's total investment, including inventory, came to only $2,500. The small investment and minimal labor expense permitted low markups, so the store could offer very attractive prices. The first Economy Store did not advertise, lest customers demand Economy Store prices in the regular store nearby. With no promotion beyond low prices, shoppers came in droves.[6]

As was the case with almost everything else they did, the Hartfords were not innovators when it came to low-price retailing. Their strength was figuring out how to turn others' innovations into profitable strategies. Their 1912 test in Jersey City showed, unsurprisingly, that a store with limited hours and a small stock of merchandise sold fewer groceries than the average Great Atlantic & Pacific outlet. But it also revealed an important lesson: lower costs could lead to a higher return on investment. The Hartfords concluded that if they opened many locations, the new format could propel both higher profits and faster growth. They called the design the A&P Economy Store, putting the initials A&P on a store's nameplate for the first time. The acronym stuck; henceforth, customers would think of the place where they did their shopping as "the A&P." With George L. keeping a close eye on costs, the Hartfords plunged in, against the resistance of most of their supervisors. In 1913, they opened 175 Economy Stores, more than 5 each week. In 1914, another 408 Economy Stores opened up, including 100 in Boston alone, giving Great Atlantic & Pacific the large local market share it had lacked. By 1915, when the company opened 864 more Economy Stores, the low-price banner accounted for more than half of total sales.[7]

The birth of the Economy Store coincided with an important political shift, for it was in 1912 that chain retailing first surfaced as a national political issue. Chains, which originated in the tea trade, were expanding across the retail sector. Some 257 sizable retail chains were operating in the United States in 1910, nearly five times as many as in 1900. The F. W. Woolworth Company was created in a 1911 merger of six "5 & 10 Cent" dry-goods chains that operated 596 stores in forty-eight states; the company was so profitable that it was about to occupy the tallest building in the world, paid for entirely in cash. The United Cigar Stores Company, organized in 1901 and closely tied to the tobacco trust that controlled cigar and cigarette production, had more than 900 stores by 1913. The growth of pharmacy chains showed that chains could penetrate even a field in which highly trained specialists were needed to manufacture and dispense the goods.[8]

Independent retailers and wholesalers tried to hobble the chains by discouraging manufacturers from dealing with them. In 1909, they convinced the Kellogg Toasted Corn Flake Company to abandon discounting. Henceforth, Kellogg would offer no volume discounts to chains such as Great Atlantic & Pacific. Instead, it would sell its cereal to wholesalers only at $2.50 per case of thirty-six boxes, less a 2 percent discount for cash payment. The wholesalers had to agree to sell to all retailers, regardless of size, for $2.80 per case. Retailers, in turn, were obligated to sell the cornflakes at ten cents per box. This system meant that a case of cornflakes sold by Kellogg for $2.45, including the cash discount, would bring $3.60 at retail, a 47 percent markup. "The one-case price is exactly the same as the 1,000-case price," a Kellogg official insisted, explaining that lowering prices for big customers would "demoralize trade." The courts, however, rejected most efforts to fix prices. In 1908, the U.S. Supreme Court ruled that a publisher could not tell a retailer what price to charge for a book. In 1911, it ruled directly that a manufacturer that tried to set the retail price of its products violated antitrust law.[9]

Their losses on the legal front pushed independent retailers and their wholesale suppliers into the national political arena. An anti-chain measure came before Congress for the first time in 1912, prohibiting premiums and trading stamps in connection with the sale of tobacco. This bill was important to independent cigar-store owners, but it was of little interest to other retailers and had no serious chance of passage. Separately, small-town clothing and hardware dealers sought to rein in the parcel-post service, established that same year, but both this proposal and merchants' petitions that mail-order retailers be required to pay local taxes wherever they sold their goods were so contrary to the interests of small-town shoppers that they fell on deaf ears. Complaining that chain stores were selling goods too cheaply was not an approach calculated to earn sympathy from the consuming public, so the organizations representing independent merchants adroitly rephrased their complaint. Their objection, they said, was not to chains or low prices but to "unfair competition." The practice on which they focused was price discrimination.[10]

Price discrimination means that the seller of a product charges different prices to some buyers than to others. Despite a name suggestive of untoward dealings, it is a common business practice. In economic terms, price discrimination often makes perfect sense: selling ten thousand cans of tomato sauce to a single customer will almost always cost a food manufacturer less per can than selling a hundred cans, and price discrimination allows the customer with the larger order to capture part of the manufacturer's saving by obtaining a lower price. But to the owners of small businesses and the residents of small towns, price discrimination was a pernicious practice that would leave them forever at a disadvantage. When these interests, forming a loose coalition known as the populists, won federal regulation of the railroad industry in 1887, they secured a strict ban on discrimination. The law required railroads to publish their rates for carrying each commodity, and to charge the same price per ton, barrel, or cubic foot to every customer. The independent merchants' dream was to achieve a similar result in the distribution system, so that the smallest grocery store could purchase its stock at the same cost as the Great Atlantic & Pacific. As the secretary of the National Association of Retail Grocers explained, "The general working rules should be, 'A fair price and the same to everybody.'"[11]

In 1912, the independents won the support of the Democratic presidential nominee, Woodrow Wilson. Corporate power was a major issue in the campaign. The incumbent Republican, William Howard Taft, and his predecessor, Theodore Roosevelt, both had attacked the trusts dominating such sectors as oil and steel, and both were running in 1912 on platforms calling for stricter regulation of trusts and monopolies. Wilson, the governor of New Jersey and a prominent political scientist, had been voicing his suspicion of big business for two decades and favored breaking up monopolies, not regulating them. He was an unabashed critic of unfair competition and price discrimination. If price discrimination could be stopped, Wilson asserted, "then you have free America, and I for my part am willing to stop there and see who has the best brains." Splitting the Republican vote, Wilson became the first Democratic president since 1897.[12]

Wilson's inauguration in March 1913, closely followed by a third Supreme Court decision barring manufacturers from setting retail prices for their products, fueled the backlash against the chains. Wholesalers and independent retailers responded to the court's ruling by creating a joint lobbying organization, the American Fair-Trade League, to seek laws against price-cutting. They received the backing of one of the nation's most prominent legal scholars, the Boston attorney Louis D. Brandeis, soon to become a Supreme Court justice himself. Brandeis had made his career as an outspoken critic of big corporations. "The evil results of price-cutting are far-reaching," he asserted in the prestigious *Harper's Weekly*. The future justice would not even concede a lasting benefit to the consumer. "The consumer's gain from price-cutting is only sporadic and temporary." Unless a manufacturer is able to avoid discounting the price of its product, Brandeis argued, it will have to lower quality in order to preserve its profits, leaving consumers unable to buy the high-value articles they desire.[13]

The American Fair-Trade League's program was introduced into Congress by Raymond B. Stevens, a New Hampshire Democrat. The Stevens bill provided that the "producer, grower, manufacturer, or owner" of a trademark or brand had the right "to prescribe the sole, uniform price" at which its product could be sold at wholesale and retail. To benefit from the law, the manufacturer would have to print the retail price on each package and file that price with the government's Bureau of Corporations. It would then have to sell its product to wholesalers or retailers at a uniform price, with no rebates or volume discounts. Retailers could depart from the retail price set by the manufacturer only if they were closing the business or filing for bankruptcy or if the goods had been damaged.[14]

The Stevens bill sparked a year of congressional hearings. The Chicago grocer S. Westerfeld endorsed it because he thought it would put an end to "the method of the retail octopuses, the damnable method of killing competition through price cutting." Ralphs Grocery Company, the largest food chain in California, opposed the bill by analogy: "When a play comes to a theatre no one has the right to tell another that every seat in the house should be the same price." Spokesmen for organizations as diverse as the Connecticut Piano Dealers' Association, the New Orleans Retail Merchants' Bureau, and the watchmaker Robert H. Ingersoll & Brother paraded through the ornate room of the Committee on Interstate and Foreign Commerce and bombarded legislators with letters and telegrams. Brandeis put in an appearance as well, urging the committee to ban quantity discounts and to allow manufacturers to set retail prices, lest price-cutting destroy business. Stopping price-cutting, Brandeis argued tortuously, would actually benefit consumers by allowing them to shop more confidently: "In order that the public may be free buyers there must be removed from the mind of the potential purchaser the thought that probably at some other store he could get that same article for less money."[15]

The climactic witness in these proceedings was an obscure young man named Max Zimmerman. Zimmerman, twenty-five, was a reporter for *Printers' Ink*, the weekly bible of the advertising industry. From September through December 1914, Zimmerman and his colleague Charles Hurd called attention to the rapid growth of chain stores in a spectacular series of articles. At the time, government statisticians collected almost no data about retailing and none at all about chains. Zimmerman and Hurd made it their business to fill that void. To universal shock, they discovered more than twenty-five hundred retail chains operating a total of thirty thousand stores. In Philadelphia, by their estimates, chains accounted for one-fourth of all grocery stores, in Chicago and New York for a sixth of all tobacco stores. In the drugstore field, chains were fewer but expanding fast. When they tried to investigate individual chains, Zimmerman and Hurd ran up against a brick wall. Most of the chains were privately held and released no information about sales or profits. Great Atlantic & Pacific was among the most secretive. "From the fact that it is continuously expanding, it is believed to be very prosperous," they wrote. "It is not a rabid price-cutter and does business along rather conservative, although progressive, lines."[16]

Zimmerman and Hurd's articles expounded at length on the reasons for chains' success. Some related to better management. In the grocery field, they pointed out, chain stores typically stocked fewer items than the average grocery and turned their stock twice as fast, so they had to finance fewer unsold items sitting on shelves. If the chains had their own warehouses, they could stash their inventory on low-cost warehouse shelves and make more profitable use of the costlier space at retail locations. They noted that food chains' purchasing costs were 15–20 percent below those of independents, highlighting the importance of price discrimination by manufacturers. Most important of all, food chains were willing to accept lower profit margins than independents. They laid many of the chains' advantages at the feet of incompetent independent merchants: "Where the chain's steam roller counts is where the ignorant or panic-stricken independent throws himself down in front of it to be promptly flattened out."[17]

But when Zimmerman came before the House Committee on Interstate and Foreign Commerce, he made clear that chain stores' growth relied on more than good management. He told of chains cutting prices in a particular store to unprofitable levels to drive out an independent, and of merchants who rejected token buyout offers from chains only to have the chain move in next door or even convince the landlord to let it occupy the independent store's space. While chains brought clear benefits to consumers, Zimmerman thought, they could abuse competition unless the government set limits. This was the problem the advocates of independent grocers complained of. Their solution was to allow manufacturers to require all retailers to charge a single price for a product, as Kellogg had done with its cornflakes.[18]

After dozens of hearings, the independent retailers and wholesalers who wanted to make price-fixing legal were sent away empty-handed. The House Committee on Interstate and Foreign Commerce refused to endorse their bill: support for small stores in their struggles against the chains was too weak, and the inefficiency of independent retailing was simply too obvious. Yet there were clear signs of a shift in the political and intellectual winds. Congress enacted two major changes in antitrust law in the autumn of 1914. In September, it created the Federal Trade Commission (FTC) to address "unfair methods of competition" and "deceptive practices," both of which were made illegal. The following month, the Clayton Antitrust Act outlawed price discrimination when the effect "may be to substantially lessen competition or tend to create a monopoly." The Clayton Act did little damage to chain stores, because it specifically permitted sellers to charge differing prices based on quality or quantity, but it did raise the prospect that in some cases price discrimination could break the law.[19]

•

The Great Atlantic & Pacific Tea Company, by far the largest chain in the grocery field, was notable by its absence from the chain-store debate. The Hartfords did not believe in lobbying. The company raised no complaints in the press and sent no one to testify during the months of hearings on the bill to ban price discrimination. The legislative archives give no indication that the Hartfords contacted any member of Congress about the issue. Instead, the company launched its first national marketing initiative. In January 1915, while the congressional committee was still taking testimony, A&P stores around the country invited boys and girls to compete for prizes by selling coffee door-to-door. In Macon, Georgia, the child selling the most would earn $3,000 in gold. In Fort Worth, Texas, the top seventy sellers would win prizes as large as $500, with any boy or girl selling at least $20 of coffee receiving a watch or a camera. Everywhere, the contest was announced in newspaper articles casting the A&P store in a favorable light—a timely antidote to the criticism of chain stores emanating from Capitol Hill.[20]

Grocery manufacturers were not enthusiastic about the explosive growth of the A&P Economy Store. One secret to the format's success was that the Hartfords used their company's size to demand special terms from suppliers: they asked manufacturers to ship goods directly to Great Atlantic & Pacific's warehouses, without going through wholesalers, and to give it the standard wholesaler's commission. This put the makers of brand-name products in a difficult spot, because Great Atlantic & Pacific was effectively paying less than other retailers. The makers of Campbell's soups and Bon Ami cleanser voiced misgivings. The Cream of Wheat Company, purveyor of a popular breakfast cereal, agreed to sell to Great Atlantic & Pacific without using wholesalers, but insisted that A&P charge retail customers at least fourteen cents a package so as not to underprice the manufacturer's smaller customers. When the A&P Economy Stores put Cream of Wheat on sale for twelve cents, the Cream of Wheat Company cut off supplies. Great Atlantic & Pacific sued, accusing the cereal company of illegally monopolizing trade by refusing to sell it Cream of Wheat.[21]

Judge Charles Hough handed the Hartfords a decisive legal defeat. The Cream of Wheat Company, he ruled in July 1915, was no monopolist, and was acting in a way that would promote competition among retailers. The true monopolist, the judge wrote, was the plaintiff, Great Atlantic & Pacific, which was using low prices to stifle competition by driving other grocers out of business. If the cereal company was forced to supply Great Atlantic & Pacific, "defendant and many retailers would be injured, and the microscopic benefit to a small portion of the public would last only until plaintiff was relieved from the competition of the 14 cent grocers, when it, too, would charge what the business would normally and naturally bear." In the eyes of the law, low-price retailing had become a highly suspect enterprise.[22]

The Cream of Wheat case revealed a shift in public sentiment: price-fixing by manufacturers, once widely condemned, was now accepted. "The reaction against the punishment of price fixers is unmistakable," *The New York Times* wrote, adding that "traders' rights are having their day, as buyers' rights had their day." Yet neither the highly publicized congressional hearings on chain stores nor the lawsuit over Cream of Wheat seems to have had the slightest effect on Great Atlantic & Pacific's business. On the contrary, business was so good that the Hartfords encountered a new sort of problem: they needed cash to expand.[23]

In more than half a century of involvement with the Great American Tea Company and the Great Atlantic & Pacific, George H. Hartford, so far as is known, had never borrowed a nickel. He had earned his equity in the firm by serving as George Gilman's partner and then, after the founder's death, by persuading Gilman's heirs that their best hope of realizing a return from the tea companies was to put all of the common stock in his hands. The Gilman descendants had received $1.25 million of preferred stock paying a 6 percent annual dividend; from the Hartfords' perspective, the attraction of preferred stock over borrowed money was that if business turned bad, the preferred dividend could be skipped. Starting in 1913, many Gilman family members decided to cash out, and by 1916 more than half the preferred stock had been redeemed.[24]

To raise the capital it needed, Great Atlantic & Pacific offered $3 million of bonds to a wildly enthusiastic public in June 1916. The five-year bonds paid 6 percent interest and were convertible into preferred stock paying a 7 percent dividend. The offering opened a window on the Hartfords' closely held finances, revealing that Great Atlantic & Pacific had earned a healthy $1.8 million in the year ending February 1916 on assets of $10 million. Although investors were not informed at the time, sales for that year were $44 million, meaning that net profit was an impressive 4.1 percent of sales. In short, the Hartfords were running an extraordinarily profitable enterprise. Management forecast earnings of $2.5 million for 1917 and $3.5 million once the stores to be funded by bond issue were opened—a doubling of profits in just two years. In a stodgy industry, this was a remarkable growth story.[25]

With the money from the 1916 bond sale and a smaller bond sale in 1917, the Hartfords opened new stores at a frenetic pace. From 480 stores in 1912, the year the first A&P Economy Store was opened, the store count had reached 1,817 by the end of 1915, then doubled over the next two years. Business boomed, due to both the growing number of stores and the inflation caused by World War I: Great Atlantic & Pacific's sales, $24 million in 1912, reached $126 million in 1917.

How the Hartfords managed this fast-growing organization is a bit of a mystery: almost no corporate records from the second decade of the twentieth century survive. This was an era of dramatically new ideas about management. The biggest businesses now had tens of thousands of employees, and executives sought new tools to keep track of diverse, far-flung operations. The answer, according to the leading management thinkers, lay in quantitative management, collecting and analyzing large amounts of data to identify rational solutions to business problems. Frederick Winslow Taylor and his acolytes barnstormed the country, teaching executives to make factories more efficient by timing and measuring each step in the production process. Howard E. Coffin, president of the American Society of Automobile Engineers, led a successful effort to rationalize auto production by standardizing parts. Arch Shaw, founder of *System* magazine, and Edwin Gay, the first dean of the Harvard Business School, preached the gospel of standardized cost accounting. As World War I raged across Europe, the government created the Council of National Defense and its civilian Advisory Commission in 1916 to prepare for possible U.S. entry into the war. The Advisory Commission's task, as Wilson explained, was to bring rational thinking to relations among business and the government, "efficiency being their sole object."[26]

The new Federal Trade Commission undertook to bring this sort of quantitative management to the retail sector. In July 1916, the FTC published *A System of Accounts for Retail Merchants*, designed as a basic guide for storekeepers. The slim booklet told merchants how to keep a daily journal, a cashbook, an invoice book, and a general ledger, and even listed the headings for each column in each book. The booklet included model forms to use in constructing a monthly business summary and a balance sheet, so the retailer might figure out whether the store was actually making a profit. The commission's chairman, Edward Hurley, introduced the booklet by emphasizing the need for the merchant to have accurate information in order to compete: "The Federal Trade Commission has found that the majority of retail merchants do not know accurately the cost of conducting their business and for this reason they are unable to price their goods intelligently."[27]

George L. and John Hartford seem to have stayed abreast of these intellectual trends. In 1916, A&P created the Managers' Benefit Association as a vehicle for training store managers. The association was organized locally in cities where the company had large numbers of stores. It served a social function, bringing isolated store managers together for dinners and recreational outings, but it also offered classes in accounting, merchandising, and the other skills a modern store manager needed to know. Members received a new magazine, *The Tattle Tale,* filled with company news and pearls of management wisdom. Store managers' pay had long included a percentage of their store's sales, but late in 1916 a company-wide profit-sharing program was added to give store managers a stake in the corporation's performance. At the end of the fiscal year in February 1917, the program paid every store manager 6 percent of salary.[28]

On August 29, 1917, George Huntington Hartford died suddenly at the age of eighty-three during his regular summer vacation at the New Jersey shore. True to form, visiting a store to check on business was one of the last acts of his life. Although his sons had been running the company for a decade, the elder Hartford remained active in the Great Atlantic & Pacific until the end. The company was imbued with his management philosophy. George H. Hartford was a decidedly paternalistic manager, but his paternalism extended strictly to the business; unlike many other paternalistic capitalists of his era, he made no effort to regulate his workers' private lives. He expected his managers to show ambition and initiative while at the same time following the company's rules, and he made sure they were paid well if they did so. In 1915, he passed on his wisdom in a booklet called *Manual for Managers of Economy Stores*. "Service to the customer and cleanliness in your store should be your aim," the elder Hartford advised. "Don't try to sell a customer something he or she does not seem inclined to buy." "Don't touch with the hands Tea, Coffee, Beans, etc., if possible, when weighing same. This is an age of cleanliness." "Don't be a pessimist. Every cloud has a silver lining."[29]

During George H. Hartford's nearly six decades with the Great Atlantic & Pacific and its predecessors, the retail business had changed beyond all recognition. George Gilman's primitive tea and leather business in the Swamp had become a lavishly promoted tea-store chain, then a mail-order pioneer, then the first chain grocery company, and then a price-slashing grocer with a radically new format that was taking the country by storm. George H. Hartford did not found the Great Atlantic & Pacific, but his managerial skill and financial acumen enabled it to prosper through depressions and to profit amid major shifts in consumers' expectations. Although he was unknown to the general public—his obituary in *The New York Times* was all of seven lines long—he was among the most capable and innovative business executives of his time.[30]

Hartford had prepared for the future with typical prudence. The house on Ridge Street went to his widow, Josephine, to be passed on to Marie Louise, the younger Hartford daughter, upon Josephine's death. Minnie, the elder daughter, already owned the property adjacent to her parents'; her father left her $40,000 in cash. George L. received the family homestead in Augusta. "This was the home of my father, Joshua B. Hartford, and I have kept it because of memories of my youthful days," George H. wrote in his will. Despite his father's wish that the property remain in the family, George L. sold it within a year to the City of Augusta for $1. The house and stables were replaced by the Hartford Fire Station, a two-story redbrick structure that, at George L.'s insistence, was capped with a clock always set to the correct time. Control of the Great Atlantic & Pacific passed into the hands of a trust, of which George L., Edward V., and John A. Hartford were the trustees. The brothers had complete control. Their debts were minor and their cash flow ample, so they could ignore the entreaties of bankers and bondholders. The company was theirs to run as they saw fit.[31]

World War I temporarily slowed the Great Atlantic & Pacific's headlong expansion. Even before the United States entered the war in April 1917, surging food prices led to riots in half a dozen major cities. President Wilson responded by creating the U.S. Food Administration to keep America fed while exporting as much as possible to Western Europe. Four months later, Congress authorized the Food Administration to control prices, limit consumption, and stop hoarding. In its first year, the agency promoted voluntary action. It asked households to observe wheatless Mondays and Wednesdays. Retailers were requested to apportion sugar equitably among customers, "so that no one of such customers receives more than his fair share," leaving it to the grocer to determine what share was "fair." The Hartfords responded with appropriate patriotic fervor. Their marketing experts prepared a show window to help the Food Administration's pledge campaign, promoting potatoes and rice as alternatives to wheat. Each store soon displayed a loaf of oat bread and a knife, alongside the sign: "Put the loaf on the table and slice as needed."[32]

As the Food Administration built its nationwide bureaucracy, it imposed more serious measures to regulate food supplies. Although the Federal Trade Commission continued to argue against the dangers of unrestrained price-cutting, the Food Administration's concern was the opposite. In the autumn of 1918, it cracked down on price gouging: grocers were told to limit their markup on eggs to seven cents per dozen, on lard to 18 percent, on canned peas to 25 percent. A rationing system likely would have followed, but most food regulations were suspended immediately after Germany signed an armistice on November 11, 1918.[33]

The Food Administration's efforts notwithstanding, the need to feed Western Europe during and after World War I had a dramatic effect on food prices. On average, the prices of twenty-two grocery items tracked by the government doubled between 1915 and 1920. Wages did not begin to keep up; an hour's work at union wages bought 17 percent less food in 1919 than it had six years earlier. Drawn by its low prices, hard-pressed shoppers flocked to the A&P. The company responded by opening hundreds more locations. In 1920, two years after the war's end, the Great Atlantic & Pacific Tea Company sold $235 million of groceries from 4,588 stores. It had become the largest retailer in the world.[34]

8

THE CHAIN-STORE PROBLEM

In the waning days of the First World War, Walter and Bertha Abbott bought a house near the docks of Portsmouth, New Hampshire. Walter, forty-seven, was a railroad man, a laborer for the Boston & Maine. Bertha, two years younger, had spent her working life at a laundry. Their new two-story home on Jefferson Street, built in 1722, would serve as more than just a place to live. It offered a way for a working-class couple to move up in the world, for the west side of the ground floor had been remodeled into a storefront. Soon after they moved in, the Abbotts opened a grocery store.[1]

Walter and Bertha Abbott were following a well-worn path. Selling food at retail may have been America's most popular career in the early decades of the twentieth century, drawing millions of workers searching for a secure living and a reputable profession. The retail trade was easy to enter, and while the workday was long, the tasks at hand were safer and less strenuous than stoking the boiler of a locomotive or digging ditches for the country's rapidly spreading networks of water and sewage pipes. Owning a grocery store, a bakery, or a butcher shop offered a certain status as well, because such people were often significant figures in the neighborhood, familiar to all who lived nearby. Best of all, opening a food store meant becoming an entrepreneur. With a little luck and a little skill, one might earn enough profit from a single store to open a second and a third, building a substantial business that could carry the family up and out of the working class to prosperity, financial security, and that cherished goal of every industrious grocer, independence.

The few square blocks of Portsmouth's dockside neighborhood were home to no fewer than 6 grocery stores in the 1920s, of which the Abbotts' Little Corner Store was only one. And Portsmouth was no exception.

Chicago had an estimated 11,865 grocery and meat stores in 1923, or one for every fifty-two households, not counting the thousands of bakeries, dairy stores, and produce shops. Atlanta, the leading metropolis of the South, boasted 1,715 groceries, bakeries, butcher shops, and other types of food stores within its city limits in 1926. This retail profusion made shopping convenient. In the urban America of the 1920s, almost everyone could walk to the grocery. In rural areas, the food trade was dominated by general stores, more than 100,000 of them selling food along with clothing and other merchandise, but even small towns had grocery and butcher shops. Everywhere, food shoppers could deal personally with the storekeeper whose name was above the door.[2]

The stores of the era were hardly temples of consumption. A typical grocery store in the 1920s was perhaps twenty feet across, the width of a brick row house, and only slightly deeper, occupying space leased at a cost of $60 per month. The floors were usually of wide wood boards, sometimes strewn with sawdust. Metal fixtures shading weak incandescent bulbs hung from the ceiling. Dark wooden counters ran down each side. Behind them, against the walls, were tall wooden shelves displaying canned goods, cleansers, and packaged teas. Bushel baskets or wood crates held a selection of whatever produce was in season, and glass cases, prominently positioned, offered candy and cigarettes. Refrigerated display cases were rare in the early 1920s, although later in the decade the store probably had a bright red machine selling bottles of Coca-Cola chilled with ice. The bulk goods—coffee, sugar, barrels of pickles, wheels of cheddar—were kept in the rear, where a scale and a coffee mill rested on a separate counter that offered a cutting surface as well. Often, a doorway hidden by a curtain of fabric or beads led to the owner's living quarters upstairs or in the back.[3]

The front door was open early in the morning, as soon as the proprietor returned from his predawn trip to the wholesale produce market, and it remained open until well into the evening. No one could afford to close if competitors were staying open. In many communities, grocery store owners agreed among themselves to close Wednesday afternoon or Saturday evening, but such pacts could be voided by the decision of a single grocer to keep longer hours. In some places, not even Sunday was a day of rest. The work was endless. "You get up at 4 in the morning. You go to the market. You work all day. Your wife works all day.

About 7 at night you close up. You go to bed," remembered the son of a Washington, D.C., grocer. Working conditions at chain stores were not much easier. Maurice Hartshorn, who managed a store for the Skaggs company in San Francisco, recalled that his shop was open six days a week, from 7:30 in the morning until 6:30 at night, except on Saturday, when business continued until 9:00. Once the doors were locked, there were still shelves to stock and a floor to sweep. "You usually got through at about 1 [a.m.] on Saturday nights because you were closed Sunday and had display windows and everything else to put in," Hartshorn remembered.[4]

Bakeries and stores selling meat typically had at least one or two paid employees, but many grocery stores, vegetable markets, and candy stores relied entirely on family labor. Often enough, the owner himself—92 percent of food-store proprietors were male—and his unpaid wife made up the entire staff. If government figures are to be believed, the tales of industrious schoolboys coming in the late afternoon to sweep the floor and deliver orders were more apocryphal than factual. Only one food store in three reported having any part-time workers on the payroll—although they may not have thought of delivery boys paid mainly by tips as employees.[5]

The storekeeper's foremost task was to wait on customers. A grocer named Clarence Saunders had opened the country's first self-service food store, Piggly Wiggly, in Memphis in 1916, but the concept had not spread widely by the early 1920s. Most stores were designed with counters in front of the shelves to keep customers (and their children) away from the food. The shopper would say what she needed, and the shopkeeper would pick each item from the shelves: two eggs, a can of beans, a box of soap powder. A "long arm," a wire loop at the end of a pole, stood ready to reach cans and boxes on the topmost shelves. Should the customer require coffee beans, the storekeeper would grind them while she waited. If she wanted vinegar, he would pump the desired amount from a barrel into a glass bottle.

Many housewives phoned in their orders rather than coming to the store, despite the warnings of advice columnists that ordering by phone could result in high prices and inferior merchandise. Whether the order was taken in person or by phone, assembling it was only part of the transaction. Mom-and-pop stores almost always provided delivery to the customer's home or apartment. Often, delivery was the after-school job of the owner's children. For a woman trying to maneuver young children up several flights of stairs to their apartment, having a teenager carry the purchases was a godsend, and she was willing to pay higher prices for the added service. At some stores, more than three-quarters of all sales required delivery. But while delivery was "free" to the customer, it was far from free to the merchant, who had to buy a bicycle or a truck and, in some cases, pay a deliveryman. The average cost of providing home delivery in 1923 came to 1.2 percent of a store's total sales, an amount equal to two-thirds of a typical store's profit.[6]

Collecting payment was perhaps the most unpleasant of the grocer's tasks. Even amid the general prosperity of the 1920s, many working families were living hand to mouth, and in the last few days before payday they often ran short of cash. Retailers in working-class neighborhoods had the choice of offering credit or seeing even fewer customers walk through the door. About half of all food stores, and the vast majority of stores not owned by chains, extended credit to their customers, usually on the basis of nothing more than a name and an address. In the 1920s, perhaps one-third of all sales, and a majority of sales involving meat, generated a handwritten entry in a credit ledger rather than a cash payment. In the poorest neighborhoods, credit commonly accounted for 70 or 80 percent of grocers' sales. "You'd ask them for money to pay and then they wouldn't come into the store no more," recalled the daughter of a Washington grocer. Often enough, the customer moved away, leaving an unpaid balance, or pleaded hardship to keep the credit line open. "If we learn that a man has lost his job, or has illness in the family, or meets with other reverses, we do not even send out a bill. We forget it," one Boston grocer explained. Stores offering credit typically charged higher prices to cover the inevitable credit losses, driving cash-paying customers to chain stores that offered no credit but lower prices.[7]

To later generations, an independent grocery came to seem vaguely romantic: a self-employed proprietor might carry unique products, local brands, or healthier foods than the mass retailer with a standardized selection. In reality, though, few of the independent grocers of the 1920s were selling tropical fruits, fine cheeses, and homemade salads. A small shop might stock as few as 450 items, of which sugar was easily the most important. The shopper—usually the woman of the house—might have to visit several different stores each day to procure her family's food, selecting from each shop's bare-bones product assortment in austere, ill-lit surroundings. In return for the convenience of personal service by familiar merchants who would sell on credit, she paid prices that were very high, relative to wages. The average urban family spent fully one-third of its budget on food.[8]

That large outlay bought distressingly poor nutrition. Although most people consumed plenty of calories, the average diet was short on nutrients such as calcium, vitamin A, and thiamine. Lack of refrigeration made it hard for retailers to keep milk, poultry, and produce fresh, so such products were frequently unavailable at the grocery store even for those who could afford them. Quality was often dubious. To keep otherwise unsalable merchandise from going to waste, Katzman's grocery store on Q Street in Washington recycled old or crumbled cookies into "grab bags" that sold for a penny apiece. At Rockmoor Grocery in Miami, the meat locker, chilled by hundred-pound blocks of ice, could not maintain a temperature far below fifty degrees, and ground beef, made daily from leftover beef trimmings, typically had a rancid taste. "While the bacteria count must have been quite high, most people then thought the taste was just characteristic of hamburger," one of the store's owners recalled.[9]

A large proportion of urban grocers were immigrants. For many of them, limited command of English posed a barrier to advancement in the wider world, but knowledge of Czech or Yiddish was an advantage in selling groceries to their fellow immigrants. In big cities, family ties and mutual-aid groups helped immigrants get a start. In Washington, D.C., for example, an aspiring Jewish grocer able to raise $100 in cash could turn to the Society of Mutual Benefits, which would lend $500 at 6 percent interest if the borrower could convince two members of the society to co-sign the loan; the borrower was to bring a $10 payment to the Jewish Community Center on Sixteenth Street Northwest every Thursday night. The society also provided advice about buying stores. A well-drawn contract would typically include a provision stipulating the sales volume claimed by the seller and requiring the seller to work in the business for a specified amount of time. If the store did not achieve the sales the seller claimed it to have, the buyer could back out of the deal.[10]

Immigrant grocers assumed an important role in explaining the ways of America to their customers. Their customers reciprocated with ethnic loyalty: when a Chicago social worker surveyed ninety immigrant families, seventy-four said they purchased all their food from grocers who spoke their language. Even where immigrants were fewer, as in Portsmouth, food stores customarily catered to particular ethnic groups. The Abbotts' customer base in Portsmouth was largely of Irish heritage; the Jews living nearby were more likely to shop at Liberson's Market; and the Italians favored Pento's. Czech grocers populated the Czech neighborhoods of Omaha, Nebraska, and Mexican grocers were common in Texas. Negro shopkeepers, who owned only one in fifty food stores, served almost exclusively an African-American clientele.[11]

In its twelve or fourteen hours of daily operation, the average grocery store generated precious little business. There was a limited supply of customers, and scant opportunity to attract more. Independent stores rarely promoted themselves beyond the occasional preprinted wall calendar. Their prices usually were not low enough to be a selling point, and in any event they lacked the money to advertise: during 1929, the average grocery store spent only $750 on all operating costs other than rent and payroll. The typical store served a few dozen families who lived within easy walking distance, and almost no one else. As the son of a Polish grocer in Chicago recalled, "If my dad had fifty customers, that's all he had, fifty. If he got fifty-one one day, it would be an odd thing."[12]

The combination of few customers and little stock had an inevitable consequence: meager revenue. The first academic studies, starting in 1918, reported an average store's sales to be in the range of $50,000–$60,000 per year, but experts agreed that the average was greatly inflated because the owners of smaller stores rarely responded to surveys. "Many grocery stores with small sales volume do not keep their records in such shape that they readily can fill out a classified profit and loss statement," a 1923 Harvard Business School study determined. A more realistic estimate came from the Census Bureau, whose first national survey, in 1929, revealed that more than one-fourth of food retailers had annual sales of less than $5,000. After paying for merchandise, rent, and operating expenses, the owner of such a store would have shown a profit of no more than a couple hundred dollars. He would have earned more as an employee in someone else's food store than as an entrepreneur.[13]

The average food store therefore had a very short life expectancy. In

Fort Wayne, Indiana, one out of every four grocery stores went out of business in the average year during the 1920s. In Pittsburgh, nearly half of new grocery stores ceased business within a year, and two-thirds were gone within three years. In Buffalo, the rate of exit was even higher; of every hundred grocery stores started between 1918 and 1928, eighty-five closed within five years. Although some stores survived for decades, they were the exceptions, not the rule; after three decades behind the counter, a grocer on the North Side of Chicago was able to boast, "Now my grocery store is the oldest on the street." In Portsmouth, the Abbotts' Little Corner Store lasted until Bertha's retirement, in 1951, only because Walter took a job with the town government, providing a regular income to supplement the pittance Bertha earned selling groceries.[14]

The mom-and-pop store was the final link in a long and tortuous food supply chain. A storekeeper with an annual turnover of $20,000, or even $40,000, was too small to gain the attention of the farmers, grain traders, food processors, and importers further up the chain. The grocer's ability to do business depended entirely upon his relationships with wholesalers.

The United States had 13,618 wholesale distributors of groceries in 1929. Of these, about a third carried a broad line of merchandise sometimes bought directly from manufacturers, sometimes from independent manufacturers' agents, sometimes from commissioned brokers who represented many manufacturers, sometimes from other wholesale merchants. Typically, they would try to purchase by the railcar load, to save money on freight, and then hold the goods in their own warehouses until a customer was ready to buy. Alongside the full-line wholesalers were several thousand specialists who handled a single category of merchandise, such as produce or delicatessen meats, that was too perishable for the general-line wholesalers to stock. The biggest wholesalers were independent, family-owned businesses that in many cases had been around for decades, but many smaller firms came and went: although thirty-six grocery wholesalers started up in Seattle during the 1920s, only eighteen wholesalers were operating there in 1930, two fewer than a decade earlier. The established wholesalers, especially in the big cities, had sales territories stretching far into the hinterlands: two-thirds of the general-line wholesalers in Chicago did business more than five hundred miles away.[15]

A wholesaler such as Corbin Sons & Company, located a few blocks north of the Chicago Loop, sent out hefty weekly circulars to keep grocers apprised of prices and market intelligence. "Broom corn is scarce and the price is tremendously high," *Corbin's Weekly Salesman* cautioned in 1923, advising grocers to stock up on brooms ahead of a price rise. Havana Sparks stogies were on sale at $1.95 per hundred; selling the cigars at the recommended price of three for ten cents would allow wide margin for profit. Sugar, to be bagged by the grocer, could be had in limited quantities at $8.70 per hundred pounds. Epsom salts, egg crates, and No. 9 corks for vinegar bottles all were available, often in very small lots. Many grocers preferred to buy that way, urged on by widely sold advice manuals that instructed grocers to forgo volume discounts in order to minimize the amount of money tied up in inventory and the risk of holding unsold goods. But stocking only enough goods for a few days' sales created risks of its own. Popular items like canned pineapple and tuna fish were to be had only sporadically. A retailer who failed to buy enough when the wholesaler had them available might end up without the goods his customers demanded.[16]

Corbin's had no shortage of competition. Chicago was home to 366 general grocery wholesalers in 1926, and hundreds of other wholesale firms specialized in meats, vegetables, or candy. Every day, thousands of wholesalers' salesmen fanned out from the Loop, competing for orders from the seventeen thousand food stores within the city limits and tens of thousands more in the country beyond. An astute shopkeeper could figure out how to play one against the other. Often enough, the decisive factor in choosing a wholesaler was credit, not price. For a perpetually cash-strapped retail grocer, a wholesaler willing to defer payment for thirty or sixty days was a godsend.[17]

Most grocery stores, though, were too small to interest big wholesalers with far-flung businesses. Instead, they often dealt with jobbers, wholesalers dealing in relatively modest quantities. Jobbers sometimes bought directly from manufacturers, sometimes from wholesalers, but they usually dealt in a limited number of items and held little inventory themselves. Critically, jobbers usually offered delivery, allowing the retailer to place his order by telephone without a time-consuming trip to the warehouse or the central produce market. Jobbers rendered themselves invaluable with intelligence on price trends and product availability and advice on displaying products. Most jobbers extended credit, which small retailers desperately needed, but they thereby exposed themselves to major financial risks. Goldman Brothers Wholesale Fruits and Produce in Breckenridge, Texas, ordinarily extended one week's credit, collecting payment for the previous week's delivery when it brought the next order. When the local oil boom went bust in 1921, the oil-town grocers vanished overnight, and their unpaid bills brought the wholesaler down as well.[18]

Each jobber carried a limited line, so independent grocers needed to do business with several jobbers to obtain all the different products they wished to sell. Since they had neither the storage space nor the cash to buy in large quantities, they might see each jobber several times a week. Competitive pressure forced jobbers to render such expensive service. "It is not uncommon to see three or four large trucks of that many wholesale or jobbing firms standing before a single small retail store," the Federal Trade Commission observed in 1919. "The cost of these individual delivery systems . . . is a large item to be figured into the wholesale prices."[19]

The wholesalers and jobbers, in turn, procured much of their merchandise from some 60,000 manufacturing plants around the country: 25,095 bakeries, 3,738 butter plants, 723 factories making pickles and preserves, 348 soap works, and so on. Some food processors were extremely large. The meat packer Swift & Company booked $800 million of sales in 1921, more than any other company in America, and the National Biscuit Company sold cookies coast-to-coast. Most food manufacturers, however, were mom-and-pop enterprises: the average cannery had a mere twenty workers, the average cheese plant no employees save the proprietor. To find buyers for their goods, these small firms used a bewildering array of brokers, each of whom earned a commission on every sale to a wholesale buyer. Some fruits and vegetables were marketed through sizable cooperatives such as the California Fruit Growers Exchange, which could move large quantities to market quickly. Most produce, however, was sold by individual farmers to small-town dealers who in turn sold to bigger dealers in nearby cities, creating a lengthy and circuitous route before perishable merchandise finally reached the retail store.[20]

Motortrucks were used within cities, but the only practical way to move food long distances in the early 1920s was by train. Shipment of canned or packaged foods by big manufacturers was relatively efficient, because major wholesalers bought entire boxcar loads and had rail sidings alongside their warehouses. When a big-city wholesaler sent a smaller lot to a small-town wholesaler or retailer, however, the freight cost could be high. Moving fresh produce was a nightmare. In Chicago, jobbers or wholesalers used horse-drawn wagons to collect incoming loads at rail yards, because the unloading platforms were too narrow for motortrucks. The freight from eighty thousand carloads a year was then drayed through downtown to the wholesale market on South Water Street. The market buildings lacked refrigeration, forcing wholesalers to sell their fruits and vegetables quickly lest they spoil. In New York City, which had no central produce market, each railroad operated its own terminal. Apples packed in barrels arrived on the New York Central, while apples in boxes came on the Erie. "The result," reported an astonished congressional committee, "is that the buyer desiring to purchase apples packed in the two types of packaging secures his supplies at two different docks some distance apart. If the same buyer desires certain other fruits or vegetables he must go to still other docks."[21]

The rapid spread of chain food stores threatened the livelihood of everyone who worked in the food industry. Before World War I, chain grocery stores were limited mainly to the Northeast and Midwest, and the larger chains collectively owned only a couple thousand stores. The Hartfords' aggressive expansion changed that picture. By 1923, Great Atlantic & Pacific alone had 9,236 outlets. Other companies, such as Kroger, Grand Union, and American Stores, could not open stores as quickly as A&P, so they raced to catch up by consolidating small chains into larger ones. The bigger chains had marked advantages over small chains and independent grocers. They could command volume discounts when buying from manufacturers. They could employ modern management techniques: Great Atlantic & Pacific turned its stock ten times in 1921, compared with seven times for the average grocery store, so it required much less working capital and storage space per dollar of sales. And the chains were willing to accept narrower margins than the independents: a chain could sacrifice a penny's profit on each dollar of sales and hope to make up the difference with higher volume, but for a store owner selling $30,000 of groceries a year, a narrower margin might seriously squeeze the family budget.[22]

Independent grocers and their wholesale suppliers generally fared well before and during World War I. Food prices were persistently high, and profit margins were wide. But as peace brought sharply lower food prices in 1920 and 1921, retail grocers' profits slumped badly, and grocery wholesalers booked losses. The downturn affected chains as well as independent stores; A&P's expenses as a share of sales soared from 15 percent in 1919 to 18 percent in 1920. But the hard-pressed independent merchants knew where to lay the blame for their plight. In 1922, the National Association of Retail Grocers debated whether there should be a limit on the number of chain stores in any community. That same year, Missouri wholesalers and retailers organized the Association Opposed to Branch Stores and urged the state legislature to tax chain stores out of existence. These efforts fell short, but many more would follow.[23]

9
WRONG TURNS

Had they occupied the executive suite at a prominent company with millions of stockholders, or had they allowed themselves to be profiled in the press as captains of industry, the Hartfords' personal lives could have brought embarrassment, and worse, to the Great Atlantic & Pacific Tea Company. Instead, when family affairs took an unorthodox turn, the company itself was entirely untouched by scandal. The Hartfords' obsessive concern with privacy, in evidence from the company's earliest days, paid off richly in the 1920s.

So far as is known, nothing untoward ever happened to George L. Hartford. Photographs show a stolid man, with a mustache and a head of thick gray hair, wearing a black suit, with the jacket fully buttoned over a vest, necktie, and white shirt. Now in his fifties, he drove the twelve miles from his Montclair home to the office in Jersey City six days a week and then drove back home in the evening. His personal life revolved around his wife, Josephine; his stepdaughter, Mabel; and Mabel's husband, Sheldon Stewart, who ran a real-estate company in Newark. Sunday outings frequently included visits to his mother, four miles away in Orange, until her death in 1925. George occasionally dined with his company's managers, but there is no record of him ever attending any society event in New York City. The notable events on his social calendar seem to have been the Montclair Junior League's annual fundraising show and, from 1926, the Montclair Horse Show, of which Sheldon Stewart was a director. Josephine was a long-standing parishioner of St. James Catholic Church in Newark, but George was not known as a churchgoer. He never held a passport; his travels seem to have taken him no farther than the New Jersey shore hotels where he spent his summer vacations, just as his father had. He was, as *Fortune* magazine later described him, an "implacably conservative" man.[1]

John's situation was rather different. In 1915, he and his wife, Pauline, separated after twenty-two years of marriage. The proximate cause was a red-haired young woman named Frances Bolger, who had come to the Hartfords' country home in Valhalla, north of New York City, to model gowns for Pauline. "He flirted with me over his wife's shoulder," Frances alleged later. Pauline embarked on round-the-world travels, riding a camel at the Great Pyramid and crossing the Pacific aboard the liner *Wilhelmina* to visit China and Japan before obtaining a divorce in 1920. John moved into a town house on West Fifty-fifth Street, but spent much of his time on the road, tending to the affairs of his burgeoning company, while continuing to raise prizewinning horses at Valhalla. Frances, who lived in the Hotel Berkley in New York, seems to have been an occasional diversion. Apparently, she wanted more. On June 28, 1923, the couple was secretly married in Danbury, Connecticut, not far from Valhalla. The marriage lasted all of six months. On December 27, John walked out. The story landed in the papers in July 1924, when Frances sued for alimony. Her lawsuit, filled with colorful detail, was met with silence from John. A divorce was quietly arranged, and the press soon lost interest.[2]

In September 1924, John applied for his first passport. He used it to visit Paris, where he and Pauline were remarried on April 4, 1925. Pauline apparently extracted certain commitments, for John resumed married life, at age fifty-three, with a newfound attention to leisure. Henceforth, the society pages would report his and Pauline's transatlantic voyages and their winter visits to Palm Beach. He bought a boat and cruised in the Atlantic. During the horse show each November, the Hartfords threw an elaborate dinner, the guest list printed in the papers. And in 1926, he and Pauline began transforming the country house in Valhalla into an estate fit for a magnate. Sitting on 310 acres in Westchester County, Buena Vista Farms included stables, a golf course, a polo field, and a twenty-nine-room Tudor mansion with gold bathroom fixtures and a private screening room. The house was an easy commute from New York City. John and Pauline took an eight-room apartment at the Plaza Hotel as their main residence and used Buena Vista Farms as a summer home. After 1927, when Great Atlantic & Pacific moved its head office into the Graybar Building, adjacent to Grand Central Terminal, John could go directly from his twenty-second-floor office to the train and be at Buena Vista Farms in forty-five minutes.[3]

The unexpected death of John's older brother Edward in June 1922 held yet more potential for commercial damage. Edward, his wife, Henrietta, and their two children, Josephine and Huntington, had moved from Park Avenue to an estate in Deal, a wealthy enclave on the New Jersey shore. According to family lore, Edward was a practicing Christian Scientist and refused to see a doctor when he fell ill, contributing to his death at age fifty-two. The family was evidently embarrassed by the circumstances. Although Edward was well-known as an inventor and manufacturer who had been prominent in New York society, the only notice of his death was a four-line announcement in *The New York Times*, stating that the funeral would be private.[4]

Under other circumstances, the two separations, two divorces, three marriages, and lavish new lifestyle of one of the nation's wealthiest men and the shocking death of his independently wealthy brother would have furnished months of tabloid titillation. The Hartfords' private affairs, however, drew surprisingly little public notice. And if they were aware of the Hartford family's affairs at all, shoppers seem not to have connected them with the neighborhood store where they shopped every day. The trade of the Great Atlantic & Pacific seems not to have been affected in the least.

Though it had several times the sales of any other grocery company, the Great Atlantic & Pacific Tea Company was in no sense a modern business. Its five thousand stores were tiny: just one of the vast supercenters that flourished at the end of the twentieth century had as much floor space as three hundred A&P Economy Stores. Where the average grocery store at the end of the twentieth century carried perhaps forty thousand different items, the average A&P, circa 1921, stocked only a few hundred. Some A&P stores allowed self-service, but usually the goods were kept out of customers' reach, behind the counters, and store clerks retrieved each can of soup or bag of coffee as the shopper made her selections.

A&P stores rarely carried meat, fish, or milk, except in cans. "Of produce commodities they handle only butter, eggs, potatoes, and some eating apples in season," one researcher found. Keeping fruits and vegetables in good condition as they passed through a complex distribution system was a problem no chain retailer had solved, but there was an entirely different reason to avoid them. The toughest task facing the executives of a retail chain was monitoring the work of store managers, who had ample opportunity to steal from the till, help themselves to the merchandise, or hurt the company's reputation by neglecting the store. The sale of nonperishables was fairly easy to keep track of: if the store had received three cases of cigarettes, three cases should have been sold, and missing merchandise could be deducted from the manager's pay. Perishables, however, could be rendered unsalable for any number of reasons, from delays in delivery to extremely hot weather to the store manager's failure to care for the products. If a manager's weekly report had indicated that fifty pounds of pears went unsold, there would have been no practical way for the company to determine the cause. Monitoring perishable products was such a daunting task in the early 1920s that most grocery chains, including A&P, avoided selling them.[5]

Its limitations notwithstanding, the Great Atlantic & Pacific possessed important advantages over its competitors in the grocery trade. Its wide footprint made A&P the only grocer that could use national magazine advertising effectively, an edge the Hartfords exploited in 1920 by mounting the first-ever national ad campaign by a grocer; it may well have been William G. Wrightson, vice president for advertising and husband of George and John's niece, who came up with the idea of portraying A&P as "the little red school house of American retailing." Volume discounts from food processors provided a significant advantage by allowing A&P to buy its goods more cheaply than other grocers, especially when suppliers were willing to circumvent wholesalers and sell directly to the retailer at wholesale prices. Most critical of all, by blanketing cities with stores—there were three hundred in Chicago alone—A&P gained powerful economies of scale. With geographic concentrations of stores, the company could run its own warehouses and delivery trucks, which in turn let it manage inventory efficiently. On average, grocery products took more than four months to get from factory to consumer in the early 1920s, and the financing charges and storage costs had to be built into retail prices. A&P, in contrast, turned its inventory once every five weeks. With comparatively few goods sitting in storage at any given time, it enjoyed much lower costs than independent grocers.[6]

The Hartfords moved to exploit these advantages with scientific precision. With ample profits to reinvest and no outside shareholders clamoring for higher dividends, the Hartfords had the resources to expand quickly. No surviving information documents the discussions between George and John in the early 1920s, but it would have been in character for John to push faster growth and George to question the payoff from new investments. In any event, teams of company real-estate experts scoured the country, drawing on A&P's detailed statistical information to evaluate buildings, measure pedestrian traffic and neighborhood wealth, and estimate how much revenue a new location might bring in. Data in hand, A&P was in control when it came time to negotiate a lease. Construction workers swarmed in, readying the store within days. Over the three-year span between February 1922 and February 1925, the gold-on-red A&P logo went up on seven new storefronts a day, a pace limited only by the company's ability to find store managers. "We went so fast that hobos hopping off the trains got hired as managers," John Hartford joked later. By February 1925, the Great Atlantic & Pacific operated more than thirteen thousand stores from Maine to Texas.[7]

As leases expired, existing stores were relocated to larger premises. The six-hundred-square-foot Economy Store, state of the art before World War I, was an anachronism by the Roaring Twenties, and the new stores were twice that size or more. Here, too, scientific thinking came into play, with A&P's designers using sales data and customer surveys to decide where to place the various departments and how to present the goods. The larger stores displayed products on counters, rather than behind them, so shoppers could serve themselves. Some stores had room for electric refrigerator cases, a new invention, to hold fresh milk and produce. Customers' new expectations extended to trading stamps. With the Economy Store, John Hartford had convinced shoppers to forgo premiums in return for low prices, but in the 1920s they expected both. By the early 1920s, A&P shoppers in some locations could once again obtain coffee mills or sherbet glasses in return for stamps handed out with every purchase.[8]

Around 1920, the Hartfords decided that their fast-growing retail business would assure a profitable outlet for manufacturing. The evidence suggests that this, too, occurred at John's urging. Vertical integration—the idea that a company should take charge of multiple facets of its business, one supplying the other—was all the rage in American industry. In 1917, the Ford Motor Company had begun building its vast River Rouge plant near Detroit, which was designed to take in iron ore, rubber, and other raw materials, turn them into mufflers, windshields, and fan belts, and combine the thousands of parts into a complete vehicle, all at a single site. John, impressed, consulted Henry Ford about applying the secrets of volume production to the food sector. The meatpacking industry was already trying to do this. The five big firms that dominated hog and cattle slaughtering had opened retail meat markets, allowing them to control the industry vertically from the fattening of animals for slaughter to the retail sale of pork chops, and one of the five, Armour & Company, had built a retail fruit and vegetable business. Federal antitrust action in 1920 forced the meat packers to exit their retail businesses, but it did nothing to hinder retailers from entering manufacturing. A&P was already vertically integrated in a modest way thanks to its Jersey City manufacturing complex, but it manufactured only a small part of the goods it sold. Reliance on outside suppliers must have seemed a disadvantage at a time when manufacturers were capturing a greater share of the food industry's profits. As George and John debated this issue, they decided that the best way to fight the growing power of grocery manufacturers was to manufacture more themselves.[9]

The first step came in 1919, when the brothers turned A&P's coffee business into the American Coffee Corporation, a wholly owned subsidiary. A&P, of course, had been selling coffee since the Civil War, and had imported coffee directly from Brazil since at least the 1890s. Its brands, however, were not the market leaders, and the name A&P was not associated with high-quality coffee. George Clews, the son of George and John's sister Minnie, took charge of American Coffee. Again, scientific thinking was put to use. American Coffee set up a buying office in Santos, the main Brazilian coffee port, and established a network of agents in the growing regions; rather than accepting whatever Brazilian exporters chose to ship, it would select the beans with the characteristics its customers preferred. Roasting and grinding plants were built across the United States so A&P could move coffee to its stores quickly after grinding. The product was enveloped in an aura of quality carefully constructed by A&P marketers. Experts were said to blend the beans in precise fashion at Santos. Trained testers sampled the coffee on the docks and again before it left the roasting plants to maintain consistency. George L. Hartford, a man who never went out to lunch, established the new tradition of visiting the tasting department at 2:00 p.m. each day to make sure the coffee tasted just right. Several weak brands were dumped so A&P could put its marketing muscle behind Eight O'Clock Coffee, its bestselling coffee.[10]

In October 1922, A&P spent $275,000 to buy the White House Milk Company at West Bend, Wisconsin. At the time, grocery stores rarely sold fresh milk, which had a short shelf life due to the lack of refrigeration. Instead, A&P sold canned evaporated milk, which the consumer could use simply by adding water, and sweetened condensed milk, similar to evaporated milk but with sugar mixed in. By acquiring White House, which produced only 400,000 cases of evaporated milk per year, the Hartfords were entering head-to-head competition with established manufacturers of brand-name canned milk, such as Borden and Carnation. John Hartford visited West Bend in 1923 and must have liked what he saw. A&P rapidly added plants across Wisconsin to purchase milk from farmers, condense it, and can it. It was soon among the biggest milk producers in America.[11]

The story was repeated with bread. Once, when its stores had been concentrated around New York City, most stores had sold bread baked at the A&P headquarters complex in Jersey City. By 1923, though, A&P had stores in twenty-three states, most of which had to be supplied by local bakers under their own brand names. These industrial bakers usually wanted to charge all retailers the same price, a situation the Hartfords saw no reason to accept. A&P went on a buying binge, purchasing existing bakeries, installing the most modern equipment, and becoming the second-largest baker in the country, with costs far below those of other bakeries. The company's mass of sales data allowed A&P's bakeries to forecast demand with a high degree of accuracy, minimizing returns of stale bread and doughnuts. Bread was delivered to stores in the same trucks that delivered other foods rather than by commissioned salesmen, a system that saved a penny per one-pound loaf at a time when the average loaf sold for a nickel. With a cheap source of supply, the stores could use Grandma's Bread and pound cakes as major customer draws.[12]

Another subsidiary, A&P Products Corporation, plunged into the salmon industry. Fresh fish were extremely difficult to transport and were rarely sold far from the docks where they were landed. Most of the catch was canned, and canned salmon had been a major grocery product since the turn of the century. The salmon-canning industry had boomed during World War I. When prices collapsed after the war, many canneries failed. A&P swooped in. It leased three canneries in southeastern Alaska in 1922 and added others. By 1926, A&P's operation, renamed Nakat Packing Company, was challenging Libby, McNeill & Libby as the leader in the $46-million-a-year canned salmon trade.[13]

The Hartfords expanded their manufacturing business in the continental United States under a subsidiary that became known as Quaker Maid. Great Atlantic & Pacific was not entirely new to packaged foods, having opened a vegetable cannery around 1907, but Quaker Maid was on an entirely different scale. A&P-owned plants began churning out everything from peanut butter to gelatin. The company's market-research department surveyed consumer preferences and massaged detailed sales data from individual stores so Quaker Maid could adjust its recipes to suit local or regional tastes. Quaker Maid was so large that A&P even owned a factory to print labels and another to manufacture cans, twenty-two million of them a year.[14]

Being a food processor vastly complicated the job of moving raw materials and finished products, and A&P created a huge logistical infrastructure. Leased refrigerator cars carried produce from growing areas to canneries and warehouses. Goods from outside suppliers were purchased by the boxcar, minimizing the purchase price and allowing the company to save about 15 percent on freight costs. As one of the country's largest shippers, A&P had the muscle to bargain with the railroads, saving $60,000 a year by winning changes in the rates for moving coffee from ports to roasting plants to warehouses. Its in-house transportation division marshaled fleets of company-owned trucks and refrigerated boxcars to get food delivered on time.[15]

By all public evidence, A&P was an amazing growth story. Its stores, warehouses, and factories had been planted in thousands of communities across the eastern half of the United States. Its new manufacturing might would give it an ever-bigger cost advantage over neighborhood grocers. Its brand was famous, promoted on the *A&P Radio Hour*, one of the earliest national radio shows, by the music of Harry Horlick and the A&P Gypsies. Its sales figures, released annually since its first bond sale in 1916, astonished the experts. "1924 Sales Were Enormous," *The New York Times* declared in 1925. The annual dividend on the common stock, which was announced each May, was raised to $3 in 1923, $4 in 1924, and $5 in 1925, seeming proof that the firm was in the best of health.[16]

The reality was otherwise. Although the numerous articles and books about the Great Atlantic & Pacific uniformly praise the Hartfords' management skill, the push to grow so quickly in the early 1920s and to diversify into manufacturing, apparently driven by John's eagerness to expand, was unwise. The Hartfords had always been parsimonious with their investment dollars, doing all they could to avoid buying fixed assets: by the company's estimate, its average store involved an investment of only $1,120 in real estate and equipment, a fraction of the $2,740 invested in the average Kroger store and the $4,543 at American Stores. But manufacturing, as John Hartford frequently pointed out, involved a great deal of "capital tie-up." He was forced to admit that the results of his push for vertical integration were disappointing. In 1924, A&P's canneries and milk plants produced a 23.6 percent return on invested capital—but while two canning plants were extremely profitable, others barely made money or even ran in the red. The bakeries as a group earned only a 17 percent return, far below the company average, and several of them lost money. Manufacturing was no gold mine.[17]

Worse, running a complex manufacturing operation caused management to take its eye off the main business of selling groceries. Although A&P's total sales rose 50 percent between 1920 and 1924, sales per store *fell* almost 50 percent. The physical volume of groceries handled in the average store declined for four consecutive years: A&P was not even keeping up with mom and pop. Among ten grocery chains, none approaching A&P's size, A&P ranked dead last in sales per store. Selling expenses, 14 percent of sales in 1920, climbed to 18 percent of sales in 1924, forcing A&P to hike prices and retreat from discount pricing. While A&P was content with a profit of three cents on each dollar of sales, American Stores, a Philadelphia-based chain, was rumored to be earning twice as much. Those impressive dividend increases merely reflected the amounts George and John Hartford chose to pay themselves and the family trust, and were no indication of the company's performance. By some measures, A&P was using more cash than it was generating.[18]

The Hartford brothers were in no danger of running out of money, but the trend lines were pointing in the wrong direction. By 1925, they could not ignore the fact that their company had grown too big and too unwieldy. It was time for a new strategy.

10

THE PROFIT MACHINE

If the modern consumer economy can be said to have a starting date, 1925 is as good a choice as any. In that year, George and John Hartford began to steer their company onto a dramatically new course, one that sought growth and profitability by emphasizing low costs, low prices, and high volume. In restructuring the Great Atlantic & Pacific Tea Company, they transformed both the nature of retailing and the expectations of the American shopper. The Hartfords' organizational changes created a retailing behemoth whose size was almost beyond comprehension and touched off a quarter century of political and legal warfare over the role of small business in the American economy.

The Hartfords' initiatives were in tune with the spirit of the times. In January 1925, the Chamber of Commerce of the United States gathered two hundred executives in Washington for the first National Distribution Conference. The featured speaker was Herbert Hoover, the secretary of commerce and the man who had mobilized the American food distribution system to feed a starving Europe in the wake of the world war. Hoover, an engineer by training, had spent years trying to standardize everything from typing paper to bricks in order to improve the efficiency of the manufacturing sector. Although far from being a socialist, he believed that capitalism naturally led to so much diversity as to create inefficiency. "The only case where unlimited diversification seems justified is padlock keys," Hoover said. Government, he asserted, could make the capitalist system more productive by helping businesses agree on standard products and procedures that would eliminate unnecessary costs. Now he was turning his engineer's eye to America's wholesale and retail trades, and he did not like what he saw. Those thousands of tiny wholesalers and retailers that made up the distribution system meant waste and inefficiency, and the public was paying for it. He called on businesses to standardize their products, their record-keeping systems, and their freight handling. If products could move more efficiently from producer to consumer, Hoover insisted, farmers and manufacturers would earn more profit, consumers would save money, and the country would prosper as workers shifted from distribution to more productive activities.[1]

The Hartfords' new strategy for A&P would put such ideas to use. They would ruthlessly purge waste and inefficiency from their business, rationalizing the process of manufacturing and distributing food. In so doing, they would improve the productivity of capital as well as of labor. Their family business would evolve into a complex organization that distributed more goods at lower cost than any retailer in history. Retailing would cease to be a personal matter between a regular customer and a merchant known by name, and instead become an anonymous transaction with a distant corporation whose only important attribute was its ability to sell food cheaply.

A&P sold $352 million worth of merchandise in the twelve months ending in February 1925. It was by any standard an astonishing figure: far more than any retailer in any country had ever sold in a single year, 63 percent more than the sales of the second-biggest U.S. retailer, F. W. Woolworth, and 18 percent above A&P's own sales the previous year. Yet despite its size, the company was run very much like a mom-and-pop business. Though there were layers of executives, every decision, from closing an underperforming store to buying a small condensed-milk plant, was liable to end up on the desks of the men who controlled all of the company's stock, George and John Hartford. "We handled all operations from headquarters in Jersey City. All departments. All divisions. Everything," John Hartford explained later. There were so many details to tend to that no one was responsible for strategic planning, or for thinking about how developments in technology, society, and politics would alter the environment in which A&P operated. There simply wasn't time.[2]

The Hartfords ran their sprawling empire with rule books and carbon paper. Headquarters issued regulations for everything: how managers should use their time, how products should be selected, how company-baked bread should be priced relative to bread from outside bakeries. To keep the central office staff up-to-date on policy changes, the Hartfords invited them to "informal" dinners—command performances that were anything but informal. "I hope that nothing will occur to prevent your presence at this 'Home Gathering' A&P family affair," John Hartford wrote to one manager invited to such an evening at the elegant Hotel Astor. In addition to fostering adherence to the rules, these gatherings gave the brothers a chance to assess their men and decide who was ready for promotion. They served to build team spirit as well: mid-level corporate managers cherished the opportunity to speak directly with Mr. George and Mr. John.[3]

There were rule books for A&P's store managers, too. The company's experts, using sales data from thousands of stores, knew the best way to organize merchandise and arrange window displays, and managers were expected to heed their advice. Store managers were to treat their clerks and bookkeepers respectfully, in line with John Hartford's belief that "after a man has worked loyally for a concern for a reasonable time, the responsibility of his employer to him is fully as great as his responsibility to his employer." Unlike other grocery chains, A&P did not require store managers to post bonds to assure their honesty; instead, it submerged them beneath piles of forms. Order sheets were to be filled out in a certain way and sent to the warehouse twice a week. Reports on sales and stock losses were to be submitted weekly. Once each quarter, each manager had to detail his store's expenses for vehicles, from truck repairs to outlays for shoeing horses. Inspectors visited each store regularly, issuing grades to the managers and designating the best-run properties as "model" stores. Compliance with company policies was treated as each manager's personal obligation to the Hartfords. "The interest that you have shown in our behalf by conforming to all our rules and regulations is indeed very gratifying," John Hartford cabled to a "model" store manager in 1924.[4]

When members of Congress first studied grocery chains, in 1921, they concluded that chains would have a tough time maintaining a competitive edge because their management and supervision costs were very high. A&P seemed to prove the case. More stores and factories led to more central office staff, driving up operating expenses. Rule books and forms with multiple copies were indispensable management tools at a time when computers did not exist and a quick phone call from New York to Chicago cost as much as a store clerk's daily pay, but at A&P so many of those forms piled up in Jersey City that important information got lost in the shuffle. Even George L. Hartford, whose extraordinarily detailed knowledge of the firm's finances ensured a firm footing for its expansion, had to acknowledge that he could no longer study the financial performance of each of his thousands of stores. By 1925, the brothers knew they needed to decentralize administration and delegate authority.[5]

As they contemplated greater reliance on their executives, the Hartfords must have been concerned about their ability to retain talent. "One of the disadvantages of chain stores is the difficulty they have in keeping their best men, for many of them, after they learn the business, leave to engage in business for themselves," a leading wholesaler commented in 1930. The Hartfords paid high-level managers well and provided unusually good job security; John Hartford's view was that if a man did not perform well in a responsible position, "we can give him another equally important post for which he is better fitted." Given that all common shares were controlled by the Hartfords, though, executives could not expect to grow wealthy thanks to a rising share price. Executives received preferred stock paying a generous 7 percent annual dividend, but lower-level managers had no financial stake in the company at all. National Tea Company, then the third-largest grocery chain, had issued common stock in 1924, allowing it to offer stock grants to executives, and it was no secret that Wall Street bankers were trying to restructure other private food chains into publicly traded companies that would then be able to use stock grants to lure away A&P managers. Keeping their best men from jumping ship would require the Hartfords to offer a similar incentive.[6]

The first hint of major changes came in January 1925, when A&P sold its headquarters, warehouse, and factories in Jersey City. The sale came as a surprise, and the public explanation was enlightening. The company's growth, an anonymous official told *The New York Times,* made it necessary to establish smaller warehouses and factories in different localities. This heralded far tighter control over costly investments and represented a shift in managerial focus. First and foremost, A&P would be a retailer.[7]

On March 1, 1925, the start of a new fiscal year, the Hartfords announced the reorganization of their company. A&P's 13,398 stores were divided into business units based on geography. The New England, Eastern, Central, Southern, and Middle Western divisions were all given their own headquarters and boards of directors, with a staff of real-estate, personnel, and purchasing experts. Underneath each division—two more would later be added—were units covering smaller territories. Some functions, such as store design, were assigned to the division level, but the forty-eight unit managers were responsible for the operations of stores and warehouses. Unit managers could stock A&P-brand merchandise, but they were also free to order from outside manufacturers. The Hartfords wanted to push responsibility for sales and pricing as far down the chain as possible, not only because unit managers and store managers were familiar with local conditions, but also because increased responsibility would help lower-level managers develop new managerial skills. There was one important exception to decentralization: the Atlantic Commission Company, a subsidiary created in 1924, would supply all of the divisions with fresh produce, so they would not compete with one another to buy from farmers and farm cooperatives. The division presidents would join company executives on a council to set company-wide policy on whatever matters seemed to require uniformity, but John Hartford insisted that the main role of headquarters was to offer "suggestions"; the men in the field would make the decisions.[8]

The third big change came in June, when the Hartfords revamped the corporate structure. They created a new holding company with the power to sell common shares to employees. Anyone who had worked for A&P for at least five years could invest up to 10 percent of the previous year's wages in A&P shares, with the company paying part of the cost. The shares were not available to the public, but inevitably some employees who had acquired them wished to sell, and outsiders could occasionally pick up five or ten shares on the Curb Market, New York's lightly regulated exchange for speculative stocks. Employee stock ownership hardly affected the Hartfords' managerial prerogatives—they still controlled more than 99 percent of the common shares—but it did provide a means for cementing managers' loyalty: many employees jumped at the opportunity to purchase as little as a single share.[9]

Along with its new stock-ownership plan, A&P announced publicly that it aimed to sell $420 million of groceries in 1925, some 20 percent more than a year before. It was an ambitious goal. A&P would achieve it with room to spare.

The new council of division presidents, which included the Hartfords and a few top executives from headquarters, met for the first time on June 25, 1925. The group plowed through a massive packet of graphs and tables. The brothers believed in managing with data, and each quarterly meeting of the division presidents involved detailed dissection of figures on every topic imaginable: labor turnover among meat clerks; outlays for electricity and paper bags; sales of A&P's brands versus outside brands of coffee. Often, the figures were calculated on a per-store basis and arranged by division or even by unit, allowing executives to spot a high rate of stock losses in the Louisville unit or to see whether Atlanta spent more on in-store displays than Albany. Drawing on the Hartfords' example, the division presidents presented numbers upon numbers at their biweekly or monthly meetings with unit heads. In those precomputer days, collecting and assembling such massive amounts of data were complicated tasks, but there was nothing to which the brothers attached higher priority.[10]

The June 1925 presidents' meeting brought a lengthy discussion of the company's mixed performance. A&P's return on investment in 1924, 24 percent, was far below that of competitors such as Kroger in the Midwest and American Stores in Philadelphia. Over the previous five years, one-fifth of the company's after-tax earnings had gone into the purchase of fixed assets such as factories and warehouses, with the biggest increases coming in 1923 and 1924. This was a major change for a company that had traditionally avoided tying up its money in buildings and equipment, and the money was not well spent: the factories, while highly profitable, earned a lower return on investment than the stores. Over the same period, inventories had ballooned. In 1919, A&P had kept a one-month supply of groceries in its stores and warehouses. By 1925, seven weeks of inventory had become the norm, a particular problem in a deflationary economy in which inventories lost value. Perhaps it was a reflection of George Hartford's chronic shyness that although he was responsible for financial matters, John Hartford took the lead in discussing the company's results, complaining to the assembled executives that "capital tie-up" was dragging down return on investment.[11]

The conclusion that A&P was making poor use of its capital had fateful implications for the company's business strategy. The planned expansion of manufacturing was abandoned; A&P would continue to run its plants, but would not add more except for bakeries, which provided an essential product for much less than the price from outside suppliers. The company's investment would go into stores, not factories. Those new stores would be larger than the Economy Stores, which had become distinctly outmoded by the mid-1920s. A&P had conducted an experiment in Detroit, opening larger stores with meat departments and learning that customers liked the convenience of buying meat in the same place they bought their groceries, so most new stores would have meat counters. The Hartfords were so eager to add stores that they took the exceptional step of purchasing seventy outlets in Kansas City from the troubled Grand Union Tea Company.[12]

The results of the push for more stores and greater regional autonomy quickly proved disastrous, turning 1925 into A&P's worst year since the war. The average store moved only 2.73 tons of groceries, a full 13 percent below the peak in 1919. As this occurred, A&P's return on investment plummeted; as John Hartford acknowledged, the $10 million invested during 1925 boosted earnings by less than $500,000, a meager return of 5 percent. Some local managers were trying to revive sales by offering delivery and even trading stamps, costly frills A&P had moved away from when it developed the Economy Store concept in 1912. "Mistaken sales and development policies" were at the root of the company's problems, John Hartford told his top executives, adding: "I think that we are steering the boat wrong . . . [We have] a low volume and a high expense rate driving us out of the Economy business."[13]

The preference for volume over margin was a matter on which the Hartford brothers did not see eye to eye. George hewed to a traditional understanding of retail profitability, preferring to maintain a generous markup on each item sold. Profits averaged an impressive 3 percent of sales from 1921 to 1925, appearing to show the success of the high-markup strategy. John, though, downplayed return on sales as a measure of profitability. He preferred to watch the company's return on investment. Historically, A&P's pretax return on investment had exceeded 25 percent in most years, and John set that as the norm. The way to boost return on investment, he thought, was to make better use of capital by pushing more merchandise through A&P's stores and warehouses. In February 1926, John convinced his brother and his division presidents to scale back store openings and focus on increasing volume per store. He inspired his executives with a secret goal: A&P would more than double its sales over a five-year period, becoming in 1929 the first retailer in history to reach $1 billion in sales.[14]

The new strategy was a decided gamble. To make it work, A&P would have to cut costs drastically: lowering prices without lowering costs would devastate profitability. The easiest way to cut costs, of course, was to slash the wages of grocery clerks and store managers, but the Hartfords, extremely paternalistic employers, would not hear of such a thing. Instead, they identified other avenues. The pace of store openings was scaled back; after opening nearly nine thousand stores between 1922 and 1926, A&P would add fewer than one thousand over the next four years. The company's thirty-six warehouses would have to run more efficiently, keeping less inventory. The bakeries would acquire the latest technology to make a thousand loaves at a time at the lowest possible cost. If stores' orders for the products of A&P's bakeries and factories allowed them to run at capacity, the manufacturing plants should earn solid returns even while supplying merchandise at low cost; those that could not would be sold or closed. Low factory production costs would enable the stores to "pass a part of the manufacturing profit along to the customer," reducing retail prices in a way independent stores would be unable to match.[15]

The most important change—one that would have grave political consequences—came in A&P's relationships with grocery suppliers. Through the early 1920s, purchasing had been rather haphazard, with warehouses, unit managers, or division managers buying directly from independent brokers, from manufacturers' sales representatives, or, in some cases, from wholesalers. The 1925 reorganization put division presidents in charge of purchasing, with the result that the company paid several different prices for a particular product. In 1926, the Hartfords put an end to such laxity. A&P bought more groceries than any other retailer in the country, and they determined that it should be treated accordingly. Headquarters took charge of relationships with the big grocery manufacturers with the frank aim of driving purchasing costs down.

Many of these companies, such as Morton Salt and National Biscuit Company, produced popular brands with hefty profit margins. A&P's new policy represented an attempt to capture some of the value in those brands. A&P demanded that the manufacturers give it advertising allowances in return for promoting their products nationally in whatever way it saw fit. Manufacturers were to sell directly to A&P, without using brokers or agents, and A&P would receive the commissions normally paid to brokers. If a manufacturer refused to play by those rules, A&P would take its business elsewhere. As the Hartfords anticipated, allowances became a major source of income. By 1929, allowances paid by manufacturers directly to A&P headquarters accounted for one-quarter of pretax profits.[16]

Manufacturers were to provide volume discounts, as they had in the past—but with A&P now placing many orders centrally, rather than at the unit level, its orders were extremely large, entitling it to deep discounts. Manufacturers almost always gave larger discounts to chains than to independent retailers, and they gave larger discounts to A&P than to any other chain. Between the volume discounts, the advertising allowances, and the brokerage commissions, A&P's cost to purchase any item should be lower than that of smaller competitors. The difference was not huge: careful estimation by the economist Morris Adelman suggests that in 1929, A&P may have paid 0.94 percent less than wholesale grocers would have paid for the same products. But in a business in which customers would go out of their way to save a few pennies, A&P's persistently lower purchasing costs gave it a leg up in retail competition.[17]

If they wanted their products on the shelves of the nation's largest retailer, suppliers had little choice but to give A&P special terms, but they received special benefits in return. A&P's orders were usually firm commitments, scheduled in advance. This allowed manufacturers to plan production efficiently, smoothing out the peaks and valleys in their business and thus lowering average production costs. While the advertising allowances it received were rarely tied to specific advertising plans, A&P was a huge buyer of newspaper advertising, and its decision to put its marketing muscle behind a product could turn an also-ran brand into a market leader. Thanks to its masses of sales data, A&P knew more about consumers' tastes in food than anyone else in the country, and it shared that information selectively with its suppliers. Philadelphians, it found, liked their butter lightly salted, with a light straw color, whereas New Englanders preferred more salt and a deeper yellow coloration. Tastes in coffee and canned vegetables varied, too. A manufacturer allowed to mine A&P's trove of market intelligence had an important advantage over its competitors.[18]

Its purchasing executives began to treat A&P's manufacturing capability as a bargaining chip. If a supplier offered a good enough price, A&P might forgo manufacturing and order from outside. In a 1926 deal, A&P agreed to stop making chocolate products and to promote Hershey's chocolate instead, and it weighed a similar arrangement with Postum, maker of Jell-O brand gelatin, and Campbell Soup, which offered to buy A&P's bean and spaghetti plants. Conversely, when vendors of coffee and evaporated milk refused to cut prices as much as A&P demanded, A&P stepped up promotion of two of its own brands, Bokar coffee and White House milk. The possibility that A&P might refuse to stock their products or relegate them to the top shelves was enough to bring even the biggest grocery manufacturers into line, making sure that A&P got better deals than anyone else.[19]

Its size also gave A&P an edge when unique opportunities arose, because its thousands of stores made its purchasing agents confident that the company could sell almost anything they bought. In 1926, for example, twelve of A&P's warehouses agreed to bid jointly when a cannery needed to dispose of eighty thousand cases of canned corn. By acting quickly, A&P saved $16,000, or twenty cents per case, off the regular price of corn. Individual stores ordered what they wanted at the low price, and the excess was sold off to other grocers. Such bargains were available to all retailers, but A&P could move faster than other potential buyers because it had little worry that it would be saddled with unwanted goods.[20]

A&P shook up the way it bought produce, too. Its national produce-buying operation, the Atlantic Commission Company, had started in 1924 by purchasing a modest forty-five hundred boxcar loads of fruits and vegetables. By 1929 it was spending $44 million, taking eighty thousand carloads a year directly from farmers who had signed contracts to grow crops for A&P, and buying another twenty thousand or so carloads on the open market. The savings were huge. Growers were willing to accept lower prices in return for an advance commitment to buy their crops, and by purchasing directly from growers, Atlantic Commission avoided paying brokerage commissions. In addition, less food went to waste, because Atlantic Commission's distribution system, including fleets of company-owned trucks and refrigerated railcars, circumvented the delays involved in moving fresh produce through wholesale produce markets, shortening the time between field and store. Once Atlantic Commission assured it a supply of low-cost produce, A&P could profitably expand produce departments in its stores. But Atlantic Commission also created new enemies. Its relationships with growers disrupted the business of thousands of produce brokers and wholesalers who now had reason to oppose the giant retailer. And because its stock of perishables rarely was a precise match for A&P's own needs, Atlantic Commission frequently entered the market as a seller, dealing its excess supply of one or another product to other retailers. Transactions with retailers other than A&P accounted for about 30 percent of Atlantic Commission's sales, and at times put A&P in the awkward situation of being an important supplier to competing grocers.[21]

Astute management of real estate was another important aspect of A&P's cost cutting. The Hartfords rarely acquired stores, because they did not want to be stuck with other operators' poor locations or long-term leases. When leases expired, stores were often moved to better locations: as the country's premier grocer, with impeccable credit, A&P was a catch for any commercial landlord. Landlords hoping for long-term leases, however, were disappointed: George Hartford used A&P's bargaining power to insist on short-term leases with optional extensions, giving the company the right, but not the obligation, to renew a lease at a specified rate. George, like other business leaders in the 1920s, was adept at convincing others to spend for A&P's facilities. When the company needed a new office in St. Louis and a warehouse in New England, it issued what would later come to be called commercial mortgage-backed securities, so A&P did not need to tie up its own money in the buildings. Concerned about the frothy property market, George ordered in 1928 that store leases not commit the company for more than a single year, leaving A&P in the driver's seat when property prices and rents tumbled following the stock market crash in 1929. He later explained his prescience thus: "I just couldn't now go along with all their big talk."[22]

The two brothers' strengths were in unique alignment. John Hartford's high-volume, low-price strategy, executed with George Hartford scrutinizing every financial detail, represented a radically new model for retailers. Many companies, including A&P itself, had undertaken some of the steps A&P initiated in 1926. Sears, then entirely a mail-order house, had opened an enormous central warehouse in Chicago in 1906 designed to fill millions of customer orders in the most efficient way. Kroger, the second-largest food retailer, was the leader in operating its own factories. Most of the larger food chains ran their own warehouses to gain efficiencies in distribution. Never before, though, had a retailer sought to squeeze out costs from every part of its business in a systematic way: even bags and boxes were recycled, bringing in $1.2 million a year. Nor had major retailers embraced the seemingly counterproductive goal of reducing their margins on the goods they sold. Rather than trying to increase profits per dollar of sales—the conventional strategy of the day—A&P was deliberately seeking to *reduce* profits per dollar sold in hopes of creating more sales. From 1915 through 1925, A&P's profit had averaged more than 3 percent of sales. Henceforth, Mr. John decreed, profits should never go above the 2.5 percent level lest volume suffer. If the company's profit margin widened, it would be not a good sign but a bad one, an indication that A&P was forsaking the cost discipline that would lead it to domination of the grocery market.

The giant retailer executed this radical strategic shift with remarkable speed. During the four-year period between 1925 and 1929, consumer food prices nationally fell 2 percent, but prices at A&P stores fell 10 percent. The advertising and brokerage allowances from manufacturers were important contributors to the large price drop: in 1928, A&P received allowances of $8.89 million, or more than 1 percent of its cost of goods. Inventories fell from 7.2 weeks of sales in December 1924 to 4.9 weeks of sales in December 1928 as purchasing agents and warehouse managers learned to move goods through the system faster. A&P's bakeries, which had yielded a puny 13 percent return on investment in

1925, earned 82 percent in 1928 as more regular orders from the stores permitted the ovens to run full blast. As John Hartford had foreseen, lower prices brought customers streaming into the stores: the grocery volume of the average store doubled from 1925 to 1928. Expenses as a percent of sales plummeted, and the number of unprofitable stores fell by half. The after-tax rate of return on investment topped 26 percent in 1928, the highest rate A&P would ever register. The Hartfords had transformed their company into a profit machine.[23]

A&P's new aggressiveness was in evidence throughout the grocery industry. By early 1927, after the new strategy had been in place for just a year, the division presidents' meeting buzzed with complaints from manufacturers angry at demands for price cuts on their goods. The bottler of Clicquot Club ginger ale was furious that some A&P stores were selling the soft drink at retail for less than independent grocers were paying at wholesale. The maker of Palmolive soap threatened to revoke all of A&P's advertising allowances. Canada Dry, another soft drink bottler, cut off sales to A&P's Indianapolis unit. A&P kept its arrangements with individual manufacturers confidential to minimize controversy, but it could not still the rumors that it was selling merchandise below cost—an illegal act in many states—to steal customers. The Hartfords instituted a new rule: no matter the price at which A&P purchased a product, its retail price could not be lower than the undiscounted wholesale price paid by small stores.[24]

A&P started a price war on bread in early 1927, slashing the price of a standard thirteen-ounce loaf from six cents to a nickel. It could wage such a war lawfully, because its bakeries turned out bread much more cheaply than chain bakeries: competitors buying from one of the big national bakery chains, such as Continental or Purity, were paying nearly five cents per loaf at wholesale. A year later, A&P cut cigarette prices, roiling the tobacco industry and causing steep drops in the prices of tobacco shares. By 1929, A&P was charging shoppers eleven cents for a pack that had sold for fifteen cents a year earlier. The first victims were two tobacco chains, United Cigar Stores and Schulte. Unlike A&P, the tobacco specialists could not accept narrow margins on cigarettes and recover them somewhere else: tobacco was all they sold. United Cigar

Stores was swept up in an accounting scandal as it sought to maintain its profits in the face of a price war. Schulte was forced to skip its dividend, cut executives' pay, and slash bonuses. Hundreds of thousands of independent grocers, newsstand owners, and cigar-store operators were caught in the cross fire. The result, predicted the New York cigar vendor Benjamin Gorlitzer, "will be only to eliminate the small cigar dealers who are entirely dependent upon their business for a livelihood."[25]

The company's impressive profits and rock-solid balance sheet financed newer and larger stores, upsetting the food trade in places where chain retailing had not previously been an issue. Chain grocery stores were rare in Texas before A&P opened its first outlet in the Dallas area around 1924. By 1927, A&P had 80 stores in Houston alone. The first red-front A&P stores opened in Montreal in May 1927, the forerunners of a sizable Canadian operation. Stores in Minneapolis and Oklahoma City followed. By 1929, A&P had 16,000 stores covering thirty-four states east of the Rocky Mountains and two Canadian provinces. In the densely populated Northeast, from Maine to Washington, D.C., A&P captured one of every eight dollars of retail food sales. When A&P made its long-awaited move into California, in 1930, it did so in force, opening 101 stores in Los Angeles in less than a year. Merchants everywhere had reason to fear it.[26]

So did wholesalers. Not only did A&P's expansion destroy wholesalers' customers, but A&P's insistence on direct relationships with manufacturers and its refusal to pay brokerage commissions meant that wholesalers sold almost nothing to A&P stores. A Federal Trade Commission investigation found that A&P bought from wholesalers and jobbers "only to meet exceptional situations." Data compiled by the commission revealed just how serious this loss of business was. The smallest chains, those with five or fewer stores, spent around 60 percent of their purchasing dollar with wholesalers. The biggest grocery and meat chains, at the other extreme, obtained just 1.5 percent of their merchandise from wholesalers. A&P's business with wholesalers was even smaller than that, because, unlike some other big chains, it bought none of its fresh produce through the wholesale channel. "This chain is becoming independent of the wholesaler by performing through its own organization a complete wholesaling function," the commission found. A&P bought milk and cream directly from farmers, purchased fish from fishermen at the Boston docks, aged most of its cheese in its own warehouses. In a single year, 1928, it moved 205,164 full railcar loads of merchandise through its own distribution system. For the wholesale grocery industry, the flourishing of A&P was unambiguously terrible news.[27]

The Great Atlantic & Pacific was by no means a monopoly or a trust, as its critics readily charged. It manufactured only 13 percent of the groceries it sold. Even where its retail position was strongest, in the suburbs of New York City, it was responsible for only one of every five dollars of food sales. But A&P transformed American retailing in the decade after World War I. The Hartford brothers implemented a strategy that changed the way Americans bought their food, and soon enough would change the way Americans shopped for other products, too. While other large retailers foundered or even failed, the Great Atlantic & Pacific grew relentlessly. By the end of the 1920s, it operated stores in thirty-eight hundred communities. One-tenth of all sugar sold in the United States passed through A&P's hands. The largest coffee buyer in the world, it sold one-eighth of the country's coffee and one-seventh of its tea. It met 10 percent of the nation's demand for Alaskan salmon, half of that from its own canneries, and furnished 12 percent of the country's evaporated milk. Its thirty-five bakeries made 600 million loaves of bread per year, more than all but one baking company in the United States. It sold more butter and more cigarettes than any other retailer in the world. It competed head-to-head with retailers, wholesalers, and manufacturers, and in its determination to have the lowest retail prices and the greatest volume, it squeezed the margins of all of them. In a country of thirty-two million households, A&P served five million customers a day. In 1929, it became, as John had predicted, the first retailer anywhere to sell $1 billion of merchandise in a single year.[28]

For all its modern methods, A&P remained as paternalistic as ever. When Clark Equipment Company, which sold A&P warehouse equipment, ran into financial problems, John Hartford proposed that the company pay its workers in scrip that A&P would redeem at face value. When the stock market crash of 1929 triggered higher unemployment, A&P accelerated planned construction work in order to provide jobs in ten different cities. Although his company now had eighty thousand employees, far more than he could ever hope to meet, John still emphasized his personal relationship with everyone who worked for A&P.

"What the average man on the job wants is a good job and a feeling that as long as he does what is right he can keep it," John wrote to his workers in 1930. "If a man is to have this feeling—and he cannot do good work without it—then the company must be loyal to him. As a matter of sound business policy, it is just as necessary that the company be loyal to the employee as it is that the employee be loyal to the company."[29]

A&P's relentless growth turned a formerly obscure grocery chain into one of the country's most prominent corporations, the object of endless curiosity and envy. Jersey City was no place for a company like this. In 1927, the Hartfords moved their headquarters into the Graybar Building, a prestigious new office tower adjacent to Grand Central Terminal in midtown Manhattan, where Mr. George and Mr. John shared an office suite on the twenty-second floor. In an indication of the business world's newfound respect for their achievements, John was invited to join important boards: the Guaranty Trust Company, the New Haven Railroad, the Chrysler Corporation. When the president of the Pennsylvania Railroad Company invited two hundred prominent businessmen and government officials to his summer home in September 1929, John A. Hartford was among the guests who mingled with members of President Hoover's cabinet. The scion of a self-made grocer, himself with little education save what he had learned on the job, was now among the nation's business elite.[30]

11

MINUTE MEN AND TAX MEN

Big Business Now Sweeps Retail Trade," *The New York Times* declared in a 1928 headline running the entire width of a page. "Huge Corporations, Serving the Nation Through Country-Wide Chains, Are Displacing the Neighborhood Store." Across the United States, the newspaper reported, some thirty-eight hundred retail chains were operating 100,000 stores. "Out of every dollar spent in retail stores today 17 cents goes into the treasury of chain corporations." Of course, most of those chains had only a handful of stores, but a few were quite large. Foremost among them was a single company operating twice as many stores as the next seven chains combined, with sales more than four times those of the next-largest food retailer. "By all odds the largest retail trade trust in the world is the Great Atlantic and Pacific Tea Company," the *Times* affirmed.[1]

The *Times* deemed A&P an "amazing concern," but most of the 2.1 million Americans who earned their livings making and selling food had a decidedly different view. The company's headlong growth and rampant price-cutting were a threat to every part of the food distribution system. A&P's demands that suppliers slash prices and provide advertising allowances cut into grocery manufacturers' profits. Its insistence that food processors, soap makers, and fruit and vegetable growers deal with it directly, without middlemen, endangered tens of thousands of agents, jobbers, and wholesalers whose purpose was to link food suppliers with individual grocers. A&P's financial strength, giving it the ability to plant a store anywhere it chose, darkened the prospects not only of the 400,000 people who ran independent food stores and their families but of uncounted numbers of men who dreamed of someday becoming merchants and of the small-town bankers and insurance agents who counted local retailers among their clients.[2]

TABLE 1: LARGEST U.S. RETAILERS, 1929

Company	*Category*	*Sales ($m)*
Great Atlantic & Pacific Tea	Grocery	$1,054
Sears, Roebuck	Department/Mail Order	$415
F. W. Woolworth	Variety	$303
Montgomery Ward	Department/Mail Order	$292
Kroger Grocery and Baking	Grocery	$287
Safeway	Grocery	$214
J. C. Penney	Dry Goods	$210
S. S. Kresge	Variety	$147
American Stores	Grocery	$143
Gimbel Brothers	Department	$125

Source: *New York Times*, January 12, 1930, and other reports.

The woes of small merchants were especially acute in the small towns of the South and Midwest, where farm-based economies reeled under sagging commodity prices even as the big cities prospered. Through the first half of the 1920s, wholesalers and independent shop owners in these regions pushed political leaders to act against the chains. The first success came in 1925, when the town of Danville, Kentucky, population five thousand, required an annual license fee of grocery stores, with "cash and carry" grocers—such as chain stores—required to pay several times as much as "regular service" grocers. The ordinance was quashed by a state court, but the reprieve for chain stores would prove temporary.[3]

New fuel was added to the conflict when the two largest catalog retailers, Sears, Roebuck and Montgomery Ward, began opening retail stores in 1925 and 1926. With their vast selections and money-back guarantees, Sears and Montgomery Ward had long taken business from small-town retailers, but their appeal was constrained by the need for customers to order by mail and wait for their purchases to arrive. The prospect that Sears or Ward's might open a store on the local Main Street encouraged hardware dealers and shoe-store owners to make common cause with grocers and druggists, who had been fighting the chains for years. In 1926, storekeepers in Petersburg, Virginia, organized a mass protest meeting. Similar groups formed to mount "trade at home" campaigns in one small town after another. State legislators responded. Four states enacted anti-chain laws in 1927. Maryland prohibited any chain from owning more than five stores in Allegany County and taxed each chain-owned store in the county $500—a tax that would have taken nearly half the profits of an average A&P store. Georgia slapped a $250 tax on each chain-owned store over five. North Carolina charged any company with more than five stores $50 per store. Pennsylvania provided that only registered pharmacists could own drugstores. These laws, as well as a $100-per-store tax enacted by South Carolina in 1928, were invalidated by courts, but their very passage demonstrated the growing political power of the forces opposed to chain retailing.[4]

The political success of state-level anti-chain efforts reverberated around the country. In April 1928, the National Association of Retail Meat Dealers—influenced by A&P's decision to begin opening meat departments—accused chain stores of misleading advertisements, short weights, and false sales. The Meat Dealers asked the Federal Trade Commission to investigate. A week later, J. H. McLaurin, president of the American Wholesale Grocers' Association, told members that "the Atlantic & Pacific . . . as now conducted, possesses the potentiality of a control of retail food distribution to such an extent as to threaten the best interests of the American public." Perhaps, McLaurin said, the Justice Department will look into things. The alarm was bipartisan. Smith Brookhart, a Republican senator from the farm state of Iowa, authored a congressional resolution directing the Federal Trade Commission to investigate whether chain retailing was creating monopoly or unfair competition. The commission also was to determine whether chain stores' growth was based upon "actual savings in costs of management and operation." The resolution led John A. Hartford to speak out on a matter of public policy for the first time in his long career. "We have nothing to fear from any such investigation," he told reporters. "If sufficient reasons appear to justify an inquiry into the industry as a whole, our company would welcome it."[5]

A 1928 study supported by the Chamber of Commerce of the United States concluded that "the death knell has been sounded for one-third of all retail outlets in the country" due to the growth of chains. Spurred by such inflammatory reports, the FTC launched two investigations—one of chain stores in general, and one focused on A&P. In June 1928, an FTC attorney sent the company pages of questions about its purchasing, pricing, and advertising practices to find out why

A&P was selling name-brand merchandise more cheaply than other grocers. A few months later, the attorney wrote to ask whether A&P "has partially abandoned cut price appeal in its advertising." Finding no wrongdoing, the commission terminated the investigation in 1929, but the reprieve would prove temporary: A&P would be under federal investigation continuously for the next quarter century.[6]

No factual investigation, however, could quell the growing concern about chain stores, for the worry had less to do with price competition than with the survival of small-town America. The chain store altered economic geography. Thousands of towns were home to grocery warehouses or the offices of small retail companies. A chain such as A&P, on the other hand, obtained economies of scale by centralizing its warehouses and offices in regional business centers. In small towns, it had only stores, with few employees and no highly paid executives. As local competitors fell by the wayside, jobs vanished with them, destroying the social fabric and leaving communities bereft of capital and civic leadership. "If businessmen become purely representatives of a large corporation without residence, property, or direct personal interest in the local community, the significance of such a change in community life is indeed apparent," one of the earliest scholars of the chain store wrote in 1927. Agreed a Michigan newspaper, "The consumer who patronizes the chain store, instead of the regular merchant, is effectually destroying the value of any property he owns in the town in which he lives."[7]

Victories only fueled anti-chain agitation. "The chain store menace is growing, and unless an intelligent population can be made to see and understand, the independent merchant will soon be only a memory," a rabble-rousing pamphlet warned in 1928. The anti-chain forces, however, understood the need for subtle changes to their message. Hundreds of independent merchants had created their own tiny chains, operating five or ten stores under common ownership; of 386 grocery and meat chains responding to a Federal Trade Commission survey, only 6 operated more than 1,000 stores in December 1928, and the vast majority owned just a few. Many other merchants had joined "voluntary" chains, in which a single wholesaler handled all distribution for stores that operated under a common banner but remained independently owned: the Federal Trade Commission counted 395 voluntary grocery chains with 53,400 stores in 1929. New terminology was needed to distinguish good chains from bad. Now the enemy was the "foreign" chain, based in a distant city, rather than the homegrown variety. In Springfield, Missouri, the chamber of commerce mounted an advertising campaign accusing chain-store managers of being "'mechanical operators,' controlled entirely by a set formula." As the advertisements explained, "Their duties, boiled down, are to 'get Springfield's money' and send it to the Home Office."[8]

Independent merchants were a notoriously anarchic group. Only a tiny percentage of them belonged to state or national trade organizations; the largest of these, the National Association of Retail Grocers, claimed a scant fifteen thousand members nationwide. Political influence required leadership. It arrived in 1929 in the unlikely person of a middle-aged businessman named William Kennon Henderson.

Born in the northeast Louisiana town of Bastrop in 1880, Henderson grew up in a prosperous family that owned an ironworks, a lumber company, and a garage. After graduating from St. Edward's, a Catholic college in Austin, Texas, he went to work in the Henderson Iron Works in Shreveport, the biggest city in northern Louisiana. He took charge of the family businesses upon his father's death in 1919 and added others, including a taxicab company and a printing company. Henderson became an influential civic leader. He acquired a thirty-five-hundred-acre estate eighteen miles north of Shreveport and called it, after his middle name, Kennonwood. Despite his subsequent reputation, Henderson was in no way an outcast or a crank. He was an educated man and a successful executive, a pillar of the local business establishment. In 1925, he was elected president of the Shreveport Chamber of Commerce.[9]

Among Henderson's acquaintances was an auto dealer named W. G. Patterson, who had established a 10-watt radio station in Shreveport in May 1922. Early radio equipment, often jerry-rigged, did a poor job of transmitting on a steady frequency, and Patterson's tiny station was being drowned out as other broadcasters occupied nearby wavelengths. Needing money for a more powerful transmitter and a better antenna location, Patterson asked Henderson to invest in the station.

Henderson discovered radio, and he liked it so much that he bought control of the station at the end of 1924 and moved the transmitter to Kennonwood. Henderson sought to rename the station WKH in honor of himself; when he was informed that call signs for stations west of the Mississippi River had to start with *K*, he chose KWKH instead. He built a studio at Kennonwood, from which he handled much of the broadcasting himself, and another at a downtown hotel. The government allowed him to increase his power from 50 to 250 watts on a frequency of 1100 kilohertz, which gave a clear signal in Shreveport. KWKH dominated the local airwaves with the slogan "KWKH on the air, Shreveport everywhere."[10]

Henderson's ambitions ran well beyond dominating the airwaves in Shreveport. In 1927, KWKH shifted to a less congested frequency, 760 kilohertz, and was authorized to boost its power to 1,000 watts. The station was strong enough to be heard at night all over the region, especially when, as frequently occurred, Henderson directed his engineers to use more signal strength than authorized by the Federal Radio Commission. Henderson attacked his regulator on the air as a tool of the big-business interests behind the nascent broadcast networks. Nonetheless, the commission allowed KWKH to increase its power to 5,000 watts in early 1929. That June, KWKH was assigned a new frequency, 850 kilohertz, which was designated as a "clear channel." KWKH had to share with the station WWL in New Orleans, which broadcast in the daytime, but no other stations in the United States could use the frequency. With a clear channel, KWKH, now beamed out with 10,000 watts of power every evening, could be heard by millions of new radio listeners, who carefully tuned their sets to enjoy the exotic experience of receiving broadcasts from afar. There was no reliable audience measurement in the late 1920s, but "Old Man Henderson," booming out his familiar greeting, "Hello, World!" and playing blues and country recordings, was among the best-known radio personalities in the United States.[11]

Henderson learned quickly that colorful language and outrageous stunts would draw an audience. In between records, he read real and invented letters and telegrams, issued retorts, and commented sarcastically on events of the day. "People don't care about gentle modest talk," he said in 1929. "They want it strong. They want to hear you ride somebody. If not, why do they spend their good money for telegrams?" During the 1928 presidential campaign, Henderson assailed Herbert Hoover, the Republican candidate, as "a harebrained ninny-com-poop," "a Quaker skunk," and "a cross between a jackass and a bulldog bitch." When the Federal Radio Commission considered whether to renew his broadcast license, he presented 163,000 affidavits of support—evidence, admitted the commission's chairman, "that KWKH is a station of considerable popularity."[12]

Radio advertising was scant in the early days, and KWKH carried none. But as more advertisers took to the airwaves, Henderson decided to get in on the action. One of his routine stunts at the microphone was to ask for a cup of coffee and then comment that it was "doggone good coffee." Inevitably, listeners asked about the coffee. In 1928, he ordered some tins bearing his image, filled them with coffee beans, and sold them over the air for $1 per pound. At a time when a pound of coffee cost ten cents at the store, Hello World coffee was no bargain for consumers, but it made a profitable business. KWKH soon began touting Bibles, insurance policies, patent medicines, and whatever else Henderson felt like selling. In 1930, readers of *Radio Digest* would vote him "most popular broadcaster in the South."

Stations such as KWKH had considerable airtime to fill, and speeches were standard fare. One of the speakers in October 1929 was Philip Lieber. Like Henderson, Lieber was no dirt-poor Louisiana sharecropper; he was an important local businessman, president of the Shreveport Mutual Building Association, which provided home mortgages. Lieber was concerned that store owners among his borrowers were having trouble paying their mortgages because chain competition was hurting their businesses. He delivered a speech titled "The Menace of the Chain Store System" to the Shreveport Chamber of Commerce. Henderson was in attendance, and invited him to repeat the speech that night on KWKH. In a florid half-hour address, Lieber praised hometown merchants and warned of "a couple of hundred over-lords and all the rest of us eternally consigned to a condition of peasantry." The retail chains, he asserted, "are taking everything out and putting nothing back."[13]

Henderson's prior interest in chains had been limited to the hated radio networks; he had never spoken about retail chains. Indeed, selling

Hello World coffee by mail undercut local grocers everywhere. But Lieber's talk inspired him. When the banker finished, Henderson returned to the microphone. "I am going to tell you what that address means," he told his listeners. "It means that these dirty, sneaking chain stores are coming into your home town and taking your money and sending it out to a bunch of crooked, no-account loafers in Wall Street." Letters and telegrams flooded into Kennonwood, and Henderson adopted the issue as his own. The wealthy, college-educated businessman made himself the spokesman for the mass of downtrodden commoners oppressed by forces beyond their control. "American people, wake up!" he proclaimed. "We can whip these chain stores . . . I'll be your leader. I'll whip the hell out of 'em if you will support me."[14]

Evening after evening, Henderson returned to the theme. He read out anguished letters from shopkeepers. His extended monologues found targets in Wall Street, "thieving chain-store scoundrels," and "gold-bellied Hartford." For variety, Henderson turned his microphone over to populist politicians such as Louisiana's governor, Huey Long, and the Alabama attorney general, Charlie McCall, who also took after the chains. "There are 3,000 convicts in Alabama who contribute more to the upbuilding of the state than all the foreign chains in America," McCall told KWKH listeners. Shopkeepers and their wives sent letters or came by for a tour of the station, and Henderson put them on the air, too. One was R. K. Calloway, owner of a corner grocery in Taylorville, Illinois, who spoke passionately about chains sucking the money out of his economically troubled coal-mining town. "What good is an education going to do your children, if the chain store method of distribution is to endure?" he asked the radio audience. "If all the thinking, planning, etc., is to be done in New York or Chicago, and all they need is a yes mam yes sir, wouldn't it be cheaper to buy a phonograph and be done with it?"[15]

The anti-chain feeling was sincere, but Henderson knew how to turn it to profit. In the winter of 1929–30, he appealed to his listeners to support the anti-chain campaign by joining the Merchants' Minute Men. For annual dues of $12—two or three days' pay for a grocery clerk—members could help alert the public that chain stores were selling short weights and avoiding local taxes. Within a year, Henderson had signed up thirty-five thousand Minute Men in four thousand communities.

The operation was less a mass movement than a fund-raising venture. Of $373,500 paid in dues for 1930, $151,800 went to pay the debts of the Henderson Iron Works, as the Federal Radio Commission subsequently revealed.[16]

Henderson's entrepreneurial approach quickly inspired imitators. Broadcasters such as Winfield Caslow, "the Main Street Crusader," in Grand Rapids, Michigan, and Robert Duncan, "the Oregon Wildcat," in Portland, launched profitable anti-chain crusades of their own. In 1930, Montaville Flowers, a lecturer best known for warning that granting citizenship to Japanese immigrants would be "the first step toward a rapid dissolution of our nationality and the loss of the soul of our civilization," took up anti-chain activities. He offered himself as a consultant to local business groups and made thirty-six half-hour radio speeches in Washington and Oregon, inviting listeners to send money for a book of his talks. When Flowers's radio attack on A&P fell short because parts of the West had no A&P stores, he simply trained his sights on the regional MacMarr chain instead. So outrageous were the anti-chain orators that in February 1930, the National Association of Retail Grocers, the independent grocers' lobby, warned its members against giving them money, explaining, "At the present time, there are in the United States literally thousands of individuals interesting themselves in anti-chain-store campaigns purely for the money they can make out of it for themselves."[17]

The Merchants' Minute Men was never an organized political force. It held but a single national convention and a few local meetings. It did not lobby at state capitols or endorse political candidates, and it had no relationship with the radio-based crusade of Father Charles Coughlin, the Michigan Catholic priest who first supported and then became a bitter critic of the New Deal. So far as is known, there were no formally organized local chapters or state-level leaders of the Minute Men, only the voice of Henderson warning against the "menace of the chain system, now seeking to fasten its fangs into the life of every community." But the loud anti-chain agitation of Henderson and his imitators transformed the political environment. The fight against chain retailers was no longer a rearguard action by inefficient shopkeepers standing in the way of progress. Now it took on elements of class struggle, with the impersonal "foreign" chains, backed by the faceless and heartless finance capital of Wall Street, accused of undermining the vitality of small-town America and destroying opportunities for the common man.[18]

The chain retailers were unprepared to do battle with a mass movement, even a poorly organized one. Two chain-store associations had been formed in the early 1920s, but both included only grocers. Neither was particularly effectual in the political realm. Amid the increasing anti-chain agitation, the two groups merged in late 1928 to create a new organization that would be open to chain retailers in all fields. The National Chain Store Association united every major retail chain in the country, with one notable exception. The Great Atlantic & Pacific, the largest chain retailer by far, stood aloof.[19]

The new association had two main orders of business. One was a public relations campaign. Speakers from the National Chain Store Association fanned out to radio stations and Rotary Clubs around the country, explaining how chains made distribution more efficient and brought lower prices to consumers. A monthly newsletter went out to selected opinion leaders, and educational materials were distributed to teachers, editors, and librarians. The association's other main undertaking was a legal effort to lobby against anti-chain legislation and fight it in the courts.[20]

Some 142 bills to tax chain stores were introduced in twenty-nine state legislatures during 1929 and 1930 as the battle raged in every part of the country but the Northeast. In Wisconsin, independent merchants' associations organized pickets of chain stores, and chain-store managers were socially ostracized. Chain-store boycotts were organized from Oregon to Florida. Legislatures in Indiana, Georgia, and North Carolina adopted tax schemes designed to overcome courts' objections to the 1927 anti-chain laws. South Carolina imposed a chain-store tax in 1930, Florida and Alabama in 1931. Portland, Oregon, enacted the first municipal chain-store tax, with a fee rising from $6 on a single store to $50 for each store over nineteen run by the same company. When the Kentucky legislature debated a chain-store tax in February 1930, six hundred people packed a state senate hearing to support it, and as the house of representatives prepared to pass the bill, one legislator took up Henderson's signature cry, "Hello, World!"[21]

The controversy was equally intense outside the legislative halls. The Federal Trade Commission began releasing results from the chain-store investigation directed by Congress in 1928, providing a flood of data for the use of partisans on both sides. Its findings, which would eventually fill thirty-four volumes, found their way into high schools and colleges, where thousands of debaters squared off over the topic: "Resolved: that chain stores are detrimental to the best interests of the American public." The American Management Association published a study of chain stores, and the American Economic Association held a panel debate. *The Nation*, one of the country's most prestigious magazines, devoted a four-part series to the chain phenomenon, concluding that "the chain principle of distribution is economically sound," but urging "new policies of community spirit" to control workers' hours and wages and to protect the interests of food producers. *The New Republic*, similarly influential, followed with a series of its own. When legislators such as Senator Arthur Capper, a Kansas Republican, tried to stake out a middle ground, praising the virtues of chain stores while proposing to allow the makers of trademarked articles to set retail prices so as to stop the "profiteering price cutter," they could hardly make themselves heard amid the anti-chain cacophony.[22]

In May 1931, Indiana's chain-store tax, enacted in 1929, was upheld by the U.S. Supreme Court in a case called *State Board of Tax Commissioners v. Jackson*. The Indiana tax charged $3 a year for a single store, rising to $25 for each store over twenty under the same management or ownership. A federal district court had rejected that fee structure, holding that Indiana lacked a legitimate basis for distinguishing between chain and independent merchants. The Supreme Court reversed. Chain stores, it ruled, were a different type of business from individually owned stores and could be taxed differently. This logic extended a blatant invitation to other jurisdictions to tax chain retailers. Among the five justices voting to uphold the Indiana statute was Louis Brandeis, still an implacable opponent of chain retailing, but now in a position where his views could directly shape the law. In *A&P v. Maxwell*, a few weeks later, the same 5–4 majority upheld the constitutionality of North Carolina's $50-per-store tax on anyone owning more than a single store.[23]

The *Jackson* and *Maxwell* decisions opened the floodgates. In the three years from 1931 through 1933, 525 chain-store tax bills were introduced in state legislatures, and 18 of them were enacted. Although chain-store taxes were invalidated by state courts in Vermont and Wisconsin, they were upheld by courts in other states. By the end of 1933, retail chains in seventeen states from Florida to Idaho were subject to special tax levies, many of them far more onerous than those in Indiana and North Carolina.[24]

No company stood to be hurt as badly by this new form of taxation as the Great Atlantic & Pacific. The specific form of tax approved by the Supreme Court linked the tax to the number of stores in a state and not to sales. For A&P, with more stores than its top five competitors combined but far lower sales per store, a fixed per-store tax meant that it would pay a higher proportion of revenue to state tax collectors than any competing grocer.

A&P's lawyers sought to block the taxes in state courts, without success. Yet as the storm confronting chain stores grew more intense, the world's largest retailer tried to steer clear of the controversy. As early as 1927, Sullivan & Cromwell, then A&P's law firm, had urged the company to combat anti-chain propaganda. The Hartfords refused, agreeing only that all press releases should be issued centrally by John Hartford's office. When the National Association of Chain Stores set up a committee in 1931 to plan an educational campaign, A&P did not participate. When the association doubled its budget to combat the taxes, A&P lent no support. A&P's own advertising said nothing of taxes on chain stores, and its magazine for store managers focused on opportunities for advancement rather than political struggles. Nor did the company hire lobbyists to plead its case. "It is not the company's policy to do any lobbying or anything that smacks of lobbying," division executives in the Midwest were instructed in 1931. Far from being the slaves of Wall Street, as critics charged, George and John Hartford were used to running their business privately, without outside interference, and they intended to keep doing so.[25]

The brothers did not take the threat of chain-store taxes seriously. Perhaps, having spent their entire lives in and around New York City, they did not understand the depth of anger toward big business in some of the nation's more rural quarters. Or perhaps, having been associated with the Great Atlantic & Pacific for their entire lives, they failed to grasp that the company they saw as so benevolent was viewed by others in a harsher light. "The public . . . would not countenance radical legislation that would penalize efficient distribution," John Hartford told a management meeting in 1928. Two years later, in a rare interview with *The New York Times*, he brushed off the risk of rising anti-chain sentiment: "Chains . . . are now recognized as rendering so great a public service that I do not believe there is any cause for worry on that score." This comfortable judgment was to prove disastrously wrong.[26]

12
THE SUPERMARKET

The year 1930 found John and George Hartford at the top of the business world. Their company had just become the first retailer ever to sell $1 billion of merchandise in a single year. A&P's after-tax profit had topped $26 million, an all-time record, yielding a solid 24 percent return on investment. Despite the worrying stock market crash in October 1929, George's stubborn insistence that A&P avoid owning property and rent stores only on short-term leases offered protection against a steep drop in revenue.[1]

The Hartfords were by no means resting on their laurels. They recognized that the way Americans got their food was changing dramatically, and they understood that their company had to keep pace.

As the Great Depression arrived, three technological developments were reshaping the grocery trade. The most important was refrigeration. Before commercial-size electric refrigerators first appeared in 1922, stores that sold meat or fresh milk struggled to keep their goods cold in coolers chilled with hundred-pound blocks of ice. Reliable electric refrigerator cases, which were widely used by the late 1920s, finally made it practical for grocers to sell perishable foods without worrying that their stock would go bad. Shoppers, accustomed to making daily visits to the grocer, the butcher, the baker, and the produce vendor, embraced one-stop shopping enthusiastically. As they did, retailing's traditional boundary lines began to erode. By 1929, one in three grocery stores sold meat and poultry, while many meat markets sold groceries and produce. In 1930, U.S. factories turned out a million home refrigerators as refrigerators outsold iceboxes for the first time. The families wealthy enough to afford them could stock up at the grocery store, rather than buying one day's fresh food at a time.[2]

The second big change sweeping through the food industry was packaging. Cellophane, a clear film derived from wood fiber, was invented in France in 1908, but it arrived in North America only after Du Pont licensed the patents in 1923. The invention of a waterproof cellophane in 1927, along with Du Pont research showing that cellophane in bright colors stimulated impulse purchases, convinced manufacturers to use it to wrap candy, baked goods, and cigarettes. Retailers could expand their product lines, selling slower-moving items without worrying that they would go stale. Cellophane was a godsend for grocery-store meat counters: shoppers resisted precut meats wrapped in brown butcher paper, but they readily accepted packaged pork chops and chicken legs when they could see the product. Coupled with the newly invented slicing machine, cellophane wrap made it practical to sell sliced loaves of bread that would stay fresh for more than a day on a grocer's shelf. Cellophane was more expensive than other types of packaging, but it could be used to competitive advantage: when makers of gelatin desserts began promoting the freshness of their products, A&P responded by advertising that Sparkle gelatin powder, produced by Quaker Maid, was the only gelatin wrapped in cellophane to ensure freshness.[3]

The other technology buffeting the food trade in 1930 was the automobile. Passenger cars were still luxuries in the early 1920s, but by the end of the decade twenty-three million private cars were on American roads. Cars brought dramatic changes in shopping patterns. Car-owning families did not need to lug their purchases home from a neighborhood store, and they were certainly not bound to an independent corner grocer who provided home delivery. Car owners could drive to the store of their choice, roaming far afield in search of the best bargains, and purchase more than they could carry in their arms. Conversely, a retailer could now appeal to shoppers outside its immediate environs. If its prices were sufficiently low, its products sufficiently attractive, or its advertising sufficiently outrageous, customers would drive from miles around.[4]

All three of these technological changes led in one direction: larger stores. Around 1930, most grocery stores, including most A&P stores, were still extremely small. The industry norm was a modest space perhaps twenty feet wide and thirty feet deep, with canned goods stacked toward the front and fast-moving staples like bread and sugar displayed near the refrigerator case at the rear. A&P, like other retailers, was gradually shifting from these spartan outlets to larger "combination" stores that carried meat, poultry, and a larger selection of produce. Combination stores were bigger than stores without meat departments—the average traditional store had two employees, including the proprietor, whereas the average combination store had three—and had much higher labor productivity, selling about 20 percent more groceries per worker. Yet the "model" combination store recommended by *The Progressive Grocer* was no more than thirty feet wide and forty feet deep, perhaps twice the floor area of a traditional store, and the magazine specifically warned readers against making their stores too big. When the Rockmoor Grocery opened in a forty-by-seventy-foot space in Miami in 1926, the owners worried that its size was excessive. Marketing techniques throughout the industry were still so primitive that *The Progressive Grocer*'s 1931 guide advised, "Every item that admits of being handled must be so displayed that it can be picked up and handled by the housewife." While experts were now advising grocers to get rid of counters and to stop displaying merchandise in barrels and boxes, the idea that an attractive store design could bring higher sales was only starting to penetrate merchants' thinking.[5]

A&P led the shift to the combination store. In 1923, it had cautiously begun adding produce to its stores, and it opened its first meat counter late in 1924. In 1926, it began introducing combination stores, usually replacing two or three traditional stores with a single, larger unit. "The chain grocery store is rapidly become a chain 'food' store, selling every article formerly sold by the old-time independent from meat to fruit and vegetables," one expert wrote in 1928. The new stores had far more decoration than the ones they replaced, and many were located in upper-income shopping areas to attract more prosperous housewives. Although most A&P stores were still of the traditional variety in 1930, the company had thirty-nine hundred combination stores and made 10 percent of its revenue from meat. A few of its new stores were quite sizable. Most, however, were small and still relied on clerks to wait upon customers. A model A&P combination store in New England in 1932 was thirty-four feet wide and fifty-two feet deep, with one side wall lined with meat cases and the other with shelving behind a wooden counter, where customers could not reach it; the only items customers could select for themselves were fruits and vegetables, which were displayed in the middle of the store.[6]

The reality was that small stores had become unprofitable even before the Great Depression. In 1928, A&P's 1,615 traditional grocery stores with weekly sales below $700 were money losers. The grocery departments in one-third of the combination stores lost money, as did more than half the meat departments. A&P's own accounting showed that scale was vital: combination stores with sales above $3,000 per week produced annual returns on investment above 80 percent. The Hartfords planned to increase store size as they opened two thousand new locations a year, increasing average sales per store by more than one-third by the end of 1933. By then they expected A&P to have twenty-three thousand stores and $2 billion of annual sales. For a company of A&P's size, the speed of the planned shift to bigger stores was ambitious. But those thousands of combination stores were never built. Instead, the shift to bigger stores was driven by a development the Hartfords had not foreseen. It would become known as the supermarket.[7]

The supermarket has many fathers. Like most innovations, it developed over time rather than springing fully fledged from the mind of a clever entrepreneur.

Large food stores had existed, in very small numbers, for three decades by 1930. Some were like department stores, with clerks in each department to wait upon the customers. Others combined sections operated by the owner with stands leased by other vendors. In Southern California, Alpha Beta, famed for arranging its products in alphabetical order, and Ralphs, a grocery company dating to 1873, both ran self-service grocery stores of up to twelve thousand square feet—the size of ten standard A&P combination stores. There were twenty-five such stores in Los Angeles at the start of 1930, with average sales twice those of the average chain-owned combination store. The big Southern California stores, though, did not feature low prices; rather, their big draw was free parking in a city that was already becoming dependent on the automobile. In any event, Southern California in those days was still a remote outpost of the U.S. economy, and its large drive-up grocery stores drew little attention in New York and Chicago.[8]

It took a brash grocer named Michael J. Cullen to shake up the industry. Cullen, the son of Irish immigrants, had learned the grocery trade as a clerk at A&P just after the turn of the century, and later worked as a regional manager for the Kroger chain in Illinois. In 1930, when he was forty-six, Cullen wrote to the president of Kroger to propose a new kind of store. The store, Cullen thought, should be "monstrous," four or five times the size of the typical grocery store. It should be located not on a busy shopping street but a few blocks away, where rents were lower and parking ample. It should offer a wide variety of branded merchandise, generating massive traffic by selling three hundred items at cost and another two hundred at cost plus 5 percent and advertising those low prices heavily. Sales would exceed $600,000 per year—ten times the average of chain-owned combination stores. The store would hold operating expenses per dollar of sales to half those of the average combination store by relying on self-service and keeping the staff small. The targeted annual profit was $16,900 per store. Relative to sales, such a profit would be no larger than A&P's or Kroger's. But Cullen's large store would need far less investment per dollar of sales. He calculated that each store would require $30,000 of equipment and inventory, so a profit of $16,900 implied a stunning 56 percent return on capital. Even A&P's pretax return of 27 percent looked anemic by comparison. "I would lead the public out of the high-priced houses of bondage into the low prices of the house of the promised land," Cullen wrote.[9]

Perhaps the management of the Kroger Grocery and Baking Company found such bombast off-putting. In any event, Cullen's letter received no response. He quit his job, moved his family to New York City, and leased a vacant garage in Jamaica, Queens. In August 1930, the King Kullen Grocery Company opened its doors. Under bright lights, cans and packages were neatly stacked on tables, and wicker baskets holding discounted specials lined the aisles. All items had prices clearly marked, allowing the shopper to make her selections without the help of a clerk. As predicted, crowds streamed in to buy seven-cent cans of Campbell's soup for four cents and three cans of Krasdale tomato sauce for a dime. Calling itself "The World's Greatest Price Wrecker," King Kullen was reported to be operating eight stores by 1932, with average sales of more than $1 million per store.[10]

Imitators arrived very soon, often financed by grocery wholesalers. During the second half of the 1920s, many wholesalers had fought back against the food chains by organizing their customers into "voluntary" chains whose independently owned members adopted a common brand name. That brand was then used on the canned goods and staples manufactured by the wholesaler, allowing the small stores to benefit from a large wholesaler's economies of scale. In many cases, the wholesaler coordinated advertising, creating much more prominent newspaper promotions than the stores could have afforded individually. Wholesalers, with far more food-retailing experience than most retailers, also provided management advice. In some instances, store owners bought shares in their wholesaler, creating a sort of cooperative arrangement. Voluntary chains gave wholesalers direct experience in retail operations. In the 1930s, wholesalers applied that expertise to helping ambitious retail grocers open larger stores.[11]

The first of these was the Big Bear market. Located on the first floor of a former Durant Motors auto factory in Elizabeth, New Jersey, Big Bear was owned by the American Grocery Company, a wholesaler, and two entrepreneurs, Robert Otis and Roy Dawson. In fifty thousand square feet of floor space—four times the area of Cullen's first store, forty times the size of an A&P combination store—they sold not only food but also paints, tires, hardware, even radios. Big Bear opened in December 1932, with a flurry of advertisements proclaiming, "Big Bear Crashes into New Jersey." In its first full year, 1933, the store purportedly sold $2.2 million of merchandise and made a net profit of $166,507 on an investment of less than $10,000. Big Bear was so successful that competitors pressured newspapers to refuse its advertisements, forcing the store to resort to handbills to tout its discount prices. Other entrepreneurs came to Elizabeth to tour the new facility and went home to open their own Big Bears in places like Boston and Columbus.[12]

The new form of competition was not a major concern for George and John Hartford. They had more pressing worries. A&P's profits soared in 1930; although sales per store fell with the onset of the Depression, profits per store hit a record $1,954. John Hartford interpreted this jump in profits as negative, not positive. Unit managers were setting prices too high, boosting profits in the short run, but eroding volume and driving business to competitors. John was especially annoyed that some unit managers had adopted the strategy of selling selected products below cost and raising prices on other items to make up the difference. He ordered a return to the basics: no drastic price cuts, no special sales, all merchandise sold with narrow markups week in and week out. His managers, he fretted, simply didn't understand his philosophy that volume was what mattered: "Sometimes the body gets so large that the pulsations fail to reach its extremities."[13]

Indeed, the pulsations were getting nowhere near the extremities. The Hartfords had pushed authority out to the division offices, so the prices for A&P's products were not set in New York. In a difficult economy, many division executives favored taking whatever profits could be had by keeping prices high. Reducing margins in order to lower prices might be good for the company's long-term growth, but it meant less profit in the short term. While that was John Hartford's desire, his managers were not in agreement. Unit managers were loath to close "red-ink stores," because the closure of a store would shift its overhead costs, including its share of warehouse operating expenses, onto the remaining stores. Putting up prices often served to make underperforming stores profitable in the near term, even if the longer-term impact was to tarnish A&P's reputation for low prices. John stumped the country, meeting with the boards of A&P's divisions and trying to persuade them of the virtues of low prices and high volume. The minutes of one division board meeting break into capital letters to repeat the message Hartford delivered: "LOWER EXPENSE RATE INCREASED TONNAGE INCREASE IN CUSTOMERS."[14]

Nothing better illustrates the wisdom of John Hartford's approach than A&P's coffee business. In the early 1920s, after organizing the American Coffee Corporation, A&P had taken extremely generous markups on coffee, selling it for almost twice its wholesale cost. Its high prices limited sales, holding A&P's share of total U.S. coffee sales to less than 5 percent. As the company slashed its markup, sales took off. By 1932, it controlled one-sixth of the U.S. coffee market, and the average A&P store was selling nearly three times as much coffee as it had seven years earlier. John Hartford's aim was to replicate this performance in other product lines, using low prices to bring customers into the stores.[15]

At the same time as John Hartford wanted to hold prices down, though, there had to be a floor. Individual store managers were perpetually facing challenges from local competitors who advertised extraordinary bargains on ketchup or soap powder. Store managers were naturally tempted to hold on to their customers by matching those prices, even if that meant selling products for less than the wholesale price. The Hartfords strongly condemned this practice. Not only did they dislike the idea of losing money on any sale, but they knew that below-cost sales could furnish ammunition for government investigations of unfair practices. In 1931, the company ordered that no merchandise be sold in any store for less than a 3 percent markup without approval from the division president, and that nothing be sold below replacement cost without approval of headquarters.[16]

In the face of such internal issues, the Hartfords were not preoccupied with the threat from large stores opened by independent retailers. "We did not take it seriously at first," John Hartford would testify years later. This neglect was not illogical. Of the $9 billion or so of retail food sales in 1933, these big stores, just becoming known as supermarkets, accounted for only 1 or 2 percent. And it was far from certain that supermarkets were the future. "It is to be hoped that gradually this type of competition will ease off," managers of A&P's New England Division concluded in 1933. "They are undoubtedly losing a great deal of money and will have to either go out of business or change their policies very soon." In any event, supermarkets' stunts and giveaways created what one writer terms a "carnival atmosphere" far from the sober, value-for-money approach John Hartford favored. A&P executives hoped that once the Depression was past and shoppers were less concerned about pinching pennies, the appeal of large, bare-bones stores far from home would wane. Even if it did not, supermarkets were a small-time business. No company owned more than a handful. No supermarket operator had the buying power of A&P, nor the canneries or bakeries or meat-buying companies or produce wholesaling operations such as the Atlantic Commission Company. If the supermarket turned out to have staying power, A&P, with its enormous logistical infrastructure, would be able to catch up quickly.[17]

Although the Hartfords never discussed the matter publicly, politics may also have had a role in A&P's reluctance to build large stores. The early supermarket operators were overwhelmingly independent grocers. A&P was already under serious attack for trampling independents, whose complaints had grown louder as competition squeezed margins across the industry. In the spring of 1932, the National Association of Retail Grocers' annual convention branded A&P a monopoly, condemning it for operating "in control of every function as grower, packer, manufacturer, broker, commission merchant, wholesaler and retailer." Retailing experts advised independent merchants to cut their costs, improve their merchandise, and spruce up their stores. A direct counterattack on independents trying to refashion themselves by opening larger and more efficient stores would have been highly impolitic.[18]

In the summer and fall of 1931, the Hartford family's private affairs titillated the American public once again. This time, the stories involved the children of Edward Hartford and Edward's widow, Henrietta. Both of the young people would presently become far more famous than their grocer uncles.

Josephine Hartford O'Donnell and Josephine's brother, George Huntington Hartford II, had grown up amid wealth and privilege, first in a Park Avenue apartment, then in the exclusive shoreside town of Deal, New Jersey. Jo, as she was known, was born in 1902 and was educated in Paris as well as New York. As many gender barriers broke down in the 1920s, she was able to follow her passions. She was a concert pianist, a tournament tennis player, an airplane pilot. Her father's death, in 1922, left her independently wealthy. She married in 1923.

In July 1931, when she was twenty-eight, Jo traveled to Reno, one of the few places in America where divorce was easy. A few weeks later, she sailed to Paris to wed Count Vadim Makaroff, a former Russian naval officer and diplomat. Makaroff, who was making a new career as a caviar importer, was a yachtsman. He may have gotten to know Josephine through her brother, with whom Makaroff sailed near Seaverge, Henrietta Hartford's "cottage" in Newport, Rhode Island, where America's wealthiest families converged each summer.

Huntington Hartford, nine years younger than his sister, was in his second year at Harvard in 1931. His mother had encouraged him to enjoy his wealth. In 1926, she had petitioned a court to increase the amount Huntington could draw annually from the Hartford trust from $100,000 to $150,000, explaining, "I do not believe that he should come into his inheritance with desires ungratified and wishes thwarted." But Henrietta herself would soon do the thwarting. Disapproving of Huntington's infatuation with a Broadway showgirl, she purportedly called upon a blond, blue-eyed pianist named Mildred King, whom she had met at a musical event in Boston, and asked her to serve as a "love pilot" and steer Huntington away from trouble—or so King claimed in a lawsuit seeking $100,000 for her services. "I never even saw this Miss King" was Henrietta's response. By the time the suit was filed, Huntington had eloped with a third woman, a college student from West Virginia named Mary Lee Eppling, and Miss King received a secret settlement.

The loves of the wealthy grocery heirs were fodder for newspapers from coast to coast. Invariably, the reports included embellished accounts of A&P's history and descriptions of the Hartford family's vast wealth. Some mentioned Henrietta's newly built home, a thirty-two-room mansion at Lexington Plantation, near Charleston, which she bought in 1930. At a politically sensitive moment, with big chain retailers standing accused of destroying economic opportunity for the average man, it was not the sort of publicity that stood the family company in good stead.[19]

Henrietta and her children would remain in the spotlight for years to come. Jo's 1937 divorce from Makaroff and her third marriage, a few weeks later, made headlines, with articles describing her "squadrons of servants" and her love of parties. The public was further engrossed by Henrietta's marriage that same year in Rome to Prince Guido Pignatelli, which brought a lawsuit by the prince's first wife contending that they had not been legally divorced. Huntington joined the A&P in 1934, after graduating from Harvard, but he lasted only a few months; his uncles fired him from his job keeping track of bread and pound cake sales after he skipped work to attend the Harvard-Yale football game. Like his sister, he would be married four times. As a theatrical producer, art collector, resort developer, and bon vivant, he would never escape the public eye.[20]

Huntington Hartford, his sister, and his mother were never involved in running the Great Atlantic & Pacific Tea Company. Years later, Jo and Huntington's constant need for cash would help speed the company's decline. But for now, their goings-on provided a ready source of ammunition for the company's critics. John A. Hartford, whose own marital travails had landed in the press a few years earlier and whose entertainments and travels with Pauline were regularly released to the society pages, may not have been bothered by the lifestyles of his late brother's widow and children. The opinion of George L. Hartford, a man who avoided flaunting his wealth and who did all he could to keep his name out of the newspaper, was not recorded.

Even amid the general prosperity of the 1920s, the growth of chain retailing discomfited many Americans. For all its mighty cities, the United States was mainly a rural country: 44 percent of the population lived in places of 2,500 people or fewer in 1930. Many more resided in small towns; the hundredth-largest city in the country, Rockford, Illinois, had only 85,864 inhabitants. Locally owned businesses were the lifeblood of these small communities. Chain stores were often seen as intruders, destroying not only the small retailer but also the local jobber that supplied it, the local stationer that printed its circulars, and the local bank that held its receipts. While there were anti-chain forces in the cities as well, young urban men at least could aspire to the many factory or office jobs being created in a growing economy. In more rural areas, where the agricultural economy was moribund through the 1920s due to falling crop prices, young men without prospects on the farm saw their aspirations to enter business blocked by the giant chains. Their best opportunity, it seemed, was to become a clerk for a company such as A&P, trading dreams of independence and upward mobility for a steady if none-too-generous weekly paycheck from a chain retailer that, it was frequently alleged, paid lower wages than independent grocers.[21]

As the Great Depression deepened, these resentments only mounted. Lack of alternatives drove even more people to try the grocery trade. Although severe food-price deflation decimated sales, cutting receipts at food stores from $10.9 billion in 1929 to $8.4 billion in 1935, the number of grocery stores rose 15 percent. Between 1930 and 1937, perhaps a quarter million independently owned grocery stores opened their doors. As A&P increased its share of the country's grocery-store sales from 14.4 percent in 1929 to 16.4 percent in 1933, at the expense of independent grocers, more people than ever before had cause to fear it.[22]

Public attack on the chains focused on their heavy use of "loss leaders"—products sold at a price that, even if not leading to actual loss, was too low to provide a normal profit. The research director of the Chain Store Research Bureau estimated that the leading chains of all sorts were selling 15 percent of their merchandise without profit in the late 1920s, and the Federal Trade Commission found that "an important aspect of chain-store price policy is the frequent use of 'leaders' consisting of specially low selling prices on particular items." Food chains used loss leaders extensively, but so did the independently owned supermarkets, whose entire strategy depended upon heavy promotion of a few very cheap items. For big stores, offering special sale items at prices that left little or no profit made great sense, as they drew customers who would then buy high-margin merchandise as well. From the viewpoint of mom-and-pop grocers, on the other hand, loss leaders, whether offered by food chains or by supermarkets, were simply unfair, a form of "destructive competition." The small grocers and their wholesale suppliers had been fighting "below-cost sales" for decades. In 1933, they finally had an opportunity to stamp out the plague.[23]

13

FRANKLIN ROOSEVELT

In March 1933, Franklin Roosevelt took office as president of the United States. Chain stores were the least of his worries. America was in its fourth year of the deepest depression in four decades. One worker in four was without a job, the banking system was on the verge of collapse, the farm sector was a disaster. Roosevelt had won election the previous November as the candidate of hope. His defeated Republican predecessor, Herbert Hoover, had offered one program after another to ease the country's distress, but nothing had brought improvement. With Democratic majorities in both houses of Congress and broad support among a desperate populace, Roosevelt had a commanding political position that freed him to try almost any policy he thought might extricate the country from depression and despair.

His ability to make a connection with average Americans was part of Roosevelt's genius. The journalist Jonathan Alter put his finger on the matter: "While FDR knew how to say 'My friends' in several different languages and appear to mean it in every tongue, Hoover could seem as if he were addressing strangers even in a roomful of friends." Hoover, one of the most accomplished men ever to occupy the presidency, had spent much of his life running large organizations in and out of government. He knew how to manage bureaucracies, but he had little feel for connecting with people, creating confidence, restoring a sense of possibility. Nor did he fathom how radio, just starting to become an important source of information, was changing the way in which people came to know their leaders. Roosevelt, an aristocratic New Yorker, was far more skilled at communicating with the common man. He understood radio and used it to powerful effect. When he spoke, whether in a formal address to Congress or in one of the series of "fireside chats" that began eight days after his inauguration, average people from Maine to California felt his empathy with their problems and their worries.[1]

Some of those average people ran grocery stores. Even before Roosevelt took office, they were begging his help to save the small retailer. "I remember in times past when your boy or mine if he could not get a job we could start him in business for a small capital and he could get along fine and be contented, but now under these chain store methods it is different," wrote Thomas Seamans of Jackson, Michigan. George Rund, owner of Universal Market in Princeton, Indiana, suggested a tax of at least $2,000 on each store over fifty owned by a single chain. F. H. McKay of Greenville, Michigan, wrote approvingly that "Germany locked up its Chain Stores because they considered them a bad thing for the economy." Mrs. Jennie Applegate, a grocer's wife from Bound Brook, New Jersey, sent the president a poem in her careful script:

The old home town has changed a lot since I was just a lad.
For in those days the home owned stores were all we ever had.
I remember how the boss could come and meet us at the door.
And he always made us feel at home when we were in his store.[2]

At the same time, Roosevelt heard from every corner about the struggles of consumers. Before the world war, consumers had rarely identified themselves as such. The consumer movement arose from the long campaign for woman suffrage, which in 1920 won ratification of a constitutional amendment giving women the right to vote. The first books promoting consumers' interests came in the mid-1920s and the formation of the first national consumer organization, Consumers' Research, in 1929. Consumer consciousness was in full flower by the time of Roosevelt's election. Prominent consumer advocates joined his administration, and federal agencies created consumer advisory councils to make sure the interests of the "citizen consumer" were represented. Roosevelt's appointees never forgot to emphasize the consumer's importance. The central role of consumer concerns, one New Deal economist asserted, was "a new development in American economic policy—a development which offers tremendous opportunities for social well-being."[3]

There is no doubt that consumers were in need of help, for the Depression was devastating living standards. Between 1929, when the stock market crashed, and 1933, Roosevelt's first year in office, total consumer spending fell by an astonishing 40 percent. Even allowing for a 32 percent drop in the consumer price index, many households' living conditions deteriorated sharply. Millions lost their homes to foreclosure or turned to charity to survive. Although workers lucky enough to hold on to their jobs saw their buying power surge because wages fell much less than prices, they were nonetheless fearful of the future. Travel fell sharply. Sales of clothing, cars, and radio sets collapsed. People worried first and foremost about keeping food on the table.[4]

One prominent version of New Deal history depicts the Roosevelt administration as the first pro-consumer government. Many decades after the fact, that depiction served a variety of political purposes, countering claims that the New Deal was too conservative and turning socialist and communist groups, women's groups, immigrant organizations, and activists of myriad other flavors into important historical actors. The consumerist story is not entirely without foundation: the 1930s saw consumers standing up for themselves as never before. Housewives organized boycotts to force down meat prices in a dozen cities, including a "meat strike" against forty-five hundred butcher shops in New York. Neighborhood committees checked poultry weights and measured the contents of food cans. Women's clubs and labor unions demanded that government take consumer interests into account in writing laws and regulations. Many of those grassroots activists drew strength from what they imagined to be the strong support of Franklin Roosevelt. "Never has there been such a wave of enthusiasm to do something for the consumer," insisted *The Nation*.[5]

Yet the claim that the New Deal was a pro-consumer program is too simple by half. An important part of Roosevelt's constituency had a very deep distrust of big business. Groups such as the Farmer-Labor Party in Minnesota, Father Charles Coughlin's National Union for Social Justice, and Huey Long's Share Our Wealth campaign were the heirs to the Populist movement of the 1890s. Their members, mainly working-class people and farmers, distrusted the chain stores as their grandfathers had distrusted the railroads, and no talk about efficiency would change their minds. The administration's own economic experts had no time for these neo-Populists; for all of their kind words about consumers, it was producers who had their attention. They overwhelmingly diagnosed the Depression as the result of excessive competition that was forcing down prices, decimating profits, and causing employers to lay off workers. Stopping deflation became one of the administration's first economic objectives. Holding up prices is as anticonsumer an activity as one can imagine, but when it came to choosing between aiding business and aiding consumers, there was no contest.[6]

The scholarly literature on the consumer and the New Deal scarcely makes mention of the Great Atlantic & Pacific. It is a curious omission, for during the presidencies of Franklin Roosevelt and his successor, Harry Truman, the world's largest retailer was under almost constant government attack. Both administrations, many members of Congress, and Roosevelt supporters in state and local governments all found it opportune to wage war on the Hartfords and their company, regardless of the cost to the consumer.

The day he took office, Roosevelt shut the nation's banks. Depositors in those days had no insurance to protect against bank failure, and as they panicked, pulling out deposits and demanding gold in exchange for their currency, they made the banks even weaker. Roosevelt's "bank holiday" was intended to stop the panic by halting withdrawals until Congress could enact a new banking law. The bank holiday quickly starved the economy of cash. Some employers gave workers scrip in lieu of paychecks. Others issued paychecks that, at least for the moment, no bank could cash. Most retailers muddled through, extending credit so their customers could buy the necessities of life. A&P did not. Hewing to established policy, A&P stores did business in cash only. They offered no credit and refused to accept scrip or to cash checks. Financially, it was a sound decision for the company. Politically, it was a poor way to start a relationship with the new administration in Washington.[7]

Truth be told, the Hartfords sought no relationship with the new administration in Washington. This was not as remarkable as it sounds. Until the 1930s, most businesses had no involvement with the federal government. The government's main role in economic regulation concerned transportation, so companies had little reason to spend time and money influencing Washington unless they were seeking higher import tariffs or lower freight rates. In any event, the Hartfords had little interest in politics. John, like most of his friends who sat on the boards of major corporations, was a Republican, but hardly an ardent one. In 1932 he donated $1,000 to William J. Donovan's unsuccessful campaign for governor of New York, in which Donovan, a Republican, was crushed beneath a Democratic landslide. That same year, Pauline Hartford donated $1,000 to help cover expenses remaining from Hoover's reelection campaign. John had no known relationships with Calvin Coolidge or Hoover, and he did not seek ties to Franklin Roosevelt. George, following his natural inclinations, avoided all contact with politicians. He would have opposed A&P's involvement in political affairs even if John had grasped that the relationship between business and government was about to change in a fundamental way.[8]

That change was codified in two laws enacted in the spring of 1933, during the congressional marathon that became known as Roosevelt's "Hundred Days." The Agricultural Adjustment Act was meant to prop up farm commodity prices by paying farmers to take land out of production and to slaughter hogs and cattle. It also required handlers of agricultural commodities to obtain government licenses, making them subject to regulations designed to "eliminate unfair practices" and to speed "restoration of normal economic conditions." That broad language gave the new Agricultural Adjustment Administration (AAA) enormous power not only over farmers and grain handlers but also over retailers such as A&P that dealt in large volumes of milk, butter, and wheat. A similar new law, the National Industrial Recovery Act, called for "codes of fair competition" governing individual industries. Such codes were to be written by industry groups supervised by the new National Recovery Administration (NRA). The codes were required to address work hours, minimum pay rates, and workers' right to union representation, and could also regulate other aspects of competition. Once accepted by the government, a code would apply to every company in the industry with the force of federal law. If a company failed to adhere to what was in effect a privately written statute, the U.S. district courts could levy a fine of up to $500 per violation per day and, in some cases, even impose prison terms.[9]

Neither law made the least mention of retailing. Yet both struck directly at the way A&P conducted its business.

The scale of the threat became clear on June 23, when the AAA convened food-industry executives in Washington. John A. Hartford was in the audience as Charles Brand, briefly serving as the agency's co-director, laid down rules that went far beyond the language of the new laws. No food distributor, Brand said, had the right to sell commodities produced from one set of materials at a loss and make up the loss on commodities produced from other materials. Though the language was obscure, it meant that the administration was joining the battle against big grocery chains. Independents had long accused the chains of selling some items at money-losing prices—loss leaders, they were called—in order to bring customers in the door. Brand's words meant that government would no longer allow some goods made from farm products to be sold at a lower profit than other goods. Nor could the retailer use advertising and brokerage allowances to reduce the price to the consumer. As A&P took in far more in advertising and brokerage allowances than any other retailer, the new rules seriously restricted its ability to set prices below those of competitors.[10]

Worse was to come. The AAA was overseeing the development of marketing agreements among distributors of some agricultural products, such as milk. As early as July 1933, AAA rules forced A&P to raise the price of White House milk, canned in the company's Wisconsin factories. A&P was required to charge at least seventeen cents for three cans of milk, executives in the Southern Division complained, while small competitors "have made inroads on our business through offering specials at 5¢ per can or less." Federal officials had no realistic way to police such violations at the hundreds of thousands of independent grocery stores, but the nation's largest grocer could not avoid compliance.[11]

Food manufacturers, wholesalers, and retailers all were expected to adopt codes of fair competition under the National Industrial Recovery Act. Administration officials made clear that grocery wholesalers were to write one code, grocery retailers another. Chain and independent grocers were to be covered by the same code. And what if they could not agree what that code should say? "The government's thought in this connection is that when an industry comes together to draw up a code, the thoughtful men in every line will pretty nearly embrace the same opinion," an AAA representative explained helpfully. The food retailers, he added, were expected to agree to "a truce in competition."[12]

Like groups in hundreds of industries, food wholesalers and food retailers spent the summer of 1933 drawing up codes of fair competition for government approval. Fair competition, as the National Recovery Administration defined the term, meant that competitors should have similar cost structures so that they could charge similar prices. The results would have the force of law, but the process was nothing like lawmaking. The grocery code was to be drafted by various state and national organizations, which were deemed to represent the interests of all firms in the industry, whether or not individual firms concurred. The draft code was to be submitted for a formal hearing, at which witnesses could object to particular provisions or offer substitute language. The NRA's consumer, industrial, and labor advisory councils could weigh in as well. After these procedural niceties, agency officials would negotiate with the groups that drafted the code, agree on final language, and submit the finished product for President Roosevelt's approval.[13]

This process allowed wholesalers and retailers to write rules that could be used to strangle competition to the advantage of small retailers. The National Association of Grocery Wholesalers, one of two nationwide wholesaler groups, dominated the writing of the food wholesale code. While the National Association of Food Chains helped draft the code for grocery retailers, its interest was the many chains owning only a few stores, not the large retailers. A&P, which had sales greater than those of the next seven food chains combined, was not an association member. Although A&P accounted for one-sixth of all sales at grocery stores in 1933, it was not invited to join the code-writing bodies. Nor did those bodies have the slightest interest in efficiencies that could reduce the cost of distributing food to consumers. The codes turned out to be competitive weapons, and A&P was in the line of fire.[14]

The grocery code, signed by Roosevelt at the end of 1933, was an independent grocer's dream. Like all NRA codes, the grocery code was stuffed with provisions to stabilize labor costs at a time when falling prices and high unemployment were pushing market wages down. Individual employees could work no more than ten hours in a day and forty-eight hours in a week. Children under sixteen could work no more than three hours per day. The minimum wage for grocery clerks would be $15 a week in large cities, $10 per week in small towns. Workers had the right to form unions to bargain with employers. But none of these provisions applied to family labor in independent stores or to small independent stores operating in rural areas. Of the 482,000 food stores in the United States, upwards of half were unaffected by the labor rules in the grocery code, while chains were uniformly forced to comply.[15]

The pricing provisions of the codes were even more damaging to the chains. The grocery code barred the sale of any grocery product for less than the invoice cost plus freight plus a 6 percent markup. This required markup on food was set lower than the independent grocers and wholesalers hoped for, and in November 1933 representatives of the National Association of Retail Grocers and the National-American Wholesale Grocers' Association visited Marvin H. McIntyre, Roosevelt's secretary, to plead unsuccessfully for a mandatory 10 percent markup. Even so, minimum selling prices on everything except meat, which was covered by a separate code, were a direct attack on John Hartford's philosophy of cutting prices to increase volume. The NRA food code would not allow more efficient grocers to operate with lower prices than competitors, even if they could do so profitably. This hardly served consumers' interests, but it served the administration's objective of keeping less efficient retailers in business to avoid adding to unemployment. Protests by the NRA Consumer Advisory Board against the ban on below-cost sales were ignored.[16]

With a stroke of the president's pen, the codes rendered many routine food-trade practices illegal. A&P and other grocery chains frequently accepted slim margins on sale merchandise to entice shoppers who would fill their baskets with more profitable items. The chains often found such sales profitable after taking manufacturers' allowances for advertising, brokerage, and fast payment into account. Now, however, allowances could not be considered in setting prices; any retail price below 106 percent of invoice price plus freight constituted unfair competition. A&P often featured low prices at new stores to build a clientele, and this, too, was barred by the codes. Selling one product with a low margin subsidized by the high-margin sale of another product was illegal. Fresh milk had to be sold at a single wholesale price across an entire region; coupled with the rules on minimum markups, this effectively meant that all retailers in a city had to charge the same price. The NRA macaroni code barred sales "below a fair and reasonable price," leaving it to bureaucrats to decide when the manufacturer's wholesale price constituted "destructive price cutting." The codes prohibited rebates of brokerage fees to grocers that did not buy through brokers, such as A&P, and required that advertising allowances be offered equally to all grocers, even mom-and-pop stores that never advertised.[17]

The list of prohibitions was extensive. Grocery stores could not remain open more than sixty-three hours a week, fulfilling a long-standing demand of independent grocers who stood behind the counter every moment their stores were open. For chains, however, the sixty-three-hour limit effectively mandated each store to close for a day and a half each week, reducing efficiency by requiring costly assets—store, furnishings, equipment—to sit idle. Premiums such as trading stamps were not permitted, a restriction that hardly affected independent stores, which rarely offered them, but did affect chains. Grocery stores could not hold two-for-the-price-of-one sales or give a discount on one product in return for the purchase of another. Separately, the codes for grocery manufacturers discouraged advertising and brokerage allowances and cash discounts, raising the effective prices manufacturers charged A&P and other big chains but leaving the prices for small grocers unaltered. The trucking code eroded A&P's cost advantage in moving foodstuffs from warehouses to stores.

These rules, and many more, were enforced by 783 local code authorities, which were charged with monitoring compliance and investigating suspected violations. Complaints were frequent. Between November 1933 and May 1935, officials registered 3,327 alleged violations of the Food and Grocery Code. Only the trucking and construction industries generated more complaints than the grocery trade. The more complicated complaints ended up at the central code office, located a couple of blocks from the White House, where seven employees devoted to food retailing sorted out such issues as when markdowns of dented cans and rotting produce were legal and when not. Smaller firms often paid little attention: a survey of 181 grocery wholesalers in New York state found one-third of them in violation of the food wholesaling code, with smallest wholesalers the most common violators. In combination, New England Division executives estimated, the NRA codes increased expenses by an amount equal to 1.5 percent of sales, while "many of our competitors, particularly the smaller chains and independents, are not adhering to the Code as rigidly as we are . . . and we find them proving very stiff competition."[18]

•

The Hartfords were slow to respond to the mounting threat. While the New Deal's policies permitted competitors to enlist Washington in their fight against A&P, Roosevelt's supporters continued their assault on chains at the state and local level. Before 1933, only a handful of states taxed chains. Between 1933 and 1935, fifteen states imposed new chain-store taxes, sometimes more than once. Minnesota, where A&P had only recently entered the market, passed a tax in 1933 that rose to $155 per year for each store in the state above fifty. Michigan, where A&P had done business for half a century, enacted an assessment that rose to $250 per year for each store over twenty-five. Florida's state senate came within one vote of banning chain retailers altogether in 1935; instead of a total ban, the legislature enacted a "privilege tax" of $10 for one store, $400 for each chain-owned store over fifteen, along with a tax of 5 percent of the gross receipts of chain stores. The most onerous levy, in Huey Long's Louisiana, taxed a chain with even a single store in the state according to the number of stores it owned nationwide, with the tax reaching $550 per store for chains with more than five hundred stores. The levy on A&P's fifteen thousand stores came to $8.25 million—half the company's total profits in 1934. Long, then a U.S. senator but still dominant in Louisiana politics, made no bones about the purpose of the tax. "I would rather have thieves and gangsters than chain stores in Louisiana," he told his constituents.[19]

The anti-chain forces made imaginative use of the day's most powerful communications medium, the talking picture. In 1934, a former NRA official, Frank Wilson, released *Forward America*, a film devoted to exposing "the anti-American business methods" of the chains. "The picture is dedicated to the American housewife," the publicity proclaimed. "It shows her how by sending her money away from home she is trading her husband out of his job, destroying the value of her home, and adding to the national problem of unemployment." Independent merchants arranged for local cinemas to show *Forward America* as the second film of double features and handed out free tickets to their customers to build support for further action against the chains.[20]

While chain-store taxation affected all chains, the Great Atlantic & Pacific was the main target. The Supreme Court had specifically ruled that a graduated per-store tax was constitutional, while taxes on chain stores' revenues or profits were not. In 1935, A&P had four times as many locations as Kroger; ten times as many as J. C. Penney, a clothing and dry-goods chain; and eight times as many as Woolworth, the king of variety stores. Unlike Kroger, A&P had stores throughout the South, where chain-tax fever ran especially high. Its chain-store tax burden, never disclosed to the public, was $2.2 million in 1935, or one-seventh of its total profit. And to the burden of state taxes must be added the municipal taxes that sprang up from Hamtramck, Michigan ($25 for a company's first local store, $1,000 for the fourth), to Fredericksburg, Virginia (up to $250 per store), to Little Rock, Arkansas, to Portland, Oregon.[21]

The proponents of state chain-store taxes were among Franklin Roosevelt's strongest backers. According to the economist Thomas Ross, the single most important variable in predicting which states would tax the chains was politics. States in which the Democratic Party controlled the governorship and both houses of the legislature were much more likely to enact chain-store taxes than states where the Republican Party shared power. Although these taxes raised consumers' costs, the pro-consumer New Dealers in Washington dared not criticize the small-town Democrats who led the anti-chain crusades. Nor did they object to the many other state laws that sought to protect small merchants and thereby raise the consumer price of food.[22]

John Hartford, standing aloof from politics, never opposed the New Deal's efforts to cartelize the food sector under the Agricultural Adjustment Act and the National Recovery Act. At the onset, in 1933, he had told his executives that while the code for the food and grocery trade "will undoubtedly place certain restrictions and burdens upon our operation," he thought "the industry as a whole" might benefit. The responsibility that came with running the nation's largest retailer may have made him hesitant to criticize the New Deal. In July 1933, he agreed to join other executives on the Agricultural Adjustment Administration's Food Industries Advisory Board, lending tacit support to the Roosevelt program, and two weeks later he publicly pledged his company's support for the codes. Perhaps the fact that the codes would constrain the new discount supermarkets, which made heavy use of loss leaders, made him hesitant to condemn the new regime. But he also refused to speak out against the rapid spread of state and local taxes on chains, which affected his company enormously but touched the independently owned supermarkets hardly at all.[23]

Odd as it may seem, such reticence was not unusual among businessmen in 1933. In the fourth year of the Depression, no one thought it strange that a trade association executive would complain that business was "being crucified on the cross of competition" or that the Chamber of Commerce of the United States, the country's leading business group, favored allowing the majority of firms in an industry to enforce price and production restrictions on their competitors. In a survey of New England manufacturers, 80 percent favored codes to eliminate unfair practices in business, and the NRA Business Advisory Committee spent much time discussing ways to end "unfair" practices such as price discrimination and below-cost selling. John Hartford must have shared some of those views, for in 1934 he agreed to join a committee to pass on loans to companies that wanted to borrow from the Federal Reserve Bank of New York, hardly a post that would have appealed to a rabid free marketer. Speaking to the board of the Central Western Division in June 1934, he "emphasized the desire of the Company to completely support all government policies and to conduct our operations in conformity with all of the codes affecting our business." If he felt the New Deal's policies were persecuting companies such as his, he never said a word to that effect in public.[24]

John Hartford's silence proved to be a profound mistake, for the New Deal dealt A&P serious damage. Unlike most of the NRA codes, which favored big businesses over little ones, the codes in the food and grocery sector favored small retailers over big ones such as A&P. "The decided price advantage we formerly held has been to a great extent lost," executives of the Eastern Division lamented in September 1934. With the federal codes and the state chain-store taxes blocking the company's low-price, high-volume strategy, customers fled. Physical volume per store fell 10 percent between 1932, the last year before the New Deal measures, and 1934. A&P's share of national grocery-store sales dropped by three percentage points over those two years. Profits plummeted, and the company's after-tax return on equity, 14.7 percent in

1932, fell to 10.3 percent in 1934. As government lawyers later explained the situation, "In 1934, A&P found that it had little advantage over independents and cooperative groups of retail grocers. Therefore A&P was unable to emphasize retail price advantage to consumers."[25]

On May 17, 1935, the U.S. Supreme Court declared the National Industrial Recovery Act unconstitutional. The codes governing retailers, wholesalers, and food manufacturers were null and void. Congress, the Court found, had no power to delegate its authority to the industry groups that wrote the codes. Nor did it adequately define what those codes were meant to limit: the term "fair competition" had no meaning under law, the Court found, and the term "unfair competition" had a very narrow meaning related only to misrepresentation. The law's direction as to how the codes should ensure fair competition and eliminate the unfair kind was thus unacceptably vague. Eight months later, the Court would invalidate the Agricultural Adjustment Act on very similar grounds.[26]

The extent to which federal policies had damped down competition in the food sector became clear almost immediately. Although the chain stores' association warned members against "hasty changes in prices wages and hour of employment," complaints about violations of the grocery code poured into NRA offices. Having lost their authority to enforce the codes, the agency's officials spent their time documenting the effects of the codes' demise. "There is considerable price cutting in this trade, which they blame on chain stores," one wrote after surveying grocers in Arlington, Texas. In northwestern Arkansas, sixteen of thirty independent grocers lengthened work hours within two months of the grocery code's abolition. "The average is probably about 60 hours a week instead of the 48 hours prevailing under the Code regulation," the Kansas Retail Grocers Association reported. Wages fell as independent grocers slashed costs in the face of "the disastrous price war now raging here," as one California groceryman described the situation. Grocery clerks tried to form unions *after* the code's labor-protection provisions lapsed, because they feared price wars would lead to lower wages. In Los Angeles, the new Food and Grocery Bureau of Southern California, claiming to represent 90 percent of local grocers, put forth a "voluntary" code requiring the same 6 percent markups as the voided NRA grocery code, but without the law behind them they had no way to keep competitors in line.[27]

As the codes fell away, consumers were the clear winners. Eggs, thirty-one cents per dozen in Los Angeles under the NRA code, fell overnight to twenty-eight cents. Sugar, fifty-one cents for a ten-pound bag under the code, tumbled to forty-one cents, saving local consumers more than $1 million per month. Loss leaders and two-for-one sales returned with a vengeance. Margins at many stores were squeezed, as independents as well as chains sold with less than the code-mandated 6 percent markup simply to move merchandise. Customers returned to the discount-minded grocery chains. In 1936, the first full year after the National Industrial Recovery Act and the Agricultural Adjustment Act had been invalidated, A&P's tonnage per store rose sharply, and its after-tax profit margin was the highest since 1933. John Hartford's strategy of boosting profit by moving high volumes at low prices was back at work.[28]

For the moment, the consumerist forces in New Deal Washington had gained the upper hand over the producers. The Hartfords prepared for a return to business as normal. But the consumerist ascendancy would turn out to be short-lived.[29]

14

WRIGHT PATMAN

Politics abhors a vacuum, and early 1935 found a leadership vacuum atop the national movement against chain stores. W. K. Henderson, having sold his radio station in 1932, no longer filled the airwaves with anti-chain tirades or sold memberships in the Merchants' Minute Men. Huey Long, now a U.S. senator from Louisiana, had moved on to other issues. Local activists such as William States Jacobs, a prominent Houston minister, made radio speeches and supported merchants' committees, but they developed no wider following and had little political influence. At the national level, the fight had been taken over by the lobbyists for independent druggists, grocers, and wholesalers. These men were at home with the bureaucrats at the National Recovery Administration and the industry committees that wrote NRA codes, but galvanizing masses of supporters was not their forte. The anti-chain movement needed a dramatically different sort of leader. One appeared quite accidentally, in the person of a populist congressman from Texas.[1]

Wright Patman's sympathy for humble men seeking opportunity was real, for he was one of them. Born in 1893 in a two-room log house in a railroad stop known as Patman's Switch, in northeast Texas, Patman grew up on a farm and then in the nearby town of Hughes Springs, population seven hundred. He rode a horse six miles each way to high school, becoming the class valedictorian. He lived as a tenant cotton farmer, just as his parents had, while studying the law by correspondence. In 1915, he entered the one-year law school program at Cumberland University, a Presbyterian institution in Tennessee that was noted for producing influential political leaders. Returning home, he tried to build a law practice. For Patman, as for so many other small-town boys, being called to the Army in the world war was a life-changing experience, broadening his horizons and fueling his ambition. After serving as a machine-gun officer, he moved back to Texas in 1919, marrying and joining a law practice in Linden, a few miles from Hughes Springs. In 1920, he won a seat in the Texas legislature. His political ascent was swift. He was appointed district attorney in 1924 and made a name for himself arresting bootleggers in Prohibition-era Texarkana. In May 1928, he paid $11 in filing fees to enter the Democratic primary in the First Congressional District against Eugene Black, a seven-term incumbent. Patman's platform was "Against monopolies, trusts, branch banking and excessive and discriminative freight rates," and opposed to the "money barons of the East." His upset victory in the primary was tantamount to election in his heavily Democratic district. In March 1929, Patman, aged thirty-five, moved to Washington to take the congressional seat he would hold for forty-seven years.[2]

Patman quickly identified a signature issue: bonuses for veterans of the world war. In 1924, Congress had voted payments for wartime service, with each individual's entitlement depending upon length of service and amount of time overseas. Only small amounts, however, were paid immediately. The fiscally conservative administration of Calvin Coolidge insisted that the government set aside the money before making payments, so most veterans received not cash but certificates that could be redeemed, with interest, only in 1945. One of the largest veterans' groups, the Veterans of Foreign Wars, demanded money right away, and Patman took up the cause. His first attempt, in 1929, failed in the House of Representatives, where the Republican Party had a large majority. Two years later, with the Depression devastating the country, he reintroduced the bill, drawing attention by arranging with the clerk of the House to have it designated H.R. 1. The House now had a Democratic majority, but after hearings in April 1932 the Ways and Means Committee reported out the bill with a negative recommendation. The following month, thousands of destitute veterans descended on Washington to demand passage of the Patman bonus bill, setting up a shantytown within sight of the Capitol and parading daily. Patman maneuvered carefully to bring his bill to a vote on the House floor despite the committee's rejection. Facing the specter of social unrest in the shadow of the Capitol, the House overruled the powerful Ways and Means Committee and approved the bill, with an appropriation of $2.4 billion, on June 14. The Republican-controlled Senate blocked it. When the Bonus Marchers refused to go home, the U.S. Army, under the command of General Douglas MacArthur, routed the veterans from their camps with bayonets and gas. Patman emerged from the uproar a hero, one of the few people in Congress dedicated to the veterans' cause.[3]

A stocky man just under six feet tall, with curly brown hair and a receding hairline, Patman did not cut a particularly imposing figure in Washington. A teetotaler, he shunned the capital's social scene—his wife, Merle, remained at home in Texas with their four sons—and did not have close relationships with other legislators. He spent seven days a week at his office, dictating endless letters to people back in his impoverished rural district. Given unimportant committee assignments, he decided to concentrate on high-profile issues that would resonate in eastern Texas, as he had with the veterans' bonus bill. In 1931, he stunned Washington by demanding the impeachment of Andrew Mellon, the highly unpopular Treasury secretary, claiming that Mellon had cheated on his taxes and done favors for several major companies; Mellon was soon persuaded to become ambassador to Great Britain. In 1932, Patman called for an investigation into the Federal Reserve Board's role in causing the Depression. In 1933, he was one of forty-nine congressmen who forced the House Democratic caucus to discuss what he called "a breakdown of the anti-monopoly laws," and he also campaigned to curb the banking industry's influence over the Federal Reserve. In 1934, he spent $1,771 to self-publish two books, *Patman's Appeal to Pay Veterans* and *Bankerteering, Bonuseering, Melloneering*, expecting that the largest veterans' organization, the American Legion, would buy copies in bulk for its posts throughout the country. Patman ended up losing money when too few people sent their quarters to Patman Publications in Paris, Texas.[4]

The bonus issue burned on after the inauguration of Franklin Roosevelt in March 1933. Roosevelt adroitly extinguished the problem by quietly encouraging Congress to pass Patman's bill, which he then vetoed in front of a joint session of Congress in the expectation that the Republicans would vote to override his veto. They did so, helping pass the bill but surrendering their ability to attack Roosevelt for the spending involved. Victorious at last, Patman needed a new cause. By chance, an issue fell into his lap. In April 1935, newspapers reported the creation of a new organization, the American Retail Federation, which claimed to serve as "the unified voice of the entire field of distribution" but was in fact dominated by the big chain retailers. Representative John Cochran demanded an investigation. "It is inimical to the welfare of the citizens of the United States to permit the organization and functioning of such a superlobby," Cochran stormed. The Missouri Democrat was named to head the special investigating committee, but a heart attack put him out of action almost immediately. Patman was named chairman in his stead.[5]

Patman seized the opportunity. He first asked the House to broaden his committee's power, giving it authority "to investigate the trade practices of individuals, partnerships, and corporations engaged in big-scale buying and selling of articles at wholesale or retail." That sweeping mandate brought everything related to retailing within the purview of the special investigating committee. When investigators examined the files of the American Retail Federation and came up with little more than the shocking fact that the group had organized lobbying efforts against anti-chain legislation, Patman used his broad investigative authority to bring A&P into the committee's headlights.[6]

A&P had, in fact, been one of Cochran's original targets: his resolution to investigate the American Retail Federation identified John A. Hartford as a member of the organization's executive committee. The claim was untrue. The Hartfords had long made it their policy to avoid industry associations, and they were not involved with the American Retail Federation. They were, however, involved with Merrill Sickles, a consultant who charged A&P $150 a month for his economic research. Sickles, who also had other food-industry clients, approached Patman in May 1935, describing himself as "formerly Washington representative of the A&P Tea Co." and proposing to handle the chain-store investigation for the committee for a fee of $2,250. The low price made the committee suspicious that the big chains were trying to infiltrate the investigation, a suspicion Sickles's testimony did little to allay. It seems unlikely that A&P paid Sickles in an attempt to influence Patman's committee. At the time, the committee was focusing on the American Retail Federation, with which the company had no connection. No matter. Though the committee found no evidence that he was working on A&P's behalf, the hint of scandal lingered in the air.[7]

More strange evidence turned up when Patman went after an entirely different organization, the Food and Grocery Chain Stores of America Inc. Its files, subpoenaed by the committee, revealed that its executive director, John A. Logan, was secretly paying $50 a week in cash to one John E. Barr, an employee of the National Anti–Chain Store League, an organization claiming to be on the opposite side of the chain-store issue. Barr thereupon vanished, to resurface only after Patman had his wife arrested for refusing to reveal his whereabouts. In what one publication described as a "queer irony," Patman, the veterans' hero, found himself compelling testimony from Logan, decorated for conspicuous bravery in the war, and Barr, formerly an official of the U.S. Veterans Bureau. Patman's discovery of a plot to undermine the anti-chain movement, however, seemed laughable after Barr provided details about the National Anti–Chain Store League. The league, he testified, was yet another anti-chain scam, a for-profit business owned by a man who sold shares to various Washingtonians whose names appeared on a "sucker list" and then used part of the proceeds to entertain members of Congress. Patman had uncovered a scandal, but not the one he wanted to find.[8]

Nor was that the end of the oddities. Patman made much of a $1,500 payment from Logan's retailer group to the National-American Wholesale Grocers' Association, a wholesalers' group, asserting that it was in some way improper. Logan shot back with allegations that Patman was deliberately aiding a different wholesaler organization, the United States Wholesale Grocers' Association, which, unlike the National-American group, opposed chain grocery stores. Logan's charge hit home, for Patman and the United States Wholesale Grocers, known for its vigorous criticism of the Great Atlantic & Pacific, had in fact become the best of friends.[9]

Within days of the Supreme Court decision in May 1935 voiding all NRA codes, the general counsel of the United States Wholesale Grocers, H. B. Teegarden, drew up a bill to prohibit price discrimination by manufacturers. The bill was meant to reestablish some of the anti-chain provisions in the NRA food and retail codes. Under Teegarden's draft, a manufacturer could give a volume discount to a retailer only if the manufacturer could prove in each instance that filling the larger order meant lower manufacturing or shipping costs, a burden that would have been almost impossible to meet. By June, when Patman introduced the bill in the House and the Senate majority leader, Joseph Robinson, submitted it to the Senate, two other provisions had been added, both aimed at A&P. One required that a manufacturer giving any store an advertising allowance had to offer proportionate allowances to all stores; if a retailer buying $100,000 of a product received a $1,000 advertising allowance, a retailer buying one-tenth as much should receive one-tenth the allowance. The other new provision, making it illegal for a retailer to own a broker, sought to end A&P's ownership of the Atlantic Commission Company, its produce-wholesaling subsidiary. The United States Wholesale Grocers lavishly praised Patman for his efforts to fight "the barons of Wall Street" and threw a dinner in his honor at the Mayflower hotel.[10]

Unfortunately for Patman, A&P proved to be an elusive target for his special investigating committee. The Hartford brothers had steered clear of the Food and Grocery Chain Stores of America, just as they had avoided the American Retail Federation. Even if Patman had identified any real wrongdoing at those organizations, he would not have been able to attach it to A&P. The inability to link the biggest and most controversial chain-store operator to allegations of illicit lobbying by chain stores undermined the original premise of the investigation. Nor was A&P linked to "the barons of Wall Street"; while investment bankers would happily have taken a stake in the company, as they had with Safeway, Kroger, and other competitors, the Hartfords had no use for Wall Street's money.

Pushing the Robinson-Patman bill against price discrimination by manufacturers allowed Patman to change tack. Instead of focusing on chain stores' wrongdoing, he used his broad subpoena power to probe chain stores' buying practices in an effort to drum up opposition to price discrimination. Although A&P had avoided being caught up in the committee's investigation of wrongdoing, the battle was shifting to a subject on which the company was highly vulnerable: size.

The special investigating committee's star witness was C. W. Parr, a vice president for purchasing at A&P. Parr provided a detailed look inside the company that accounted for one of every seven dollars spent in U.S. grocery stores in 1935. A&P, he revealed, had forty-five to fifty warehouses serving its stores, which were organized into six geographic divisions. The company purchased through a dozen buying offices in major cities as well as the Atlantic Commission Company, which bought fresh fruits and vegetables from farmers or farm cooperatives. Each of the six divisions had its own purchasing director, but headquarters took responsibility for the arrangements that were Patman's real interest—the 343 contracts in which suppliers agreed to furnish A&P with advertising allowances, payments in lieu of brokers' fees, or quantity rebates above and beyond those appearing on invoices. In the previous year, Parr testified, these allowances had come to $6 million, representing a hefty chunk of the company's $16.7 million after-tax profit.[11]

Parr insisted that A&P's huge volume entitled it to discounts that grocery manufacturers' smaller customers did not deserve. Its large orders provided manufacturers with order backlogs that reduced their risks, he said. And, he claimed, the manufacturers themselves derived benefit from the various discounts A&P received. The advertising allowances supported newspaper and radio advertising, window and counter displays, and advertising circulars, while in return for brokerage discounts A&P provided nationwide distribution and promotion of a manufacturer's product. A&P expected to pay 5 percent or more below the standard wholesale price for all merchandise, and would usually not carry undiscounted products. Parr offered examples of A&P's arrangements with suppliers. General Foods extended advertising and brokerage allowances coming to 5 percent on A&P's purchases plus various quantity discounts, with the total reaching $450,000 per year. Standard Brands provided advertising allowances of $97,164 per year on Chase & Sanborn coffee and $38,000 on Royal gelatin, along with a $144,000 advertising allowance and a 10 percent quantity discount on yeast. The California Packing Corporation rebated 5 percent in return for a firm order for 2.5 million cases of Del Monte canned fruits and vegetables. Quantity discounts on Diamond matches left A&P paying 75.11 cents for 144 packs, versus the standard wholesale price of 82 cents.[12]

To Patman, Parr's testimony was proof of naked market power. Other chains received rebates as well, but A&P seemed to get far more than its share; it had four times the sales of Kroger but took in nine times as much in advertising and brokerage allowances and quantity discounts. Patman grilled witnesses from the food manufacturers. Yes, a vice president of General Foods said, other grocers could obtain a twenty-five-cent-per-case quantity discount on Diamond salt, although no other grocer purchased the requisite 200,000 cases a year. Advertising discounts were available on yeast, said a vice president of Standard Brands, but A&P and Kroger were the only merchants to sell the 300,000 foil packages a month needed to qualify. Why, Patman demanded, could independent stores not receive such discounts if they advertised the yeast? The reason, he was told, was that Standard Brands sold its yeast to merchants for 2.5 cents a packet. Only a chain with many stores in a market would have the volume to justify advertisements for such an inexpensive product. And selling to A&P was cheaper than selling to independents, because Standard Brands could send all its invoices to the central office and receive a single payment, resulting in "tremendous" saving.[13]

The cold financial details revealed in days of such testimony presented a compelling yet simple story. Firm orders from a retailer with the size and national scale of the Great Atlantic & Pacific Tea Company enabled grocery manufacturers to lower their production costs and promote their products in ways that would otherwise have been impossible, and in return the chain expected a share of the manufacturers' gains. But while business school professors saw such testimony as evidence of economic rationality, the anti-chain forces read it precisely the opposite way. A&P's prices were "close to 10 percent" below his own, testified the grocer Harry Wadsworth of McKeesport, Pennsylvania, "and if I had their discounts and allowances, I could meet them easily."

In any event, evidence about efficiency would never address the underlying concerns of Wright Patman and millions of others, who feared the demise of a society in which personal relationships were all-important and hardworking men had the opportunity to rise through their own efforts. Where experts pointed to scientific management and consumer benefits, Patman saw "the huge chain stores sapping the civic life of local communities with an absentee overlordship, draining off their earnings to his coffers, and reducing their independent business men to employees or to idleness." The disagreement concerned worldview far more than economics, and it could not be bridged with explanations about the cost of advertising yeast.[14]

Fighting the chain stores became Patman's full-time crusade. It was appreciated back in Texas, where chain stores were an important political issue—and where many ardent supporters of President Roosevelt were heavily engaged in the same fight.

In November 1934, James Allred, a populist Democrat, had captured the governor's office on a platform calling for a chain-store tax. Only thirty-five years old, Allred had served as the state's attorney general, aggressively attacking monopolies and corporate interests. He asked the legislature to impose a graduated tax, depending upon the size of the chain, "to equalize unfair competition between the great foreign chain stores, with their tremendous capital, and the little home owned stores." Handwritten letters of support from Depression-stricken merchants poured into the governor's office. N. F. Howard, San Antonio: "Put the tax so high they must get out." W. L. Neel, Neels Grocery, Wichita Falls: "Something must be done to protect the independent merchant." Many small-town residents echoed the sentiments of L. D. Steffens, a traveling salesman, who sent Allred a copy of his plaint to President Roosevelt: "I will site you, sir, to my old home town of about 3300 population. Several years ago they had a wholesale grocery company there that worked about 8 men. There were four good sized General Stores that employed from 7 to 15 men per store. Today, three of these stores are gone and one remains with five people where they had about fifteen. The wholesale house closed and moved away . . . In these stores these employees were making a living, and the owners were, also, and everyone was happy."[15]

When the legislature convened in Austin in September, Allred again pushed the chain-store issue. Citing the work of Patman's special investigating committee, he asserted that the nefarious methods used by chain stores to defeat anti-chain legislation showed the need for action. The legislature opened hearings on September 30, 1935, with Patman, who had conveniently arranged for his special investigating committee to hold its own hearing in Austin, as the first witness. His comments hinted at corruption in the halls of the state capitol. Patman explained that fourteen general-merchandise chains had joined forces with Safeway to engage the Washington lobbyist Robert W. Lyons as their agent in Texas. Lyons, he implied, had suborned two former state senators to work on his behalf. Their tactic supposedly was not to oppose the bill but to amend the definition of "chain" so that independent stores in voluntary chains would be taxed the same way as A&P and Safeway and would therefore turn against the bill. His accusations caused an uproar as former senators came to defend themselves and legislators spoke on behalf of their former colleagues.[16]

It was more than dislike of monopoly that motivated Allred's commitment to the cause. He was desperately searching for revenue to support a New Deal–style program of his own, including old-age pensions, better highways, and improved education. Texas, he complained, still had the tax system of a rural economy, when the state was increasingly populous and increasingly urban. A chain-store tax, along with taxes on liquor and a new system for collecting fees due the state, were among his ideas for raising revenue. His proposal hung in the balance until the last days of the legislative session, when the real wheeling and dealing began. When it was over, retailers operating in Texas faced a $1 annual tax on the first store and $25 on the third, rising to $750 per store for all stores beyond fifty owned by a single company. Although all stores were taxed, the highest rates applied only to the grocery chains, for only they operated dozens of stores in the state. For A&P, the tax would consume the bulk of the profits of its Texas stores.[17]

Patman's special investigating committee hearings continued sporadically through 1935 as the Robinson-Patman antidiscrimination bill awaited action in the House Judiciary Committee. That committee was chaired by Patman's fellow Texan Hatton Sumners. Sumners, eighteen years Patman's senior, grew up poor in Tennessee before his family moved to Garland, Texas, where his formal education ended after one year of high school. After farming and working as a grocery-store clerk, Sumners moved to Dallas, taught himself the law, and passed the state bar exam in 1897. A self-made man who became a constitutional scholar, Sumners had more than a little sympathy with Patman's desire to preserve opportunity for men of humble origins. On the other hand, he distrusted Patman's constant quest for publicity, and he had opposed the veterans' bonus bill. Sumners was one of the barons of the House, and his relations with his younger colleague seem to have been rather formal.[18]

In 1937, Sumners would fall out with Franklin Roosevelt by opposing the president's plan to add administration-friendly justices to the U.S. Supreme Court, but in 1935 he was still an ardent New Dealer. He would steer Patman's bill however the administration wished—but the administration wished only that the entire chain-store issue would go away. President Roosevelt was aware that many of his most enthusiastic supporters, especially in the South, were avid foes of chain stores, and that many of his best-known critics, including several radio commentators, had made hay with the chain-store issue. On the other hand, grocery chains had been well established in northern industrial centers for decades, and Roosevelt knew that his working-class voters appreciated the money they saved by shopping at them. Roosevelt had delivered a bland endorsement of "increased efficiency in moving the essentials of life from the producer to the consumer," but had also said at a press conference in February 1935 that loss-leader merchandising could inflict hardship on small merchants. He told reporters, in a very general way, that some regulation of chain stores might be necessary, but he remained deliberately vague about what sort of regulation he might support.[19]

The organized support for the Robinson-Patman bill was led by the United States Wholesale Grocers' Association, which drafted it, and the National Association of Retail Druggists, representing pharmacists who owned their own stores. The proposed ban on price discrimination and allowances was wildly popular with both groups. According to government studies, two-thirds of tobacco manufacturers, half of grocery manufacturers, and one-third of drug manufacturers gave special allowances to retail chains. Chains typically received larger allowances than the wholesalers serving independent merchants, and while the vast majority of allowances were less than 10 percent, a handful of chains received much larger allowances from certain manufacturers. The smaller merchants and wholesalers naturally found this situation unfair. But opinion among merchants was badly split, reflecting the diversity of ways in which business was done. Lumber wholesalers opposed the Robinson-Patman bill because it prohibited discounts for buying wood by the railcar load, long the practice in their industry. The National-American Wholesale Grocers' Association, the group Patman had attacked in the spring of 1935, was opposed as well. The American Fruit and Vegetable Shippers Association asked for an exemption, as market prices changed "almost hourly," potentially giving rise to endless claims of price discrimination as some buyers paid different prices than others. The National League of Wholesale Fresh Fruit and Vegetable Distributors, on the other hand, was strongly in favor of the bill. Allowing chains to expand, the league's secretary told the House Judiciary Committee, was "generosity with the producer and shipper's money . . . taking it right out of his pocket and giving it to the consumer," making clear his view that the consumer had no right to save money.[20]

Robinson-Patman's advocates presented the legislation as help for manufacturers victimized by "concentration of power in the buying field." As H. B. Teegarden, the attorney for the United States Wholesale Grocers' Association, explained helpfully, "The law must help the manufacturer to resist the unfair demands of the large buyer." Many manufacturers did not see things that way. Monsanto Chemical Company, a maker of pesticides, deemed the legislation "unsound and impractical." General Mills objected that some of its customers would inevitably pay different prices than others because of constant fluctations in flour prices, but the bill might deem these price changes discriminatory. Cigar company executives opposed the bill because they feared that if the big grocery chains could no longer receive discounts on large orders of cigars, they would manufacture their own. The same concern led most makers of kitchen matches to oppose the Robinson-Patman bill. As one match company executive explained, "The large companies are always fearful that the large Corporate Chains such as A&P, Kroger, Safeway and a couple of others will manufacture their own matches unless they are given a special concession."[21]

Independent merchants, notably grocers, were the poster children of the anti-chain campaign. But while small food retailers, by far the most numerous group of merchants, overwhelmingly favored the legislation, their opinions did not much matter. Their national organization, the National Association of Retail Grocers, was hapless, and most of its state affiliates depended on contributions from wholesalers or food manufacturers. Even their friends, such as Carl Dipman, the editor of *The Progressive Grocer*, admitted that tens of thousands of grocers lacked basic business skills and were bound to fail, and "no amount of legislation can stop the carnage." The fact that most grocery stores and butcher shops survived for only a few years meant that shop owners were rarely influential even at the local level: in Texarkana, the largest city in Wright Patman's congressional district, 37 percent of the independent grocery stores that opened their doors between 1925 and 1935 failed during the first year. In the big northern and Midwestern cities, food retailing was dominated by immigrants who in many cases spoke little English and were not even citizens eligible to vote. The independent grocers would never have been able to bring the Robinson-Patman bill to final approval. It was the druggists and the food wholesalers, pillars of their communities running well-established businesses, who drove the train.[22]

Patman was unable to advance his bill in 1935, as Congress had far more momentous legislation on its agenda—bills granting workers the right to form unions and bargain collectively, regulating electric and gas utilities, and establishing a national pension and social insurance scheme, Social Security. Patman maneuvered for Roosevelt's support to pass the price-discrimination bill in 1936. On November 16, 1935, he asked Marvin McIntyre, a White House aide, to arrange an appointment with the president just before Christmas. Two weeks later, he offered a more ambitious plan, proposing to bring wholesalers and independent retailers from each state to meet with Roosevelt on December 30 in Washington. If that were to happen, he promised, "the Republicans would quickly forget politics and follow the President." McIntyre passed Patman's request to the president with his own cover note: "I don't think the movement sponsored by Patman would work very well." Roosevelt steered clear, seeing Patman instead at his annual New Year's Day reception, where the congressman told him about his chain-store investigation.[23]

The president understood he was on treacherous ground. Since 1933, his administration had made much of its commitment to the consumer, creating various consumer advisory councils and styling itself the first administration to give the consumer a voice. Now those consumer groups wanted to be heard. They strongly opposed the Robinson-Patman bill: what Patman called price discrimination they thought of as discount pricing, and they wanted more of it, not less. Six women's organizations, including the national League of Women Voters and the federations of women's clubs in Chicago and Cleveland, joined forces to object that the bill would reduce purchasing power. "This is clearly a WOMAN'S CAUSE," they proclaimed. Patman would not allow such statements to go unanswered. "When all independent merchants can receive the same prices from manufacturers that the banker-controlled retailers receive, competition will be preserved and the consumer protected," he thundered. Patman skillfully orchestrated grassroots support. Hundreds of petitions poured into Congress, signed by grocers and candy-store owners all over the country. Druggists sent Roosevelt handwritten letters referring to "the rumor that the administration is blocking the passage" of the bill.[24]

The administration was not blocking the Robinson-Patman bill. In fact, it was divided on the subject. The Federal Trade Commission, which had taken on responsibility for fighting monopoly, thought the legislation too weak and proposed that quantity discounts, which "as a rule work in favor of monopoly," be put under FTC regulation. The Commerce Department took no stand, but its Business Advisory Council, which included prominent chain-store executives, proposed further study "to understand pricing behavior" before passing the bill. R. E. Wood, the president of Sears, Roebuck, and Edward Filene of Filene's, the Boston department store, both wrote to the White House in opposition. When the National Conference of Independent Businessmen brought 1,500 people to Washington for the "March of the Little Men" in March 1936, a few retailers visited Roosevelt to ask his support for Robinson-Patman, but the president avoided taking a stance. The White House let it be known that "he is not personally interested in this legislation and it will have to pass under its own steam."[25]

In the end, the Democratic leaders in both houses of Congress decided to accept an altered version of the Robinson-Patman bill. They understood full well the consumer benefits brought by chain retailers, and they also understood that price discrimination had an economic logic that could not be legislated away. But in 1936, a vote for Robinson-Patman had less to do with economics than with trying to hold together a society that was fraying badly after six years of the Depression. As Hatton Sumners, the chairman of the Judiciary Committee, wrote eloquently in a confidential letter to an old friend, if Congress failed to help the small businessman, "some man like Huey Long" might come along and demand that government take over big companies. Sumners added: "I believe I can read with some degree of accuracy the signs of the times. These things give to me the deepest concern."[26]

With his usual parliamentary skill, Patman proposed that Robinson, the Senate majority leader, pass the legislation through his chamber first to press the House Rules Committee to put the bill on the House's crowded calendar. The Senate added numerous amendments and sent it to the House. On May 28, the House passed its version of the ban on price discrimination with an overwhelming vote of 290–16. House leaders pointedly excluded Patman from the conference committee that reconciled the differences between House and Senate legislation. The Robinson-Patman Act was finally approved on June 6, and signed by President Roosevelt without objection.[27]

Economists have spent decades debating the economic effects of the Robinson-Patman Act. The financial effects, however, are beyond debate. The average publicly traded grocery company lost 58 percent of its stock market value between June 11, 1935, when the bill was introduced in the House of Representatives, and December 1937, even as the Dow Jones Industrial Average rose about 8 percent. The price collapse of supermarket stocks suggests that investors expected the law to have a severe impact on profitability. That expectation proved correct. Chain supermarkets were forced to raise prices, as they were no longer able to use advertising and brokerage allowances to lower the cost of groceries. As they could no longer obtain merchandise far more cheaply than independent stores, their price advantage declined, and their share of food sales plummeted. A&P was seriously affected as well. Prior to 1935, the company's profits had never been less than 2 percent of sales. From 1935 onward, profits would never exceed 2 percent of sales. For independent retailers, especially those in the grocery trade, the Robinson-Patman Act was a lease on life.[28]

The Robinson-Patman Act served Patman's political needs as well. His radio speeches against the chains made him a national figure. He undertook to install broadcasting equipment in the Capitol, and also ordered an expensive sound system for his campaign rallies. Back in Texarkana, his main political problem was a rumor that Merle had been seen coming out of the Safeway store with a big bundle of groceries, requiring Patman to declare that he never shopped at chain stores and had asked Mrs. Patman to avoid them as well. Patman campaigned vigorously against token opposition, holding dozens of rallies in the three weeks before the July primary election and lavishly praising the president who had kept him at a distance. Patman had an almost pathetic need for Roosevelt's approval. "Dear Mr. President: I just want you to know that I still believe in you and your administration," he wrote in October 1936, enclosing a $500 campaign contribution. "This information is given to you solely for the purpose of letting you know my faith and belief in your sincerity, honesty and ability." In November, Patman coasted to victory in the Roosevelt landslide.[29]

Patman knew the cause of his success with the chain-store issue. "One certain concern had really caused the passage of this act, the A&P Tea Company," he said later. Through the months of investigation into their business and their supposed influence peddling, the Hartfords refrained from attacking Patman or his bill. Congressional files and administration records reveal absolutely no effort by the country's largest retail chain to influence the legislation save the testimony of C. W. Parr, which was provided at the request of Patman's committee. Even in January 1936, when he spoke publicly about possibly selling off stores to their managers and turning A&P from a retailer into a wholesaler, John Hartford pointed only to the cost of chain-store taxes, saying nothing about the Robinson-Patman bill. But as he watched the political process in Washington lead to a law that undermined the very foundation of his family's business, John Hartford reached a concluson that went entirely against his natural instincts: he and his brother could afford to stay silent no longer.[30]

Established 1861.

The Great American Tea Company

Receive their Teas by the Cargo, from the Best Districts of China and Japan, and sell them in lots to suit at

CARGO PRICES.

To give our readers an idea of the profits which have been made in the Tea trade, we will start with the American houses, leaving out of the account entirely the profits of the Chinese factors.

1st. The American house in China or Japan makes large profits on their sales or shipments—and some of the richest retired merchants in the country have made their immense fortunes through their houses in China.

2d. The Banker makes large profits upon the foreign exchange used in the purchase of Teas.

3d. The Importer makes a profit of 30 to 50 per cent. in many cases.

4th. On its arrival here it is sold by the cargo, and the Purchaser sells it to the Speculator in invoices of 1000 to 2,000 packages, at an average profit of about 10 per cent.

5th. The Speculator sells it to the Wholesale Tea Dealer in lines at a profit of 10 to 15 per cent.

6th. The Wholesale Tea Dealer sells it to the Wholesale Grocer in lots to suit his trade, at a profit of about 10 per cent.

7th. The Wholesale Grocer sells it to the Retail Dealer at a profit of 15 to 25 per cent.

8th. The Retailer sells it to the consumer for ALL THE PROFIT HE CAN GET.

When you have added to these EIGHT profits as many brokerages, cartages, storages, cooperages, and waste, and add the original cost of the Tea, it will be perceived what the consumer has to pay. And now we propose to show why we can sell so very much lower than other dealers.

We propose to do away with all these various profits and brokerages, cartages, storages, cooperages, and waste, with the exception of a small commission paid for purchasing to our correspondents in China and Japan, one cartage, and a small profit to ourselves—which, on our large sales, will amply pay us.

By our system of supplying Clubs throughout the country, consumers in all parts of the United States can receive their Teas at the same prices (with the small additional expense of transportation) as though they bought them at our warehouses in this city.

Some parties inquire of us how they shall proceed to get up a club. The answer is simply this: Let each person wishing to join in a club, say how much tea or coffee he wants, and select the kind and price from our Price List, as published in the paper or in our circulars. Write the names, kinds, and amounts plainly on a list, as seen in the Club Order in the next column, and when the club is complete send it to us by mail, and we will put each party's goods in separate packages, and mark the name upon them, with the cost, so there need be no confusion in their distribution—each party getting exactly what he orders, and no more. The cost of transportation the members can divide equitably among themselves.

Parties sending Club or other orders for less than $30, had better send Post-Office Drafts or money with their orders, to save the expense of collection by express; but larger orders we will forward by express, to collect on delivery.

Hereafter we will send a complimentary package to the party getting up the club. Our profits are small, but we will be as liberal as we can afford. We send no complimentary package for Clubs of less than $30.

Parties getting their Teas of us may confidently rely upon getting them pure and fresh, as they come direct from the Custom House stores to our Warehouses.

We warrant all the goods we sell to give entire satisfaction. If they are not satisfactory, they can be returned at our expense within 30 days, and have the money refunded.

The Company have selected the following kinds from their Stock which they recommend to meet the wants of Clubs. They are sold at Cargo Prices, the same as the Company sell them in New York, as the list of prices will show.

PRICE LIST OF TEAS.

OOLONG (black), 70c., 80c., 90c., best $1 per lb.

MIXED (green and black), 70c., 80c., 90c., best $1 per lb.

ENGLISH BREAKFAST (black), 80c., 90c., $1, $1 10, best $1 20 per lb.

IMPERIAL (green), 80c., 90c., $1, $1 10, best $1 25 per lb.

YOUNG HYSON (green), 80c., 90c., $1, $1 10, best $1 25 per lb.

UNCOLORED JAPAN, 90c., $1, $1 10, best $1 25 per lb.

GUNPOWDER (green), $1 25, best $1 50.

Consumers can save from 50 cents to $1 per pound by purchasing their Teas of

GREAT AMERICAN TEA COMPANY,
Nos. 31 and 33 Vesey Street,
Post-office Box, 5643 New York City.

Coffees Roasted and Ground Daily.

GROUND COFFEE, 20c., 25c., 30c., 35c., best 40 cents per pound. Hotels, Saloons, Boarding-house keepers, and families who use large quantities of Coffee, can economize in that article by using our FRENCH BREAKFAST and DINNER COFFEE, which we will sell at the low price of 30 cents per pound, and warranted to give perfect satisfaction.

CLUB ORDER.

EDWARDS, ST. LAWRENCE CO., N. Y.,
June 3, 1867.

THE GREAT AMERICAN TEA COMPANY,
31 and 33 Vesey Street, New York.

DEAR SIRS: I herewith send you another order for Tea. The last was duly received, and gives general satisfaction. As long as you send us such good Tea, you may expect a continuation of our patronage. As a further evidence that the subscribers were satisfied, you will observe that I send you the names of all those that sent before who were near out of tea, with a large addition of new subscribers. Accept my thanks for the complimentary package. Ship this as the other, and oblige

Your obedient servant, DAVID C. McKEE.

Order	Name	Price	Amount
4 lb Japan	J. Havens	at $1 25	$5 00
5 do Japan	J. Havens	at 1 00	5 00
1 do Gunpowder	J. Havens	at 1 50	1 50
1 do Japan	S. Curtis	at 1 25	1 25
2 do Young Hyson	S. Curtis	at 1 00	2 00
1 do Japan	N. Shaw	at 1 00	1 00
1 do Young Hyson	N. Shaw	at 1 00	1 00
3 do Young Hyson	R. McCargen	at 1 25	3 75
2 do Green	R. McCargen	at 1 25	2 50
4 do Green	Wm. Barraford	at 1 25	5 00
1 do Gunpowder	A. H. Perkins	at 1 50	1 50
And ten others	Total		$51 05

N. B.—All villages and towns where a large number reside, by CLUBBING together, can reduce the cost of their Teas and Coffees about one-third *(beside the Express charges)*, by sending directly to "The Great American Tea Company."

BEWARE of all concerns that advertise themselves as branches of our establishment, or copy our name either wholly or in part, as they are *bogus* or *imitations*. We have no branches, and do not, in any case, authorize the use of our name.

POST-OFFICE orders and drafts make payable to the order of "The Great American Tea Company." Direct letters and orders to

GREAT AMERICAN TEA COMPANY,
Nos. 31 and 33 Vesey Street,
POST-OFFICE BOX, No. 5643 NEW YORK CITY.

From its earliest days, the Great American Tea Company advertised massively to bring in orders by mail. This advertisement, from 1867, features detailed instructions for ordering by mail and a critique of the bankers, importers, wholesalers, and retailers who profited from the tea trade. Note the date of the company's founding: 1861. (Hartford Family Foundation)

George H. Hartford around 1863, when he was a thirty-year-old clerk for the Great American Tea Company. (Hartford Family Foundation)

The date of the company's founding is uncertain. At various times George H. Hartford's sons gave the founding year as 1858, 1859, 1861, or, as shown by this 1931 medal, 1856. (Hartford Family Foundation)

By the 1870s, the Great Atlantic & Pacific Tea Company was making heavy use of trade cards for promotion. Grandma (*left*) would be a company icon for decades. (Library of Congress)

George F. Gilman, a promoter in the style of P. T. Barnum, retired from the Great American Tea Company in 1878, leaving its management to George H. Hartford. Few photos of Gilman exist; this one was published by the *Connecticut Post* in 1932. (Bridgeport History Center, Bridgeport Public Library)

In the 1880s, store openings often were heralded by a team of horses pulling a tea-laden wagon through the city. (Hartford Family Foundation)

In the 1890s, Great Atlantic & Pacific slowly added packaged foods and bulk staples sold from barrels to its traditional selection of teas, coffees, sugar, and baking powder. (Library of Congress)

In 1903, this Great Atlantic & Pacific store in downtown Baltimore was an elaborate temple of consumption. (Hartford Family Foundation)

Thousands of Great Atlantic & Pacific wagons delivered groceries in cities and peddled from farm to farm. This photograph dates from around 1905. (Hartford Family Foundation)

Despite the shift to the Economy Store, many Great Atlantic & Pacific stores continued to offer trading stamps; this photograph, location unknown, dates from around 1915. (Hartford Family Foundation)

The Boston lawyer Louis Brandeis was among the earliest and most influential critics of chain retailing. This cartoon shows "Privilege" and "Wall Street" lamenting his appointment to the U.S. Supreme Court in 1916. (Library of Congress)

The U.S. Food Administration, responsible for supplying Western Europe during World War I, criticized waste in the U.S. food distribution system, drawing attention to the efficiency of chains such as A&P. (Library of Congress)

An A&P storefront in 1924. The company's bakeries let its stores sell bread for less than competitors, creating a powerful advantage. (Library of Congress)

Greeting listeners with the cry "Hello, World!" W. K. Henderson, a college-educated millionaire and Louisiana radio personality, made the anti-chain-store movement a nationwide phenomenon in the late 1920s. (Archives and Special Collections, Louisiana State University at Shreveport)

George L. Hartford's conservative financial policies kept A&P solvent through the Great Depression. Although he ran one of the largest companies in America, he was rarely photographed. This image dates from the mid-1920s. (Hartford Family Foundation)

John A. Hartford was the marketing genius behind A&P's relentless expansion. A flashy dresser, he favored custom-made suits and Sulka ties. (Hartford Family Foundation)

After unions in Cleveland went on strike in October 1934 to demand that A&P sign union contracts, the Hartfords ordered all Cleveland stores closed and had the merchandise loaded into boxcars for shipment to Pittsburgh. The strike was settled a few days later after federal intervention. (New York World-Telegram / Library of Congress)

Wholesalers complained that A&P's produce brokerage, the Atlantic Commission Company, monopolized the produce trade. From A&P's point of view, Atlantic Commission was an efficient alternative to archaic distribution centers like Washington Market in New York City, shown here in 1939. (Library of Congress)

By 1933, most A&P stores carried fresh produce and operated on a self-service basis. The supermarket was yet to come. (Hartford Family Foundation)

Carl Byoir, shown here at the groundbreaking for the Biltmore Hotel in Coral Gables, Florida, in 1925 (second from left), became John Hartford's key adviser in fighting the anti-chain campaign. Also pictured here is former secretary of state William Jennings Bryan (fourth from left). (State Library and Archives of Florida)

Marvin H. McIntyre, secretary to President Franklin D. Roosevelt, was one of Byoir's back-channel contacts to the president. (Library of Congress)

The Texas congressman Wright Patman (left) and Representative Robert Doughton of North Carolina, chairman of the House Ways and Means Committee, in 1939. Doughton avoided bringing Patman's chain-store tax bill to a vote. (Library of Congress)

The Temporary National Economic Committee, charged with investigating the concentration of economic power, held its first meeting on July 1, 1938. The chairman, Senator Joseph O'Mahoney of Wyoming, is at the head of the table. The vice chairman, Representative Hatton Sumners of Texas, is at the right corner in the light-colored suit. Patman, leader of the anti-chain-store forces in Congress, was excluded from the committee. (Library of Congress)

At the start of 1938, A&P still had more than thirteen thousand stores from coast to coast, like this one, photographed by Ben Shahn in Somerset, Ohio. Within four years, the store count would drop by more than half as the company shifted to supermarkets. (Library of Congress)

After a crash program to build supermarkets, A&P had more large self-service food stores by 1939 than all other retailers combined. This large store, photographed in 1940, was in Durham, North Carolina. (Library of Congress)

A&P's supermarkets, with large meat and fish departments, were barely profitable during World War II because of rationing and price controls. (Hartford Family Foundation)

Shoppers in the Bronx lined up when their local A&P reopened on October 22, 1946, following a five-week strike by the Teamsters Union. Urban supermarkets such as this were obsolcte within a few years as competitors opened larger stores and as increasingly prosperous customers moved to the suburbs. (New York World-Telegram / Library of Congress)

Thurman Arnold, head of the Justice Department's Antitrust Division from 1938 to 1943, pushed for an investigation of the food industry. The probe led to the conviction of A&P and the Hartford brothers on criminal antitrust charges in 1946. (National Archives)

15
THE FIXER

The demise of the National Industrial Recovery Act in May 1935 changed the political environment surrounding chain retailing. By ruling out codes of conduct as a means of restraining competition, the Supreme Court decision gave a decisive impetus to direct legislative attacks on big retailers. For George and John Hartford, though, the most important effect of the law's invalidation had nothing to do with politics. With the National Recovery Administration's codes of conduct dead and buried, A&P was free to undertake a major change in strategy.

In the early 1930s, when the supermarket concept first arrived in New York, the Hartfords had ignored it. Although their decision not to open supermarkets in 1931 and 1932 has been roundly criticized by later writers, it proved fortuitous. From May 1933, when Congress enacted the National Industrial Recovery Act, until May 1935, when the Supreme Court overturned it, the retail prices of most items on grocers' shelves were effectively set by manufacturers. The NRA Food and Grocery Code made it hard for A&P to win wholesale price concessions from manufacturers and mandated at least a 6 percent markup over wholesale on all items at all grocery stores. Had A&P opened supermarkets, the stores could not have passed their lower operating costs through to customers in the form of lower prices. An investment in new supermarkets would have been difficult to recover, for under the codes large stores had no competitive advantage.[1]

The end of the NRA restored price competition in food retailing, and supermarkets made sense once again. As independently owned supermarkets cut into A&P's market share, John A. Hartford was eager to start opening large stores. George L. Hartford, per usual, took a more conservative stance. "We had a conflict at headquarters whether we should adopt that type," John testified later. "Some said it wouldn't last—you can't operate without selling under cost, and that we won't do."[2]

The decision to adopt a new type of store was far more complicated for a retailer the size of A&P than for independent operators. An independent could install a store in any suitable space, but the Hartfords needed to find a format they could replicate widely. Independents could position themselves as wild-eyed price-cutters—the image conveyed by such banners as Big Bear and Big Bull—whereas A&P, whose name was a household word, had to develop a format consistent with its established identity. Many independently owned supermarkets staged marketing stunts reminiscent of the Great Atlantic & Pacific in the era of George F. Gilman, with free prizes, product giveaways, and cooking demonstrations before hundreds of customers. One even hired a hypnotist to put a woman to sleep; while the subject slept in a store window, the hypnotist granted private interviews to shoppers. The day when A&P could promote itself so shamelessly was long past. In retailing, it was the establishment, not the upstart, and it had to position itself accordingly.[3]

Pressed by division and unit managers, who saw their sales leaking away to supermarket competitors, the brothers agreed to a trial. In 1935, A&P opened its first supermarket in Paducah, Kentucky. The goal was to hold expenses to 12 percent of sales, far below the company-wide average of 17.6 percent. At first, that goal seemed unattainable, but as the store lowered its prices, sales soared with little increase in operating costs, and the expense ratio began to fall. John Hartford liked what he saw, and he encouraged other experiments to raise volume by lowering prices. These trials showed that if they were located properly, supplied efficiently, and operated on a self-service basis rather than with clerks waiting on shoppers, supermarkets could be highly profitable. In some stores, expense rates fell to less than 11 percent, more than a third below the company-wide average.[4]

In March 1936, John spoke to the division presidents about developing more supermarkets. He was plainly worried about A&P's competitive position. Unless the company moved faster to shed low-volume stores and build big stores, he said, it would face increasing difficulties. George Hartford said he was less pessimistic about A&P's outlook but supported "conservative" development of supermarkets. A few more were opened, giving A&P twenty in all by the end of 1936. But it was clear the brothers were not of one mind. In October 1936, they disagreed openly at a division presidents' meeting, with George insisting that "too much emphasis had been placed on the procuring of a large volume" even as John complained that "we have not progressed nor adapted our business in pace with the changing times." There was no getting around the financial facts: profits were down almost by half from their peak in 1930, and the pretax return on investment was only half John Hartford's target of 25 percent. A&P's thousands of older stores, the ones that did not even sell meat, were downright dowdy, and many of the combination stores with meat counters, innovative in the 1920s, had become obsolete and unattractive. In too many places A&P was no longer the low-cost grocer.[5]

As A&P's profits collapsed in early 1937, George changed his mind. He agreed to slash markups in order to increase sales volume, always John Hartford's preferred approach. John ordered a concerted effort to replace underperforming stores with supermarkets. But in a company the size of A&P, the boss's order was not always heeded. John's instruction went to the division presidents, who in turn told their unit managers to find sites for supermarkets. Some did; some did not. The Eastern Division, in the New York City area, promised to open sixty-four supermarkets in the first quarter of 1938, but only twenty were ready. In Olean, New York, part of the Central Division, the unit manager opened a supermarket in 1937 but refused to close the four traditional full-service stores, destroying profitability. "Do you realize that we have gone all this quarter with only two supermarkets being opened in the entire Division?" J. J. Byrnes, head of the New England Division, wrote to the head of his Providence unit in 1938. "I shall have to go in again and try to offer alibis, which I dislike very much doing, as to the reasons why we have not procured more supermarket locations."[6]

Opening supermarkets posed a troublesome management problem, because it was difficult to introduce the lower-price format without destroying the profitability of the company's older stores nearby. The Hartfords preferred price discrimination: when A&P opened a new supermarket, it would advertise its low supermarket prices while charging higher prices for the same products in conventional stores. This approach, of course, hurt the conventional stores' sales, leaving profits in tatters and employees bewildered. It is no wonder that John Hartford's enthusiasm for supermarkets was not widely shared.[7]

The brothers may have controlled A&P's shares, but turning their huge company required Herculean effort. John visited division-level management meetings to talk up supermarkets. At the December 1937 meeting of division presidents, John "emphasized the importance of doing this quickly," and George said he was "completely convinced that the rapid carrying out of the program outlined by Mr. John is the only salvation of the business." The gears began to mesh. From 1929 through 1936, A&P had closed an average of 356 stores per year, a small fraction of the number that were losing money. In 1937 and 1938 combined, more than 4,000 older stores were closed down, and 750 supermarkets were opened. The new stores all had meat, produce, and dairy departments and far more shelf space than the combination stores. Wide aisles allowed shoppers to take advantage of another innovation of the 1930s, the shopping cart, in which a large volume of purchases could be wheeled directly to the shopper's car in the parking lot adjoining the store.[8]

Supermarkets offered economies of scale in almost every area of store operations. The bigger, the better: labor costs, restocking costs, store rental, and administrative costs all were much lower, relative to sales, in large supermarkets than in small ones (Table 2). In the largest supermarkets, operating costs were barely half those of traditional A&P stores. Supermarkets allowed A&P to capture economies of scale—and the company's sheer size permitted it to capture those scale economies in a very big way. The sole exception was advertising expense: because big stores drew customers from a large geographic area, they required

TABLE 2: OPERATING COSTS OF A&P SUPERMARKETS, 1938

Average weekly sales per store	$4,100	$6,100	$8,400	$12,400	$17,500
Operating cost (% of sales)	14.40%	11.63%	10.53%	9.60%	9.22%

Source: Adelman, *A&P*, 59. Figures pertain to stores in Central Western Division.

much heavier spending on circulars and newspaper advertisements to spread the word about their low prices and special sales.

John Hartford pushed his company into supermarkets for the most traditional of business reasons, retaining customers and rebuilding market share. But there was an important side benefit. By 1937, more than half the states imposed chain-store taxes, almost all of which were based on the number of stores owned by a chain. Replacing several small stores with a single supermarket let A&P markedly reduce its taxes. A&P's store count, which hovered around fifteen thousand in the mid-1930s, fell 27 percent between February 1936 and February 1939, shrinking its tax bill accordingly. The state chain-store taxes, meant to shelter small grocers and wholesalers against the depredations of giant chains, gave chains such as A&P an added incentive to shift to large stores that would provide even tougher competition for mom and pop.[9]

For Wright Patman, the enactment of his bill against price discrimination in June 1936 was not an end but a beginning. Fighting for the independent businessman was to prove rewarding, personally as well as politically, and it would occupy the Texas congressman for the next decade.

A few weeks after the Robinson-Patman bill became law, Patman signed a contract with the Thomas Brady Speakers' Bureau, which sent him on tour in the fall of 1937. The congressman traveled the country, speaking to civic associations and small-business groups from coast to coast. The trip was a triumph—until word leaked out that McKesson & Robbins, a drug wholesaler, had paid part of the cost. McKesson supplied drugs to independent pharmacies and therefore had a direct interest in legislation that protected independent druggists against pharmacy chains. Patman later denied allegations that McKesson had paid him $18,000 and bought him a new car; his speaking fees, he claimed, were only $4,000.[10]

What Patman did not disclose, and what was never revealed, was that he had done far more for McKesson than give speeches. He introduced the company's president, F. Donald Coster, to Jesse Jones, then head of the Reconstruction Finance Corporation, a powerful federal lending agency, in 1937, and tried unsuccessfully to arrange a meeting between Coster and President Roosevelt in March 1938. Coster, well-known in business circles, was a man of substantial wealth, owner of a 133-foot yacht and of a twenty-room house in Fairfield, Connecticut, where he attended the local Methodist church. But there were a few things about his patron that Patman almost certainly did not know. Even as McKesson & Robbins was financing the anti-chain campaign and positioning itself as the protector of independent retailers, the company was secretly assembling a retail drug chain of its own. Also, Coster was not his sponsor's real name. As Philip Musica, he had a background as a smuggler, bootlegger, and gunrunner with a federal bribery conviction on his record. He would shortly come under federal investigation for looting his company along with his brothers, who, it turned out, also were serving as McKesson executives under assumed names. After the fraud was unveiled, Coster-Musica committed suicide in December 1938.[11]

None of this caused Patman much damage back in his northeastern Texas district. The region was one of the poorest parts of the country, and getting poorer. The eleven counties in the First Congressional District would collectively lose 53,300 residents between 1930 and 1960, with three consecutive decennial censuses showing population decline. Hughes Springs, Patman's hometown, had 1,000 residents in 1929, but only 767 in 1940. As tenants fled drought-stricken farms and as small towns withered, resentment of distant forces making it hard for a man to earn a living ran very strong. Martin Dies, the Democratic congressman from a district adjoining Patman's, explained this feeling eloquently in 1937: "If a man undertakes to go into the grocery business, there is hovering above him the shadow of the Great A&P." Although A&P controlled one-fifth of the grocery business in Texarkana, Patman's constituents shared the views of most Americans, as revealed in a *Fortune* magazine survey: most households bought their food at chain grocery stores but also favored restricting them. The chain-store issue was one Patman could ride.[12]

The passage of the Robinson-Patman Act immediately unleashed a new round of political warfare. Patman told supporters that he had two other bills in mind. One would prohibit manufacturers from engaging in retailing, so large merchants could not circumvent Robinson-Patman's restrictions on volume discounts by running their own factories. His other idea was to force wholesalers and distributors selling in towns where they did not pay local taxes to pay a federal tax instead. This, Patman argued, "would remove a discrimination against local merchants in favor of absentee distributors."[13]

A&P, though, was not sitting idle. At the start of 1936, in the midst of the battle over the Robinson-Patman Act, John A. Hartford had taken what by A&P's standards was a truly radical step. He appointed an outsider, Caruthers Ewing, as the firm's general counsel. Ewing, then sixty-five, had been on the verge of retirement after a prominent career as a corporate lawyer in Memphis and New York. He had long been John Hartford's personal attorney, but he owed nothing to the company. Quite unlike every other top executive—the man he replaced as general counsel was John Hartford's cousin and an employee since the turn of the century—Ewing had not spent his entire career at A&P. John had decided he had been passive too long in the face of political attack, and he wanted Ewing to test the limits of the new law.[14]

First, Ewing sought to find a way around the ban on retailers accepting brokerage commissions. In July 1936, headquarters informed its regional brokerage offices that they would henceforth be known as field buying offices and should no longer accept commissions from food processors and other suppliers. However, as the field offices were saving suppliers the expense of using outside brokers, they could insist—according to A&P's interpretation of Robinson-Patman—that A&P deserved lower prices than competitors because its account cost the suppliers less to service. One month later, in August, A&P required suppliers to sign two amendments to its standard contract. One committed the supplier to pay A&P a 6 percent advertising commission, in return for which A&P accepted only a general obligation to advertise the supplier's products. The other specified that A&P would receive a 5 percent volume discount. Both forms required the manufacturer to certify that it was not engaging in illegal price discrimination by avowing "its willingness to make the same agreement as is hereby made with any other purchaser similarly situated and on proportionately equal terms."[15]

Ewing's approach seemed to allow A&P to protect the low purchasing costs that let it sell groceries so cheaply. Its open flaunting of the law, though, provoked the Federal Trade Commission to start an investigation, which upheld A&P's new policies on advertising allowances and quantity discounts but objected to A&P's insistence on payments in lieu of brokerage commissions. The FTC soon discovered that the R. J. Peacock Canning Company in Lubec, Maine, gave A&P a 3 percent discount from list price on sardines and that A&P's bakery division purchased Fleischmann's yeast at fourteen cents a pound while smaller bakers paid twenty-five cents. These favorable prices were the result not of advertising allowances or quantity discounts but of A&P's demand that suppliers charge it less than their list price. Suppliers that refused price concessions went on the "unsatisfactory list." After Stokely Brothers, a canner, announced on August 31 that it would no longer pay brokerage allowances or other rebates, A&P canceled options to buy more than ten thousand cases of tomato soup. For A&P, these tactics were intended to hold prices down and protect its position as America's biggest grocer, but to the Federal Trade Commission they looked suspicious. In January 1937, the commission charged A&P and some of its suppliers with violating the Robinson-Patman Act. No longer passive, A&P fired back defiantly, declaring publicly that the Robinson-Patman Act was unconstitutional.[16]

Even as A&P came under legal attack, another piece of anti-chain legislation was moving through the U.S. Senate. The Miller-Tydings Act was crafted to overturn the Supreme Court's old rulings that manufacturers' attempts to fix retail prices violated antitrust law. Miller-Tydings permitted each state to allow the maker of a branded or trademarked product to require its customers to agree to charge at least the specified minimum retail price, thereby assuring small merchants they could not be undersold by chains. Roosevelt opposed the bill at the request of the Federal Trade Commission, but support in Congress was strong, and the House majority leader, Sam Rayburn, convinced the president not to stand in the way. Miller-Tydings, though, offered little to independent grocers: coffee processors and vegetable canners could not set retail prices by contract, because their wholesale prices fluctuated constantly as commodity markets moved. Patman tried to add something for the grocers, coupling Miller-Tydings with a heavy tax on chain stores in the District of Columbia, where A&P was a leading grocer. That plan passed the House but failed in the Senate, which approved the Miller-Tydings Act in August 1937.[17]

The anti-chain forces were swarming state capitols as well. In 1935, a group called the Anti-monopoly League, which claimed to represent eighty thousand independent merchants, announced its intention to drive chain retailers out of California. The league pushed two bills through the legislature in Sacramento. One was a steep tax on chain stores. Any company with nine or more stores in the state faced a tax of $500 per store, nearly half the profits of the average A&P. The other new law, the Unfair Trade Practices Act, prohibited retailers from selling any item below cost, including an imputed share of the cost of doing business, and also required any chain to charge uniform prices throughout the state save for differences attributable to transport costs. Quite aside from the fact that competitive conditions in San Diego might be very different from those in Eureka, nearly seven hundred miles to the north, assuring uniform pricing was almost impossible for a food chain: the wholesale prices of many foodstuffs fluctuated frequently due to changing commodity prices, and a retail grocer violated the law every time it failed to change an item's price in all of its California stores at the same moment.[18]

Unlike in other states, retailers in California, led by Safeway, the state's largest grocery chain, mounted a sweeping counterattack. They went to court to overturn the Unfair Trade Practices Act, winning an injunction in early 1936. To fight the chain-store tax, they decided on a different course. California's constitution provided an opportunity for voters to reject any state law by referendum. By September 1935, pro-chain forces collected the requisite 116,487 signatures to put the chain-store tax on the November 1936 ballot, giving them fourteen months to organize support. Their vehicle was the newly formed California Chain Stores Association, with sixty-five member chains. The association hired an advertising agency, Lord & Thomas, to run the campaign. The Lord & Thomas strategy was to show the advantages of chains while avoiding attacks on independent shopkeepers. Chain-store managers were directed to join local civic groups to counter charges that chain stores had no interest in their communities. Advertisements discussed the chains' role in providing a better life for average families and described the many small chains based in California. Educational tours took housewives through chain-store warehouses and factories.

Opportunity fell into the chains' lap when the California Canning Peach Growers asked the Chain Stores Association for help unloading a surplus of peaches. Food chains, including A&P, which had 104 California stores, undertook a nationwide campaign to convince Americans to eat more peaches. The campaign led to legislative hearings on the connection between chain stores and farm prices, allowing an A&P executive to explain how his company played the role "of a coordinating factor between the producer and the American consumer." Similar campaigns for beef and dried fruit followed, helping the chains collect important friends in California's huge agricultural industry. Then scandal hit the anti-chain campaign, when it was revealed that its chief fund-raiser kept 40 percent of everything he collected from mom-and-pop merchants across the state. Just ahead of the vote, Lord & Thomas shifted from promoting the virtues of chain stores to direct attacks on the tax, calling it "a Tax on You." The slogan worked: majorities in fifty-seven of the state's fifty-eight counties voted to repeal the tax, demonstrating that on this controversial and emotional subject, public opinion was ripe to be molded.[19]

California offered the first evidence that the anti-chain crusaders were overreaching. More such evidence came from Oklahoma, where independent merchants failed to collect enough signatures to obtain a referendum on the most onerous tax plan yet, imposing an annual tax of $7,500 on each store over seventy-five owned by a single chain. Yet in most of the country, the anti-chain fervor remained strong. Kentucky, where A&P had 178 stores, passed an unfair trade practices law similar to California's in 1936. The Food and Grocery Conference Committee, an organization of grocery manufacturers, wholesalers, and retailers, tried to stave off more draconian legislation in other states by endorsing a "model" state law to require a minimum 6 percent markup on all grocery products, a proposal that would have hurt A&P. In 1937, bills to restrict price-cutting by retailers were debated in twenty states. Legislatures in four additional states—Georgia, Montana, South Dakota, and Tennessee—adopted taxes on chain stores, while Minnesota required retailers to sell all merchandise for at least 10 percent above the manufacturer's or wholesaler's list price. In Florida, one house of the state legislature overwhelmingly approved a bill prohibiting chain stores altogether.[20]

Most worrying to A&P, anti-chain-store sentiment was spreading to the highly urbanized states of the Northeast, where shoppers had been patronizing chain grocery stores for three decades. In June 1937, Pennsylvania's governor, George Earle, signed a bill imposing a tax of $500 per store on any company with more than five hundred stores in the state. A&P, with two thousand Pennsylvania stores, faced a tax bill of $1.05 million a year and promptly closed eighty stores that, it claimed, the tax rendered unprofitable. Even in New York, where A&P was based and where it was far and away the largest grocer, the company had been threatened with the loss of its milk license for selling milk too cheaply in 1936. By 1937, a chain-store tax bill was thought to have a serious chance in the coming year's legislature. This represented a dangerous threat, because New York, home to twenty-four hundred A&P stores in early 1937, accounted for one-sixth of A&P's pretax profits.[21]

George L. Hartford's attitude was unchanged: he thought the company should ignore the controversy and concentrate on selling groceries. But with the business under mounting assault, John Hartford understood A&P could no longer remain aloof from politics. In the winter of 1937, Waddill Catchings, a well-known New York investment banker and economist, invited John to the Cloud Club, the elite luncheon club near the top of the Chrysler Building, to make the acquaintance of Carl Byoir.[22]

Byoir, forty-eight years old in 1937, had already enjoyed a long and colorful career by the time he met John Hartford. He first made his mark in 1911, while attending Columbia University Law School, when he bought the American rights to the works of the Italian educator Maria Montessori and introduced the Montessori method into the United States. After selling advertising for the Hearst newspapers, he served on President Wilson's Committee on Public Information during World War I, distributing propaganda films and creating a front group, the League of Oppressed Nations, to support the Allies' cause. He attended the Paris Peace Conference to tout Wilson's peace plan. The Committee on Public Information brought Byoir into close contact with Edward Bernays, one of the early practitioners of public relations. After the war, Byoir represented Thomas Masaryk, the president of newly independent Czechoslovakia; joined with Bernays on a campaign for Lithuanian independence; and represented the developer of the Biltmore

Hotel in Coral Gables, Florida. In 1928, he visited Havana because he heard that the climate would be good for his sinus problems. He soon bought two English-language newspapers, made friends with politicians, and developed a lucrative specialty working with Americans seeking to invest in Cuba. "When their business gets down to brass tacks, they 'see Byoir,' who now almost amounts to President Machado's Department of Commerce," reported *Time*, presumably at Byoir's behest.[23]

While still living in Cuba, Byoir talked his way into a lunch with Herbert Hoover in July 1931 to discuss using public relations to improve America's mood. The following year, he moved back to the States for good. Building on an idea hatched by members of an Elks Club in Muncie, Indiana, he publicized the "War Against Depression," a national campaign asking one million employers each to add one job for six months, putting a million people back to work. The campaign won the support of the American Legion and the American Federation of Labor, giving Byoir entrée to two of the most important organizations in the country. In 1933, Carl Byoir & Associates took on two highly controversial clients. One was the German tourism ministry, which tasked him with promoting tourism to Nazi Germany. The other was Henry L. Doherty, the founder and controlling shareholder of Cities Service Company, a New York–based oil, gas, and pipeline company. Doherty was a wealthy but unsavory character, his reputation tarnished by claims that he evaded income taxes and misled investors into buying Cities Service stock. He liked to spend time in Florida, where the warm winters offered him relief from crippling arthritis. Doherty had acquired a string of Florida resorts at Depression prices. He hired Byoir to manage some of his hotels and to revive Miami's moribund tourism industry.[24]

Byoir first knocked on Franklin Roosevelt's door in May 1933, two months after the inauguration. An intermediary in New York asked Marvin McIntyre, Roosevelt's secretary, to arrange a five-minute interview between the president and Byoir, whom he identified as "a personal adviser to Bernarr Macfadden." Macfadden was the controversial publisher of lowbrow magazines with vast circulations and a well-known advocate of health food and bodybuilding, and he wanted Byoir to discuss some business matter with Roosevelt. That meeting never occurred, but Byoir did not need to wait long for access to the president. The opportunity came in the form of a call from Keith Morgan, a Roosevelt friend who raised money for the Warm Springs Foundation to seek a cure for infantile paralysis—a cause near and dear to Roosevelt, a victim of the disease. When Morgan asked Byoir whether Henry Doherty might contribute to the foundation, Byoir suggested Morgan speak with Doherty directly. He did, telling Doherty he should support the cause "because it might get an old pirate like you into heaven." Doherty and Byoir formed a committee, which hit upon the idea of arranging fund-raising balls across the country on Roosevelt's birthday. On July 13, 1933, Morgan, Doherty, and Byoir discussed the matter personally with the president at the White House.[25]

The President's Birthday Ball, held in thousands of towns on the evening of January 30, 1934, was a roaring success, raising $1.1 million for the Warm Springs Foundation, and became an annual event. As the general director, Byoir was the man most responsible for organizing the nationwide extravaganza in support of the president's favorite cause. In return, he had access, strengthened by close ties to McIntyre and to Stephen Early, the president's press secretary. In late 1936, McIntyre and his wife vacationed at the Doherty-owned Biltmore in Coral Gables as Byoir's guest, and Byoir tried to hire Early as a partner in his firm. During Roosevelt's first four years in office, Byoir paid fourteen recorded visits to the White House. On October 10, 1934, he met with the president to offer a plan to put people back to work. In November 1935 and again in 1938, high-ranking White House staffers scrambled to respond to Byoir's desire for a promotion from lieutenant colonel to general in the Army Reserve. On January 7, 1937, Byoir and eight businessmen met with Roosevelt. The evening before Roosevelt's second inauguration, January 19, 1937, Byoir dined with the president at the White House.[26]

In short, Carl Byoir was one of the best-connected people around. Over lunch at the Cloud Club in early 1937, he explained to John Hartford what public relations advisers did. Hartford discussed the anti-chain campaigns, which he felt were targeting A&P. "I remember him saying that it seemed to him it had gotten so that a man is almost ashamed to work for chain stores—so many people believe this stuff," Byoir recalled eight years later. They made no arrangement, as John could commit to nothing without his older brother's agreement. Three months later, John Hartford asked Byoir to come to the Graybar Building for a talk with Mr. George. The encounter did not go well. George Hartford made clear he had no use for public relations, saying, "Well, now, Mr. Byoir, we have tried to run this business clean, and we have tried not to hurt anybody, and if a lot of people want to believe all these lies about us, it just does not bother me very much." The brothers thanked him for coming.[27]

Another three months passed before Byoir heard again from John Hartford. In September 1937, John proposed to engage Byoir's services, but not at the corporate level, which would have required George's involvement. Instead, John wrote to ask Byoir to meet with William Byrnes, president of A&P's Eastern Division in New York. Byrnes told him of the bill in the New York state legislature to impose a tax on chain stores, a tax that would cost A&P $2 million a year. Byoir was offered a contract to organize a public relations campaign against the bill. He was not to lobby directly by contacting legislators. The politics of the situation seem to have been a bit unusual. In most parts of the country, support for taxing the chains was strongest in small towns and rural areas. In New York, however, the lead sponsor was Jacob Schwartzwald, a Democratic senator from Brooklyn, suggesting that it was immigrant grocers, bakers, and butchers who were most worried about chain competition. No retailer would have been affected more by his bill than A&P.[28]

Byoir had not been involved with the 1936 California campaign, but he drew lessons from its success. Carl Byoir & Associates contacted several hundred consumer, farm, and labor organizations to explain the legislation. It wrote to every farm group it could find in New York state to expound upon the advantages of chain stores. It met with the editors of farm magazines and small-town newspapers, with economics professors, and with union leaders. It may even have encouraged A&P to strike some deals: federal investigators later claimed, although never proved, that through the efforts of a public relations man A&P shifted its milk purchasing in Buffalo to a dairy controlled by the Dairymen's League, in return for the league's aid in fighting the Schwartzwald bill. But the Dairymen's League had plenty of company. The senate committee hearing on Schwartzwald's bill lasted for four hours as the likes of the Brooklyn Consumers Committee, the Women Investors of America, and the New York State Turkey Association stood to oppose chain-store taxes alongside the New York Board of Trade, the most powerful business group in New York City. Byoir managed to orchestrate this successful lobbying effort without leaving fingerprints. New York's newspapers linked neither him nor A&P to the tax bill's demise.[29]

John A. Hartford, who had once thought it improper to meddle in political issues, was converted. He immediately engaged Carl Byoir to handle A&P's political problems nationwide.

16

FRIENDS

Toward the end of 1937, Wright Patman determined to renew his attack against the Great Atlantic & Pacific. His proposal to prohibit manufacturers from selling at retail, which would have dealt A&P a serious blow, had gone nowhere in Congress because it required impossible legal distinctions: barring A&P from combining manufacturing with retailing also would have kept family-owned bakeries from vending their own bread. But A&P's blatant challenge to his treasured Robinson-Patman Act convinced Patman that further legislation was needed. In January 1938, he invited other representatives to become "one of the original congressional sponsors of a national anti-chain store movement" and a co-sponsor of a federal anti-chain bill. A few days later, the Federal Trade Commission ruled that A&P was violating the Robinson-Patman Act by receiving discounts from manufacturers in lieu of brokerage commissions. A&P, it found, "is thereby enabled to resell such commodities at prices substantially lower than those at which its competitors can resell them." By pressing suppliers so it could sell to consumers more cheaply than other grocers, A&P had broken the law. The commission entered a cease-and-desist order, exposing A&P to fines in the event of future violations.[1]

The bill Patman proposed to introduce overflowed with populist language. Labeled a bill "to prevent monopoly in the field of retail distribution," it began with the claims that "chains of retail stores operating under absentee ownership and control are approaching a condition of monopoly"—a questionable assertion, given that A&P, the largest chain by far, collected only one of every ten dollars Americans spent at the grocery store. There was more: "The economic values inherent in the chain store method of distribution are outweighed by the pernicious social consequences of absentee ownership and control of distribution." And more: "A democracy of opportunity and the freedom of individual initiative cannot survive in competition with the unnatural and inherent economic and financial advantages of the chains."[2]

Patman's co-sponsors persuaded him to erase most of that inflammatory wording before introducing the bill on February 14. What remained, sponsored by seventy-five legislators from thirty-three states, was a tax on companies owning ten or more stores. The basic tax would start at $50 annually for the tenth store and rise to $1,000 for each store over five hundred. Chains operating across state lines, however, faced a far steeper burden, because a company's tax liability would be determined by multiplying the basic tax by the number of states in which it operated. The large majority of chains, those with fewer than ten stores or annual sales below $250,000, would pay no tax. A&P, at the other extreme, would be devastated. In February 1938, when the bill was introduced, A&P owned 13,200 stores, some 9,000 more than any other retailer, and operated in thirty-nine states plus the District of Columbia. As proposed, the tax would cost it half a billion dollars a year—more than half its sales. A&P's annual profit had never exceeded $2,000 per store, but Patman's bill would tax it $38,000 per store. Its tax liability would be six times that of F. W. Woolworth, seven times that of Kroger, eight times that of the dry-goods retailer J. C. Penney. Were the Patman bill to pass, A&P's tax bill would be roughly equal to that of all other retail chains combined.[3]

Patman described his legislation as "a bill to regulate selfishness and prevent greed." To prove that his intent was to help small merchants, not to hurt the chains, he agreed to reduce the levy for two years after enactment. That would give the big retailers time to sell their stores "and give other people, especially local citizens, a chance." For A&P, Patman's offer of a transition period was an empty gesture. If his law passed, it would cripple the company. The many state chain-store taxes and the growing number of local taxes, in combination, cost the company less than $3 million a year. Patman's bill would cost it 160 times as much. And while the Roosevelt administration had conspicuously failed to endorse a federal chain-store tax, it had not condemned the proposal, either. Just a month earlier, on January 3, 1938, Roosevelt had sent Congress a message criticizing "practices which most people believe should be ended . . . unfair competition which drives the smaller producer out of business." Although Roosevelt might not favor the bill, he might sign it if enough members of Congress wanted it badly, just as he had done with the Robinson-Patman Act.[4]

Patman's proposal changed the terms of debate. Until then, Congress had sought to cripple big retailers by halting discount competition so small retailers could survive. The Patman tax bill went much further, imposing taxes so onerous that interstate chains could not survive. Claims about big retailers' "unfair trade practices" gave way to assertions that size itself was evil. "Regulation obviously is not the aim of the Patman bill," *The Wall Street Journal* commented acidly. "The tax rates are entirely too steep for any such purpose—the objective is the destruction of the big, national chain-merchandising corporations."[5]

The bill was introduced too late in the Seventy-fifth Congress to have a chance in 1938, but it brought the topic of concentration in the U.S. economy to center stage. On March 1, the New York Board of Trade announced plans for a national organization to combat the chain-store bill. In a nationwide radio broadcast on March 6, the New York congressman Emanuel Celler accused Patman of trying to "murder the chain stores." Patman counterattacked in a broadcast that same evening, using one concern "that now owns more than 15,000 retail grocery stores" as an example of the evils he wished to combat. Patman barnstormed the country to mobilize support. He spoke for the tax on the Columbia Broadcasting System and talked up local ownership on the NBC Red Network. In March, he told a joint session of the South Carolina legislature that chain stores were a form of Yankee exploitation. In May, at a meeting of lumber dealers, he re-created a vanished past: "I remember when we did not have absentee ownership in this country. Then, I believe, we had a far better country than we have today. At that time, we did not have relief rolls; we did not need them." In Chicago, he debated Godfrey Lebhar, editor of *Chain Store Age*, before newspaper business editors. In Los Angeles, he spoke to local drugstore owners. He won endorsements from an anti-chain leader in Indiana and a union of strawberry farmers in Louisiana. He arranged for state pharmacy associations to send out 41,450 copies of his anti-chain speeches in envelopes bearing his name, with the government covering the postage.[6]

Patman tried to maneuver Roosevelt into supporting his bill. When the president's advisers decided that concern about monopoly was intense enough to justify a message to Congress, Patman sent him a special-delivery letter urging him to go on the attack against the "feudalistic chain store system." Patman suggested Roosevelt propose letting chain retailers keep the stores they already had but prohibiting further growth. Alternatively, the president might back a plan to restrict chain stores to a single state. Roosevelt ignored the suggestions. His message affirmed "the right of the well-managed small business to make reasonable profits" but proposed no restrictions on chain stores. All that came of it was the creation of the Temporary National Economic Committee, comprising six members of Congress and six administration officials, to study the concentration of economic power. Patman was not named to the committee.[7]

Through the winter of 1938, as chain-store advocates and opponents faced off around the country, the Great Atlantic & Pacific was silent. Preparing to do battle, Patman asked the Library of Congress to compile a list of every court case and federal regulatory complaint involving the company since 1928. But A&P said nothing publicly during the New York legislature's debate over a chain-store tax in March, nor did it comment on Patman's proposed federal tax. Only the most careful watchers of events in the Graybar Building would have detected a sign that the company's attitude was about to change. In April 1938, *Fortune* printed a sympathetic profile, suggesting that A&P suffered from too much commitment to its longtime employees and too little political savvy. That A&P would welcome a reporter was surprising. That the reclusive George L. Hartford would sit for an interview was unprecedented.[8]

Almost certainly, the Hartfords opened up to *Fortune* on the counsel of their new public relations adviser, Carl Byoir. Fresh from defeating the proposed New York state chain-store tax in Albany, Byoir had entered the Hartfords' inner circle. His official job was to organize a national campaign to blunt political attacks against chain stores. Together with Caruthers Ewing, he was to find a way to keep Patman's chain-store tax bill from passing Congress. Behind the scenes, he was to advise John Hartford and other top executives on protecting the company's public image.[9]

On March 15, 1938, Byoir created a new entity, Business Organization Inc. Carl Byoir & Associates had many clients; Business Organization

Inc., with offices one floor below at 10 East Fortieth Street in New York, would handle only the A&P account. A&P agreed to pay Business Organization $75,000 a year, plus costs and personnel expenses, to conduct public relations efforts on its behalf. To help run the campaign, Byoir hired thirty-two-year-old Victor Schiff. Like Byoir himself, Schiff, a former journalist, had learned the public relations trade at the feet of the great Edward Bernays.[10]

On April 16, 1938, Franklin Roosevelt directed his secretary, Marvin McIntyre, and his press secretary, Stephen Early, to schedule a fifteen-minute appointment the following week with John A. Hartford. Nothing was arranged, but following a handwritten reminder from the president, McIntyre offered Hartford an appointment on May 19. Hartford declined, averring, "I have not at the moment anything in mind which would enable me to be of service to him," leading McIntyre to respond that Hartford was welcome to an appointment with the president anytime he wished.[11]

Why, seemingly out of the blue, did Franklin Roosevelt want to see John Hartford? And why, in May 1938, did Roosevelt ask his staff to set up meetings with "Pres. Retail Grocers Assoc." and the head of the Independent Grocers' Alliance of America? It is no stretch to imagine that Carl Byoir was attempting to enlist the president to mediate a cease-fire in the chain-store wars—but if that was his purpose, why would Hartford, his client, have rejected the president's overture? A more likely explanation is that the initiative came not from Byoir but from Wright Patman, who had a personal meeting with Roosevelt at the White House on April 5. Patman had reason to urge Roosevelt to meet with John Hartford, as any compromises by A&P would have handed Patman a political victory. Hartford may have smelled the trap, which would explain why he took the extraordinary step of declining an invitation to a private meeting with the president. Whatever the case, the effort to involve Roosevelt directly in the battle over chain retailing failed. It appears that none of the meetings requested by the president ever took place.[12]

Byoir and Schiff assessed the political situation and quickly determined that A&P needed friends. They found them first in a most improbable place: the labor movement.

Unions in the grocery trade dated to the turn of the century, when clerks at the era's tiny stores banded together to seek community-wide agreements limiting opening hours. Since the typical grocery store had only two or three workers, the decision to join the union was typically made by the store manager, who worked at least as long and hard as his clerks. As extremely paternalistic employers, George and John Hartford paid their store managers well, avoided layoffs, and did not welcome unions. The rules of the A&P Managers' Benefit Association, created in 1916, barred members from joining unions, and the Hartfords had introduced a pension plan for store managers during the 1920s in part to deter unionization. Various groups of A&P workers had won union contracts from time to time, but with no federal law structuring labor-management relations, those contracts were perpetually at risk of lapsing; when employees at the Jersey City warehouse went on strike in 1922, the Hartfords threatened to close the warehouse and then made good on their threat, moving the operation to Brooklyn. As A&P installed meat counters in the late 1920s, the Amalgamated Meat Cutters' union tried to persuade the company to hire union butchers, but A&P refused. Only a handful of A&P workers were unionized in the early 1930s.[13]

The unions in the grocery sector had correspondingly little love for the chains. "Low Wage Chains Pile Up Profits," *The Retail Clerks International Advocate* headlined, explaining: "The story from the inside of these stores reveals underpaid unjustly treated personnel." The Amalgamated Meat Cutters put A&P on the union's "unfair" list in 1930. When state legislatures and city councils took up chain-store taxes in the late 1920s and early 1930s, the unions were often on the pro-tax side, because the taxes aided the independent grocery stores and butcher shops where most of their members worked.[14]

The Food and Grocery Code adopted under the National Industrial Recovery Act late in 1933 required grocers to recognize unions, and labor leaders decided to make A&P a test case. In October 1934, eight unions demanded that A&P agree to employ only union members in Cleveland, one of the country's biggest industrial centers. When the company refused, the unions of retail clerks, meat cutters, and bakery workers declared strikes. Union "flying squads" went from one store to another, demanding that the stores close. The Teamsters Union stopped deliveries by independent truckers so effectively that even armed escorts could not get merchandise delivered to the stores. On Saturday evening, October 27, A&P shocked the city with newspaper ads announcing that it had closed all 293 of its Cleveland stores and discharged twenty-two hundred workers. Rumors that George Hartford had made an extraordinary visit to the city were false, but John Hartford was there, and he abandoned his normal aloofness to blast the mayor and the president of the local labor federation for condoning violence and failing to protect the trucks, leaving A&P the choice of hiring armed guards or leaving town. "We chose the latter course to avoid bloodshed and disorder," he asserted, adding, "The whole thing is the most ghastly situation I have ever encountered. The wreckage of our entire Cleveland business in the short space of a few days is difficult to understand." Thanks to George Hartford's foresight, all the stores were on short-term leases, limiting the cost of A&P's departure.[15]

The conflict made headlines nationwide, and the Roosevelt administration, which had previously declined John Hartford's requests to intervene, summoned the parties to Washington. After an all-night bargaining session with John Hartford himself, the unions called off the strike, and A&P agreed to reopen its stores and reinstate the fired workers. The company made a public statement that it had no objection to its workers joining a union, but the unions' victory proved empty. The agreement was not a labor contract, and it did not require the parties to reach a contract. Instead of bargaining with the Teamsters, the Amalgamated Meat Cutters, and other national unions, A&P signed a contract with an independent union that claimed to speak for all of its Cleveland employees. Only with the passage of the National Labor Relations Act in July 1935, establishing an election process for unions to win employer recognition, did the national unions make headway at A&P, and even then progress was spotty. In most of the country, as officials of the Amalgamated Meat Cutters' union complained, a "bitter anti-union policy" dominated at A&P.[16]

The Hartfords still imagined that their paternalistic approach might inspire their employees, many of whom had purchased nonvoting shares since 1926. "My brother and I often look back longingly to the days when the Company was small enough for us to know almost every person in it," John Hartford wrote to his store managers at the end of 1936.

"Then we could take a man by the arm, as our father used to do, and talk things over with him." When they wanted to make important changes, the Hartfords invariably sought approval from their division presidents, whose endorsement was never in question. In October 1936, the division presidents voted to give paid vacations to full-time clerks and managers, to provide company-paid disability insurance, and to give clerks overtime pay when they worked extra hours. The workweek was shortened to five and a half days from six. But one thing the Hartfords refused to do: negotiate with the unions that claimed to represent their nearly ninety thousand employees.[17]

Byoir, the fixer, called another fixer. Chester Wright was a public relations man in Washington who managed to work simultaneously for the American Federation of Labor (AFL) and its archenemy, the National Association of Manufacturers. Among other things, he published *Chester Wright's Labor Letter,* designed to help employers navigate through the crosswinds of intense organizing activity, widespread worker unrest, and conflict between the two large labor confederations, the American Federation of Labor, whose member unions each covered a single craft, and the Congress of Industrial Organizations (CIO), which tried to bring each industry's workers into a single union across craft lines. Wright and Byoir had known each other since their days as propagandists during the world war, and Wright had lent a hand with the President's Birthday Balls.[18]

Almost immediately, the involvement of Byoir and Wright led to a new tone at the Graybar Building. "After twenty-five years of bitter opposition our International has sufficiently sold itself to the A&P Tea Company to the extent that they are treating with us and signing our contracts," Patrick Gorman, leader of the Amalgamated Meat Cutters and Butcher Workmen, told his executive board in March 1938. Around the same time, William Green, president of the AFL, met with A&P executives, probably including John Hartford. The makings of a deal were obvious: if A&P would sign contracts with the AFL unions, the unions would oppose the Patman bill. As Byoir undoubtedly pointed out, this was by no means the worst possible outcome for the Hartfords. Much as they disliked unions, the deal with the American Federation of Labor reduced the risk that A&P would have to deal with more confrontational CIO unions, such as the United Grocery Workers Union and the United Warehouse Workers Union in Chicago and some of the radical chapters of the Retail, Wholesale, and Department Store Union in New York.[19]

The new relationship blossomed. In August 1938, Wright worked out a tentative agreement allowing unionization of all A&P employees in Washington and Baltimore, including bakery workers and bread-truck drivers. Byoir met with Gorman in September. "I got along splendidly with him and believe we agreed upon a program that will establish for us a more general, friendly relationship with the Company," Gorman reported. Among Gorman's suggestions was that A&P appoint a single person to be in charge of labor relations. At its annual convention in October 1938, the AFL backed away from its normal condemnation of A&P's anti-labor attitude. Although enough of its member unions remained suspicious of the company that a resolution condemning the Patman tax bill could not win approval, the federation voted to undertake a study of "taxes of discriminatory and punitive character," such as chain-store taxes.

The Hartfords reciprocated, abandoning their long-held opposition to unions among their workers. Following Byoir's guidance, in November they made Charles Schimmat, a regional executive from Chicago, responsible for all union contracts nationwide. Almost immediately, A&P and five unions signed contracts covering employees in Washington and Chicago. Union contracts followed quickly in Milwaukee, St. Louis, and Toledo. "The past few weeks has witnessed one of the largest increases in membership in the Association that has been experienced for some time," *The Retail Clerks International Advocate* proclaimed. The company agreed to have all its printing done in union shops (although it took boycott threats from the Teamsters before the company moved the printing of *Woman's Day* to a union plant). A&P also hired one of Chester Wright's businesses, the International Labor News Service, to include chain-friendly articles in its twice-weekly news bulletins to union newspapers around the country. The fact that Byoir paid Wright $80,000 for one year of pro-chain propaganda was not disclosed.[20]

Building bridges to labor was only part of Byoir's effort to change the political environment. In the spring of 1938, an opportunity arose to cultivate the consumer movement. Ada Taylor Sackett, a writer and hotel convention manager in Atlantic City and an officer of a local women's club, had become involved in efforts to repeal the municipal chain-store tax enacted in 1935. In the spring of 1938, Business Organization Inc. offered to help her establish similar groups in other towns. The Emergency Consumers Tax Council of New Jersey was not entirely A&P's creation, but Business Organization Inc. financed the venture and provided manpower to aid Sackett in organizing 150 local councils around the state. Byoir announced the company's gift publicly, and with it A&P's new policy of supporting groups to study "hidden taxes" such as those levied on retailers.[21]

Byoir took the concept nationwide, creating the National Consumers Tax Commission in June 1938. Unlike its New Jersey precursor, the National Consumers Tax Commission was no grassroots organization. Housewives constituted the nominal leadership: Byoir recruited the head of a consumer group in Texas, Mrs. Kenneth C. Frazier, to be the president. The national secretary was Milton M. Sittenfield, a Byoir employee, and Business Organization Inc. paid the bills. With a staff of seventy-two based in downtown Chicago, the National Consumers Tax Commission sent out organizers to create discussion groups on women's issues. For local leaders, it tapped affiliates of the General Federation of Women's Clubs, one of the largest civic organizations in the country. Each discussion group developed its own locally oriented program, but "hidden taxes" were invariably among the topics. Business Organization's "research department" helpfully furnished discussion guides. *Why Pay Taxes in the Dark?* was the title of one of the commission's pamphlets, which contended that the price of a $5.60 pair of shoes included $1.60 in taxes. Another publication offered a colloquy:

> Q. Is the primary purpose of the chain store taxes to produce revenue?
>
> A. No. Of the 22 states which impose chain store taxes, 18 derive less than 1 percent from this source.

The effort burgeoned: by September 1939, the National Consumers Tax Commission claimed to have six thousand study groups with more than 650,000 members. Among them were the wives of many A&P employees, who signed up at John Hartford's request.[22]

Bringing consumer groups to A&P's defense was an easy feat for

Byoir to accomplish. Studies confirmed that chain-owned grocery stores underpriced independent stores by 10 to 15 percent, in good part because the chains did not provide credit or delivery. A 1938 survey found chains' prices below independent grocers' prices on 96 percent of the items examined. Consumer groups thus had every reason to oppose taxes on chain stores. The government, which later made Byoir a defendant in antitrust suits against A&P, alleged that he tried to keep the company's involvement in the National Consumers Tax Commission secret, but that assertion was incorrect. Although the commission's description of itself as a nonpolitical organization of "average American housewives" was far-fetched, its member newsletter publicly thanked John Hartford for A&P's financial support. Byoir constructed a masterful narrative, planting newspaper stories that described John A. Hartford as an "angel" generously supporting women who wanted to delve into civic affairs.[23]

On Thursday, September 15, 1938, Byoir's carefully constructed campaign against the Patman tax bill burst into full public view. Readers across the country opened their newspapers to find a five-column advertisement headlined, simply, "A Statement of Public Policy by The Great Atlantic & Pacific Tea Company." Over the signatures of George L. and John A. Hartford, the dense text outlined why the Patman bill was against the interests of A&P employees, consumers, farmers, and labor. The bill, it said, would "wipe out" 30 percent of the distribution machinery of U.S. farmers and raise living costs for wage earners. "We have arrived at the decision that we would be doing less than our full duty if we failed to oppose, by every fair means, legislation proposed by the Honorable Wright Patman," the advertisement announced. "We will not go into politics, nor will we establish a lobby in Washington for the purpose of attempting to influence the vote of any member of the Congress. We expect only a full and fair opportunity to present the case for the chain stores." The advertisement ran in sixteen hundred publications, and Byoir then sent a press release to thousands of other newspapers calling attention to it.[24]

The advertisement resounded through the business world, where the Hartfords' reluctance to engage in political matters was well-known. In years past, when various retailer groups had defended chain stores before Congress, the Roosevelt administration, and state legislatures,

A&P had remained aloof. Nor had it allied itself with lobbying groups like the American Retail Federation and the National Association of Chain Stores. The fact that the huge retailer was prepared to devote its vast resources to the opposition cause immediately reshaped the political landscape. "I think the A&P advertisement is one of the most constructive things that has been done for business generally in a long while," a department-store executive told *The New York Times*. "If I had any criticism to make, it would be that the ad and the educational campaign should have appeared five years ago."

17
DEFYING DEATH

For the first time since winning his congressional seat in 1928, Patman faced serious opposition in the July 1938 Democratic primary. He blamed the opposition on chain-store interests, but there was more to the story. Democrats in Texas, and in other parts of the country, had finally split over the New Deal, and conservative Democrats took on Roosevelt supporters in many of that year's primary races. In Texarkana, though, Roosevelt remained highly popular. Patman portrayed himself as Roosevelt's man, and his opponents made hay when the president failed to stop in the district on his train trip to California in early July. "This has reached the point I earnestly urge you to send me telegram of some sort as primary only few days off," Patman telegraphed to Roosevelt in San Francisco on July 15. A frantic telegram to Marvin McIntyre, Roosevelt's secretary, followed the next morning. Roosevelt, about to embark on a Pacific cruise, evidently had no desire to become entangled with the volatile congressman. Patman heard back from McIntyre, not Roosevelt: "The president asked me to wire you and express his regret that he could not come to Texarkana on his trip across Texas." Patman used McIntyre's tepid telegram as best he could, issuing a press release: "President Roosevelt Wires Personal Regards to Congressman Patman."[1]

Patman won his primary, and immediately made known his desire to replace a defeated Texas congressman on the House Ways and Means Committee. The position was much coveted, for the committee had jurisdiction over all tax matters, including the chain-store tax bill. Patman's Texas colleague Sam Rayburn, the House majority leader, controlled the appointment. Another Texas congressman also wanted the job, and Rayburn advised Patman to seek support from other members of the state's delegation. Patman did so aggressively, writing to his colleagues, their supporters, and their local newspaper publishers. "It is very probable I will be a member of the Ways and Means Committee," Patman wrote to a supporter in September. But there were problems. Several Texas congressmen strongly opposed the chain-store tax and refused their support. "It looks like the chains are trying to block my selection," Patman wrote to the head of the Texas Wholesale Grocers' Association in late October. Rayburn urged him to seek out Vice President John Nance Garner, another Texan and former Speaker of the House, who by this point had broken with Roosevelt and favored more conservative policies. "Dear Sam: I am not going to see Mr. Garner," Patman rejoined. At the start of 1939, Rayburn and William Bankhead, the Speaker of the House, sent Patman a blunt rejection letter expressing "our desire that you not further consider becoming a member of the Committee on Ways and Means but remain a member of the Committee on Banking and Currency."[2]

Someone more skilled in reading signals might have drawn certain conclusions from Roosevelt's studied avoidance, Rayburn's hesitation, and Bankhead's remoteness. These men, occupying high positions in the national government, faced serious worries in 1938. In Europe, an aggressively expansionist Germany was swallowing Austria, threatening Czechoslovakia, and resorting to increasingly violent repression at home. In China, Japan was waging full-scale war. In the United States, labor unrest was rife, and overcoming isolationist sentiment to rebuild U.S. military strength was becoming the administration's highest priority. Confronted with such weighty issues, Roosevelt and the congressional leadership must have viewed Patman's high-profile chain-store crusade as a nuisance. The chain-store debate even influenced a congressional investigation of Nazi influence peddling when the Texas congressman Martin Dies, head of the Committee on Un-American Activities as well as an ardent foe of food chains, went after Carl Byoir for associating with a purported Nazi propagandist.[3]

Patman refused to desist. He had pushed the veterans' bonus bill through Congress against the wishes of the leadership in 1935, and he planned to repeat the trick with the chain-store tax. In late July, he asked the clerk of the House to assign his bill the number H.R. 1 in the Congress that was to convene in January 1939, the better to promote it. And he laid new plans to go after George and John Hartford. In late September 1938, a few days after A&P's loud newspaper blast against the chain-store tax, he asked the Department of Justice to investigate the truth of A&P's advertisement and to gather information about the Hartfords' tax payments. In November, after voters in Colorado overwhelmingly refused to repeal their state's tax on chain stores, Patman wrote to Roosevelt suggesting a compromise: "Let A&P keep their fifteen thousand stores and the others the number of retail outlets they now own, but make the prohibitive tax apply to additional outlets. This will not be as drastic as my proposal and I believe will satisfy ninety-eight per cent of the small business men of the country." Roosevelt responded with a cold thank-you.[4]

The November 1938 elections brought sweeping change to Congress. The economy had slumped back into recession in 1937, seriously denting Roosevelt's popularity, and the president's controversial plan to add administration-friendly justices to the U.S. Supreme Court turned many old allies against him. Roosevelt's decision to back liberal insurgents against some Democrats who had opposed parts of the New Deal program exacerbated the split in his party. Although the Democrats retained majorities in both houses of Congress, eighty-one seats in the House of Representatives shifted into the Republican column. Of the seventy-five legislators who had co-sponsored the chain-store tax bill in February 1938, twenty-five did not return to Congress in 1939.[5]

Patman's tax bill was reintroduced in January as H.R. 1, but it faced opposition as never before. At year's end, Ralph Sharbrough, head of A&P's research department, told the American Statistical Association's annual meeting that "proponents of chain store taxes have resorted to the use of half-truths and distorted reports and figures." Two days later, John A. Hartford granted an interview in which he criticized "punitive" taxation. These public statements were part of Byoir's master plan. So were new endorsements. Business Organization Inc. had sent out feelers to farm interests, reminding them that A&P had often staged large-scale promotions to help dispose of surplus produce. They responded promptly: two farm groups that often disagreed on political matters, the American Farm Bureau Federation and the National Grange, passed resolutions in November 1938 opposing "discriminatory and punitive taxes." The National Drainage, Levee, and Irrigation Association, an existing organization, was transformed into a secret A&P front, receiving money in return for opposing the chain-store tax.[6]

Real-estate groups joined the anti-tax campaign as well. Along with its monthly rent checks, A&P enclosed letters urging landlords to consider the effects of the chain-store tax on their businesses. Patman spoke before the National Association of Real Estate Boards in October 1938, arguing that the chain tax would benefit property owners, but—thanks to spadework by Byoir—the group adopted a resolution declaring that Patman's bill would dislocate the real-estate market. Byoir also created a front group, Business Property Owners Inc., to oppose the bill. "So secret was the sponsorship by A&P of this group that bankers and employees in A&P field offices found it necessary to write to Headquarters to ascertain the views of the Company as to this organization," government lawyers later claimed.[7]

Byoir left no stone unturned. After A&P published its "Statement of Public Policy," he collected the ensuing press commentary and mailed it off to newspaper publishers to drum up yet more commentary. His agency sent a weekly packet of news articles, including a financial column and photographs suitable for publication, to newspapers around the country. In January 1939, he put out a press release asserting that anti-chain agitation actually helped chain stores by reminding the public of chains' low prices. In February, his contacts encouraged the West Virginia Horticultural Society to speak out against the bill. Byoir invited Roosevelt's press secretary, Stephen Early, to join him for golf in Florida and asked him to bring along Pat Harrison, the Mississippi Democrat who chaired the Senate Finance Committee, whom Byoir did not know. Early could not come, but Harrison, whose committee would have jurisdiction over the chain-store tax bill should it pass the House, golfed with A&P's political strategist in Palm Beach. And quite separate from Byoir's efforts, 135 chain-store operators, not including A&P, financed a national advertising campaign against the Patman bill. Meanwhile, Postmaster General James A. Farley, long Roosevelt's key adviser on matters of politics and patronage, was rumored to be considering a lucrative offer to become a lobbyist for a large chain-store operator; the firm in question is unknown.[8]

•

On March 29, 1939, in the midst of this intense maneuvering, Caruthers Ewing, A&P's general counsel, received an unexpected telephone call. The caller was William Sirovich, a New York physician, playwright, and banker who was serving his sixth term as a U.S. representative from New York City. Sirovich, a longtime friend of Ewing's and also of Franklin Roosevelt's, told him of a recent conversation with Roosevelt. The president said his son Elliott wanted to borrow $200,000 in order to purchase a radio station. Roosevelt thought that Sirovich's friend Ewing could probably approach the Hartford brothers about such a loan. "Why doesn't he go to a bank?" Ewing asked. Elliott's securities were not suitable collateral for a bank loan, Sirovich responded, but they were worth $750,000. Ewing immediately transmitted the request to the Hartfords.[9]

George Hartford was unwilling to lend money to anyone. John, however, was attuned to the political implications, and he told Ewing it was unfair for Elliott to be handicapped by being the president's son. With the intermediation of G. Hall Roosevelt, the brother of Elliott's mother, Eleanor, Elliott Roosevelt was invited to John Hartford's apartment at the Plaza Hotel. Hartford asked whether his father knew of the loan and said he would not make it without the president's approval. "Let's get dad on the telephone," Elliott responded, and placed a call to Franklin Roosevelt in Warm Springs, Georgia. After some preliminary conversation Elliott handed the receiver to Hartford, who had never met Franklin Roosevelt. "I said, 'Hello, Mr. President,' and I heard a familiar voice, a voice I had heard over the radio many times, said, 'Hello, John,'" Hartford recalled later. "I then told him that Elliott was in my apartment and asked him what did he think about this $200,000 loan Elliott wanted to make in connection with the radio business and the President said that he was entirely familiar with it, that it looked good and gave assurance to me that it was a sound business proposition and a fine thing." No one said anything about A&P, John continued, but "after the President was so enthusiastic about it I felt that I was on the spot and I had to make a decision right then and there and I did not want to do anything to incur the enmity of the President." He agreed to the loan, which was secured by two thousand shares of stock in the radio venture, Texas State Network Inc.[10]

The entire episode would have remained a closely guarded secret had Elliott been reliable about paying his debts. He was not. At the end of 1941, with Elliott serving as a brigadier general in the Army and the radio stations struggling, Franklin Roosevelt asked Jesse Jones, head of the Reconstruction Finance Corporation, a huge government financing agency, to meet with Elliott's creditors. Jones called Ewing to say "the Roosevelt family" wished to settle Elliott's debt. He discussed the matter with John Hartford on December 31, 1941. Hartford, according to Jones, said the money was insignificant to him, as 90 percent of his income went for taxes, and added that he did not want Elliott's notes in his estate. They met again in March, when Hartford agreed to Jones's offer to settle the debt for two cents on the dollar. A few days later, Jones handed Caruthers Ewing a $4,000 check; Ewing thereupon took a scissors and cut up the notes to excise John Hartford's name. Hartford claimed a $196,000 income tax deduction for his loss on Elliott Roosevelt's debt. The deduction was upheld by a federal tax examiner.[11]

Elliott Roosevelt's loan from John A. Hartford came to light only in June 1945, after Franklin Roosevelt's death. The House Ways and Means Committee looked into the matter that summer, collecting affidavits and testimony from Hartford and other creditors as well as Ewing and Elliott Roosevelt. It turned up no evidence supporting gossip that Elliott had used his station to support chain retailing, nor to back up Wright Patman's claim that Hartford wanted to use Elliott's twenty-five-station radio network to push for repeal of the chain-store tax in Texas. The Democratic majority found that Hartford was probably entitled to his $196,000 tax deduction. The Republican minority objected, futilely, that if the loan represented a loss to John Hartford, then it must represent a gain to Elliott Roosevelt and should be taxed. The question of whether the loan was, in the words of *The Washington Post*, "a highly satisfactory investment in White House good will" has never been clarified.[12]

By February 1939, the press was speculating that Patman's tax bill would not even come up for a vote. The North Carolina congressman Robert Doughton, the chairman of the Ways and Means Committee, declined to schedule a hearing. Roosevelt remained studiously disinterested, declining an invitation from the National Association of Retail Grocers to endorse its "trade independent" campaign. When he spoke on May 22 to the American Retail Federation, the group Patman had investigated in 1935, he said not a word about chain stores or the tax bill, despite Patman's pleas; Patman thought Roosevelt's friendliness to the group might be related to the fact that his son John worked for the federation's president, Louis E. Kirstein, vice president of Filene's department store in Boston. Two days later, Roosevelt quashed a Patman-supported bill to let manufacturers fix retail prices in the District of Columbia.[13]

As the economy revived, the steam was going out of the anti-chain campaign. A *Fortune* magazine survey in February 1939 found 47.9 percent of respondents opposing further regulation of chain stores and only 6.3 percent wanting to put chains out of business. "Independents aren't howling for chain scalps the way they once did," *Business Week* reported. Legislative defeats of state anti-chain measures, favorable court decisions, and moves to repeal existing state and local chain-store taxes were publicized as evidence that the tide had turned. Yet opposition to chain retailing was by no means dead. More chain-tax bills were introduced in state legislatures in 1939 than in any year since 1935. New state taxes were enacted in Montana and North Carolina, and new municipal taxes in Georgia, North and South Carolina, and Virginia. Most important of all, on September 22 the U.S. Court of Appeals upheld the Federal Trade Commission's finding that A&P had violated the Robinson-Patman Act by demanding discounts and brokerage fees from its suppliers. By refusing to purchase from suppliers that would not give it discounts, the unanimous court said, A&P "injured competition."[14]

Patman pressed his case, reaching an agreement with Doughton and Sam Rayburn on June 7 that the Ways and Means Committee would hold hearings on the chain-tax bill early in 1940. Five weeks later, on July 16, a group called the Independent Business and Professional Men, comprising delegates from around the country, met in Washington to urge action against the chains. Fewer than a hundred delegates showed up for the Sunday cruise down the Potomac River to Fort Washington, and even fewer were at the Willard Hotel on Monday to endorse the Patman tax bill. "It was poorly organized and poorly handled all the way through," recorded a spy who attended. Although speakers called for building a $2.5 million war chest to fight for the chain-store tax, delegates pledged only $4,500. The main organizer of the fiasco was the author and lecturer Charles Daughters, who had started the Freedom of Opportunity Foundation to sell his 1937 book, *Wells of Discontent*, as well as to fight chain stores. Seeing that his putative supporters among the Independent Business and Professional Men failed to provide funding, Daughters came up with an even more unlikely approach, proposing to hire an associate of Byoir's to raise money for the cause Byoir was opposing.[15]

Keeping the anti-chain movement going fell to Patman himself. He likely had a hand in dumping the inept Daughters, for on September 15 he circulated a letter, on his official letterhead, stating that the Freedom of Opportunity Foundation was being run by the former Minnesota governor Theodore Christianson and that "Mr. Charles G. Daughters is no longer connected with this movement so far as I am concerned." A few weeks later, he urged George Schulte, editor of the anti-chain organ *Interstate Merchant*, to attack the U.S. Department of Agriculture for being too cozy with the food chains. But in the changed political climate, longtime friends of independent merchants, such as the Kansas senator Arthur Capper, shied away from Patman's tax bill. Patman was so worried that Doughton would renege on the promised Ways and Means Committee hearing that in November he asked Roosevelt to intervene, antagonizing both Roosevelt and Doughton in the process.[16]

In an increasingly desperate search for congressional votes, Patman revised his bill in January 1940. The tax rates on chains were cut in half. Companies operating fifty or fewer stores within a hundred miles of a single city were exempted altogether. The provision multiplying the per-store tax by the number of states in which a chain operated was suspended for seven years—but only if the chain agreed not to open new stores or relocate old ones. Patman presented this as a milder, less onerous bill, but it would still have cost A&P, which had around nine thousand stores at the start of 1940, nearly $200 million a year, eleven times annual profits. As one critic jibed, "Cutting the tax rate in half had about the same practical effect as reducing the prison sentence of a convict from 998 years to 499 years." No votes were swayed.[17]

The long-awaited hearings on the chain-store tax bill were an anticlimax. After Patman threatened to force his bill to the House floor with a discharge petition—the same technique he had used to win a vote on the veterans' bonus bill—Doughton created a seven-member subcommittee to hold hearings. He pointedly included no legislators from the South or the West, the regions where anti-chain sentiment ran strongest.

One after another, representatives of the groups so carefully cultivated by Carl Byoir came to Capitol Hill to testify against a bill that, a few years earlier, many of them would have endorsed. State labor federations in places with strong anti-chain movements, such as Texas and Louisiana, now opposed the federal chain-store tax. So did the International Typographical Union, whose members did A&P's printing. "Mass production methods are here to stay as long as consumers demand them," said Patrick Gorman of the Amalgamated Meat Cutters' union, adding that sixty-three hundred of the ninety-four hundred A&P butchers now belonged to his union. Matthew Speedie of the Retail Clerks association praised chain stores while criticizing "unsanitary and uninviting" mom-and-pop stores, which "constitute a menace to the retail industry, because they divert a certain part of the trade from other merchants and operate without profit." Edward O'Neal of the American Farm Bureau testified that the chain-store tax would force up food prices and thereby limit consumption, reducing farmers' potential sales. The National Council of Farmer Cooperatives opposed the scheme, and so, at the other end of the political spectrum, did the National Association of Manufacturers. Consumer groups also appeared in force, with Harriet R. Howe of the American Home Economics Association and Caroline Ware, speaking for the American Association of University Women, criticizing Patman's tax for raising shoppers' costs.[18]

With the chain-store tax headed for certain defeat, the Roosevelt administration finally showed its hand. "We think it would be unwise and unnecessary to give up the economies which have been brought about by chain store distribution," Agriculture Secretary Henry Wallace wrote to Doughton in opposition. The Commerce Department's Business Advisory Council opposed the bill because "it kills efficiency in distribution and encourages inefficiency," and Edward J. Noble, the acting secretary of commerce, echoed the advisory council's views. The Treasury Department's tax office deemed the bill unconstitutional. Patman met with Thurman Arnold, the assistant attorney general for antitrust, to solicit support, but Arnold opposed the tax bill. The Federal

Trade Commission, which had aggressively investigated A&P two years earlier for violating the Robinson-Patman Act, declined to endorse the tax, suddenly discovering that it lacked up-to-date information about chain stores. Sam Rayburn, who had tolerated his fellow Texan's anti-chain efforts for years, now steered clear; the mail from his constituents in rural northern Texas ran heavily against the tax. In desperation, Patman sought the support of the retired Supreme Court justice Louis Brandeis, a critic of big business since the turn of the century. Brandeis, then eighty-three, responded with a friendly letter carefully worded to avoid an endorsement.[19]

In the second week of May, as the hearings ground to a close, Patman made a last-ditch effort to save his bill. For eight consecutive nights, he held forth on the Columbia Broadcasting System, arguing his case to radio listeners nationwide. Moving from the book of Genesis to Leonardo da Vinci to the American farmer, he returned again and again to the idea that the independent merchant was the nation's bulwark against monopoly. The following week, on the NBC Blue Network, he went even further. "We, the American people, want no part of monopolistic dictatorship in either our American government or in our American business," he said. "Think of Hitler. Think of Stalin. Think of Mussolini. Let's keep Hitler's methods of government and business in Europe."[20]

Such inflated rhetoric did not serve Patman's cause. Nor did Patman's last-minute attacks on Byoir on the House floor and then on a national radio broadcast, in which he referred to the A&P strategist as Hitler's "first agent" in the United States and suggested that he had disclosed military mobilization plans to Germany. On June 18, the Ways and Means subcommittee, headed by the Massachusetts Democrat John W. McCormack, refused to report out the bill to the full committee, effectively killing it. If fear of monopoly justified legislation, McCormack said, "such legislation should be of a regulatory nature and not punitive through the exercise of the taxing power."[21]

As a political movement, the anti-chain campaign was dead. Political scientists have speculated ever since about the reasons for its demise. Some point to the movement's lack of leadership. Others emphasize the difficulty of maintaining a coalition of small, widely dispersed merchants with very diverse interests. Some find explanations in the economic recovery that drove unemployment in 1940 to the lowest rate in nine years, or in the evident rise in wage levels, or simply in Americans' increasing familiarity with chains. Whatever the case, a cause that had burned fiercely for years no longer resonated in 1940.

Yet seen in another way, the anti-chain movement was a remarkable success. Against long odds, it held back the chain-store tide, withstanding pressure from Wall Street and big business to preserve the livelihoods of hundreds of thousands of people engaged in wholesaling and retailing. In 1929, before the start of the Great Depression, 1.4 million Americans ran family-owned retail stores, nearly one-third of them in the food line. A decade later, the ranks of small merchants had swelled to 1.6 million, and there were more mom-and-pop grocers than ever (Table 3). Independent grocers' share of the nation's food sales, 66 percent in 1939, declined only two percentage points over the decade. The number of wholesale establishments rose 19 percent during those years—and the number of unincorporated wholesalers, the small firms that gained the most from restraints on chain retailing, rose even faster. If their cause was to preserve opportunity for the independent merchant, the warriors of the anti-chain-store crusade succeeded beyond all expectation.[22]

This job preservation came at a cost: through the 1930s, the distribution of grocery-store products became more, not less, of a burden on the economy. One measure of that burden was the gross margin of participants in the grocery distribution chain—the difference between the price they paid for their goods and the price at which they sold them. In the retailing of manufactured foods, non-manufactured foods, and

TABLE 3: STRUCTURAL CHANGE IN RETAILING IN THE 1930s

	1929	*1939*	*Change*
Retail employees	4,286,516	4,600,217	7.32%
Retail proprietors	1,434,704	1,613,673	12.47%
Retail establishments	1,476,365	1,770,355	19.91%
Wholesale employees	1,510,494	1,559,586	3.25%
Wholesale proprietors	90,772	117,651	29.61%
Wholesale establishments	168,820	200,573	18.81%

Source: 1939 *Retail Census*, vol. 1, pt. 1, 57; Albright, "Changes in Wholesaling."

cleaning supplies, gross margins were far wider in 1939 than they had been in 1929, an indication that grocery stores had become less rather than more efficient. Much the same was true of food wholesalers. In 1929, shoppers buying non-manufactured foods such as produce paid 47.9 percent more than the amount received by farmers. By 1939, with chain retailers restrained from cutting prices and more mom-and-pop stores in business than ever before, that margin widened to 58.5 percent.[23]

To be sure, mom and pop were not getting rich. In the food trade, the largest single slice of retailing, the ranks of independent merchants included 179,335 keepers of traditional grocery stores, with average sales of about $8,000 in 1939, and 166,276 proprietors of combination stores selling an average of $20,255. These businesses were tiny even by the standards of the time: the average chain-owned combination store had five times the sales of the average independent store. But no matter how marginal they were in economic terms, these independent stores sustained millions of people during the U.S. economy's most difficult decade, when jobs of any sort were hard to come by. In that sense, the opponents of chain retailing could justifiably claim victory. And despite their political weakness, they were not done fighting.

18

THE FOURTH REVOLUTION

By the end of the 1930s, fifteen years of attacks and investigations had left their mark on the Great Atlantic & Pacific. A&P remained the world's largest retailer by far, but it operated under a microscope. Although the NRA's price restraints had been overturned and the federal chain-store tax defeated, the Robinson-Patman Act was in full force, complicating the company's efforts to command discounts from suppliers and to use profits from its factories to hold down prices in its stores. At the state level, chain-store taxes and "fair trade" laws requiring uniform prices and minimum markups played havoc with the most routine business decisions. A Kansas official visited a store in Kansas City to buy three packages of coffee for forty-nine cents, then purchased the same brand in Topeka at three packages for fifty-three cents to accuse A&P of illegal price disparities. A county attorney threatened to arrest the manager of a new supermarket in St. Paul for having prices below those in other A&P stores. A regional circular advertising Waldorf tissue at five boxes for nineteen cents had to be withdrawn because that price, legal in Indiana, where the circular was printed, was illegally low at stores across the state line in Ohio. The wholesale price of Sparkle gelatin from A&P's Quaker Maid factories, 3.035 cents per package, was too high to resell at three for ten cents once Arizona's state-mandated markup was factored in, but Quaker Maid refused to reduce the wholesale price a few hundredths of a cent per package lest sales from one A&P division to another be deemed too cheap.[1]

Such legal assaults contributed to a sharp drop in profitability. In 1937, George Hartford was forced to abandon the cherished $7-per-share dividend because profits were too small to cover the cost. Even after doubling since that low point, A&P's after-tax earnings remained far lower than they had been a decade earlier. In 1939, which saw the best performance in six years, earnings per share of the company's stock were down 42 percent from their peak. At the start of the decade, investors had scrambled to buy five or ten nonvoting shares whenever employees were willing to sell on the New York Curb Exchange, but now, according to *Barron's*, A&P was "a stock that has lagged far behind the average." Shares that had changed hands for $260 in 1930 could be had for as little as $36. The Hartfords even offered to repurchase shares from employees who had invested with great enthusiasm in the late 1920s and had seen the value of their holdings collapse.[2]

For a company listed on the stock exchange, owned by impatient investors demanding increased dividends and a higher share price, such performance would have been disastrous. George and John Hartford, however, controlled all of A&P's voting shares, and they had no need to answer to anyone. They could do as they pleased. They stuck with the strategy they had finally agreed upon in early 1937, closing older, smaller stores and opening supermarkets. In 1937, when A&P had been stripped of almost all its cost advantages, 44 percent of its retail outlets had lost money. By February 1940, after 5,950 store closures in three years, the proportion of "red-ink" stores was below 18 percent and headed into single digits. In place of these outmoded stores, where wages and operating expenses ate up 17 percent of every dollar of sales, A&P rapidly rolled out supermarkets where expenses took less than twelve cents per dollar of sales. Its new stores lacked the flash of independent competitors' stores; as *Fortune* magazine described matters, "A&P's entries in the field are like wrens in a flock of noisy parakeets." But those wrens proved to be extremely profitable. Three years after the start of A&P's transformation, supermarkets accounted for half the company's profits.[3]

The supermarket was a shock to the tens of thousands of longtime employees at A&P. When A&P had begun to shift from traditional grocery stores to combination stores in the late 1920s, the main changes at store level had been the installation of meat counters and the employment of butchers. Outlets had relocated to slightly bigger premises gradually, over a period of many years, but the work of store clerks and store managers barely changed. The shift from combination store to supermarket was far more abrupt. A full-service combination store, of which A&P still had thousands, might occupy a space twenty-five feet wide and fifty feet deep on the ground floor of a narrow building. New supermarkets were four or five times as large. A combination store, on average, had sales of $1,400 a week at the start of 1940. New supermarkets were expected to have weekly sales of $10,000 or more. Fixtures, displays, lighting, and even scents were carefully thought out to attract more prosperous shoppers. Employees' jobs changed, too. Clerks were no longer meant to chat with customers, pick their purchases off the shelves, and ring up the sale; now supermarket stock clerks—largely male—specialized in moving boxes and keeping the shelves filled, without disturbing shoppers, while checkout clerks—mostly female—were more like assembly-line workers, serving unending queues of customers. The shrinking store count meant that many erstwhile store managers no longer managed, and those who remained had so many employees to oversee and so many items to keep in stock that they rarely labored alongside their clerks, as they had in the past. Even high-ranking executives had difficulty adjusting to these changes. At the end of 1938, as he was pressing his staff to open more supermarkets, the head of the New England Division asked all workers to make sure "no customer is allowed to leave our stores until at least one item has been suggested"—a demand for just the sort of face-to-face contact the supermarket was intended to eliminate.[4]

A&P's vast manufacturing and distribution system was well suited to keeping these large new stores stocked at favorable prices. Due to the Robinson-Patman Act, A&P could not buy branded goods from outside producers for less than its competitors paid, except where it could justify volume discounts. But its factories and bakeries gave it brands other retailers could not offer. If it organized orders properly, those plants could operate steadily near maximum capacity, driving down the cost of producing each can of green beans and each loaf of bread. With demonstrably lower production costs, A&P's factories could set their wholesale prices below those of outside suppliers, allowing the retail stores to price below the competition without running afoul of the law. So important was in-house manufacturing that A&P set up a merchandising committee in late 1938 to find ways to get more of its own products into its growing number of supermarkets. "A&P products are the largest single source of profits which A&P has," the committee agreed. "To increase these profits is our one aim."[5]

Supermarkets had far larger produce sections than the combination stores they replaced, giving the Atlantic Commission Company, A&P's produce wholesaler, a critical role in the business. Atlantic Commission was controversial, because by the standards of the fragmented produce trade it was an extremely large operation, handling 9 percent of U.S. shipments of fresh fruits and vegetables in 1940. Most produce in those days was sold through local grower associations; when an area's pea harvest or plum crop came in, individual farmers would haul their output to the association's warehouse, where it would be auctioned to specialized brokers. The brokers, in turn, would move the produce in smaller lots through wholesale markets in major cities. Atlantic Commission sometimes joined those auctions, but it could also circumvent them. Unlike the independent brokers, it had agents at big-city markets in addition to a hundred buying offices around the country. Their close communication enabled it to decide whether, on any given morning, Atlantic Commission would bid at the apple auction run by the Yakima Valley Growers Association in Yakima, Washington; strike private deals with the association or individual apple growers; or buy nothing in Yakima and meet its requirement for apples at the market in Chicago or New York. Atlantic Commission was big enough to obtain volume discounts by purchasing dozens of railcar loads at a time and to control risks by contracting for farmers' potato harvests in Kern County, California, before the crop was even planted. Its scope and scale gave it advantages smaller brokers could not match.[6]

Purchasing in volume, circumventing brokers and wholesalers, and minimizing losses in transit brought lower costs: in 1940, A&P estimated that moving a box of oranges from California to a store in Jersey City would cost forty-six cents with a broker but only twelve cents through Atlantic Commission. Even allowing for exaggeration, the cost saving was huge. Atlantic Commission's marketing muscle allowed it to balance supply and demand in a way a smaller dealer could not. It could organize regional or national promotions of fruits that were in oversupply, redirect shipments to places where a commodity was scarce, and sell excess to other retailers when it had more peaches or carrots than A&P needed in a particular location. In 1941, Atlantic Commission bought up 26 percent of Maine's potato crop and organized ships to take the potatoes to ports in the South and Southeast, allowing A&P supermarkets to stock Maine potatoes in towns where they were normally unavailable. Atlantic Commission enabled A&P to gain efficiency in a highly inefficient corner of the food distribution world, filling the new supermarkets with an unprecedented array of produce from all over the country.[7]

The spread of supermarkets also opened new possibilities for A&P's huge bakery division. Until the late 1930s, the thirty-five bakeries served principally to supply cheap sliced bread; A&P's grocery stores had neither space nor equipment to sell more perishable baked goods, and the bakeries rarely produced them. The supermarkets, however, had room to display cakes, pies, and pastries attractively, assuming A&P could figure out a way to deliver the goods quickly enough to keep them fresh. In 1939, A&P began to train its bakers to make cakes and pies on an industrial scale. To convince customers that the goods were as fresh as those in any bakery window, A&P wanted to display them on sheet pans rather than in packages, so its engineers developed a galvanized container to transport sheet pans safely from bakery to store. Glass display cases appeared in the supermarkets, where clerks were taught to sell and wrap baked goods. With the creation of a heavily advertised bakery brand, Jane Parker, sales took off. Retail sales of baked goods jumped 35 percent in three years, and may have accounted for half the company's profits by 1941.[8]

In hindsight, it is difficult to appreciate the speed with which the mammoth retailer restructured a business that operated from Florida to Alaska and Quebec to California. By the end of 1941, two-thirds of the A&P stores that had been open in 1937 no longer existed. In their place were bigger stores operating far more efficiently. While food prices rose only a few percentage points over those four years, sales at the average A&P store increased 236 percent, and the physical volume of merchandise moving through the average store nearly quadrupled. Sales per employee rose by half. With prices held constant, expenses fell by one-third in four years, relative to sales. By 1941, A&P's operating costs, per dollar of sales, were half what they had been in 1925.

The company's advance would have been even more rapid had it not heeded the counsel of Carl Byoir to slow the pace of supermarket openings. Byoir frequently participated in A&P management meetings to advise on public relations. In June 1939 he warned that simultaneous supermarket openings in individual cities might "be detrimental to the company in a public relations way." The order went out from headquarters to move more slowly. Unit managers were advised to take care to avoid the perception that A&P was trying to dominate the local grocery trade anywhere.[9]

The supermarket was the fourth retailing revolution through which George and John Hartford had guided the Great Atlantic & Pacific. With their father, they had turned George Gilman's tea company into the first grocery-store chain in the 1890s. Starting in 1912, their Economy Store had changed the grocery trade from a haphazard enterprise of uncertain profitability into a large-scale business based on careful control of costs and prices. In 1925, the Hartfords had reorganized the company to take advantage of vertical integration and economies of scale with the aim of boosting profits by increasing volume. Now, with little ado, they brought about yet another transformation by moving quickly from the combination store to the supermarket. They were by no means the inventors of the large self-service food store. Their contribution came in figuring out how to use this new format to increase efficiency and lower costs. In the space of a very few years in the late 1930s and early 1940s, A&P turned the supermarket from a wild marketing concept of uncertain profitability into the main place American families bought their food. In 1939, the first time it examined the supermarket phenomenon, the U.S. Census Bureau counted 1,660 self-service food stores with sales exceeding $250,000 per year. A&P had more stores fitting that description than all other food retailers combined.[10]

The numerous government investigations of A&P have left an unusually detailed picture of how the Hartfords managed their company through the 1930s, a decade of extraordinary economic and political challenges. In the tens of thousands of pages of surviving company documents, though, George L. Hartford remains an enigma. By the second half of the 1930s—George turned seventy in 1935—his appearances at company meetings were limited to the quarterly reunions of his highest-ranking executives, such as the division presidents. Even in earlier years, the only division board meetings he attended were those of the Eastern Division, which were held at the Graybar Building; he would normally arrive at a prearranged time, speak his piece, and leave. There is no record of him traveling to company functions outside New York. The minutes of corporate meetings cite him only occasionally. When he is mentioned, his utterances either are benign generalities—"He mentioned that we were passing through some trying times, but he felt that our company was in splendid shape to weather any storm"—or concern financial performance, the sorts of comments one might expect from a corporate treasurer, not from the chairman of the board.[11]

Beyond a handful of top managers, Mr. George was a distant presence to A&P employees. Few of them ever laid eyes upon him. For most, he was more a legend than a man to whom they related personally. A&P's public relations department helped burnish his image by crafting myths such as his supposed forays to taste A&P's coffee each day at two. Managers, though, seemed to feel he was out of touch. A&P had difficulty obtaining the best locations for its new supermarkets because it would not sign leases for more than five years; while competitors leased desirable parcels of land for twenty years and spent their own money to build stores, A&P would not, because George focused more on the risk of a long-term commitment to an unsuccessful store than on the growth potential. When the chairman of the Southern Division told his division president to slash prices to build business, he offered one caveat: "But there is one thing and it is most important: do not advertise a standard brand of coffee at cost, or 1 cent above cost. I think you understand that Mr. George Hartford feels very strongly against this sort of thing." His brother was not beyond using George's remoteness to advantage, insisting that policies be obeyed because George demanded it. When the president of the Middle Western Division requested John's permission in 1937 to sell below cost in Joliet, Illinois, for a single weekend in order to meet competition, John slapped him down, responding, "I would hesitate even to bring up this matter to Mr. George."[12]

John A. Hartford, on the other hand, seems omnipresent in the company records. Far more vigorous than his older brother, he traveled widely, conferring with division-level boards of directors in Detroit, Boston, Pittsburgh. He visited bakeries, sat with executives of the National Meat Division, met with produce suppliers and grocery vendors. When the division presidents convened each quarter, he participated from beginning to end. There was hardly a meeting at which John's thoughts were not cited, even if he was not personally in attendance. What emerges from the records is a company in which Mr. John was the driving force and Mr. George, more often than not, was manning the brake.

John, always dapper in his tailored suit and polka-dot bow tie, was A&P's public face. When speaking to the press was deemed useful, John took on the task. Internally, he represented the company to A&P's own employees. He responded personally to their letters. When headquarters wanted to communicate with store managers, whether to explain a recent labor dispute or to threaten firing of any manager alleged to have sold short weights, the communication often took the form of a personal letter from John. When he was on the road, he occasionally gathered local store and warehouse managers to meet him over dinner or at special events with the singer Kate Smith, who was featured in A&P's advertisements and radio programs. Although he often spoke in the first-person plural, representing his brother as well, to employees, it was Mr. John who personified A&P.[13]

But John was no front man. Since 1912, when he convinced his father and brother to let him test the Economy Store concept, he had been the company's visionary. The reorganization of 1925–26, in which A&P curbed its investment in manufacturing to focus on increasing sales volume in its retail stores, was largely John's achievement. The campaign against the Patman tax bill, which saved the company from annihilation, had come at his initiative, against his brother's opposition. The company's quick transition to the supermarket between 1937 and 1940 was John's doing as well, often against the resistance of his brother and longtime executives. At the same time, John was a hands-on manager with detailed knowledge of the company's business.

In principle, the brothers had removed themselves from day-to-day operating responsibilities in 1925, when they decentralized store management and manufacturing and put an experienced executive in charge of each division. The Hartford philosophy was that men should be given responsibility and left to do their jobs. "As much responsibility as possible should be thrown upon the key men as it is only in this way we discover a man's capabilities," one division president told his managers, echoing John with every word. In practice, though, John Hartford had a hand in everything, and no A&P executive, no matter how senior, made a significant decision without his knowledge. When the quarterly meeting of division presidents resolved on June 25, 1931, that no merchandise would be sold at a markup below 3 percent without the approval of the division president, it was carrying out John's wishes. When they agreed, against their better judgment, to reduce margins in stores in an attempt to sell more groceries, they did so because John wanted it done. When a truck driver sued the company, alleging injury from a knife thrown by an A&P clerk, John, according to company lore, practiced throwing knives at the distance claimed until he convinced himself that the incident could not have occurred.[14]

John's management style was a curious mixture of quantitative analysis and old-fashioned paternalism. A&P was a leader when it came to finding ways to quantify performance. Its armies of office clerks collected numbers on everything, and participants in management meetings pored over thick packets of figures, neatly typed on stencils and duplicated on mimeograph machines. No subject was too unimportant to be broken down by division or unit, allowing for easy comparisons. If one division or unit lagged others, the executive in charge was well-advised to come armed with a plan to fix the problem. Store managers who failed to attain sales and profit goals found themselves replaced: in 1927, a time when rapid expansion forced the company to promote large numbers of untested men to run stores, one-third of all managers were replaced in a nine-month period. Managers who met their profit goals by overcharging customers were prone to lose their jobs as well if detected by the company's ubiquitous auditors or by the "secret shoppers" who checked to make sure prices were posted clearly on the shelves.[15]

Yet John also assumed personal responsibility for people who had devoted themselves to A&P. If a manager who tried to follow company policies nonetheless failed in his job, John believed, the fault lay with the company's inadequate training; rather than being fired, he should be moved into a position to which he was better suited. Store managers who could no longer do the job due to age or physical infirmities but wanted to continue working were kept on the payroll as clerks. While his paternalism had limits—A&P hired few black workers before World War II, and female clerks and secretaries had little chance for promotion—his unwillingness to displace thousands of loyal employees was partly to blame for delaying the shift to supermarkets, which eliminated seven thousand jobs, mainly those of store managers, between 1937 and 1940.[16]

John's paternalism often brought him into conflict with his executives. Division managers and their subordinates, the unit managers, were meant to keep costs low, but they were to do so by careful management—finding good store locations, minimizing inventory, advertising wisely, bargaining hard with vendors. John's fervor for cost control did not extend to squeezing workers. Although very few A&P workers were represented by unions before 1938, John is often to be found urging district and unit executives to raise wages and improve benefits. During the Depression, when many employers slashed wages, the Hartfords refused to do so. Division presidents were urged to grant paid vacations, and in July 1931, John asked the Southern Division to raise clerks' wages "to make our proposition more attractive to the young men in our organization, who are really entitled to further remuneration." In 1935, he told the unit managers of the Central Western Division, in Chicago, that he was "apprehensive" of the salaries of store clerks. "He has received letters from clerks who have terminated their services with the company, in which charges have been made that their positions had been eliminated in order to make way for a new clerk at a lower wage," the division's minutes report. "He felt that the excess we earn over our dividend requirements should be thrown back into the business to further reduce our retail prices and to improve the income and working conditions of the managers, and particularly the store clerks." A year later, he wrote to the Southern Division asking that it institute sick pay.[17]

Division managers often failed to heed John's advice, because raising labor costs, in the short term, lowered profits. When that occurred, John could not dictate a change in policy—he had, after all, decentralized authority—but he could embarrass the local management by raising the issue again and again. After the Central Division in Pittsburgh ignored John's suggestion that it raise pay in 1935, he persisted. According to the minutes of a division board meeting in January 1936, "Mr. Hartford has brought up the subject of our low clerk salary in practically every meeting he has attended in the Central Division during the last few years, and it was humiliating to the committee for him to bring it up again. It was felt that he was justified in taking any steps he thought wise to bring about a higher wage for the clerks however it was still felt we could correct the situation." The division's board met again the following Monday and did as Mr. John had dictated, bringing average pay for full-time clerks to $17 per week. "It is hoped that Mr. Hartford will not again find it necessary to bring to our attention that we pay our clerks too little," the minutes affirmed. As A&P opened more supermarkets, he was concerned that division managers failed to appreciate that running a supermarket was far more difficult than managing a much smaller combination store, and he repeatedly urged pay raises for store managers and assistant managers. He believed "the future of this type market depends to a large extent on the personnel, and they should be compensated according to ability and achievement," the 1940 minutes of the Eastern Division record.[18]

Such issues were addressed in personal visits and in voluminous correspondence, all of it formal. A&P's competitors were far less starchy. At Safeway headquarters in Oakland, California, President Lingan A. Warren was prone to address his managers as "Dear Tom" or "Dear M.L.," and many of them wrote back to "Dear Ling." At Kroger's general offices in Cincinnati, executives frequently sent out brief memos on standard forms rather than resorting to letters. There was no such familiarity in the Graybar Building. Even an executive such as the Southern Division's chairman, O. C. Adams, who had worked with the Hartfords since 1894, was addressed as "Mr. Adams," and Adams corresponded with his subordinates in the same vein. John's courtliness was an integral part of his image, but it must have seemed very old-fashioned to new A&P employees in the late 1930s.[19]

Decentralization or not, John could not resist becoming involved in details. He wanted his executives to know that he knew about their businesses, and he poked his nose into everything. Auditors advised headquarters whenever they found a store selling merchandise below cost, and John personally reprimanded offenders. In 1936, after a court in Washington, D.C., found A&P guilty of selling short weights of meat, he personally signed an individual letter to each of forty-five thousand store employees warning that anyone accused of cheating customers would be fired. In March 1939, he telephoned the chairman of the Southern Division to ask about the wide margins reported by two supermarkets in Georgia. In November 1939, the Atlantic Commission Company's methods of purchasing oranges from a Florida cooperative were on his personal agenda. In 1940, he looked into large stock gains at certain stores in Virginia, which could mean that the managers were setting prices higher than the company desired. In 1941, he had an extended interchange with the president of the New England Division on the way a regional competitor accounted for depreciation. But there may be nothing that illustrates John Hartford's management style more fully than the case of G. D. Keller.[20]

Keller, the former manager of A&P's store in Oberlin, Ohio, sent Hartford a three-page handwritten letter on April 16, 1939. Keller explained that he had left A&P after eleven years in a dispute with an assistant superintendent, whom he accused of having affairs with female store clerks. He had then raised the money to open his own grocery store in Oberlin, only to find that A&P had lowered prices in its store to put him out of business. "I had the pleasure of meeting you in Cleveland at Kate Smith's party and do not believe you are a man to condone such tactics," Keller wrote.

On April 19—no more than a day after receiving Keller's letter—Hartford wrote to D. F. Meier, head of the Cleveland unit, asking him to look into the situation. Meier explained that Keller had a drinking problem and that the assistant superintendent had been trying to help him. The Oberlin store was one of fifteen in the unit where prices had been cut, he said. On May 5, Hartford sent Meier's response to C. A. Brooks, president of the Central Division and Meier's boss, and asked him to investigate to make sure Keller had not been treated unfairly. Brooks wrote to Meier, then phoned him, and wrote to Hartford that the price reductions in Oberlin were not intended to hurt Keller. Hartford wrote back almost immediately, demanding the dates and store locations where prices had been cut. Brooks again wrote to Meier, who supplied more details. Hartford refused to drop the matter. He telephoned Brooks, then sent him a stern letter on June 7. "I believe in carrying out this plan of action in this store you made a very grave mistake," he wrote. "After developing this story through my correspondence with you, I feel it to be indicated that we did exactly what Mr. Keller describes in his letter." Hartford's executives knew when to grovel. "Your valued favor of the 7th received," Brooks replied to Hartford. "I agree with you that it was a mistake, and I believe unintentionally on the part of Mr. Meier." Brooks phoned Meier once more, and the unit manager paid a personal call on Keller to apologize and let him know the local A&P would be raising its prices. Only then did Hartford contact Keller directly: "I wish to take this opportunity to thank you for writing to me in this regard."[21]

That the president of the largest retail organization in the world would even read a three-page handwritten letter from a disgruntled former employee is remarkable enough. That he would intervene personally with high-ranking executives on four separate occasions concerning a problem at one of his company's nine thousand stores, repeatedly challenging their explanations and ultimately accepting the former employee's story over theirs, is extraordinary. But if such interventions could be humiliating for the employees concerned, they were a critical management tool. Mr. John was watching everything, or so he wanted his people to believe. And every A&P employee knew that if there was something wrong, Mr. John would try to set it right. That remarkable loyalty extended even to ex-employees such as G. D. Keller. In April 1940, a year after his first letter to John Hartford, Keller sent Hartford another handwritten note to say that business was better and he hoped soon to be out of debt. "I want to thank A&P for teaching me the grocery business," Keller wrote.[22]

John A. Hartford took an extremely long-term view of his family's business. For A&P executives, John's demands could be infuriating. Rather than urging higher profit margins, he often insisted on the opposite. His view that A&P should focus on return on investment rather than profits as a percentage of sales was not widely shared within the company. To his division presidents, who were overseeing thousands of stores or substantial industrial operations, a large profit, relative to sales, indicated good performance. To John, though, a large profit was a warning light, signaling an attempt to maximize short-term returns by paying workers inadequately or by holding prices too high. Either way, too much profit in the short term was bad for the company's position in the long term. As he saw it, excessive prices would reduce volume. Once that occurred, A&P would be forced to spread the fixed costs of its warehouses and factories across a smaller customer base, which would require it to raise prices even higher. No matter what the short-term implications for the bottom line, damaging A&P's reputation as the low-price grocer was a risk he was unwilling to take. In 1940, John went so far as to tell his division presidents the company should not attempt to earn more than $7 per common share; if earnings were above that, then their prices were simply too high.[23]

So long as it could hold down costs, A&P could undercut the competition even under the tight legal constraints on prices. The supermarkets brought lower costs, and their lower prices brought customers flocking back. In 1940, according to the company's estimates, it captured 10 percent of the available business in the places it had stores—more than it had held before the National Industrial Recovery Act, state chain-store taxes and fair-trade laws, and the legislative efforts of Wright Patman. In Pittsburgh, where its pre-Depression market share had been around 12 percent, A&P sold 20 percent of the groceries in 1940. In Chicago, its market share climbed from 11 percent to 14 percent, in Detroit from 10 percent to 15. Perhaps, John Hartford suggested, the relentless political attacks on A&P had backfired by focusing public attention on the fact that A&P was the cheapest place to shop. Whatever the cause, A&P found itself in a virtuous circle just as he had predicted: low prices brought higher volume, and volume boosted the bottom line. A&P's pretax return on equity climbed above 15 percent in 1940 for the first time since 1933. The fourth revolution, bringing A&P quickly into the supermarket age, proved to be the company's salvation.[24]

19
THE TRUSTBUSTER

The demise of his bill to tax chain stores in June 1940 brought an end to Wright Patman's hopes of pushing anti-chain legislation through Congress. It also doomed Patman's ambitions to enter the U.S. Senate. Patman had long coveted a Senate seat, and the death of Senator Morris Sheppard in April 1941 created an opening. When he tried to rally support across his huge state, though, Patman found he lacked for friends as well as money. The flamboyant populism that endeared him to voters did not appeal to potential patrons such as Sam Rayburn, now the powerful Speaker of the House, and Franklin Roosevelt. Roosevelt's support went to a young congressman, Lyndon Johnson, who then lost to the conservative governor, W. Lee "Pappy" O'Daniel, in a fraud-ridden election. Patman, humiliated, abandoned the race and sent a pitiable missive to the Democratic Party boss, Edward J. Flynn: "Having been a loyal Administration supporter, I am hoping that I will be considered the next time a situation arises in Texas that will warrant an evaluation of my merits."[1]

The tax bill's crushing legislative defeat did not mean the end of the anti-chain crusade. Far from it. The cause was taken up by a most unlikely protagonist, Franklin Roosevelt's antitrust chief, Thurman W. Arnold.

Arnold shared Wright Patman's small-town roots, but not much more. Born in Wyoming in 1891, Arnold had struggled through Princeton before flourishing at Harvard Law School. He opened a law practice in Chicago in 1914, handling divorces, collecting debts, and struggling to make ends meet. The call to military service was timely. In 1916, his National Guard unit was ordered to Texas to help track down the Mexican guerrilla leader Pancho Villa, and that adventure was followed by wartime service in France. Following his military career, Arnold moved back to Wyoming and won a seat in the state legislature, where he was the only Democrat. His most famous initiative involved nominating himself to be Speaker of the House, rising to second his own nomination, and then rising once more to proclaim: "Mr. Speaker, some irresponsible Democrat has put my name in nomination and I wish to withdraw it."[2]

In 1923, Arnold became mayor of Laramie, a city of sixty-three hundred that was home to the University of Wyoming, where he taught law. He moved east when a former Harvard Law classmate recruited him to become dean of the law school at West Virginia University. An offer to teach at Yale Law School, one of the most prestigious legal faculties in the country, came in 1930. At Yale, Arnold developed classes on leading-edge subjects such as psychiatry and the law, and his writings made him one of the best-known professors at the school. Easily identified by his three-piece suits, his neatly trimmed mustache, and the cigar that was often between his fingers, Arnold was a colorful character with many friends in New Deal Washington. During vacations and sabbaticals from Yale, he worked in the Agricultural Adjustment Administration (whose counsel was his former Yale Law School colleague Jerome Frank), the newly established Securities and Exchange Commission (headed by his former Yale Law School colleague William O. Douglas), and the tax division of the Department of Justice. Arnold turned down appointments to the National Labor Relations Board and the Securities and Exchange Commission. "An academic seat on the Atlantic Seaboard is more to my liking than anything else I can possibly think of," he wrote to the Harvard Law professor Thomas Reed Powell in March 1938. When the offer to head the Justice Department's antitrust division came in 1938, it was one he could not pass up.[3]

Antitrust law was not Arnold's field of expertise, and his nomination brought forth protests from senators who thought him insufficiently concerned about the economic dominance of big business. His record suggested as much. At Yale, he was associated with a group known as legal realists, who were more interested in the ends to be achieved with the law than in philosophical consistency or political ideology. Realism left him skeptical that antitrust policy was an effective way to encourage competition. He thought the antitrust laws were a subterfuge, serving to "promote the growth of great industrial organizations by deflecting the attack on them into purely moral and ceremonial channels." But the worries about his commitment to activist competition policy were unfounded. As a Westerner, Arnold shared the West's deep suspicion of eastern capital and of large, centralizing institutions. During the five years of Arnold's tenure at the antitrust division, from 1938 to 1943, it would undertake almost as many investigations of corporate power as it had since passage of the Sherman Antitrust Act in 1890. The division's 215 investigations would lead to ninety-three court cases, a number limited only by Arnold's ability to hire additional investigators and prosecutors.[4]

The political situation Arnold faced was difficult, for the Roosevelt administration's attitude toward competition was nothing if not confused. On the one hand, the New Deal favored restraints on competition in the interest of raising prices and wages; the National Industrial Recovery Act, to take the most extreme example, lent the federal stamp of approval to price-fixing across the economy between 1933 and 1935. On the other hand, Roosevelt was always willing to criticize the monopolistic tendencies of big business. In the spring of 1938, just after Arnold's appointment, he had launched a blistering attack on "the concentration of economic power in American industry and the effect of that concentration upon the decline of competition." The president's ambivalence about a matter that did not deeply interest him permitted Arnold great freedom. He regarded the legal assaults on companies deemed too big as intellectually unsound. Arnold determined to focus on "not the evil of size but the evils of industries which are inefficient or do not pass efficiency on to consumers."[5]

The food industry was one of many that came into Arnold's sights. Although he had no patience with Patman's plan to use the tax system to punish big retailers, Arnold shared his concern about competition in food retailing. In June 1940, as Patman's tax bill was going down to defeat, Arnold's staff recommended a "systemic nationwide attack" on restraints of trade in the food sector. Arnold jumped on the idea. Food was a huge part of the average household's budget, and both farm interests and consumers would applaud policies that might shrink the gap between the prices farmers received and the prices consumers paid. "In my opinion there is no excuse for not cleaning the Augean stables of food distribution," Arnold wrote in a 1940 book arguing that their control of "bottlenecks" in the distribution system enabled companies to exploit consumers.[6]

Patman urged him on—and specifically urged him to investigate Carl Byoir. Byoir, the mastermind of the effort to block the chain-store tax, had boasted of its defeat in a series of triumphant twenty-four-page pamphlets: *What Farmers of America Did to Defeat the Patman Bill and Why, What Manufacturers of America Did to Defeat the Patman Bill and Why,* and so on. Patman was bent on revenge. The congressman's appointment books, which are largely blank, refer to meeting after meeting to discuss Byoir between 1940 and 1942. He talked about Byoir with Arnold on March 16, 1940, with a State Department official on May 27, and with a New Jersey woman on June 2. On July 21, he attacked Byoir in a statement to the Associated Press. A discussion of Byoir appears on Patman's calendar again on August 17. Patman's staff gave information about Byoir to Martin Dies, who was looking into Byoir's work for the German Tourist Information Office in 1933; after Byoir testified before Dies's committee that certain interests "were paying Patman what I would consider large sums of money" to fight chain stores, Patman responded with the claim that "big business is cooperating with Nazi agents for the purpose of having this country follow an appeasement policy." On September 20, Byoir was the subject of a meeting between Patman and Arnold's top deputy, Wendell Berge, after which Patman's staff furnished derogatory information to Arnold's investigators concerning Byoir's role in the antitax campaign.[7]

In 1941, the antitrust division set up an office in New York specifically to pursue antitrust violations by chain grocers. Indictments followed quickly. On May 23, A&P, First National Stores, and several wholesalers were charged in Connecticut with conspiring to fix prices through an organization called the Connecticut Food Council. Five days later, A&P and John Hartford, along with several other retail chains and some labor unions, were indicted in Washington, D.C., on charges of fixing the price of bread. On September 25, 1941, a grand jury in New York indicted A&P and ninety-one other organizations on charges of using the Monday meetings of the Cuba Cheese Board in tiny Cuba, New York, and of a similar board in Gouverneur, New York, to fix cheese prices for the entire state.[8]

The theory behind the food investigation was that, while A&P accounted for just 12 percent of U.S. food sales and four other big chains jointly took 20 percent, "they are a monopoly in actual practice or effect." Yet the economic logic behind Arnold's attack on the chains was muddled. The Connecticut Food Council was blatantly anticompetitive, which is why all defendants, including A&P, pleaded guilty to antitrust violations. Yet this "conspiracy" was no secret; as one of many organizations set up by grocers and food wholesalers to control competition after the NRA's demise in 1935, it had been tolerated and even encouraged by the Roosevelt administration until Arnold attacked it. The main evidence of price-fixing in the bread case was that bread cost more in Washington than elsewhere; a federal judge thought the government's case so weak he dismissed the charges. The cheese case dragged on for three years before A&P and other defendants eventually pleaded no contest, relieving the government of having to explain how there could be a secret conspiracy with ninety-two participants.

Confusing matters further, in September 1941, Corwin Edwards, the antitrust division's chief economist, said that "the protection of all grocers, in their ability to buy goods on equal terms," was the greatest antitrust issue facing food retailers. Allowing all grocers to buy on equal terms, as Edwards demanded, is exactly what the government sought to stop in the Connecticut Food Council, bread, and cheese cases. Indeed, even as the antitrust division was suing chain grocers for keeping food prices artificially high, the State Department was signing deals with twenty countries to artificially hold up the prices of coffee, sugar, and other commodities. Rather than straightening out the administration's ambivalent approach to antitrust enforcement, Arnold continued it, at least where chain stores were concerned.[9]

A&P fought back with an image-shaping campaign that bore Carl Byoir's fingerprints. At the end of 1940, John Hartford announced that employees would receive up to 20 percent of their wages for one year if they entered military service, a policy duly noted in the newspapers. He issued a year-end statement, widely reported, emphasizing that efficient distribution would leave the country with more resources for defense. Another Hartford statement, in March 1941, asserted that vegetable and fruit shippers received fifty-three cents from each dollar of produce A&P sold in 1940, up from forty-seven cents in 1937—evidence,

Hartford said, of the efficiencies created by the Atlantic Commission Company.[10]

The following month, Hartford announced that A&P employees in the New York area would henceforth work only five days a week instead of six, receiving the same pay for a forty-eight-hour week that they previously earned for fifty-four hours. Even a modest decline in profits was treated as good news, a result of "the company's traditional policy of passing along to consumers, producers and employees the savings resulting from the constantly increasing efficiency," Hartford said. The distribution of $700,000 to twenty-six hundred employees serving in the military, which once would have been handled quietly, merited a press release, as did the award of $1.5 million in Christmas bonuses. At the end of 1941, three weeks after the Japanese attack on Pearl Harbor brought the United States into the war, A&P published advertisements in three thousand newspapers calling for the government to control food prices.[11]

Such efforts may have burnished A&P's public image, but they did not soften the views of the antitrust division of the Department of Justice. Teams of investigators fanned out across the country, soliciting complaints from organizations whose members had been hurt by A&P's aggressive growth, from the National League of Wholesale Fresh Fruit and Vegetable Distributors to the Independent Grocers & Meat Dealers of Omaha, Nebraska. Investigators interviewed hundreds of shopkeepers, citrus growers, and vegetable shippers. They collected documents from the giant retailer's files in New York, Los Angeles, Seattle, and regional offices in between. By early 1942, prosecutors were outlining two separate types of cases, some charging unfair competition by virtue of purchasing practices, the others against several chains that supposedly conspired to eliminate competition. Patman met Arnold for lunch on February 12, and while the two were in no way close, it seems highly probable that chain stores were on the menu.[12]

Almost everything the investigators turned up raised suspicions. Internal Justice Department memos highlight examples of normal business dealings that seemed outrageous to the lawyers on the case. Produce handling: "The Commission Company's files clearly indicate that the best quality of all shipments handled by it are diverted to the Tea Company while the poorer quality on which the multiple commissions, brokerages and discounts are taken, finds its way into the hands of the independent trade." Wholesaling: "A&P store managers do not have the liberty of buying their supplies from independent wholesale distributors." Manufacturing: "It manufactures no product whatsoever that is not an imitation of a well-known advertised brand which some manufacturer has invented and introduced to the consuming public at great expense." Retailing: "In all A&P stores popular brands are displayed in the most inaccessible places. The fighting imitations are kept in the most conspicuous places and everything possible is done to suggest to customers the disparity in price between the originals and the imitations." Even A&P's remarkably rapid shift from combination stores to supermarkets exemplified monopoly at work: "We get a vivid picture of the power of this organization to control and dominate when we see how it has been able to reduce the number of its stores by more than one-half and at the same time increase the volume of its retail sales to unprecedented heights." If fewer stores were able to sell more merchandise, the trustbusters believed, then something illegal must be going on.[13]

In addition to their concerns about the food business, Arnold's investigators had a particular incentive to pursue A&P. By early 1942, with war mobilization in high gear, Arnold's attacks against industrial cartels and monopolies had triggered a backlash within the federal government. The Army, the Navy, and mobilization agencies such as the War Production Board were concerned that antitrust investigations were distracting corporate managers and diverting attention from efforts to boost industrial production; Arnold's argument that monopoly was the main cause of production shortfalls cut little ice. In an unusual memorandum of understanding signed in March 1942, the War and Navy departments were given veto rights over antitrust prosecutions, and they exercised those rights frequently. But while Arnold's ability to investigate manufacturers and transport companies was considerably limited, the military had no reasonable grounds to block an antitrust probe of a retail chain. In this sector, the antitrust division had free rein.[14]

On November 25, 1942, Arnold's prosecutors persuaded a federal grand jury in Dallas to indict twelve A&P-related companies, Carl Byoir and his firm, and sixteen A&P executives, including George and John Hartford, on charges of "combination and conspiracy to restrain trade."[15]

The indictment laid out twenty-five allegations, ranging from publishing false comparisons of store prices to coercing suppliers to sell to other wholesalers and retailers on terms dictated by A&P. At the heart of the complaint was the claim that A&P had "the power to dominate and control the production prices and distribution of a substantial part of the food and food products produced, marketed, sold and consumed in the United States." The U.S. district judge quickly threw the case out, ruling that the indictment was filled with irrelevant and inflammatory statements. The government appealed, and a federal appeals court reinstated most of the charges; it agreed, however, that there was no case against Carl Byoir. Prosecutors, realizing that a trial in Dallas would be run by a judge who was evidently hostile to their case, withdrew the complaint on February 26, 1944. The same day, they filed new charges against all the original defendants, including Byoir, eight hundred miles away, in the unlikely venue of Danville, Illinois, where A&P's presence consisted of a single ten-thousand-square-foot supermarket.[16]

So it was that the epic criminal antitrust case landed in the courtroom of Walter Lindley in the three-story limestone-fronted post office on Hazel Street in Danville. Public interest was intense; as the Danville newspaper commented, "The Hartford family and A&P has always and still is synonymous. Our mothers and grandmothers for the most part have known and trusted them . . . the Attorney General's office has attacked a company that has been one of the institutions of the food merchandising world for 86 years." Swarms of lawyers, witnesses, and reporters crowded Danville's hotels. Extra court reporters were laid on for the occasion. Lindley wanted to try the case before a jury, but all the parties felt otherwise. They preferred to leave it to the judge to be both the interpreter of the law and the finder of fact.[17]

The trial in the Danville antitrust case began on Monday, April 16, 1945, when all defendants save George L. Hartford, who was not present, rose at the request of the defense attorney W. M. Acton to enter pleas of "not guilty." By any measure, the case was extraordinarily long and complex. Prosecutors subpoenaed more than 260,000 documents from A&P's files. The trial transcript runs to 21,000 pages, the government's closing brief to 1,105. The government introduced some forty-five hundred exhibits, the defense over a thousand more. Although wartime travel restrictions made it difficult to book train tickets to Danville, 191 witnesses, from A&P produce buyers to a sausage manufacturer to the head of a Chicago noodle company, passed through the post office's revolving doors, climbed the stairway to the second floor, walked down the narrow, marble-lined corridor, and pushed through the green leather doors into Lindley's courtroom. Forty additional prosecution witnesses were brought to Danville at government expense but were not called to testify. The presentation of evidence dragged on through eighty-six trial days until October 24, with a two-month break dictated by the fact that the high-ceilinged courtroom lacked air-conditioning. George L. Hartford claimed to be too ill to testify in his own behalf. The final witness, late on a Tuesday afternoon, was John A. Hartford. Then seventy-three, Hartford appeared in his standard gray suit, gray shirt, and bow tie, captivating the audience "both with his rather striking appearance and his knack for expression," according to a reporter on the scene.[18]

Despite the mountain of evidence, there was little dispute about the facts. Indeed, almost every document in the record was from A&P's own files: statistical reports, minutes of company meetings, correspondence with suppliers, letters between headquarters executives and employees around the country. The issue was not what A&P and its executives had done over the previous two decades, but what they had achieved. In A&P's view, its aggressive efforts to cut purchasing costs, narrow its own margins, and reduce consumer prices in order to build business were exactly what a company was supposed to do in a competitive economy. In the view of Thurman Arnold and his prosecutors, A&P's behavior amounted to illegal restraint of trade.

The logic of the government's case is worth considering, because it reflected a very peculiar understanding of economics—an understanding quite at odds with the contention of one of Thurman Arnold's biographers that "his entire antitrust program was oriented toward the benefit of the consumer." A typical antitrust case involves the claim that the defendant is attempting to control the supply of some product with the aim of driving prices higher than they would be in a competitive market. In many cases, the objectionable conduct includes mergers by which a company gains greater control of its markets. *U.S. v. New York*

Great Atlantic & Pacific was nothing like that. There had been no mergers of consequence; A&P had grown not by buying businesses but by building them. And the government's case had to do not with monopoly but with *monopsony*, the use of A&P's power as the nation's largest buyer of meat, produce, and packaged groceries to force suppliers' prices down. As Holmes Baldridge, one of the government's special prosecutors, explained in the Danville court, "A&P sells food cheaply in its own stores because it is a gigantic blood sucker, taking its toll from all levels of the food industry."[19]

What made A&P "a gigantic blood sucker," in the government's view, was vertical integration. The idea that a company could be engaged in a variety of different activities related to its business—in A&P's case, manufacturing, warehousing, produce brokering, retailing, and even publishing a women's magazine—deeply disturbed many critics of big business. Vertical integration was hardly a new concept; decades earlier, the Ford Motor Company had raised soybeans that it made into a plastic which it used to manufacture horns for its automobiles. Over time, vertical integration had waxed or waned in particular industries as economic factors dictated; in many instances, it was not the cheapest way to do business. But A&P, prosecutors argued, gained an unfair competitive advantage by doing so many things in-house. It could organize orders from its store to run its bakeries and canneries full blast, generating greater profits than manufacturers whose flow of business was less regular. It could use its manufacturing capabilities and its clout as the nation's largest buyer of groceries to pressure suppliers to give it lower prices than any other buyer received. It could, and did, refuse to order merchandise from manufacturers that insisted on selling through brokers, or that declined to grant it advertising allowances, or that wanted higher prices than A&P felt were warranted. It could accept low profits from running stores because the stores enabled other parts of the company to be very profitable.[20]

The trial testimony included many examples of A&P's use of vertical integration to cut costs. One involved Ralston Purina, which had invested $1 million in a factory mainly to manufacture private-label breakfast cereal for A&P. In the summer of 1939, A&P declared it would start manufacturing cereal itself unless Ralston lowered prices. This was not an idle threat; A&P had studied the matter carefully, determining that Ralston's prices were so inflated that if A&P invested $175,000 to expand an existing plant to make the cereals, its investment could earn an annual return of 73 percent. After much bargaining, Ralston agreed to grant A&P various rebates and allowances on corn, bran, and wheat flakes. Although the government prosecutors focused on these "rebates" and "allowances" as nefarious departures from some official list price, in an economic sense they were nothing more than price concessions; the only thing that really mattered was A&P's ultimate cost per box of cereal. In the event, A&P had leverage because Ralston, apparently unwisely, had expanded its plant without a firm commitment from the largest buyer of its cereals. If it had not struck a deal with A&P, its factory might have stood empty.[21]

The government attached great significance to the fact that many of A&P's stores lost money, although one reason for those apparent store-level losses was that manufacturers paid the various price concessions directly to A&P's headquarters, rather than deducting them from the factory price of each bottle of fruit juice and each can of sardines shipped to A&P's warehouses. Integration, in short, allowed A&P to cross subsidize, using profits from some parts of its vast operation to support other parts, which simple wholesalers or retailers could not do. The complaint of the Dallas grocer L. S. Culwell that many of A&P's retail prices were below the prices he paid at wholesale was held up by the government as an example of the unfairness arising from A&P's system. As Horace L. Flurry, another of the special prosecutors, told the court, "A&P's programs of expansion were predicated upon its price advantage over competition, resulting from the use of the integrated power."[22]

The Atlantic Commission Company, A&P's produce-brokering subsidiary, was a particular sore point for the prosecutors. It was wrong, prosecutors contended, for Atlantic Commission to function as a broker, selling produce to retailers that competed with A&P, at the same time it served A&P. This supposed conflict of interest was said to damp competition among wholesale buyers of produce while forcing other grocers to pay higher prices. The trial, though, provided scanty evidence on both points. Sales to other retailers were between a quarter and a third of Atlantic Commission's overall trade, and as a business strategy they made great sense: Atlantic Commission could obtain the best possible prices by purchasing very large quantities, knowing it could dispose of unneeded produce by selling to other retailers, and it could balance its own supply and demand in individual localities by selling surplus fruits and vegetables rather than throwing them out. Lindley found that Atlantic Commission's "multiple, irreconcilable functions" inevitably served to restrain competition; in particular, he objected to Atlantic Commission's practice of selling to A&P's stores at prices reflecting a cash discount from produce shippers while selling to outside customers at higher prices. Yet the fact that other retailers chose to purchase from Atlantic Commission suggests that its prices were competitive with those of other produce brokers. In any event, Atlantic Commission's sales to buyers other than A&P came to a mere 3 percent of U.S. growers' total produce sales. How it could have restrained price competition in produce brokerage, a field with thousands of competitors, was not analyzed rigorously at the Danville trial.[23]

The government freely admitted that A&P's strategy enabled its customers to buy food cheaply. However, Baldridge argued, "The consumers who buy food in stores competing with A&P pay part of the low cost of A&P's operations." This assertion implies that manufacturers met their profit targets by raising prices to other stores to compensate for their price breaks to A&P. But why would manufacturers have charged other retailers less if only A&P had paid more? Any sensible, profit-maximizing manufacturer would have tried to charge each retailer as much as it could get, regardless of the price paid by A&P—and no retailer would have needed to pay an above-market price for readily available commodities such as cereal or tomato sauce. The behavior posited by the government's lawyers would have been odd.[24]

Eventually, Baldridge predicted, its low prices would force retail competitors out of business, giving A&P a monopoly, which "will place them in position to sell at whatever price they choose." This is the standard concern about the practice known as predatory pricing, the setting of prices at unprofitably low levels in the short term in order to drive out competitors and establish very high prices in the long term. But the government did not contend at trial that A&P engaged in predatory pricing, and it would have had a difficult time showing that it had done so. The company was far from unprofitable even in the depths of the Great Depression, when many companies were bleeding red ink. Between 1931 and 1941, the last year before the government's original antitrust complaint was filed in Texas, its average pretax rate of return on investment was 14.4 percent; there was only one year, 1937, in which it fell below 11 percent. A&P clearly was not setting prices at levels that caused it to lose money. And even if A&P had somehow been able to use predatory behavior to create local food monopolies, those monopolies would have been impossible to sustain. "The business of food distribution is just about the last business I can think of in which it would be feasible for anybody to develop a monopoly," the Harvard Business School professor Malcolm McNair, the only academic expert to testify, told the court. Even if a retailer were to lower prices so far as to drive all competitors out of business, "nobody is going to award any kind of public franchise"; as soon as the company tries to exploit its monopoly by raising prices, McNair said, other competitors would enter the market.[25]

Lindley found almost all of the defendants guilty as charged. He acknowledged that John Hartford's strategy of trying to lower gross profits, or markups, saved money for shoppers, but he thought A&P's ability to shift profits within the organization created unfair competition for other retailers. He disapproved of A&P's aggressive bargaining with suppliers, finding it to be an unjustified source of competitive advantage. The fact that consumers benefited, he ruled, was not relevant to the question of whether A&P was violating antitrust law. On the contrary: "Combination that leads directly to lower prices to the consumer may, even as against the consumer, be restraint of trade." The defendants were fined $10,000 each, and A&P was required to pay the prosecution's costs.[26]

The convictions did no damage to A&P's business. The Hartfords continued to run their company as they always had, certain that Lindley's ruling would be overturned. But on February 24, 1949, the circuit court of appeals ruled against them. After reviewing Lindley's findings regarding A&P's business methods, the three-judge panel agreed fully with his conclusions. Wrote the judges: "The inevitable consequence of this whole business pattern is to create a chain reaction of ever-increasing selling volume and ever-increasing requirements and hence purchasing power for A&P, and for its competitors hardships not produced by competitive forces, and, conceivably, ultimate extinction."[27]

The case against A&P was one of three antitrust complaints filed against big food chains in 1942 and 1943. The others, against Kroger and Safeway, were quite different; both firms had undertaken many mergers that reduced competition, and the government turned up evidence that they had made arrangements to avoid competing with each other in places like Omaha and Oklahoma City. Neither case went to trial. Both Kroger and Safeway eventually pleaded no contest to the criminal charges and paid small fines.[28]

U.S. v. New York Great Atlantic & Pacific Tea Co. provided fodder for decades of academic debate. Morris Adelman, later a preeminent energy economist, was a Harvard University graduate student in the late 1940s, and turned his dissertation into a closely reasoned attack on the lack of economic logic undergirding the government's case. Among the government's supporters was another young economist, Alfred E. Kahn, who would become famous as a proponent of economic deregulation during the 1970s; in 1952, however, he and another economist, Joel Dirlam, argued that A&P's attempts to force suppliers to discriminate in its favor justified the guilty verdicts. Carl H. Fulda, later a renowned scholar of international law, offered a defense of Lindley even as he agreed that consumers had suffered no harm. The Justice Department's files bulge with hundreds of requests for information from students writing senior papers, master's theses, and dissertations, an indication of the intensity with which A&P's business practices and its conviction were debated around the country.[29]

By the time the court of appeals rendered its verdict upholding Judge Lindley in 1949, Thurman Arnold was long gone from the scene. The Roosevelt administration lost enthusiasm for antitrust prosecutions, especially at a time when it was encouraging businesses to work together to help win the war. After winning huge spending increases for the antitrust division during his first four years, Arnold saw his division's budget slashed by nearly one-fourth in 1943, and many of his investigations were blocked in the name of national security. He took the hint that his services were no longer desired, accepting a nominal promotion to become a judge on the U.S. court of appeals in Washington. The job, the pinnacle of many a lawyer's career, evidently bored him. After only two years, he resigned to enter private law practice. Arnold, known for his irreverent wit, is said to have explained, "I would rather be speaking to damn fools than listening to damn fools." His firm would soon become known for defending, without charge, people accused of disloyalty in the second term of Roosevelt's successor, Harry Truman. It would eventually become one of the most influential corporate law firms in Washington.[30]

Truman had his own views when it came to antitrust policy, and they were far more consistent than Roosevelt's. A former merchant himself, he was suspicious of big business, cartels, and price-fixing. In his State of the Union message to Congress in January 1947, he emphasized antitrust enforcement as a key part of his economic program. The war, he said, accelerated the trend toward economic concentration, so "to a greater extent than ever before, whole industries are dominated by one or a few large organizations which can restrict production in the interest of higher profits." Republicans won sweeping majorities in both houses of Congress in the 1946 election, and key Republican senators sought to block prosecutions. Truman responded by proposing large budget increases for antitrust enforcement and directing his antitrust officials to think big, pursuing large cases involving entire industries rather than going after individual companies.[31]

The Danville case against A&P, originally filed in Dallas in 1942 and refiled in Danville in 1944, was not a Truman administration project. Truman's trustbusters were much more interested in the monopolistic tendencies of heavy industry than in chain stores. While Wright Patman continued to introduce new versions of his bill to tax chain stores into the House of Representatives, public interest in the subject largely waned after the antitrust convictions of A&P and of George and John Hartford in 1946. But when, at the start of Truman's second term in office, the appeals court upheld the convictions, the battle against chain stores was back in the headlines again.

20

MOM AND POP'S LAST STAND

Americans were eating well at the start of the 1940s. With unemployment shrinking and incomes rising rapidly at last, spending on food rose sharply, and the food chains experienced a remarkable revival. Chain grocers' sales rose 23 percent in 1941 and even faster in the first months of 1942, far outpacing the growth in food sales overall. Grocers found themselves facing a novel problem: lack of labor. After a decade in which workers were begging for jobs as grocery clerks, war industries were hiring at far higher wages than retailers could offer. The food chains were left with fewer and less capable workers, providing a strong incentive to improve efficiency. All over the country, smaller stores gave way to supermarkets designed to sell far more food for each man-hour of work. The Great A&P was atop the wave. Its sales jumped 39 percent from early 1940 to early 1942, even as it shuttered one-third of its stores. As consumers turned to chain supermarkets, public opinion turned with them; in their 1941 sessions, Carl Byoir proudly told A&P's directors that June, not a single state legislature increased taxes on chain stores, and one state let its chain-store tax expire. Although "fair trade" laws continued to limit chains' price-cutting, independent grocers struggled. From 1939 through June 1942, the failure rate for food stores was half again as high as that for retailers in other lines.[1]

War changed everything. The Japanese bombing of Pearl Harbor brought the United States into World War II in December 1941. The government immediately moved to mobilize the economy, and measures to stave off consumer-price inflation while dealing with shortages of consumer goods followed quickly. The Emergency Price Control Act, signed on January 30, 1942, gave the federal Office of Price Administration the power to place price ceilings on all products save agricultural commodities, to regulate apartment rents, and to ration goods in short supply. Under the General Maximum Price Regulation handed down in April 1942—known to almost everyone in America as "General Max"—the office's director, the longtime New Dealer Leon Henderson, and his deputy, a young Canadian economist named John Kenneth Galbraith, froze prices on about 60 percent of food products. Until further notice, no seller could charge more than the highest price it had charged in March for any item, and prices were to be "generally fair and equitable." Across the country, a staff of administrators and price checkers soon to reach sixty-five thousand, aided by an army of volunteer housewives, stood ready to object to unauthorized price increases.[2]

Initially, the ceiling-price system worked to the advantage of small stores. Chains, in general, kept prices fairly steady, whereas independent grocers typically combined high everyday prices with special sales. Those high everyday prices became the independents' ceilings, while the chains faced lower ceilings as the result of their lower prices in March 1942, and with supplies scarce the independents could sell every can and box they could lay hands on despite their higher prices. But the system quickly became an administrative nightmare. General Max applied to canned vegetables, fruits, and preserves from the 1941 harvest. As the 1942 crop came in and the government set new, higher ceiling prices, grocers holding goods canned the previous year were supposed to adhere to the former ceilings until their inventories were depleted: 1941 string beans were to sell for less than 1942 string beans. Compliance proved impossible to monitor. Controls were extended to products whose supply varied seasonally, such as butter and citrus fruits, which meant that price ceilings had to change seasonally. Increases, temporary exceptions, seasonal adjustments, and changes in coverage left both shopkeepers and consumers confused about what ceilings were in effect. "The result at the moment is more regulations than any retailer could be expected to read and abide by," Galbraith acknowledged in late 1942.[3]

In October, Galbraith proposed shifting from product-specific price ceilings to maximum markups on food, with the allowable markup varying by type of food store and class of commodity. His thinking was that a relatively efficient operator, such as A&P, might be authorized to charge a 12 percent markup on eggs and 10 percent on bread, while a mom-and-pop store might be allowed larger markups. That plan was problematic, not least because consumers would have a hard time identifying violations of the price regulations if different price ceilings were in effect at different grocery stores. Instead, the Office of Price Administration used the average profits of various sectors of the retail industry to determine whether price increases would be permitted. A&P's profit margins were well below the average for grocery stores, so price hikes approved with the average grocer in mind should have permitted it lavish profits. But the story was more complicated than that.[4]

A&P's prewar cost advantage came largely from its supply chain, which imported coffee by the shipload, commanded deep discounts by purchasing huge volumes of processed foods, and minimized inventory costs by moving goods quickly from farms and factories to its warehouses and then into its stores. Amid the general wartime mobilization, such logistical feats were no longer possible. The military had first claim on foodstuffs, buying up 13 percent of all U.S. food production in 1942 and annulling A&P's ability to gain a cost advantage by buying in huge volumes. The need to move troops and military freight meant that civilian transport was restricted, making it hard for grocery chains to ship large quantities of goods. No longer could A&P learn of a canner's surplus of peaches and agree on the spot to buy a dozen railcar loads at a deeply discounted price; neither the goods nor the railcars were to be had. "Markets and delivery routings are in such a chaotic state that there is no means of determining the exact source of the merchandise sold today and just how replacements will be routed," A&P's research director reported soon after Pearl Harbor.[5]

In practice, the price controls were a constant headache for chain retailers, which risked damage to their reputations if consumers thought they were flouting the law. In Palestine, Texas, A&P had to produce records to refute a customer's complaint that it had raised the price of Grape-Nuts Flakes from thirteen cents to fifteen cents. It won permission to raise the price of pork and beans packed in glass jars, but not in tin cans. It was denied the right to claim a wholesale markup on bananas because its banana-handling operation was not separately incorporated as a wholesaler. A&P claimed to be losing 1.81 cents on every ten-cent loaf of Marvel bread it sold in Pennsylvania and New York, but the government forced it to cut the price rather than allowing a price increase. In the spring of 1942, A&P stores ran out of Dexo, a store-brand shortening manufactured for it by the Durkee Company. The government had imposed a price ceiling on cottonseed oil, a key ingredient, but none on the seed itself; shortening manufacturers that owned crushing mills could buy cottonseed on the open market and make all the oil they required, but shortening manufacturers without mills, such as Durkee, found no cottonseed oil for sale at all.[6]

In addition to the price controls on most products, gasoline, motor oil, and tires all were rationed to discourage civilian consumption of critical raw materials. Car owners responded by cutting back sharply on driving. Before the war, growing numbers of shoppers had gotten in the habit of motoring to one of the new supermarkets offering free parking. Under wartime conditions, gasoline was precious, and due to rationing and short supplies there was less money to be saved by using it to drive to the supermarket. Many shoppers returned to buying their groceries at the corner store.[7]

The result of all this was a disaster for the big grocery-store operators. Although A&P's operating costs reached record lows—its cost of doing business came to less than 13 percent of sales in 1942, a drop of six percentage points since it began the conversion to supermarkets in 1937—profits were slim due to limited supplies of food and high wartime taxes. The other grocery chains also fared poorly. "The fact is that the chains have not been able to operate under the regulations on any kind of an economic basis," *The New York Times* reported in 1945. Chains' share of all grocery-store sales plummeted nine percentage points over the course of the war. The largest chains fared notably worse than the small ones, with the profit margins of the four biggest chain grocers trailing those of much smaller competitors throughout the war. A&P was hit badly, its sales falling 11 percent in 1943. The construction of new stores was suspended to conserve building materials and labor, giving the independent grocers a prolonged lease on life.[8]

The end of the war in August 1945 did not bring immediate change: manufacturers needed time to shift from tanks and bombers to cars and home appliances, and demobilizing more than ten million soldiers, sailors, and airmen took two years. Price controls initially remained intact;

in early 1946, the maximum wholesale price of lima beans still depended upon whether they were to be canned, frozen, or sold fresh at retail, and whether they had been grown in Idaho, Michigan, or Virginia. "If we lifted the lid today, there would be a substantial rise in cost of living," Agriculture Secretary Clinton Anderson warned in February 1946. But amid an uproar over a scarcity of meat, controls were allowed to expire over the summer on all foods save rice, sugar, and sugar products. As the economy returned to normal in the second half of the year, with merchandise in ample supply and ration coupons no longer needed, the chain-store business exploded. In 1945, chains accounted for 31 percent of grocery sales. Just two years later, their share was 37 percent. A&P was at the top of its game. While consumer spending on food rose by half between 1945 and 1948, A&P's sales doubled and its profits trebled. Earnings per share, which had ranged between $4.65 and $5.45 during the war years, reached $18.21 in 1947, permitting George L. Hartford to reinstate the cherished $7-per-share dividend.[9]

With building supplies available once more, the supermarket revolution that had begun before the war resumed in full force. In 1946, developers spent $801 million to build stores, restaurants, and garages—twenty times as much as in 1944. The number of supermarkets nationwide, around two thousand in 1941, hit fifty-six hundred in 1948. For the first time, the supermarket was a national phenomenon. And most notably, it was a suburban phenomenon. Before the war, grocers had built supermarkets mainly in fancier urban neighborhoods, using one structure perhaps fifty by seventy feet to replace several combination stores one-third that size. Now, though, farm fields blossomed into suburbs as housing construction boomed: of the 931,600 housing units started in 1948, 82 percent were single-family homes and 44 percent were in "rural, non-farm" areas, mainly on the outskirts of big cities. These developments provided room for food stores with large parking lots. The new stores were still far from the fifty-thousand-square-foot supermarkets that would become the norm by the 1990s; in 1947, a seventeen-thousand-square-foot store qualified as "huge." Even so, as bigger stores opened and smaller ones closed, sales at the average A&P rose 139 percent between 1945 and 1948.[10]

The new stores had far more to offer than their prewar counterparts. Before the war, the average conventional grocery store stocked perhaps fifteen hundred items and offered clerk service, credit, and home delivery. The average prewar supermarket had about three thousand items in stock and had no credit or delivery but, like conventional stores, made heavy use of sales clerks, especially to sell meat and produce. In the late 1940s, new supermarkets typically carried four thousand or so items and featured self-service meat and produce sections. Only 22 percent of the nation's grocery stores operated wholly on a self-service basis, but they accounted for 64 percent of grocery sales. This put the squeeze on independent grocers. If an independent store owner cut out clerk service, telephone orders, credit, and delivery, he would eliminate the important features distinguishing his store from chain supermarkets. Continuing to offer such amenities, on the other hand, would create an impossible cost disadvantage. Eliminating the clerks standing at attendance behind wooden counters was the only feasible choice.[11]

The new supermarkets devoted careful attention to aesthetics. Prewar grocery stores were utilitarian, often displaying merchandise in bushel baskets set out on wood floors. "If food stores were built primarily for men shoppers, they might be fairly simple, possibly even slightly mechanical, with not much attention paid to store atmosphere. But with women it is different," *The Progressive Grocer*, the leading trade magazine, told its readers in 1946. Light colors, bright illumination, and attractive floor coverings were now essential, but owners were advised to pay close attention to their customers' expectations; fancy shelving and decoration in a store serving price-conscious working-class customers might drive them away. Survey after survey showed that cleanliness was housewives' top concern. This meant more than sweeping floors. In 1944, A&P joined with the Ohio Agricultural Experiment Station to test prepackaged produce at ten stores in Columbus: alongside loose produce, the stores stocked vegetables that had been trimmed in a warehouse, placed on a cardboard tray, wrapped in cellophane, sealed, and machine labeled. The produce sections looked neater, losses from damaged produce fell by half—and the company discovered that shoppers would pay a premium for prepackaged carrots with their tops cut off. After the war, A&P took the concept one step further, setting up produce packinghouses in California to do the trimming and packaging before the produce was shipped east.[12]

New items began to fill the shelves as industrial-scale food manufacturing took hold. In 1946, A&P began opening bakeshops in its stores. Initially, the shops sold unwrapped cakes and pies produced in A&P's bakeries and took orders for custom products: using a color catalog, the shopper could order a birthday cake of a particular type, style, and icing and pick it up the following day. To cut costs further, much of the baked-goods line was soon put on a self-service basis, with cakes and pastries boxed at the bakery. A&P had long sold poultry feed for customers who kept chickens, and in 1947 it sponsored a contest to design the "chicken of tomorrow," promising "a chicken with breast meat so thick you can carve it into steaks." The larger A&P stores were getting freezer cabinets by 1946. Frozen vegetables and seafood, while still luxury items, gained popularity as freezer compartments became standard in household refrigerators, and manufactured meals in metal trays were introduced in the late 1940s. Frozen orange juice, previously known for its astringent taste, became a consumer staple after government scientists found a better way to make it—and after a juice manufacturer hired the singer Bing Crosby as a celebrity promoter. Production went from 7 million cans in 1945 to 600 million in 1951, making orange juice concentrate "perhaps the most dramatic single new product of the past 25 years," in *The Progressive Grocer*'s judgment.[13]

By 1948, the supermarket format had captured one-quarter of all grocery sales. The chain-store wars no longer raged. Wright Patman, now chairman of the Select Committee on Small Business, struggled to keep the cause alive, entering scathing attacks on A&P in the *Congressional Record* and mailing them to supporters in massive quantities. He put forward anti-chain bills in every session of Congress. In 1945, 1947, and again in 1949, he proposed to amend the tax code to prohibit retail chains from subtracting losses at money-losing stores when determining their taxable income; the Truman administration was strongly opposed, and Patman could not even secure a committee hearing. Another Patman bill, to bar manufacturers from offering quantity discounts unless they publicized that similar terms were available to all customers, went nowhere. As late as 1949, four years after the Ways and Means Committee concluded its look at the subject, a Patman investigator was still trying to prove that John Hartford's 1939 loan to Elliott Roosevelt was intended to allow A&P to use Elliott's radio stations to push repeal of the Texas tax on chain stores. But now, with chain supermarkets all around them, even the congressman's erstwhile supporters in rural eastern Texas rejected his crusade. "The A&P has done more to raise the living standard of the people of the U.S. than any other industrial business," one constituent wrote to Patman by hand in 1949.[14]

It was on February 24, 1949, that the U.S. Court of Appeals for the Seventh Circuit upheld Judge Lindley's ruling convicting A&P, George and John Hartford, and other A&P executives of engaging criminally in restraint of trade. A&P chose not to appeal to the U.S. Supreme Court. The Department of Justice quickly moved to use the criminal conviction as the basis for a civil antitrust suit. On September 15, it asked a federal court in New York City to order the breakup of A&P.

The civil suit was the culmination of a quarter century of government attacks on the world's largest retailer. The leadership of the Department of Justice had changed once more, and the civil suit was the first case brought by the new attorney general, J. Howard McGrath. McGrath, a Democratic senator from Rhode Island who had managed Harry Truman's 1948 election campaign, had been named attorney general in August, and one of his first decisions was to press ahead with the case being developed by Herbert Bergson, the twelve-year Justice Department veteran who had taken charge of the antitrust division in 1948. The Truman administration signaled its support: on September 15, the day the civil suit was filed, Truman nominated Sherman Minton, author of the appeals court ruling upholding A&P's criminal conviction, to the U.S. Supreme Court. The same day, he nominated Lindley to Minton's seat on the U.S. court of appeals in Chicago—a nomination the laconic Lindley greeted with the words "Well, that's something."[15]

The criminal case had resulted in relatively small fines for the defendants, and had led to only one important change in the way A&P ran its business: in view of Lindley's objection to the Atlantic Commission Company acting as both a wholesale buyer for A&P's stores and a wholesale seller to other retailers, the produce brokerage now bought only for A&P. In its civil suit, the government sought far more sweeping changes. It asked the court to order each of A&P's seven retail divisions to be spun off as an independent company. It wanted A&P's food-processing plants reorganized into a stand-alone business, with "the complete and perpetual separation" of manufacturing from retailing. And it wanted many of A&P's central functions, including the Atlantic Commission Company, the national egg and poultry department, and the national butter department, abolished altogether.

As with the government's other antitrust complaints against A&P, the economic logic behind the civil suit was hazy. The suit asserted that A&P's ownership of manufacturing and distribution, as well as retailing, made it "impervious to competition." But the claim that A&P was exercising monopoly power rested on shaky ground. The company's sales in 1948, $2.9 billion, amounted to 9.3 percent of that year's sales at food stores and only 7.3 percent of consumer spending on food for at-home consumption, hardly enough to allow it to set food prices nationally. The suit made no claims regarding A&P's pricing power in particular cities, in some of which it held 15–20 percent of the grocery market; the government's economic analysis did not go into such detail.

A&P's profits in 1948 came to 1.3 percent of sales—more than during the war years, to be sure, but far below the 2.1 percent average of the 1930s or the 2.7 percent average of the 1920s. Its diminished profits made clear that A&P was not behaving like a monopoly, controlling supply to drive up prices. Far from it: vertical integration and the replacement of smaller stores with supermarkets were holding costs and retail prices down. McGrath trotted out the familiar argument about cross subsidies, contending that shoppers at some A&P stores were being forced to pay extra-high prices to subsidize losses at other A&P stores. Why those supposed victims would willingly pay high prices rather than shopping around he did not explain. In a similar vein, Bergson contended that suppliers charged higher prices to other grocers to make up for "the losses they have sustained through doing business with A&P." Why would suppliers have sold to A&P at a loss? How, unless the suppliers themselves held monopoly power, would they have been able to force other grocers to pay more because A&P paid less? The government's files reveal no economic analysis of such questions.[16]

A&P's reaction to the lawsuit was virulent. "The whole basis of this attack is the fact that we sold good food too cheap," an anonymous A&P spokesman—presumably Carl Byoir—proclaimed the day the suit was filed. Byoir arranged for A&P to buy advertisements in every one of the country's two thousand daily newspapers and in another five hundred weeklies to tell its side of the story. In response, McGrath and Bergson mounted national speaking tours. "If a businessman outsells his competitors because he has unreasonably restrained trade, he has fought unfairly," McGrath asserted in Cincinnati. The government is "not going berserk in the china shop of American business," Bergson told the American Retail Federation, shortly after issuing a statement condemning A&P's "false and misleading advertising." A&P countered with still more advertisements, spending $5 million, one-seventh of its after-tax profits for 1949, in the space of three months. Its most memorable entry featured a photograph of the Empire State Building with the caption: "It's Far Too Big. It Ought to be Seven Buildings."[17]

Independent grocers and wholesalers were told to ignore A&P's advertising, lest their responses give A&P yet more opportunities to push its case, but the controversy mushroomed nonetheless. The National Federation of Independent Business launched a newspaper and radio campaign in support of the government's case. "Americans have always fought oppressing!" the ads proclaimed. "In 1899, 1917, and 1941, Americans have fought and died to try and insure a fair deal for everybody. And often, the oppressors had big, powerful and loud propaganda organizations, but Americans have never been swayed by propaganda." Patman made daily speeches castigating A&P, using his congressional mailing privilege to send out thousands of copies of each speech at government expense. The American Trucking Association condemned the suit on the ground that it would cause "severe curtailment" of its members' business. Even the anti-chain Bureau of Education on Fair Trade, an arm of the National Association of Retail Druggists, took a shot at the antitrust division, claiming that it showed "colossal inconsistency" with respect to below-cost selling.[18]

Some twenty-nine hundred letters, overwhelmingly opposed to the lawsuit, poured in to the Justice Department in the fall of 1949. "The A&P was the best concern we ever sold to in all our business career," wrote the former proprietor of the Richmond Pickling Company in Virginia, recounting how A&P's chemists discovered that his company had left out the celery seed from three hundred cases of pickles and rightly forced it to correct its error. "Their desire for quality and their demand for honest business practices mark them as a company, not to be broken up or looked upon in disfavor, but, rather, to be admired and respected," asserted a Maryland crab packer. Sensitive to the public relations implications, Bergson or his deputies responded to every letter. In congressional testimony, Bergson accused the company of receiving "discriminatory rebates" that would be disclosed as the civil suit proceeded. But A&P's quick response had won public opinion to its side. A Gallup poll in November showed that two-thirds of voters questioned had heard about the A&P case—and that almost twice as many sided with the company as with the government.[19]

A&P filed its reply to the suit in April 1950. "By its very nature this industry is one in which monopoly is impossible," its brief asserted. Another advertising campaign followed. Citing a letter in which Judge Lindley wrote, "I have not made a finding which could be the basis for a suit of dissolution," full-page newspaper advertisements accused the government of wanting to put A&P out of business. Again, the company succeeded in drawing a large public response. The Justice Department's archived records include four large cartons of letters concerning the civil case against A&P, many of them handwritten. "Dear Sir," a Massachusetts woman wrote to Attorney General McGrath, "I am dropping you a line to see if you will try and help us housewives save our A.&P. stores. We surely could not make our money go so far in small stores and will cause hardship on large familys." Concurred a Tennessee man in a handwritten letter to Harry Truman, "If it were not for big chains like the A&P my family could not eat as well as we do." In Texas, A&P store clerks pleaded with Sam Rayburn to help save their jobs. The manager of the A&P in Paris, Texas, sought help from Patman, who responded: "I would like to see you own the store instead of two childless brothers in New York."[20]

In September 1950, Herbert Bergson resigned his position as head of the antitrust division to pursue a better-paying career in private practice. His post was left vacant until January. With its chief antitrust enforcer gone and the political tides running in A&P's favor, the Truman administration sat on its hands. No trial was scheduled.[21]

Meanwhile, the A&P public relations machine continued to operate in high gear. The Hartford brothers granted an unprecedented five-hour interview to *Time*, arguably the nation's most influential magazine, with which Carl Byoir had close connections. John Hartford visited an

A&P store with a researcher and a writer from *Time*, lamenting the high cost of radishes, and raked leaves with them at Buena Vista Farms. The result was a cover story humanizing the brothers and warning that the breakup of A&P would drive up the price of food. "I don't know any grocer or anybody else who wants to stay small," John Hartford told the magazine. "They all dream about building something bigger. The whole country's growing—our cities, schools, labor unions, everything. I don't see how any businessman can limit his growth and stay healthy." In his annual year-end statement, John pointed out that Americans were eating more and better food than ever before. A few months later, John received even more gushing attention in *Coronet* magazine, which devoted a five-page article to the folksy philosophy of "the enlightened head—and heart—of the world's largest grocery chain." If it was going to press its case, the government would evidently need to show the public why it was persecuting two nice old men.[22]

Delay worked in A&P's favor. In January 1951, an influential study group headed by the former dean of Harvard Law School suggested repealing the Robinson-Patman Act. Four months later, the U.S. Supreme Court dealt a devastating blow to state "fair trade" laws, holding that retailers could not be compelled to sell above minimum prices set by manufacturers unless they had signed contracts agreeing to do so. The decision opened the door to a new type of enterprise—discount retailing.[23]

21
THE FALL

On September 20, 1951, following a board meeting of the Chrysler Corporation, John A. Hartford collapsed with a heart attack in an elevator in the Chrysler Building in New York. He was not immediately identified, because he had left his wallet in his office, a block away. A physician declared him dead on the scene. His funeral, at Buena Vista Farms, drew four hundred mourners, so many that some had to listen through loudspeakers set up on his private golf course. With John's death, A&P lost its most visible leader and the man most responsible for navigating the company through changing markets and political headwinds. Even after substantial gifts to the John A. Hartford Foundation during his lifetime, John's assets were valued at $55.6 million—the equivalent of half a billion dollars in 2011. Almost everything, including the mansion, was left to the foundation, a charity he had set up in 1929 but had never taken an active role in running.[1]

John was seventy-nine years old at his death. He and George had made careful preparations for succession. They had named David T. Bofinger executive vice president in 1947, and had put him in charge of the grocery business in February 1949. Bofinger, sixty-three, had joined A&P as an office boy in 1899, and had run the vital purchasing operation for three decades. His post as president cast him in a public role for the first time. In December 1949, the Senate Agriculture Committee asked him to testify on the price of coffee, and threatened him with a subpoena when he requested a delay. Two weeks later, Bofinger died of a heart attack at a company banquet, leaving the succession plan in tatters.[2]

The brothers' second choice was an executive unknown outside the company, Ralph W. Burger. Burger, then sixty, was also an A&P lifer.

His father had worked for A&P at the turn of the century, and Ralph had joined in 1911, working as a part-time store clerk and then helping on a horse-drawn wagon. In 1912 he had moved to the Jersey City office as a bookkeeper, working directly with George L. and John Hartford, and had later become the corporate secretary. Since 1927, when headquarters moved to the Graybar Building, his office had been between George's and John's on the twenty-second floor, literally putting him in the middle of every major decision. He had never run a store or a factory, purchased an advertisement, or negotiated with a supplier. Like the Hartford brothers, he was childless. In the late 1940s, after Pauline Hartford's death, Burger and his wife spent most weekends with John Hartford at Buena Vista Farms, frequently accompanying him to visit stores. As a longtime executive said of Burger in 1945, "The average person at headquarters looks upon him as an assistant to Mr. John Hartford."[3]

John Hartford's death left Burger in an entirely unaccustomed position. Long a backstairs operator, he was now head of the fourth-largest business enterprise in the United States, ranked by sales. George L. Hartford was still chairman of the board and came to the office daily, but at age eighty-six he wanted no management responsibilities. A&P was Ralph Burger's to run, but he had to run it without John Hartford's vision to aid him. Burger had another job as well. John Hartford's will directed that he become president of the John A. Hartford Foundation. John had convinced Burger to take on the position, but Burger had refused the proposed $25,000 salary. Instead, the two had agreed on a fee of one carnation per day—often, a red carnation, of a strain developed and worn by John Hartford.

Burger's priority was to end the quarter century of conflict between the government and A&P. The 1949 antitrust suit still threatened A&P's breakup. Truman's latest antitrust chief, H. Graham Morison, seemed sympathetic to the company, as he criticized state laws restricting price discounting and called for repeal of the Robinson-Patman Act. But scandals enveloped the Justice Department in the autumn of 1951, and Attorney General J. Howard McGrath's resignation in April 1952 was followed by Morison's departure at the end of June. Settlement of the lawsuit had to await the inauguration of Dwight Eisenhower in January 1953 as the first Republican president in thirty years. A deal was struck late that year: A&P would close down the Atlantic Commission Company, its controversial produce brokerage, but the government would abandon its other demands to break the company apart. For the first time since the 1920s, A&P could do business without Washington watching over its every move.[4]

The company Ralph Burger took over was a dominant force in American retailing. A&P's balance sheet was extraordinarily solid, thanks to George Hartford's aversion to debt. Its market share had rebounded from wartime lows: in 1951, A&P accounted for 12 percent of all sales at U.S. grocery stores. It operated in forty of the forty-eight states, making it the only grocer with a national footprint. Sears, Roebuck & Co. was the only retailer in the United States with even half its sales (Table 4). A&P was still, by a very wide margin, the largest retailer in the world. Although price controls and an excess-profits tax enacted in response to the Korean War decimated profits, they also meant that A&P faced few competitive threats to its position.[5]

When wartime controls ended in 1953, though, all bets were off. With steel for construction available once again, food chains raced to the suburbs with bigger, fancier stores, building more supermarkets in 1953 than in any year since 1940. Those new stores, on average, were twice the size of the stores built in the late 1940s, and frequently featured

TABLE 4: LARGEST U.S. RETAILERS, 1951

Company	*Sector*	*Sales ($ million)*
Great Atlantic & Pacific	Grocery	$3,393
Sears, Roebuck	Department	$2,757
Safeway	Grocery	$1,455
Montgomery Ward	Department	$1,106
J. C. Penney	Department	$1,035
Kroger Grocery and Baking	Grocery	$997
F. W. Woolworth	Variety	$684
American Stores	Grocery	$521
Federated Department Stores	Department	$389
First National Stores	Grocery	$372

Source: Company reports. Fiscal years vary.

two amenities unknown a few years earlier—air-conditioning and regular evening hours. The cost of building a supermarket was three or four times what it had been in 1948, putting new construction beyond the reach of many independent grocers. In 1954, Congress changed federal tax law to provide generous tax benefits for owners of new retail buildings, further stimulating construction of suburban shopping centers with supermarkets. America's new way of selling food attracted worldwide attention: when Britain's Queen Elizabeth visited Washington, D.C., in October 1957, she requested her State Department hosts to arrange for her to visit a supermarket.[6]

As supermarkets surged, mom-and-pop grocers were roadkill. In 1948, the retail census had recorded 504,439 food stores in the United States, including many small stores bought or started by ex-servicemen using low-cost government loans. The store count had dropped nearly one-fourth by 1954, despite robust population growth, and another 30,000 food stores disappeared between 1954 and 1958. Independent stores still held two-thirds of all grocery sales, but most of the thriving independent stores were supermarkets whose owners had ascended into the upper middle class, with homes of their own, 1.7 cars, kids in college, and an average income six times that of all Americans. Although the vast majority of food stores had three or fewer paid employees, those traditional grocery stores, collectively, sold only one-fifth of the nation's food. One-third of all food was purchased at stores with thirty or more employees and sales exceeding $1 million. The world Wright Patman feared had come to pass: in food retailing, there was almost no way an ambitious young man could go into business for himself and hope to make a living.[7]

Yet even as the grocery chains triumphed, the world was beginning to turn away from A&P. The 1950s were California's golden years. The state's population grew by half as it added 5.1 million residents. A&P, though, had only a modest presence in Los Angeles, and no stores at all in most other California cities. The Los Angeles stores were an afterthought, managed as part of the Eastern Division, based in New York. There were no high-ranking executives located in the Golden State, and no one in A&P's executive ranks pushed hard to expand there. A&P, led entirely by men who had spent their entire careers east of the Mississippi, chose not to invest in the state that would have the nation's fastest population growth in each decade through the end of the twentieth century.[8]

In those places where it was expanding, A&P's fiscal orthodoxy began to have dire consequences. Burger had inherited the financial views of George L. Hartford, who preferred to avoid owning real estate and rarely agreed to long-term leases. This caution had saved the company during the Great Depression, but it was disastrous in an era when developers were building new shopping centers designed around the needs of specific tenants. A&P was locked out of the most modern structures in the best locations, because its competitors would sign long-term leases while A&P would not. Its new supermarkets were disproportionately located in older buildings in the urban neighborhoods that upwardly mobile households were starting to flee, not along the highways where affluent suburban housewives went to shop.[9]

Nor did A&P push to broaden its product line. Other supermarket operators in the 1950s dedicated space in their large new stores to nonfood items, from pots and pans to ready-to-wear clothing, which typically offered much wider profit margins than food. By 1959, the average supermarket carried fifty-eight hundred items, some two thousand more than at the start of the decade. A&P resisted the trend. Its stores did not even carry toothpaste and shaving cream until it undertook a cautious test of one hundred items in the autumn of 1951—by which time 85 percent of supermarkets were selling nonprescription drugs and toiletries. A brief trial of magazines and comic books, which other supermarkets sold profitably, was discontinued in 1954. "We have always considered ourselves food merchants," Ralph Burger told a reporter. That attitude, reflecting the inbred nature of A&P's top management, would strand the company on the wrong side of economic change. In 1951, when Burger took charge, more than 21 percent of consumer spending bought food and alcoholic beverages for at-home use. A decade later, food and drink for at-home consumption captured barely 17 percent of the consumer's dollar as rising incomes gave Americans the money to spend on cars, clothes, and household goods—things A&P did not sell.[10]

A&P's conservatism brought disaster. While its largest competitors were adding popular product lines to big stores in the best locations in fast-growing parts of the country, A&P voluntarily confined itself to its traditional line of business in places it had operated for decades. No longer was there a voice in the executive suite insistently pushing the company to change with the times.

Of all of A&P's strategic missteps in the 1950s, perhaps the most serious was forgetting John Hartford's dictum that volume was the key to growth. Gaining market share by discounting should have been easier than ever, because the spread of large retail outlets was turning public opinion against anti-discounting laws. Only fourteen states had chain-store taxes by the middle of 1953, down from twenty-nine states in the late 1930s, as legislatures repealed their laws or state courts voided them. A New Jersey court threw out a state law allowing only pharmacies to sell aspirin and cough syrup in 1953, and in early 1955 courts in Georgia, Arkansas, and Nebraska annulled those states' laws letting manufacturers fix retail prices. Two months later, a federal antitrust advisory committee condemned such laws. "It seems evident that the absence of competitive pricing under 'fair trade' results in higher pricing for the consumer," said Eisenhower's attorney general, Herbert Brownell, recognizing a trade-off that the Roosevelt and Truman administrations had been unwilling to acknowledge.[11]

Such powerful assertions of consumers' interests freed A&P to slash its margins without political repercussions for the first time in thirty years—but it did no such thing. Instead, perhaps chastened by decades of legal battles over pricing, Burger seems to have backed away from John Hartford's insistence on being the lowest-price grocer in any local market. Although A&P still had the slimmest profit margin among the ten largest food chains, its margins edged wider, irreparably damaging A&P's cherished position as the price leader—with precisely the disastrous consequences of which John Hartford had frequently warned. From 1950 to 1960, while A&P's sales were rising 65 percent, each of its four top competitors saw sales growth above 200 percent. A&P's customers began defecting in droves.

George L. Hartford commuted almost daily to the Graybar Building until 1955, when he was ninety years old. Two years later, on September 23, 1957, he died in the New Jersey house where he had lived since 1908. He was buried in the family mausoleum in Orange, accompanied to the grave by an honor guard of longtime A&P executives. His entire estate, including one-fifth of A&P's shares, was willed to the John A. Hartford Foundation, instantly making it one of the largest charitable foundations in America.[12]

Mr. George's death was the end of an era. Under the arrangements made by his father in 1915, the George H. Hartford Trust was dissolved upon the death of his last surviving son. Forty percent of the shares, representing the ownership stakes of George L. and John, were turned over to the John A. Hartford Foundation. The remainder was divided among the two children of Edward V. Hartford, the two children of Marie Louise Hartford Hoffman, and the six grandchildren of Minnie Hartford Clews Reilly. Ralph Burger, not a family member, owned little stock, but he held a position of strength nonetheless. He was the boss of the thirteen other members of A&P's board of directors, whose total service to the company came to more than six hundred years, and as president of the John A. Hartford Foundation he had sole power to vote 40 percent of the company's shares.[13]

The ten Hartford heirs who held the other 60 percent had few sentimental ties to the company run for so long by their uncles and granduncles. Just one worked for A&P, as did the spouse of another. The others knew little about the performance of the firm whose shares they had just been given. Around the time of John Hartford's death, seven of the heirs had signed a legal agreement to pool their voting power as soon as they received it. Collectively, though, these seven descendants of George H. Hartford controlled only 40 percent of the shares. The balance of power rested with Rachel Carpenter, a granddaughter of Minnie Hartford Clews Reilly, and Edward Hartford's daughter, Josephine Hartford Bryce, a noted philanthropist and sportswoman. Each of the women had 10 percent of the votes. Josephine Bryce sat with Burger on the board of the John A. Hartford Foundation and was thought to be friendly with the chief executive. With her support, Burger was in a position to maintain control.

In anticipation of a public stock sale, the price of the company's nonvoting common stock, mainly held by employees, rose from $175 in October 1957 to $485 in November 1958. That month, fourteen months after George Hartford's death, A&P announced two major changes. Six outsiders were appointed directors—the first non-employees ever to sit on A&P's board. At the same time, the company was reorganized. Preferred stock and nonvoting common shares were exchanged for common stock with voting rights, putting 18 percent of the shares in the hands of some twelve thousand people unrelated to the Hartfords. The shares were listed on the New York Stock Exchange, giving family members and the John A. Hartford Foundation a way to sell. Huntington Hartford and his cousin Marie Hartford Robertson each put 900,000 shares on the market almost immediately, allowing outside investors to acquire a further 8 percent of A&P. That sale, at $44.50 per share, placed a market value of $1 billion on the entire corporation.[14]

There may never have been a major company so ill suited to public share ownership. A&P was still extraordinarily secretive, as it had been under George L. and John A. Hartford and under their father before them. When researchers from the government's Bureau of Labor Statistics came to check prices for the monthly consumer price index, A&P sent them away. When the National Labor Relations Board sought to interview supervisors to resolve union complaints, A&P refused. A&P, unlike its competitors, declined to provide data on sales of individual items to A. C. Nielsen, the market-research service; it alone saw proprietary value in its internal information—an attitude that would be emulated half a century later by Walmart. Unlike other retailers with publicly traded shares, which published their financial results once a quarter, A&P released its financials only once a year and omitted information routine in other retailers' reports, such as the cost of goods sold.[15]

The public listing of A&P's shares subjected A&P to attack from shareholders and investment analysts, two unfamiliar sources of criticism. News articles drawing on information from unhappy family members highlighted A&P's conservatism, pointing out the embarrassing fact that the giant company still operated several door-to-door truck routes first served with horse-drawn wagons in the nineteenth century. Analysts noted that A&P's sales were growing far more slowly than those of most other chains, and more slowly even than those of independent grocers. When a stockholder asked at the first public shareholders' meeting in December 1958 why A&P did not increase its profits, the chairman and president could offer only a strained explanation: "The company does not believe in profiteering on food." It was only in January 1959, in his eighth year of leading one of the largest companies in America, that Burger finally granted his first interview to the press.[16]

The speed of A&P's decline was shocking. At the start of 1961, it was still the largest retailer in the world, with 4,351 stores selling an average of $1.2 million of groceries. Its profits in 1960, up 13 percent on the previous year, hit a record as a growing economy helped A&P achieve the highest sales in its history. Yet signs of rot were everywhere.

John A. Hartford had always kept an eagle eye on A&P's gross profit—the difference between the amount it paid for goods and the amount it received by selling them. In the years before the 1925 reorganization and again in the early 1930s, when the company refused to cut wages despite falling grocery prices, gross profit had been over 20 percent of sales. For John, a high gross profit was a warning, a signal that the company was failing to hold down operating costs. Between 1933 and 1941, his constant push to make A&P more efficient had driven gross profit down from 22 percent to 13 percent of sales, creating huge savings for A&P's customers and bringing in throngs of shoppers. In the 1950s, after John's death, gross profit began to creep higher, year after year. Gross profit was rising across the industry, but the rise at A&P was especially steep. In 1960, A&P resumed handing out trading stamps for the first time in decades, and that alone raised costs by around 2 percent of sales at the stores where stamps were given. In 1968, gross profit would top 20 percent for the first time since 1934. Its wide margins meant that A&P was no longer delivering bargains to shoppers, and shoppers responded, as John Hartford always feared they would, by taking their patronage elsewhere.[17]

At the store level, higher prices meant lower volume; dollar sales at the average A&P store would not exceed the 1960 level until 1969, and the company's total grocery tonnage would be lower in 1970 than it had been in 1952. Inventories were rising rapidly, a sure sign of poor management; by 1964, A&P's inventories, relative to sales, would be the highest since 1947. While A&P still had hundreds of small urban stores with minimal parking and few amenities, shoppers were flocking to bigger, newer stores, often featuring clothing, toys, small appliances, and phonograph records along with food. By 1961, discount stores collected around 2 percent of all grocery-store sales, selling food slightly cheaper than supermarkets and personal-care products at much larger discounts. A&P couldn't decide whether to embrace the discount-store concept or run from it. In early 1960, Burger declared that the average housewife, possessing a bigger refrigerator and more cabinet space than ever before, was buying so much food on each supermarket visit that she did not want to shop for anything else. A year later, reversing course, A&P discussed joint ventures with a discount operator and a drug chain. Then it opened its own nonfood discount store in Pennsylvania as a test—only to close it two years later. The company had lost its way.[18]

Many poor decisions in the early 1960s sped A&P's downfall, but one factor stands out: A&P paid generous dividends. From the time of its public share listing in late 1958, shareholders both inside and outside the family called for dividend increases. The John A. Hartford Foundation was A&P's largest shareholder, and it is here that the dual role of Ralph Burger, serving as head of both A&P and the foundation, was problematic: high dividends may have been in the foundation's interest even if they damaged the company's long-run prospects. In the year ending February 1961, nearly half of A&P's earnings went for dividends. In 1962 and 1963 the payout topped 70 percent.[19]

High dividends, alongside construction of a huge cannery, a new bakery, and the company's first dairy, starved A&P's stores of investment. The investment needs at store level were immense: the average supermarket, a thirty-six-hundred-square-foot space with eleven employees in 1951, grew to a fifteen-thousand-square-foot establishment with forty-five employees in 1961, so even stores built within the previous decade were badly outmoded. A&P lacked the funds to replace them. The number of new stores it built each year was around 4 percent of its total store count, meaning that on average a supermarket would be replaced after twenty-five years—not rapidly enough to keep the stores up-to-date at a time of great change in the way Americans shopped for food. A&P's aging store base drove customers away. In Cleveland, where A&P had operated since the early 1880s, A&P's grocery market share plummeted from 22 percent in 1960 to 15 percent in 1965, and market research showed that A&P was not among the four chains most favored by high-income households. Shareholder meetings featured complaints about dingy stores and wilted produce, and comments about A&P's poor maintenance began to appear in the press.[20]

The outside directors recognized that things were not going well, and they began to push for new management. In January 1963, the seventy-three-year-old Burger announced he would resign as president while staying on as chairman. As his successor, he proposed John Ehrgott, the company's vice president and treasurer. Ehrgott, then sixty-seven, had been employed by A&P for forty-six years, since the era of the Economy Store. As corporate controller, he had worked closely with the Hartfords and Ralph Burger for decades. Like Burger, he had never managed a store, run a manufacturing plant, or overseen a warehouse. He was a numbers man. The reaction by A&P's board was rare in the annals of American capitalism. All fourteen A&P executives serving on the board voted in favor of Ehrgott's promotion. All six outside directors voted no. After the board meeting, the six issued a most unusual statement urging the promotion of "younger executives."[21]

Dissident directors forced Burger to surrender the chairman's job to Ehrgott later in 1963, but the change did not stanch the flow of bad news. In 1963, when almost all of its competitors saw sales gains, A&P's sales fell 2 percent, despite the addition of forty supermarkets. Profits per store declined 5 percent. Earnings per share were off 3 percent. When the full-year totals were in, sales at Sears, Roebuck, the department-store chain and mail-order house, exceeded those at A&P. After a forty-three-year run, the Great Atlantic & Pacific was no longer the largest retailer in the world.

A&P, its executive ranks filled with men who had joined the company back when Henry Ford was making Model Ts, now fell victim to the creative destruction it had once dispensed. It could not adapt to a world in which novelty—new stores, new products, new ways of shopping—was an essential part of the consumer experience, and in which suburbia was where most Americans lived. In 1962, the variety-store operator S. S. Kresge opened its first Kmart discount store, and Dayton's, a Minneapolis department store, inaugurated a discount format called Target. Shoppers crowded department and clothing stores in enclosed malls far from the city centers that were A&P's traditional home. The competition was no longer mom-and-pop stores but flashy new supermarkets, run by companies as tightly managed as A&P. A&P had no counterpunch. Its stores seemed as tired as its brands, like Ann Page and Eight O'Clock Coffee, which stood as emblems of a store where Grandma might once have shopped. A&P no longer had anything special to offer.

As Ehrgott was taking charge, Huntington Hartford, George and John's nephew, inaugurated his Gallery of Modern Art in a curved marble building on New York's Columbus Circle, at the edge of Central Park. The gallery was Huntington's dream, a place where connoisseurs could experience non-abstract paintings, many of them owned by Hartford himself, for a $1 admission fee. His enthusiasm was not widely shared. After the *New York Times* architecture critic Ada Louise Huxtable called it "a die-cut Venetian palazzo on lollipops," the structure was universally derided as the "lollipop building." Few art lovers came, leaving an operating deficit of $580,000 per year plus $320,000 in annual interest and amortization payments. Unable to dispose of the gallery, Hartford sold most of his remaining A&P stock in June 1966 to cover the costs. He used the small stake that was left to launch public attacks on the company, holding press conferences and writing articles to denounce Ralph Burger for using the John A. Hartford Foundation to exercise control.[22]

Investors abandoned the company that only a few years earlier had been a glamour stock. In 1961, A&P's stock had traded at $70.50 per share. In mid-1964, despite a 20 percent rise in U.S. share prices overall, A&P's stock sagged to $34.50. In his first-ever newspaper interview, Ehrgott shrugged off investment analysts who called for A&P to raise prices, reaffirming the basic strategy of selling food as cheaply as possible. "I don't think we will ever change that," Ehrgott said. But A&P's disastrous performance brought vultures swarming. In July 1968, a group headed by Nathan Cummings, the retired chairman of Consolidated Foods Corporation, offered the Hartford Foundation $284 million for its one-third stake in A&P. The offer was rejected. Four months later, a computer-leasing company, Data Processing Financial & General Corporation, proposed to buy the foundation's holding for $330 million, but that bid, too, was turned down. Burger, although seriously ill, remained in charge of the foundation until his death in 1969, and he was not ready to turn its huge stake in the Great Atlantic & Pacific over to outsiders. In 1973, after A&P omitted its dividend for the first time ever and its share price fell below $17, Gulf & Western Corporation, a conglomerate, offered $20 per share for 19 percent of A&P's stock, but A&P's lawyers blocked the offer in court.[23]

The foundation's failure to sell its shares promptly would prove a tragic mistake. In 1959, after receiving the proceeds of George L. Hartford's estate, the John A. Hartford Foundation was the fourth-largest foundation in the United States. The Hartford brothers having directed only that they "strive always to do the greatest good for the greatest number," the foundation's trustees decided to focus on bringing medical research findings into clinical use, and the foundation became a major source of funding for research into arteriosclerosis, diabetes, and other ailments. But under Burger's leadership and after his death, the trustees imprudently failed to diversify their assets, which consisted almost entirely of 8.4 million shares of A&P common stock. As the company's shares spiraled downward, the foundation had less money to dispense; after making more than 270 grants per year in the late 1960s, it was able to finance only a handful of new projects in 1973. By May 1976, when the foundation sold 1.75 million of its shares to the public, it received $12.50 per share, one-sixth of what they had been worth at the peak.[24]

In the fall of 1978, the foundation's trustees finally decided that the game was up. The investment banker they hired to peddle their shares found Tengelmann, a German grocer that was eager to expand in America, and that did not understand how far A&P had fallen. Tengelmann bought effective control in February 1979 by acquiring 42 percent of A&P's stock. The price set an implied value of a mere $190 million on a company that had been worth $1 billion twenty years earlier. After fending off decades of government efforts to destroy it, A&P had all but destroyed itself.[25]

22
THE LEGACY

In their wildest dreams, George and John Hartford could not have imagined the palatial supermarket their company would come to own on the Upper East Side of Manhattan. Over two levels stretching the length of an entire block, shoppers could browse among hand-dipped chocolates and organic shade-grown coffees, have veal chops cut to order at the butcher counter, and select perfectly shaped nectarines grown half a world away. But in 2009, when the Great Atlantic & Pacific Tea Company celebrated what it claimed to be its 150th anniversary, A&P's Food Emporium was not in on the party. Almost nothing in the store, from the labels on the store-brand canned goods to the receipts handed out at the cash register, mentioned the connection with the world's oldest grocery chain.

The omission was no accident. Long before 2009, the A&P name had lost its luster. The firm that had been the world's largest retailer for more than four decades, the first company to sell groceries from coast to coast, the powerhouse whose every move sparked fear in competitors across the United States and Canada, had shrunk to be a modest regional operator. The warehouse and bakeries had been closed, the Canadian stores sold off, the Eight O'Clock Coffee brand dealt to a private equity fund. The Great Atlantic & Pacific reached no closer to the Pacific than Philadelphia. Most of its remaining stores did not even bear the company's banner. A&P, which had thrived on competition in its first century, was driven into bankruptcy by competition in its second.[1]

Competition is the lifeblood of a prosperous economy. At the level of the individual firm, competition forces managers to find more efficient ways of doing business, motivates entrepreneurs to come up with new products to sell, and encourages shareholders and corporate boards to get rid of underperforming executives. For the economy as a whole, such changes result in higher productivity as firms use fewer inputs of labor, capital, and natural resources to produce each unit of output. Such productivity gains are the way living standards improve as a society becomes wealthier. Competition has another benefit as well: it helps economies change and adapt. Competition is certainly no prerequisite for economic growth; many countries in which competitive forces are weak have grown at impressive rates. Sooner or later, however, such economies tend to stumble, because they lack the ability to renew themselves in the face of altered technology, demography, environmental conditions, and resources. Where competition is intense, on the other hand, renewal is continuous, because firms that cannot adapt quickly enough to change are driven from the market.

Competition is often conflated with capitalism, but they are not at all the same. Capitalism involves private ownership of the means of production and distribution, but the word implies nothing about the way in which privately owned firms do business. Capitalism is perfectly compatible with a society in which a powerful state doles out favors to private monopolies, protects some enterprises from others, or even sets the prices privately owned firms may charge for their products. Indeed, while capitalists tend to praise the virtues of competition, many of them would just as soon avoid it. Wright Patman, the Hartfords' longtime nemesis, was not unusual in embracing capitalism while distrusting competition. Many business owners trying to earn a profit and workers eager to hold on to their jobs shared his views. While they were all for private enterprise, they understood that term to encompass small firms run by people such as themselves, who were putting their net worth at risk every time they opened for business. They saw large corporations based in distant places as predators that, if left unchecked, would drive true capitalists out of business.

Through the first half of the twentieth century, George L. and John A. Hartford stood at the center of a conflict between competition and capitalism that raged all across America. That they themselves were capitalists, there is no doubt; their company had used the slogan "An organization of capitalists for the distribution of teas and coffees at one small profit" as early as 1863. Yet they, like their father before them, were also fervent believers in no-holds-barred competition. Their competitive passion distinguished them not only from the millions of men and women who were satisfied to eke out a small profit from a single tiny store but also from the industrialists and railroad executives who routinely agreed with their competitors to fix prices or simply bought them out to the same effect. Other leading grocery-store operators often bought up small chains to consolidate the market in one city or another and sometimes exchanged properties to avoid competing head-to-head. So far as is known, the Hartfords did neither: George L. Hartford was loath to take on other companies' problems and obligations. Nor is there evidence that the Hartfords joined cartel arrangements to fix prices until, under the New Deal, the U.S. government effectively told them to do so. Price-fixing was not in their DNA.[2]

A&P's century-long record of growth was due not to mergers or cartels but to astute management. John Hartford's success in putting others' innovative ideas to use in the stodgy field of food retailing dovetailed with his brother's insistence that the company maintain a solid financial footing. But in a country that took competition for granted, the Hartfords' sharp competitive elbows ultimately got them into trouble. As A&P flourished, America's understanding of itself as a free-market economy came into conflict with an equally potent myth, one that places small business at the core of a democratic society.

Small business, in the public dialogue, is venerated as the wellspring of innovation and economic dynamism, the boundless source of job creation, and a bulwark against the overwhelming power of large institutions. Entrepreneurs who built giant businesses out of sweat and smart ideas, from Thomas Edison to Bill Gates, are important cultural icons, and the venture capitalists who back start-up companies are heroes in their own right. As Attorney General J. Howard McGrath asserted in 1950, "The continued existence of healthy independent business enterprises is essential to a democratic society."[3]

To portray entrepreneurship as the engine of economic dynamism and innovation is to paint an imagined landscape. Most small businesses neither grow nor innovate. Like Walter and Bertha Abbott's Little Corner Store, they provide livelihoods and, in many cases, a degree of financial independence to the proprietor. To the extent that they are located in small towns with few other sources of economic activity, they provide customers for local merchants, lawyers, and insurance agents.

But undercapitalized small businesses, wholly reliant on the proprietors' abilities, have no economic magic. The magic comes from the relative handful of enterprises, whether small or large, that grow by introducing successful products, finding new ways of doing business, and putting new technologies to use. It is these changes that bring higher productivity, the bedrock of higher living standards.[4]

The Hartfords performed such magic in ways that seem, at first blush, quite unremarkable. George L. Hartford was in no sense an innovator; had he been running the company on his own, he would have been happy with higher profits, slower expansion, and a traditional approach to food retailing. George's insistent focus on detailed operating data from every store, warehouse, and factory was critical to controlling expenses, but it would not have enabled A&P to stand out from the retail crowd. Fortunately for their company, his brother and partner, John, had an extraordinary talent for latching on to new ideas and applying them to the grocery trade. This was no modest accomplishment. A corner store's method of displaying canned goods was of no interest; to be useful to A&P, ideas had to be replicable, so they could be employed in dozens of warehouses or thousands of stores. Just as Henry Ford standardized auto production, the brothers pushed to standardize stores and later bakeries to minimize the amount of capital investment per dollar of sales. They used their size to demand, and often win, price discounts from suppliers. They cut out middlemen simply by refusing to deal with them or pay their commissions. They integrated vertically by using their vast retail network to assemble a steady flow of orders for their factories, avoiding the ups and downs that played havoc with manufacturers' production schedules. These practices, unexceptional in the twenty-first century, brought opprobrium and political and legal retaliation in the twentieth—instigated by small businesses that summoned the power of the state to protect them from competition.

In truth, the abuse of market power by big business is a perpetual problem in a capitalist economy. Businesses engage in bare-knuckle conduct on a daily basis, whether by forming cartels, monopolizing access to critical inputs, or forcing customers to buy unwanted products in order to obtain the ones they really desire. The line between aggressive competition and anticompetitive behavior can be a thin one; a company that demands a sharp price cut from a supplier, to take one example, may be promoting competition if it is one of many potential purchasers of that supplier's products but quashing competition if the supplier has few other markets. Given that businesses have strong incentives to find ways to keep input costs low and the prices they charge customers high, there is no alternative to legal oversight: in a market economy, maintaining competition is a basic governmental responsibility.

In the chain-store wars, though, the federal government and many states intervened not to promote competition but to crush it. Their interest was not in encouraging low retail prices to the benefit of consumers, but precisely the opposite: they wanted to keep prices high so that an inefficient distribution system could survive. The competition enforcers were sheep in wolves' clothing, pretending to be tough on big business to benefit the common man while in fact forcing the common man to pay more than necessary for his groceries in order to keep small businesses rolling in profit.

What is striking about the decades of attacks on A&P is how little economic analysis lay behind the legislation and the lawsuits. In its criminal complaint in 1943 and again in its civil antitrust suit in 1949, the federal government repeatedly raised the prospect that A&P would underprice competing retailers, force them out of business, and then, having established itself as a monopoly, raise prices to consumers. In some areas of the economy, such a concern might have been plausible; had the leading aluminum manufacturer used money-losing prices to force its rivals from the market at a time when high tariffs precluded imports, it might have been able to use its monopoly status to sustain high prices for years or decades. In food retailing, on the other hand, there was little chance that A&P could control the nation's supply of tea or tomatoes, and opening a store was so easy that had A&P succeeded in pushing up prices, new competitors would have appeared overnight. Perhaps the risk of long-lasting market domination would have been higher in a small town where A&P had a crushing market share—but in all its years of investigating A&P, the federal government raised few concerns about anticompetitive conduct at the local level.

The same lack of economic logic pervaded the government's relentless attacks against the Atlantic Commission Company, A&P's produce brokerage. The Justice Department's antitrust division made much of the fact that Atlantic Commission was both a buyer of produce for A&P's stores and a wholesaler selling to grocers that competed with

A&P. In his verdict at the Danville trial, Judge Lindley found that Atlantic Commission had an "inconsistent legal position," charging artificially high prices when acting as a wholesaler to bolster A&P's profits. Had Atlantic Commission dominated the produce market nationally, in any particular location, or in any single commodity, its dual role might in fact have been problematic. In reality, however, Atlantic Commission's share of the nation's wholesale produce sales, by dollar value, never exceeded 12 percent and in most years was under 10 percent. With such a small market share, Atlantic Commission would have been hard-pressed to force other grocers to pay excessive prices for low-quality produce, as the government asserted; any grocer who thought Atlantic Commission was overcharging for apples could have bought apples elsewhere. The government's contention that A&P was such a large buyer of produce that it could manipulate prices was based not on evidence about price patterns in any city or any product but on complaints from growers that it paid less than they wanted, or less on one day than on another. A logically rigorous explanation of how Atlantic Commission's dual role allowed it to overcharge consumers or other grocers is nowhere in the trial testimony or the government's pleadings.[5]

And what of the endless attacks on A&P's vertical integration? According to the federal government's trustbusters as well as the authors of state "fair trade" laws requiring minimum markups, A&P's ownership of factories, warehouses, and transport fleets gave it an unfair advantage: it could accept minimal profits in its stores because of the money it earned from manufacturing and from brokerage and advertising commissions paid by other manufacturers. Here again, though, the unfairness is hard to find when exposed to economic scrutiny. A&P's manufacturing plants earned money because the company learned to use the flow of orders from its stores to run the plants steadily at full capacity, reducing the waste that comes from expensive factory equipment that is not fully utilized. This was a cost advantage that most other food manufacturers did not have. And A&P's strategic use of its own manufacturing and distribution abilities to demand cost reductions from suppliers also squeezed out wasteful practices, such as the payment of commissions to brokers whose services provided no benefit. The economic gains from vertical integration were very real and very large.[6]

The parties injured by A&P's revolutionary approach to the grocery trade, then, were businesses, not consumers—and especially businesses that profited from the inefficiencies the Hartfords systematically sought to wring out of food distribution. The gains to American families from a more efficient food supply chain represented losses to many wholesalers, retailers, and manufacturers that had thrived in the days of relatively isolated local markets but could not survive the changes in transportation, communication, and manufacturing processes that, after World War I, made it feasible to sell groceries on a national scale. The investigations, fair-trade laws, chain-store taxes, and antitrust suits aimed at A&P all served to prolong the lives of businesses that had become obsolete. A&P's antagonists included Republicans as well as Democrats, politicians whose views ranged from socialist to ultraconservative, chambers of commerce as well as organized labor. Support for independent shopkeepers in their battles against Wall Street crossed all political boundaries, and never mind that the Hartfords had nothing to do with Wall Street.

A&P was only the most visible example of government efforts to limit competition in the U.S. economy. Later, especially on the political right, Franklin Roosevelt's New Deal would come to emblemize the heavy hand of government regulation of business, but the A&P story shows such claims to be fallacious: efforts to rein in chain retailers were embraced by the presidential administrations of the Democrat Woodrow Wilson, remembered as a social progressive, and the Republican Calvin Coolidge, recalled as a rock-ribbed conservative, long before the New Deal took root in Washington. While many restrictions to protect small merchants faded away as Americans learned to love discount shopping in the 1950s and 1960s, others remained in place far longer, endorsed by politicians of diverse ideologies, with their purpose hidden from view.

Retailing is far from the only sector in which capitalists have prevailed upon government to limit competition. The United States is unique among major countries in having literally thousands of banks, in good part because a variety of government supports and restraints on competition kept small banks in business: as late as 1990, Illinois limited banks to no more than five offices, so small-town bankers would not have to go head-to-head against their big-city cousins. New-car dealers, often pillars of the local business establishment, exist thanks to state laws that prohibit vehicle manufacturers from selling directly to consumers, thus forcing the manufacturers to sell through independent dealers—a fact conveniently ignored when, in 2009, a political uproar ensued after the bankrupt auto manufacturers General Motors and Chrysler revoked the franchises of dealers they deemed unprofitably small. In most states, brewers, vintners, and distillers may not distribute alcoholic beverages except with the intermediation of a wholesaler; in 2010, alcoholic beverage distributors in Washington beat back a ballot measure that would have devalued their franchises by allowing retailers to purchase wine and beer directly from manufacturers. In Louisiana, prospective florists must pass a licensing exam that makes it hard for newcomers to enter the field, and a similar requirement applies to would-be window glass installers in Connecticut.[7]

By the lights of many twenty-first-century consumers, the Hartfords' achievements may seem anything but praiseworthy. Neither George nor John had the slightest fondness for the family farmer or for local distinctiveness. They played a major role in industrializing and homogenizing the food sector such that prepackaged products with heavy doses of preservatives became standard fare. Their constant demands on suppliers favored large food processors with nationwide scope, destroying the jobs of tens of thousands of bakers, canners, and cheese makers who turned out unique products on a far smaller scale. They achieved unprecedented cost saving in produce distribution, but in so doing adopted standardized varieties shipped long distances from factory farms instead of fresh fruits and vegetables grown nearby. They made food, once the most local of industries, into a sector dominated by huge corporations that respected neither the diversity of nature nor the needs of small communities for which food was a vital part of the economic base.[8]

Chain-store taxes, anti-discounting laws, and laws such as the Robinson-Patman Act, all crafted to keep shoppers from benefiting from the efficiencies created by big businesses, effectively taxed consumers so that small, inefficient wholesalers and retailers could survive. The consumers most affected, inevitably, were the least affluent. During the Great Depression, roughly half the urban families in the United States spent one-third or more of their incomes on food. Various studies undertaken in the late 1920s and early 1930s showed chain grocers'

TABLE 5: NUTRITIVE VALUE OF DIETS OF POOREST THIRD OF URBAN HOUSEHOLDS

	Consumption per person per day				
	Protein (g)	*Calcium* (g)	*Thiamine* (mg)	*Riboflavin* (mg)	*Ascorbic Acid* (mg)
1936	66	0.64	0.79	1.20	58
1942	76	0.86	0.97	1.64	103
1948	86	1.02	1.26	2.07	116
1955	94	1.00	1.42	2.04	94

Source: *Historical Statistics of the United States*, 328.

prices to be 6 to 15 percent below those in independent stores. Forcing up chain grocers' prices to the level of independents' prices created a heavy burden on low-income households, potentially raising their cost of living by 2 to 5 percent.[9]

The spread of supermarkets and the industrialization of food production were good news for families of modest means. They enabled the average American to consume 10 percent more food in 1950 than in 1930, with poorer households showing startling improvements in the quality of their diets (Table 5). American families ate better at far lower cost than ever before, in part because they had to pay much less to move their food from farm to table. The rise of the food chains was especially important to African-Americans. While the Hartford brothers were no more egalitarian with respect to race than most other Americans of their era, a disproportionate number of their stores were in older urban areas occupied by working-class blacks during World War II and the years thereafter, providing reasonable prices to shoppers who otherwise faced extremely high food bills from independent inner-city stores.[10]

Look further, and there are striking parallels between the objections to A&P in the first half of the twentieth century and those raised against Walmart in the twenty-first. Walmart was widely accused of destroying the trade of small-town merchants; similar charges were raised against A&P from 1869 into the 1950s. Walmart's relentless squeeze on suppliers mirrors that attributed to A&P as early as 1915; it was A&P, not Walmart, that pioneered the practice of carefully dissecting manufacturers' costs to determine what prices they should receive for their products. Walmart's paternalistic management methods and vociferous resistance to labor unions had their parallels in A&P's aversion to unions before 1938, when it changed its tune in return for union support in defeating anti-chain legislation. Even the claims that Walmart's insistence on shaving costs led inexorably to the sale of dangerous and unsafe products echoed complaints raised eight decades earlier that A&P kept prices down by selling short weights of chicken and inferior grades of canned goods. Walmart's competitors, like A&P's many years before, sought to slow the retail giant's growth by tapping into public anxieties arising from the disruption of familiar ways, the loss of local uniqueness, the vulnerability to distant economic forces. Even Walmart's astute use of public relations and advertising to overcome opposition to new stores and to counter criticism of its business practices followed in the footsteps of Carl Byoir's efforts on behalf of A&P, starting in 1937.[11]

Together, George L. and John A. Hartford worked at the Great Atlantic & Pacific Tea Company for 144 years. When George L. came to work with his father in 1880, tins of fish were still welded shut one at a time by skilled can makers, baking powders consisted largely of ineffective starches, and soaps and breakfast foods were produced by thousands of tiny firms unknown beyond their hometowns. By the time of his death, in 1957, big businesses dominated everything. A handful of beef and pork processors controlled the meat trade nationwide. Makers of branded foods had consolidated, as had manufacturers of toiletries and housekeeping products, in order to shave warehousing and delivery costs and command better advertising deals from national television networks. The seven biggest retail grocery chains sold one-fourth of all the food in the entire country. Mr. George and Mr. John did as much as anyone to turn the personal routines of local commerce into an impersonal series of anonymous transactions, in which shoppers rarely think of the people who supply their daily needs.

For seven decades, the collective and complementary strengths of George L. and John A. Hartford allowed their company to respond deftly to rapid changes in economic conditions, competitive circumstances, and consumer tastes. But as much as they deserve full credit for A&P's stunning rise and its prolonged ascendancy, they also bear responsibility for its rapid collapse. The values they prized in their managers—experience, loyalty, and adherence to company rules—made for an organization that was highly competent, but not highly adaptable. Again and again, John A. Hartford intervened personally to persuade his reluctant executives to try new ideas. The Economy Store, the installation of meat counters, and the shift to supermarkets all faced foot-dragging by managers who were happy doing things the old way. Yet for all that resistance, John and his brother stood by their men. They recruited new blood into the executive ranks only once, when the belated realization that A&P faced a potentially lethal threat from the anti-chain movement led them to hire John's personal lawyer as chief counsel and to engage Carl Byoir for public relations advice. The company never headhunted executive talent from its competitors, from other retailers, or from other industries. If they thought A&P had anything to learn from outsiders, the brothers were extremely reluctant to say so.

Such inwardness was not toxic so long as John A. Hartford was on hand to steer the ship. He remained vigorous until the day of his death at seventy-nine, constantly challenging his managers to keep up with the demands of a fast-changing country. But with John's death in 1951, the dynamism went out of A&P. He and his brother had failed to cultivate a successor generation of executives who had the broad experience, imagination, and acute cultural antennae to go along with their financial acumen. They left behind a corporate structure under which the new chief executive reported to a board of directors that never challenged his decisions because its members all reported to him. A company that desperately needed new blood and new thinking was put in the charge of leaders more concerned with conserving the past than with shaping the future. From that point on, A&P's downfall was assured. What the anti-chain broadcasters, New Deal code authorities, populist politicians, and ardent trustbusters failed to accomplish in decades of trying, creative destruction took care of quickly.

NOTES

ABBREVIATIONS

AG: *American Grocer*
CHS: Chicago Historical Society
Danville Trial Documents:
  Dx: Defense exhibit
  Gx: Government exhibit
  Tr: Transcript
FDR: Franklin Delano Roosevelt Presidential Library, Hyde Park, N.Y.
  OF: Office Files
  PPF: President's Personal Files
FTC: U.S. Federal Trade Commission
HFF: Hartford Family Foundation Archive
JHSGW: Jewish Historical Society of Greater Washington, Washington, D.C.
JOC: Journal of Commerce
JPMC: J. P. Morgan Chase Archives, New York
KSHS: Kansas State Historical Society, Topeka
LSUS: Louisiana State University at Shreveport Archive
NARA-C: National Archives and Records Administration, Great Lakes Region, Chicago
NARA-CP: National Archives and Records Administration, College Park, Md.
NARA-LA: National Archives and Records Administration, Legislative Archives, Washington, D.C.
NARA-NY: National Archives and Records Administration, Northeast Region, New York
N-YHS: New-York Historical Society
NYMA: New York Municipal Archives
NYPL: New York Public Library
NYT: *New York Times*
SRP: Sam Rayburn Papers, Dolph Briscoe Center, University of Texas, Austin
TSL: Texas State Library and Archives, Austin
WPP: Wright Patman Papers, Lyndon B. Johnson Presidential Library, Austin, Tex.
WSJ: *Wall Street Journal*

1: THE VERDICT

1. "Walter Lindley, U.S. Judge, 77, Dies," *NYT*, January 4, 1958; "Cannon Leaves $500,000 Estate to 2 Daughters," *Chicago Tribune*, January 16, 1927; "16 Candy

Jobbers Are Found Guilty," *NYT*, April 12, 1929; "Landis Is Upheld in Fight on Rule," *NYT*, April 22, 1931; "Impeachment Action Against 2 Judges Fails," *Chicago Tribune*, May 30, 1934; "Proposed for High Court," *NYT*, March 21, 1930; "Judge in G.M. Case Chides High Court," *NYT*, October 26, 1939.

2. "3 Concerns, 3 Persons Assessed as Some Others Are Cleared," *NYT*, December 13, 1940; "Judge in G.M. Case Chides High Court." The case was formally styled *United States v. New York Great Atlantic & Pacific Tea Co.*, 67 F. Supp. 626 (E.D. Ill., September 21, 1946). It is referred to hereafter in these notes as "Danville trial."
3. "Crowd Fills Court to See John Hartford," *Chicago Tribune*, October 24, 1945.
4. Rentz, "Death of 'Grandma,'" MS, 2; John Updike, "A&P," in *Pigeon Feathers and Other Stories* (New York, 1962), 187–96; Davis, *Don't Make A&P Mad*.
5. Opinion, Danville trial, 67 F. Supp. 676, 636.
6. J. C. Furnas, "Mr. George & Mr. John," *Saturday Evening Post*, December 31, 1938; "Red Circle and Gold Leaf," *Time*, November 13, 1950.
7. See, for example, Merle Crowell, "You Don't Have to Be Brilliant," *American Magazine*, February 1931, 20.
8. U.S. Department of Commerce, *Census of Distribution: Kansas City, Missouri*, mimeo, October 25, 1927. The 1930 Census of Retail Distribution counted 481,891 food stores and another 104,089 general stores that sold groceries in 1929, for a total of 585,980 stores whose main business was selling food. On wholesalers, see U.S. Bureau of the Census, *Fifteenth Census: Census of Distribution. Wholesale Distribution (Trade Series): Groceries and Food Specialties* (Washington, D.C., 1933), 16, 38, 42–44. That census shows 47,132 establishments "producing goods sold through grocery trade channels," but the tabulation does not include the 2,443 meat and poultry plants and numerous plants making such items as candles, patent medicines, toiletries, and tobacco products shown in U.S. Bureau of the Census, *Statistical Abstract, 1933* (Washington, D.C.: 1933), 697–716. The United States had 29.9 million families in 1930; *Statistical Abstract, 1933*, 48.
9. Total employment in food retailing in 1929, including employees and proprietors in food stores and general stores selling food, was 1.2 million. Employment in food wholesaling was 187,766 and in manufacturing 753,247, yielding a total of more than 2.1 million workers out of a nonfarm workforce of 38 million. Industry employment from *1930 Retail Census*, 45, and the 1930 *Census of Distribution*.
10. Food accounted for $17.9 billion of the $71.8 billion of consumer spending in 1925, or 25 percent. Based on patterns a few years later, for which more detailed information is available, approximately 80 percent of all food spending was for at-home consumption, with purchased meals and alcoholic beverages accounting for the rest. The food component alone thus accounted for roughly twenty cents of every dollar of consumer spending. U.S. Bureau of the Census, *Historical Statistics of the United States*, 319, ser. 419–22; 320, ser. 470–71; 323, ser. 844–45; and 326, ser. 773–74. With the 1967 level set equal to 100, food consumption per capita in 1925 was 86; not until 1940 did the index reach 90. Although diets had plenty of calories, they were short on nutrients such as calcium and thiamine. See *Historical Statistics of the United States*, 328, ser. 849–65.
11. Schumpeter, *Capitalism, Socialism, and Democracy*, 83.

12. Karl Marx and Friedrich Engels, *Das Kapital*, vol. 3 (Hamburg, 1894), 303; William Graham Sumner, "The Forgotten Man" (1883), in *The Forgotten Man, and Other Essays*, ed. Albert Galloway Keller (Manchester, N.H., 1969), 491.
13. Ian Melville, *Marketing in Japan* (Oxford, 1999), 195; *Journal Officiel de la République Française*, December 30, 1973, 14142.
14. "Retailers Protest Controversial Law," *Prague Post*, December 16, 2009.

2: THE FOUNDER

1. Great Atlantic & Pacific Tea Co., *Three Score Years and Ten*, 5. This official company version of history was accepted in the most widely cited work on U.S. chain retailing, Godfrey Lebhar's *Chain Stores in America*, 21, and propagated in such prominent places as a front-page article in *The Wall Street Journal*, "A&P's Saga Includes a Pagoda, Price Wars, and Buying Brigades," *WSJ*, December 19, 1958, and *Barron's*, February 20, 1922, 10. The official story was reiterated in the announcements that accompanied the opening of new stores, prompting further embellishment. For example, the *Hartford Courant*, October 25, 1924, reported that the store George H. Hartford opened on Vesey Street in 1859 was "the first grocery store to operate on a strictly cash basis. The front of the store was painted a brilliant red and this was the origin of the red-front chain-store idea." In fact, both the sale of groceries and the red color scheme developed many years after 1859, and many other firms sold groceries on a cash-only basis much earlier. Peter Coclanis wrote in *The Encyclopedia of New York History*, ed. Kenneth T. Jackson (New Haven, Conn., 1995), that Great Atlantic & Pacific "was formed as a partnership in 1859. It initially had one tea shop on Vesey Street." No available evidence supports the date, the address, or the existence of a partnership. The company contributed to the confusion surrounding its origins by changing its foundation myth several times. An 1867 advertisement stated that the Great American Tea Company, indisputably the predecessor of Great Atlantic & Pacific Tea Company, was "established 1861"; *Commercial Enterprise*, Great American Tea Company, HFF. When Great Atlantic & Pacific issued bonds for the first time in 1916, it told investors, "The present business was started in 1858"; *WSJ*, June 15, 1916. In advertising a dozen years later, it described the Great American Tea Company, progenitor of A&P, as "Roasters of Good Coffee Since 1856." See "The Great American News," folder 431, HFF. The story of George H. Hartford buying an entire cargo of tea in 1859 was presented in court in 1945 by an attorney for the company; Tr 84.
2. As one example of the legends and misstatements of fact that developed over time, a website of the Harvard Business School library offered the following history: "The Great Atlantic & Pacific Tea Company arose from the partnership created in 1859 between George Huntington Hartford and George Francis Gilman. Using Gilman's connections as a grocer and son of a wealthy ship owner, Hartford purchased coffee and tea from clipper ships on the docks of New York City. By eliminating middlemen, the partners were able to sell their wares at 'cargo prices.' This venture was so successful that in 1869 Hartford and Gilman opened a series of stores under the name Great American Tea Company"; www.library.hbs.edu/hc/lehman/chrono.html?company=the_great_atlantic_pacific_tea_company_inc,

accessed May 10, 2009. There is no evidence that Gilman was ever a grocer or that he and Hartford were partners in 1859. The earliest known use of the Great American Tea Company name was in 1863.

3. Norcross, *History of the New York Swamp*, 124–25. *The New York Business Directory for 1840 and 1841* (New York, 1840), 55, confirms that Nathaniel Gilman was running Gilman, Smull & Company at 11 Ferry Street in Manhattan in 1840. The description of Nathaniel Gilman is from "Long Fight Presaged over Gilman Millions," *NYT*, March 24, 1901. For background on the leather trade in New York, see Scoville, *Old Merchants of New York City*, 252–62, and Ellsworth, "Craft to National Industry in the Nineteenth Century" (Ph.D. diss.), 100–29.
4. *Rode's New York City Directory, 1851–52*, compiled in the spring of 1851, showed George F. Gilman with a hides business at 35 Spruce Street and his older brother, Nathaniel Gilman Jr., with a leather business at 72 Gold Street, which was also the location of Nathaniel Gilman & Son, leather dealers. The following year, *Rode's* listed George's hides business at 17 Ferry Street, just down the block from the leather business of his brother Winthrop W. Gilman at 7 Ferry Street, while the 35 Spruce Street location was occupied by Nathaniel Gilman Jr. and Nathaniel Gilman & Son. Winthrop was still at 7 Ferry, where he would remain for many years. Winthrop, born in 1808, had moved to Sullivan County, New York, in 1846, where he bought forests and built tanneries at a place that became known as Gilman's Station. That area, in the town of Forestburgh, is said to have had thirty-nine tanneries producing 100,000 sides of leather annually in the 1850s. "A Millionaire's Lonely Death," *NYT*, December 8, 1885; en.wikipedia.org/wiki/Forestburgh,_New_York, accessed May 1, 2009.

   Nathaniel senior also was known for lending money; *Trow's New York City Directory* for 1856–57, 316, gives George Gilman's business as "exchange," suggesting that he may have collected debts for his father.
5. The 1850 census has a leather dealer named Nathaniel Gillman, age thirty-five, born in Maine, living in Ward 2, Brooklyn, with his wife, two children, and three servants. On construction of the Gold Street building, see Norcross, *History of the New York Swamp*, 38; the 1857 William Perris map of New York, sheet 5, shows 98 Gold to be a frame building with a store attached. New York City tax records show that the two buildings on the site were replaced in 1858 with a five-story structure containing about seven thousand square feet of space; see *Record of Assessments, 4th Ward, 1858*, 26, and *1859*, 24, NYMA. *Trow's* for 1859 lists George F. Gilman, hides, at 98 Gold Street and at 55 Frankfort Street, just around the corner. Many newspaper reports have the wrong date of death for Nathaniel Gilman, and some confuse him with his eldest son, also Nathaniel, who predeceased him.
6. *Trow's New York City Directory* for 1860–61, which was compiled prior to June 2, 1860, shows both a John S. Hartford and a George W. Gilman in "Teas" at 98 Gold Street.
7. This version of George Hartford's life appears in Whittemore, *Founders and Builders*, 209, which was probably checked with George H. Hartford. Avis H. Anderson, *A&P*, 9, states that George Hartford met Gilman in St. Louis and began working for him there; their common roots in central Maine would have provided a natural link. According to an alternative explanation of the Gilman-Hartford relationship, John S. Hartford is said to have known George Gilman from living in the same

town in Maine and supposedly asked Gilman to allow him to store tea in the Gold Street warehouse and finance him to peddle tea across the country. John S. Hartford's health then supposedly worsened, and George H. Hartford came from St. Louis to take over the tea wagon. "O.W.S. Biography—Initial Notes (1700 through 1874)," HFF. This story is not credible for a variety of reasons: the Hartfords and Gilman did not live in the same town in Maine; John Hartford is listed in a directory as an "agent" for Gilman's leather business in St. Louis; and the brothers appear to have moved to New York around the same time. The 1850 census, Boston Ward 9, Suffolk, Massachusetts, roll M432_337, 192, image 39, shows a George W. Hartford, aged eighteen, and a John S. Hartford, fifteen, boarding in the house of Ignatius Sargent and his wife, Sarah. It is not certain that these are the correct Hartfords; George's correct middle initial was *H*, not *W*, and both ages given are one year older than the brothers' actual ages in June 1850. However, the age spread between the two is correct, both are listed as having been born in Maine, and neither appears in the 1850 census record for Maine, indicating that they were living in another state. John S. Hartford filed a passport application in Boston in January 1855, giving his age as nineteen and his birthplace as Maine. It is uncertain where he traveled. *Kennedy's St. Louis Directory, 1859* confirms that Gilman had an office in St. Louis and that both Hartfords were working for him there in 1859 while living at 75 North Fifth Street.

8. The Hartfords' presence in Maine in June 1860 is confirmed in U.S. Bureau of the Census, *United States Federal Census, 1860, Augusta, Kennebec County, Maine*, M653_441, 121–22. Despite the lack of evidence that either Gilman or Hartford was selling tea or coffee in 1859, the Great Atlantic & Pacific Tea Company, long since free from the Hartford family's control, held fast to the story; in September 2008 it received a U.S. trademark for the slogan "America's Coffee Provider Since 1859," U.S. Patent and Trademark Office, registration number 3,522,886. Wilson's *New York City Business Directory* for 1860 listed George F. Gilman as "Hide and Leather Dealer" and Gilman & Company as "Importers of Tea" at 98 Gold Street. Gilman is also shown as being in the leather business in an 1860 credit-agency book. See Roy J. Bullock, "The Early History of the Great Atlantic & Pacific Tea Company," *Harvard Business Review* 11 (1933), 290.
9. Gilman had sufficient wealth and income to be liable for the wartime income excise tax imposed in 1863. The carriages, watches, and piano, along with an income of $4,959, appear on the 1866 tax report, series M603, roll 82, frame 507, NARA-NY. On the increasing separation between firm owners and workers, see Wilentz, *Chants Democratic*, and Beckert, *The Monied Metropolis*.
10. Albion, *Rise of New York Port*, 189, 203, 401. *JOC*, February 4, 1859, as one example, carried seven advertisements from hide dealers, although Gilman & Company appears not to have advertised in the newspaper either before or after it began to sell tea. While packet ships had made the trip from China in less than three months since around 1840, the clippers were typically larger and could carry much more cargo. John H. Morrison, *History of New York Ship Yards* (New York, 1909), contains detailed information on many of the American-built clippers. On the new fashion for tea, see, among other articles, "Tea," *Atlantic Monthly*, February 1858, 446; "Tea Culture in the United States," *Harper's New Monthly Magazine*, November 1859, 762; "Tea for the Ladies, and Where It Comes From,"

Godey's Lady's Book, May 1860, 301; "Tea-Growing in India," *NYT*, March 23, 1862.

11. Bullock, "Early History," 290, and "History of the Chain Grocery Store" (Ph.D. diss.), 18–21; Albion, *Rise of New York Port*, 187, 283–84; Carhart, "New York Produce Exchange," 214. A tea chest did not have a standard weight, and could contain anywhere from 80 to 110 pounds of tea, depending upon the origin; "half-chest" was a euphemism for a small chest, which typically held more than half the weight of a full chest. Coffee and tea auctions were held several times a week at merchants' rooms in lower Manhattan around 1860; on February 2, 1859, for example, L. M. Hoffman & Company, auctioneer, sold 150 packages of undamaged teas arriving on the vessels *Argonaut*, *Horace*, and *Eagle Wing*, and 5,000 packets and bags of Java coffee damaged on the voyage. The auction was conducted at its premises in Hanover Square; *JOC*, February 2, 1859. Albion, *Rise of New York Port*, 283, states that coffee was auctioned at the New York Produce Exchange in the 1850s, but this could not have been true, as the exchange was organized only in 1860 and opened its building in 1861; exchange records for the 1860s make no mention of tea or coffee being traded there.
12. *NYT*, April 23, 1858, reported poor prices at an auction sale of tea and said that the announcement of a coffee auction the following day had depressed private coffee trading. The weekly *United States Economist*, November 12, 1853, 69, said many tea merchants "have closed their places of business until such time as there is any chance when they can dispose of their goods at a paying price." Although some of the price and quantity information was obtained from public auctions, the vast majority concerned private sales and was derived from sources that were rarely disclosed. Quotation is from D. Stoddard, Boston, to Solomon Townsend, New York, October 9, 1847, in Townsend Family Papers, box 4, N-YHS.
13. On conditions in the Swamp during this period, see Norcross, *History of the New York Swamp*, 126; and Ezra R. Pulling, M.D., "Report of the Fourth Sanitary Inspection District," in *Report of the Council of Hygiene and Public Health of the Citizens' Association of New York upon the Sanitary Condition of the City*, 2nd ed. (New York, 1866). The Gold Street location appears in *Trow's New York City Directory, 1860–1861*, 326, the Front Street location in *Trow's New York City Directory, 1861–1862*, 323. The 1861 date for the establishment of the Great American Tea Company was used in the company's advertising not long after; see, for example, the notice in *New York Teacher and American Educational Monthly* 5 (January 1868), back cover. The New York *Record of Assessments, 1st Ward*, shows that a Jno. Lecount, variously identified as Jona Lecount, purchased 129 Front Street in 1860 and owned it for years thereafter.
14. Albion, *Rise of New York Port*, 266; *New York Produce Exchange, As It Was and As It Is* (New York, 1959), n.p. The ledgers of Brown Brothers & Company, one of New York's leading financial firms during this period, offer scattered clues as to how the business functioned. On April 9, 1866, Brown Brothers disposed of damaged coffee from the ship *Maria* for the account of M. G. Crenshaw & Company, a merchant; only $5,845.29 of the total sale price of $8,212.59 ended up in the Crenshaw account. Brown Brothers & Company Records, vol. 74, 495, NYPL. Addresses of Sturges and Scrymser firms are in *Shipping and Commercial List*, January 21, 1860.

15. Minute Book, 1–4, 33, and New York Commercial Association Membership List, 1861–63, New York Produce Exchange Papers, N-YHS. Other Produce Exchange records, such as the Complaint Book and the Visitor's Book, offer no evidence that Gilman or anyone connected with his firm was involved with the exchange in any way through at least 1873. The Produce Exchange dealt only in physical commodities during this period; exchange trading in futures contracts had yet to develop.
16. "News from Washington," *NYT*, December 24, 1861; E. M. Brunn, "The New York Coffee and Sugar Exchange," *Annals of the American Academy of Political and Social Science* 155 (1931), 110; Wakeman, *Lower Wall Street*, 94; U.S. Bureau of the Census, *Statistical Abstract of the United States* (Washington, D.C., 1878), 129.
17. Later in the 1860s, Great American's advertisements stated that the company was "Established 1861." See, for example, *New York Teacher and American Educational Monthly* 5 (January 1868), back cover. Without exception, the merchants belonging to the New York Produce Exchange during the 1860s operated under the names of their owners or partners, and even the city's largest retail merchants, such as A. T. Stewart & Company and R. H. Macy & Company, were called after their owners. The Great American stores operating in May 1863 were at 73 Catherine Street, in the Fourth Ward; 314 Second Street and 372 Grand Street, on the Lower East Side; 545 Eighth Avenue at Thirty-ninth Street; and 45 Vesey Street, a couple of doors down from the new headquarters. *New York Herald*, May 30, 1863. None of these premises was owned by Gilman; see *Record of Assessments, 3rd Ward*, various years, NYMA. No descriptions of these shops survive. Gilman's earliest surviving federal tax assessment, for $10, was paid at the end of 1864.
18. *New York Herald*, May 27 and 30, 1863. On retailer advertising in this period, see Laird, *Advertising Progress*, 23–31.
19. AG, November 12, 1870, acknowledged that tea "has become the controlling power in the grocery trade," indicating its importance to retailers. Tedlow, *New and Improved*, 190; *Trenton Daily State Gazette*, July 28, 1863; *Atlantic Democrat and Cape May* (N.J.) *Register*, August 15, 1863; *Columbus* (Ohio) *Crisis*, September 16, 1863.
20. Many sources tell Barnum's story, not least Phineas Taylor Barnum, *The Life of P. T. Barnum, Written by Himself* (New York, 1855). A website prepared by the American Social History Project, www.lostmuseum.cuny.edu/intro.html, provides a good introduction. On Great American's horses, see Wakeman, *Lower Wall Street*, 94. *NYT*, June 16, 1833; *New York Sun*, October 28, 1863. Bullock, "Early History," 292, contends that the company used little newspaper advertising during its early years; he apparently was unaware of the many advertisements that appeared starting in May 1863.
21. *Columbus* (Ohio) *Crisis*, September 16, 1863; *New York Herald*, September 4, 1863. Circulars announcing the move are in HFF. Already in the 1860s it was possible to engage an advertising agent such as George P. Rowell, who would place a one-inch advertisement in one hundred newspapers for a fee of $100; see Laird, *Advertising Progress*, 73.
22. *National Celebration of Union Victories* (New York, 1865), 16; Wakeman, *Lower Wall Street*, 95.

23. The prices quoted in the company's circulars appeared even lower than they were, because they were for New York delivery, leaving customers to pay shipping costs. The economics of Great American's operation are not fully understood, as no records are extant. See Bullock, "Early History," 292–95, and Tedlow, *New and Improved*, 190.
24. *The Brooklyn City Directory for the Year Ending May 1st, 1862* (Brooklyn, 1862) is the first to list Hartford, showing his occupation as "clerk." The next directory in which he appears, the 1864–65 edition, lists him as "book-keeper." His title of treasurer is reported in *Orange Journal*, March 30, 1878. Observations on his personality are from *Orange Journal*, March 16, 1878; Whittemore, *Founders and Builders*, 208; Pierson, *History of the Oranges to 1921*, vol. 4, 270.

3: THE BIRTH OF THE GREAT A&P

1. Internal Revenue Assessment Lists for New York, Records of the Internal Revenue Service, RG 58, ser. M603, roll 53, frame 643, and roll 58, frame 209, NARA-NY. Great American used 31–33 and 35–37 Vesey as warehouses and offices, and 45 Vesey for both warehouse space and grinding.
2. "Light-Weight Dealers," *New York World*, December 17, 1868.
3. *Brooklyn Daily Eagle*, April 8, 1865; *Shipping and Commercial List*, May 15, 1867; "The Commercial Enterprise," file 430, HFF.
4. On the marriage, see Avis H. Anderson, *A&P*, 47. Marie Josephine Ludlum Hartford, twenty-four at the time of their marriage, was said to be from a well-established family in Goshen, New York, but her name does not appear in the 1860 census reports. *The Brooklyn City Directory for the Year Ending May 1st, 1865* lists George H. Hartford as a "book-keeper" living at 67 Powers Street, a few doors down from his initial residence. The edition published in May 1867 has him living at 286 Franklin Avenue in the leafier environs of Bedford-Stuyvesant, but the family apparently had relocated to Orange by the time this was published. Record of Hartford's draft status is in "Registry of Drafted Men, 2d Cong Dst," line 7477, RG 110, entry 1531, NARA-NY; Peter Bruin's enlistment as Hartford's substitute is in "Navy and Marine Enlistment for 2nd Congressional District of New York," RG 110, entry 1535, and personal information about Bruin is in "Medical Register," RG 110, entry 1534. For background on the draft, see Peter Levine, "Draft Evasion in the North During the Civil War, 1863–1865," *Journal of American History* 67 (1981), 816–34; Eugene C. Murdock, "New York's Civil War Bounty Brokers," *Journal of American History* 53 (1966), 259–78; and McKay, *Civil War and New York City*, 215. Hartford's reported income is derived from Internal Revenue Assessment Lists for New York, District 2, ser. M603_44 (1864) and M603_45 (1865). According to McKay, *Civil War and New York City*, 219, a well-paid clerk at the A. T. Stewart department store earned $500 a year in 1863, but $300 was more typical.
5. On Lucy Stone, see Clark, *Orange, New Jersey*, 25–26, 42.
6. An 1870 city directory, the earliest extant, lists a George H. Hartford, whose business was "teas," as a boarder at 4 Centre Street. *Orange Directory for 1870* (Orange, N.J., 1870), 56. This was likely a temporary residence. The location of the Ridge Street house, at the corner of White Street, is now an apartment complex. Information on the occupants is from U.S. Census Bureau, *Ninth Census of the United*

States, 1870, Orange Ward 1, Essex, New Jersey, ser. M593_861, roll 324, image 126, RG 29, NARA. On the conversion, see "O.W.S. Biography—Initial Notes (1700 through 1874)," HFF.

7. New York had a hundred tea dealers in 1870. Bullock, "History of the Chain Grocery Store" (Ph.D. diss.), 15. Store count is from Roy J. Bullock, "The Early History of the Great Atlantic & Pacific Tea Company," 291. The description of the new store appeared in *The Brooklyn Daily Times* and was reported in *Peterson's Magazine* 53 (May 1868), 394; the employee count was in *Peterson's Magazine* 54 (July 1868), 76. Both of these articles emphasized how big and busy Great American's stores were. The company may have sought to emphasize its size and solidity to make mail-order customers confident enough to send in their money.
8. Tradition has the railroad completed with the driving of a golden spike with a silver maul, but this may well be apocryphal; see J. N. Bowman, "Driving the Last Spike at Promontory, 1869," *California Historical Quarterly* 36 (1957), 263–74.
9. *Trenton Daily State Gazette,* October 15, 1869; Bullock, "Early History," 296. The claim that George H. Hartford's association with A&P dated to 1869 was repeated in Pierson, *History of the Oranges to 1921,* vol. 4, 270–71. Hartford's census declaration is in the 1870 census records, ser. M593_861, roll 324, image 126, RG 29, NARA. The story of the name change was posted for many years on the company's website, www.aptea.com/history_timeline.asp, accessed February 7, 2009. Great American Tea Company was sold to its employees in 1965; see Progressive Grocer, *A&P: Past, Present, and Future* (New York, 1971), 11.
10. Wakeman, *Lower Wall Street,* 94; *Harper's Weekly,* February 8, 1868, 1; AG, December 10, 1870, 581.
11. AG, November 15, 1869. Assuming that the average chest weighed 100 pounds, 36,000 chests would have equated to 3.6 million pounds of tea. Net U.S. tea imports in 1869 were 40.8 million pounds. U.S. Bureau of the Census, *Statistical Abstract, 1878,* 129.
12. The Great American name was attached to a tea shop as late as the end of 1898, when a newspaper article described its store, still at the corner of Vesey and Church streets, as containing "a miniature Chinese pagoda, resplendent with gilt and brilliant carmine." *Evangelist,* December 6, 1898. On Thea-Nectar, see Bullock, "Early History," 297; *Atlanta Daily Constitution,* May 23, 1872; "A New Business," *Daily Constitution,* October 31, 1880. *Thea* was the name formerly used for the tea-plant genus, now referred to as *Camellia.*
13. On the growth of brands, see Mira Wilkins, "When and Why Brand Names in Food and Drink?" in Jones and Morgan, eds., *Adding Value,* 15–40; Koehn, "Henry Heinz and Brand Creation in the Late Nineteenth Century"; "New Business."
14. "The Tea Trade and Certain Monopolies," AG, November 12, 19, and 26 and December 3, 1870.
15. Bullock, "Early History," 294; "Tea Trade and Certain Monopolies," AG, November 19, 1870, 491.
16. Avis H. Anderson, *A&P,* 30–31. On chromos, see Laird, *Advertising Progress,* 76–91. On premiums, see Bullock, "History of the Chain Grocery Store," 42; and Roy J. Bullock, "A History of the Great Atlantic & Pacific Tea Company Since 1878,"

Harvard Business Review 12 (1933), 60. Essay by Louise Slater, Harrisburg, Pennsylvania, May 22, 1877, binder 8B, HFF.

17. The story about Hartford's actions cannot be verified, but it appeared in a hometown newspaper, *Orange Chronicle*, March 16, 1878, six and a half years after the event; see also J. C. Furnas, "Mr. George & Mr. John," *Saturday Evening Post*, December 31, 1938, 53. A&P's official history states that the company shipped large donations of food to Chicago. The advertisements using Grand Duke Alexis appeared in the *Chicago Tribune* on December 3 and 24, 1871, and on other dates.
18. On store locations, see Bullock, "History of the Great Atlantic & Pacific Tea Company Since 1878," 59; *Boston Daily Globe*, January 9, 1875; *Hartford Courant*, May 6, 1875.
19. *Orange Journal*, July 8 and November 4, 1876. A quiet Election Day was so unusual that when the 1879 municipal election transpired without incident, *The Orange Chronicle*, March 15, 1879, found the lack of disorder worthy of comment.
20. *Orange Journal*, November 27, 1876, February 8 and 15, 1879; *Orange Chronicle*, February 9 and 16, 1878, February 15, 1879. Estimate of number of hat workers is from *Orange Chronicle*, September 14, 1878, in an article reprinted from *New York Daily Graphic*, September 6, 1878.
21. This strange sequence of events is recounted in *Orange Journal*, March 16, 1878, *Orange Chronicle*, March 16, 1878, and Whittemore, *Founders and Builders*, 208.
22. *Orange Journal*, March 16, 1878; *Orange Chronicle*, March 16, 1878. The number of newspapers, two in English and two in German, is taken from *Quarter-Century's Progress of New Jersey's Leading Manufacturing Centres* (New York, 1887), 176.
23. *Orange Journal*, March 30, 1878.
24. Sales and the date of the partnership agreement are recounted in "Gilman's Tea Business," *Hartford Daily Courant*, October 25, 1901. See also Bullock, "History of the Great Atlantic & Pacific Tea Company Since 1878," 60. For details of the altercation, see "Long Fight Presaged over Gilman Millions," *NYT*, March 24, 1901. The store count appears in *Orange Chronicle*, March 16, 1878. *Hartford v. Bridgeport Trust Company*, 143 F. 558 (U.S. Cir. C., D. Ct., February 12, 1906); *Matter of Estate of George F. Gilman, Deceased*, 80 N.Y.S. 1122, February 1903.

4: THE GROCER

1. Joshua Hartford, George L. and John A. Hartford's paternal grandfather, died in 1877. Louis Ludlum, suffering from consumption and Bright's disease, died in the house on May 25, 1878, a few weeks after George H. became mayor. *Orange Journal*, June 1, 1878. Martha Hartford passed away the following November 2 at age seventy-nine. "On Saturday she was unusually bright and cheerful, and was about the House" before suddenly dying, the *Orange Journal* reported, November 9, 1878. Information on domestic servants and on John Clews is from U.S. Census Bureau, *1880 Census, Orange, Essex, New Jersey*, roll T9_780, image 104.3000. Anderson gives Clews's birth year as 1857, in which case his age in 1880 would have been twenty-two or twenty-three.
2. The story about George L. stoking the boiler appears in Merle Crowell, "You Don't Have to Be Brilliant," *American Magazine*, February 1931, 21; this version, however, has George L. beginning his career at the company in 1877, when he

would have been only eleven or twelve years old. The story about his work at the Newark store is in Great Atlantic & Pacific Tea Co., *You . . . and Your Company*, 9. According to that source, the Newark job was George L.'s first position with A&P, but it seems unlikely that a fourteen-year-old would have been charged with handling significant sums of money. Yet another tale of the start of George L. Hartford's career, reported in J. C. Furnas, "Mr. George & Mr. John," *Saturday Evening Post*, December 31, 1938, has the fourteen-year-old "counting and checking cash receipts from all stores"; Furnas does not consider the implausibility of such a young man counting receipts from nearly a hundred stores. George L.'s record at St. Benedict's was confirmed in personal communication from Father Augustine Curley, August 19, 2009.

3. Avis H. Anderson, *A&P*, 10; "A Fine Store Room," *Summit County* (Ohio) *Beacon*, April 7, 1880. The paper termed the interior of Great Atlantic & Pacific's new store in Akron as "the finest in the city so far as ceiling and wall decorations are concerned."
4. The 1882–84 ledger for the store in Port Chester, New York, is item 291, HFF.
5. A&P stores could be found in such out-of-the-way locations as Jeffersonville, Indiana, and Oswego, New York. A full listing of locations, including street addresses, appears on the back of the trade card. On George L.'s role, see Avis H. Anderson, *A&P*, 31.
6. The company may also have had modest sales of spices in its first two decades. Spices were never mentioned in advertisements; the only reference to a spice business is in an August 1866 tax record showing George F. Gilman as a "Grinder of Coffee and Spices" at 45 Vesey Street. Records of the Internal Revenue Service, RG 58, ser. M603, roll 58, frame 6209, NARA-NY. In 1870, the duty on tea was cut from twenty-five cents per pound to fifteen cents, on coffee from five cents a pound to three cents. Two years later, customs duties on coffee and tea were cut to zero; see Stanwood, *American Tariff Controversies*, 173, 183, and Taussig, *Tariff History*, 185–88. The value of tea imports in 1870 averaged twenty-nine cents per pound, and the twenty-five-cent tariff brought the import price to fifty-four cents; the 1870 tariff reduction effectively reduced the price at dockside to forty-four cents, and the 1872 import price, tariff free, was thirty-seven cents. The import value of coffee was ten cents per pound in 1870, so the dockside price including the tariff fell from fifteen cents to thirteen cents. Coffee imports in 1871, just after the first round of tariff cuts, were 27 percent higher than in any previous year; U.S. Bureau of the Census, *Statistical Abstract 1878* (Washington, D.C., 1878), 129; *Statistical Abstract, 1891* (Washington, D.C., 1891), 202–203. Gross import figures in U.S. Bureau of the Census, *Historical Statistics of the United States*, 901–902, are different, but demand and price trends are similar. Company sales figure is from Bullock, "History of the Great Atlantic & Pacific Tea Company Since 1878," 61. On the new roasting process, see *Boston Daily Globe*, February 9, 1885.
7. Other tea companies also added new products around this time; see Hall, "Barney Builds a Business."
8. Levenstein, *Revolution at the Table*, 32–33. The wartime sugar tariff, enacted in 1864, was five cents per pound, nearly 50 percent of the average import price; it fell to two cents in the 1880s; Stanwood, *American Tariff Controversies*, 129; Taussig, *Tariff History*, 285; U.S. Bureau of the Census, *Historical Statistics of the United*

States, 331, 901–902. U.S. government policy in this period focused on extracting more value from sorghum, a drought-tolerant grass, rich in sucrose, which was grown across the Midwest. Sorghum was used mainly for animal feed, but the government supported a major effort to make white sugar from it. The leader of this effort was Harvey W. Wiley, chief chemist of the U.S. Department of Agriculture, who was later known for his role in winning enactment of the Pure Food and Drug Act of 1906. See Oscar E. Anderson, *Health of a Nation*, 27–29, 32–66.

9. Port Chester ledger, HFF.
10. Avis H. Anderson, *A&P*, 29, 38. Bullock, "History of the Great Atlantic & Pacific Tea Company Since 1878," 62, dates the sale of baking powder to 1890, but advertisements and trade cards show it was sold much earlier.
11. U.S. Department of Agriculture, Bureau of Chemistry, *Foods and Food Adulterants, Part 5: Baking Powders* (Washington, D.C., 1889), 562–66.
12. Ibid., 588; Law, "Origins of State Pure Food Regulation," 1117. Several A&P trade cards bore the Doremus endorsement, which was dated July 7, 1888.
13. Levenstein, *Revolution at the Table*, 25; Smith, *Robert Gair*, 73.
14. *AG*, February 15, 1870, carried an early advertisement for "Metropolitan Paper-Bag Manufactory, Robert Gair Manufacturer and Printer of Paper and Cotton Bags and Jobber of Paper and Twine, 143 Reade St New York." See also Smith, *Robert Gair*, 42, 64–66, and Wilbert Henry Ruenheck, "Business History of the Robert Gair Company, 1864 to 1927" (Ph.D. diss.), 9–17.
15. Hunt, *Fruits and Vegetables*, 9, 35, 43; U.S. Department of Agriculture, Bureau of Chemistry, *Foods and Food Adulterants, Part 8: Canned Vegetables* (Washington, D.C., 1893), 1020; Brown and Philips, "Craft Labor and Mechanization in Nineteenth-Century American Canning," 746; Levenstein, *Revolution at the Table*, 37.
16. Levenstein, *Revolution at the Table*, 34.
17. Avis H. Anderson, *A&P*, 15–16, 74; *Atlanta Constitution*, October 15, 1882; *Summit County* (Ohio) *Beacon*, January 3, 1883.
18. Furnas, "Mr. George & Mr. John," 54; "Red Circle and Gold Leaf," *Time*, November 13, 1950; John A. Hartford to Arthur Buysee, March 26, 1937, file 157, HFF.
19. *Orange Chronicle*, March 1, 8, and 15, 1890; "Divided on Whisky," *NYT*, June 12, 1890; "Sold Out the Ticket," *NYT*, November 11, 1890.

5: THE DEATH OF GEORGE F. GILMAN

1. *George F. Gilman v. Anna K. Gilman*, 52 Maine 165, 176 (1863).
2. On Nathaniel Gilman's death and burial, see "Deaths," *JOC*, December 28, 1859; "Long Fight Presaged over Gilman Millions," *NYT*, March 24, 1901; "Will of Nathaniel Gilman," *NYT*, April 19, 1860; "For the New Surrogate, the Interminable Case of Nathaniel Gilman," *NYT*, December 31, 1887. Joanna's court case is *George F. Gilman v. Joanna B. Gilman*, 53 Maine 184, 193 (1865). Anna Gilman seems to have been obsessed by the belief that she and her mother were being treated unfairly and continued legal actions for many years.
3. "Long Fight Presaged over Gilman Millions."
4. "George Francis Gilman Dead," *NYT*, March 4, 1901; "Gilman's Place of Residence a Big Issue," *NYT*, March 13, 1901; "Black Rock Mansion Seized," *New-York*

Tribune, March 23, 1901; "Gilman's Idiosyncrasies," *Hartford Courant*, October 28, 1901; "The House That Premiums Built Will Fall," *Bridgeport Post*, November 22, 1926; Mary K. Witkowski, *Bridgeport at Work* (Charleston, S.C., 2002), 83; "Gilman Horses Sold," *New-York Tribune*, April 17, 1901.

5. "Gilman Chattels at Auction," *New-York Tribune*, May 16, 1901; "Frazier Gilman's Petition," *NYT*, April 10, 1901.
6. "Mrs. Hall At Last Tells Her Secret," *NYT*, April 11, 1901.
7. "Gilman's Tea Business," *Hartford Courant*, October 25, 1901; *Hartford v. Bridgeport Trust Company*, 143 F. 558; *Norton v. Hartford*, 113 F. 1023 (1902).
8. According to "Gilman Heirs Fight New Claim," *Evening World*, June 6, 1901, the lawyer representing Gilman's heirs asserted in court that "there was nothing in the books to show that Hartford had a dollar's interest, and he appeared as a salaried official or employee." "Accuses Gilman Partner," *NYT*, June 7, 1901; "The Great Atlantic and Pacific Tea Company Certificate of Incorporation," HFF. Hartford's status as a Home Insurance director is confirmed in that company's advertisement in *NYT*, July 11, 1900, and his role at Second National Bank of Orange in *NYT*, January 10, 1901. Pierson, *History of the Oranges to 1921*, has an undated photograph of George H. after page 270.
9. "No Tangible Assets," *Hartford Courant*, March 26, 1901; *Bridgeport Trust Company, Administrator, Appeal from Probate*, 77 Conn. 657 (1902).
10. *In re Administrators of the Goods*, 82 A.D. 186 (1902); "Certificate of Amendment of Charter and Increase of Capital Stock," October 20, 1902, HFF; *Hall v. Bridgeport Trust*, 122 F. 163 (1903); *Hall v. Gilman*, 79 N.Y.S. 303 (1902); "Gilman Estate Settled," *New-York Tribune*, July 1, 1903; *In re Administrators of the Goods*, 92 A.D. 462 (1904); "Ends Claim on Riches," *NYT*, January 9, 1904.
11. AG, August 12, 1903. The October 1902 amended certificate of incorporation lists Geo. L. Hartford as president, not George H. Hartford; it is unclear whether this was an error.

6: GEARING FOR BATTLE

1. Financial information was included in George H. Hartford's court filings in his request for an injunction against the Gilman estate, *Hartford v. Bridgeport Trust Company*, 143 F. 558, and was reported in "Gilman's Tea Business," *Hartford Courant*, October 25, 1901, and "Legal Notes," *NYT*, April 18, 1903; David Nasaw, *Andrew Carnegie* (New York, 2006), 587.
2. On Goldberg, Bowen, see AG, January 3, 1900, 10. The motto belonged to *American Grocer* and appeared just below the publication's name.
3. On bargaining and the social tensions involved in grocery shopping, see Tracey Deutsch, *Building a Housewife's Paradise*, 14–22. On incorrect measures, see AG, October 26, 1910, 11. The advice on barrels appeared in AG, July 15, 1903, 8; Bacon, *Beauty for Ashes*, 75; Pennsylvania Department of Agriculture, *Annual Report, 1908*, 26–29. When the Connecticut legislature appropriated $2,500 for special tests of food purity, state officials found that 254 of 848 samples were not as claimed; AG, July 22, 1896. On similar tests in Minnesota, see AG, October 17, 1906, 10. On the hazards of cans, see AG, February 18, 1903, 11.

4. AG, September 16, 1896, 9; October 27, 1897, 7; December 1, 1897, 8.
5. Barger, *Distribution's Place*, 148.
6. Bullock, "History of the Great Atlantic & Pacific Tea Company Since 1878," 61–62, estimates that Great Atlantic & Pacific had approximately 150 stores in 1890 and reached 200 only in 1901. On competing chains, see Bullock, "History of the Chain Grocery Store" (Ph.D. diss.), 51–53, 60–61, 70–72; Hall, "Barney Builds a Business," 306, 310; AG, July 7, 1897, 7; July 15, 1908, 14; and July 26, 1905, 6.
7. The new Tunison Grocery Company in East Orange, New Jersey, for example, billed itself as a "low price store" at its opening in 1898. AG, January 26, 1898, 10; March 29, 1905, 5; June 17, 1903, 10; and November 25, 1908, 8. The Art Deco logo appears on premium coupons dated 1903 in HFF; the globe logo in *New Orleans Daily Picayune*, January 15, 1901, 1; the one-line logo in *Washington Evening Star*, January 12, 1906, 10.
8. AG, April 1, 1903, 15.
9. The claim to being a "direct importer" was made frequently in Great Atlantic & Pacific's advertising; see, for example, the advertisement reprinted in AG, September 16, 1896, 9. The leading coffee importers are listed in AG, January 12, 1898, 22; and January 18, 1905, 26. AG, November 10, 1909, 23, reports Great Atlantic & Pacific receiving relatively modest consignments of coffee aboard two steamships arriving from Santos, Brazil. On the battle between the coffee and the sugar interests, see "The Sugar-Coffee Fight," *NYT*, October 6, 1898, and AG, October 14, 1896; December 23, 1896; January 20, 1897; and January 3, 1900.
10. Reported inventory at the time of George Gilman's death was over $830,000, and monthly sales were slightly above $400,000; "Gilman's Tea Business." AG, February 1, 1905, 7, cited an unnamed grocery in a "great manufacturing center" that turned its stock eleven times a year, versus six times for Great Atlantic & Pacific. By comparison, food retailers in the late twentieth century typically carried inventories equal to about three weeks' sales.
11. The store count was given as 198 in June 1903, when a federal judge approved the terms of the Hartfords' takeover; "Gilman Estate Settled," *New-York Tribune*, July 1, 1903. The company is estimated to have had 450 stores by 1912; see Avis H. Anderson, *A&P*, 18. The number of wagon routes is taken from *Jersey City of To-Day* (Jersey City, 1910), 105; see also Bullock, "History of the Great Atlantic & Pacific Tea Company Since 1878," 65. One example of the company's new advertising style appeared in the *New York Evening World*, March 28, 1904.
12. Rick James, "Warehouse Historic District, Jersey City, NJ, State & National Registers of Historic Places Nomination," 2003, www.jclandmarks.org/nomination-warehousedistrict.shtml, accessed June 1, 2009; *Jersey City of To-Day*, 105.
13. J. C. Furnas, "Mr. George & Mr. John," *Saturday Evening Post*, December 31, 1938, 38.
14. Avis H. Anderson, *A&P*, 16, has a 1903 photograph of a store promoting A&P Elgin Creamery butter. A&P gelatin was advertised in the *Daily Picayune*, June 15, 1901, 1. Grandmother made one of her earliest appearances in *Cleveland Medical Gazette* 3 (1888), 290.
15. On the use of the A&P brand in newspaper advertising, see AG, October 31, 1906, 14; lima bean prices are from AG, October 30, 1912, 14. On manufacturer resistance, see AG, March 18, 1908, 9.

16. Wage and price measurements were primitive in the early twentieth century, but the government's Bureau of Labor estimated that wages rose significantly faster than food prices; see *AG*, July 22, 1908, 10. On canned salmon, see *AG*, September 15, 1909, 32. On Uneeda Biscuits, *AG*, May 29, 1907, 10.
17. Photographs of stores showing premium selections are in Avis H. Anderson, *A&P*, 15–16. The coupons were published in various shapes and sizes; HFF owns a selection.
18. Great Atlantic & Pacific Tea Co., "Premium Catalog" (n.d., but after 1907), HFF. The catalog includes a large selection of furniture, including a couch-bed (650 points) and a carved rocking chair with an imitation leather seat (367 points). Customers who aspired to such gifts would have needed to collect coupons for years. On the relationship with Sperry & Hutchinson, see *AG*, June 5, 1912, 14.
19. *AG*, May 3, 1911, 8.
20. *AG*, July 17, 1907, 8.
21. *AG*, January 24, 1900, 7; February 8, 1902, 10; December 5, 1906, 12; U.S. Senate, Committee on Post Office and Post Roads, *Hearings of the Subcommittee on Parcel Post Under Sen. Res. 56*, November–December 1911 (Washington, D.C., 1912), 22, 29, 404–42. Retailer opposition delayed enactment of a parcel-post law until 1912.
22. *AG*, January 28, 1903, 6; January 4, 1905, 12; June 7, 1905, 6; October 18, 1905, 10; January 10, 1906, 7; July 4, 1906, 7; September 12, 1906, 8; January 1, 1908, 8; May 5, 1909, 8.
23. Resolution of Boston Wholesale Grocers Association, January 20, 1908, RG 233, Records of the U.S. House of Representatives, 60th Cong., Petitions and Memorials, Committee on Interstate and Foreign Commerce, box 703, HR60A-H16.3, NARA-LA; *AG*, January 4, 1905, 8; August 7, 1912, 7.

7: THE ECONOMY STORE

1. Avis H. Anderson, *A&P*, 48, 50, 63.
2. On the source of Edward Hartford's invention, see Ruth Reynolds, "Spotlight Hits Shrinking Hartfords," *New York Sunday News*, January 9, 1938. The Reynolds article contains numerous inaccuracies, and further detail is available at www.planetspring.com/pages/04_history.htm, accessed August 29, 2009. The original device was developed by Jules Michel Marie Truffault, an engineer in Paris, but Edward and George H. Hartford acquired the rights in 1903; see U.S. patents 743,995, issued November 10, 1903, and reissue 12,399, dated November 7, 1905. George H. seems to have held a 49 percent stake in the business. Edward's improvements were protected by patent 803,589, issued November 7, 1904, and subsequent patents. John A. Hartford's involvement in the auto-parts company is unknown, but he served as a witness on a 1910 patent application filed by Edward; see patent 1,124,612, issued December 10, 1910. The Hartford Shock Absorber was advertised with the slogan "Makes Every Road a Boulevard" in *The Automobile*, December 30, 1915, 220. Edward apparently liked to write about automotive technology as well as developing it; see his article "What Is a Rotary Motor?" *Automobile*, November 11, 1915, 879.
3. Letter is quoted in "O.W.S. Biography Notes from 1875–1889," HFF. The National Horse Show, opening the day after Election Day in November, started in 1883 and

quickly became one of New York's premier society events. The newspapers provided ample coverage not only of the competitions but also of the society luncheons, dinners, and late-night suppers that surrounded the event. For a brief history, see "National Horse Show on Nov. 5 to Inaugurate Formal Entertaining of Society in the City," *NYT*, September 25, 1938. Mr. and Mrs. J. A. Hartford are listed in *Dau's Blue Book* for 1914 (New York, 1914), 154. John was a member of the National Tea Association.

4. Pennington, "Relation of Cold Storage," 158.
5. On Taylor, see Kanigel, *One Best Way*, 370–74, 440. Barger contends that the average retail markup in the grocery industry expanded from 35.5 percent in 1899 to 38.1 percent in 1909; see *Distribution's Place*, 70. King, "Can the Cost of Distributing Food Products Be Reduced?" 206; "Reducing the Cost of Food Distribution," *Annals of the American Academy of Political and Social Science* 50 (1913). On peddlers, see Deutsch, *Building a Housewife's Paradise*, 28–31.
6. A Chicago wholesaler proposed to create a new retail chain on scientific principles in 1911; see *AG*, June 24, 1911, 7. The only available reference citing the address of this store is "Background Material on John A. Hartford and the A&P," binder 1, HFF. See comments of the A&P executive O. C. Adams, who had helped launch the Economy Store, in Progressive Grocer, *A&P: Past, Present, and Future* (New York, 1971), 18; Bullock, "History of the Great Atlantic & Pacific Tea Company Since 1878," 66; "Red Circle and Gold Leaf," *Time*, November 13, 1950.
7. In 1914, the average Economy Store booked sales of $18,159, whereas the average "traditional" Great Atlantic & Pacific store had sales of $50,845. "Stores and Dollar Sales (Fiscal Years)," notebook 8B, HFF; Bullock, "History of the Great Atlantic & Pacific Tea Company Since 1878," 67.
8. FTC, *Chain Stores: Growth and Development of Chain Stores*, 56; Paul Gaffney, "Dime Stores/Woolworth's," St. James Encyclopedia of Pop Culture, findarticles .com/p/articles/mi_g1epc/is_tov/ai_2419100342/, accessed July 26, 2009.
9. *AG*, September 15, 1909, 28; December 8, 1909, 12; *Bobbs-Merrill Co. v. Straus*, 210 U.S. 339; *Dr. Miles Medical Co. v. John D. Park and Sons*, 220 U.S. 373.
10. On the tobacco premium measure and mail-order merchants, see letters from independent merchants in RG 233, Records of the U.S. House of Representatives, 62nd Cong., Papers Accompanying Specific Bills and Resolutions, Committee on Interstate and Foreign Commerce, HR62A-H14.21, box 646, NARA-LA.
11. Marc Levinson, "Two Cheers for Discrimination: Deregulation and Efficiency in the Reform of U.S. Freight Transportation, 1976–1998," *Enterprise and Society* 10 (2009), 178–88; comment of John A. Green cited in *Printers' Ink*, May 28, 1914, 92.
12. Wilson's comment is cited in Retail Grocers Protective Union of Pittsburgh and Vicinity to John M. Moran, n.d., RG 233, Records of the U.S. House of Representatives, 63rd Cong., Petitions and Memorials, Committee on Interstate and Foreign Commerce, HR63A-H12.16, box 465, NARA-LA. Wilson had long been suspicious of big business, having written as early as 1898 that "the modern industrial organization has so distorted competition as sometimes to put it into the power of some to tyrannize over many." *The State*, rev. ed. (Boston, 1918), 61.
13. The case, *Bauer v. O'Donnell*, 229 U.S. 1, made clear that even the owners of patents could not control the prices at which patented goods were sold to the public;

Louis D. Brandeis, "Competition That Kills," *Harper's Weekly*, November 15, 1913. McCraw, *Prophets of Regulation*, 102–105.

14. U.S. House of Representatives, Committee on Interstate and Foreign Commerce, *To Prevent Discrimination in Prices and for Publicity of Prices to Dealers and the Public* (Washington, D.C., 1915), 3–4.
15. For Westerfeld, see ibid., March 13, 1914, 258; Elmer L. Ralphs (vice president, Ralphs Grocery Company) to C. F. Curry, September 4, 1914, RG 233, Records of the U.S. House of Representatives, 63rd Cong., Petitions and Memorials, Committee on Interstate and Foreign Commerce, HR63A-H12.16, box 465, NARA-LA. Brandeis's testimony is in *To Prevent Discrimination*, January 9, 1915, 14.
16. Charles W. Hurd and M. Zimmerman, "How the Chains Are Taking Over the Retail Field—IV," *Printers' Ink*, October 8, 1914, 36–37; "Taking the Chains by Fields and Their Number in Each—V," *Printers' Ink*, October 15, 1914, 71–72.
17. Charles W. Hurd and M. Zimmerman, "How Big Retailers' Chains Outsell Independent Competitors—XI," *Printers' Ink*, December 3, 1914, 66; "How Accounting Helps the Chains Outbattle the Independents," *Printers' Ink*, December 17, 1914.
18. *To Prevent Discrimination*, 89.
19. 38 Stat. 730, secs. 2 and 3. Members of the House Committee on Interstate and Foreign Commerce noted that while small retailers and wholesalers wanted to let manufacturers fix retail prices, manufacturers themselves evidenced little interest in the subject; many of them happily sold in quantity to chains. Charles W. Hurd and M. Zimmerman, "Why Advertisers and Dealers See Danger in Chain Stores," *Printers' Ink*, September 17, 1914, 68.
20. *Macon Daily Telegraph*, January 13, 1915; *Fort Worth Star-Telegram*, January 20, 1915.
21. Bullock, "History of the Great Atlantic & Pacific Tea Company Since 1878," 67; *Great Atlantic & Pacific Tea Co. v. Cream of Wheat Co.*, 224 F. 569.
22. *Great Atlantic & Pacific Tea Co. v. Cream of Wheat Co.*, 224 F. 574. When Great Atlantic & Pacific appealed Hough's decision, it received an even more stinging rebuke from the appellate judges: "We have not yet reached the stage where the selection of a trader's customers is made for him by the government"; 227 F. 49.
23. E. A. Bradford, "Price Cutting and Price Fixing," *NYT*, August 15, 1916. Among the fierce intellectual defenders of manufacturers' right to fix retail prices was a young graduate student named Sumner H. Slichter, soon to be one of the nation's most prominent economists, who contended that "price maintenance is not an *aggressive* device, but on the contrary it is a *protective* device." "Cream of Wheat Case," 411.
24. Repurchases of preferred shares are listed in "New Jersey Co. Transfer Journal," HFF.
25. The offer notice for the bond issue appeared in *WSJ*, June 15, 1916. Orders for the bonds "largely exceeded the amount offered"; *NYT*, June 16, 1916.
26. Robert D. Cuff, "Creating Control Systems: Edwin F. Gay and the Central Bureau of Planning and Statistics, 1917–1919," 590–95; Kennedy, *Over Here*, 113–16.
27. FTC, *System of Accounts for Retail Merchants*.

28. Avis H. Anderson, *A&P*, 39; "Bonuses for A&P Store Managers," *NYT*, March 9, 1917.
29. "O.W.S. Biography Notes from 1875–1889," HFF; J. C. Furnas, "Mr. George & Mr. John," *Saturday Evening Post*, December 31, 1938, 38.
30. "George H. Hartford," *NYT*, August 30, 1917.
31. Will of George H. Hartford, April 7, 1915, and codicil, June 23, 1916, Office of the Surrogate, Essex County, N.J., Will Book T-5, 171–73; Avis H. Anderson, *A&P*, 46.
32. Helen Zoe Veit, "'We Were a Soft People': Asceticism, Self-Discipline, and American Food Conservation in the First World War," 167–70; U.S. Food Administration, *Proclamations and Executive Orders by the President Under and by Virtue of the Food Control Act* (Washington, D.C., 1918), 3, 7, 14.
33. In 1918, the Federal Trade Commission recommended that companies be allowed to file proposed prices with an unspecified government agency; the agency could reject or revise any proposed price, but if it approved it, then all retailers would have to charge the approved price. The recommendation did not result in action. FTC, *Resale Price Maintenance*; U.S. Food Administration, "Official Statement No. 1," June 16, 1918, 4; "Official Statement No. 5," October 1, 1918, 16; "Official Statement No. 6," November 1, 1918, 29; and "Official Statement No. 7," November 15, 1918, 18. Some government officials exhorted citizens to do far more than regulations required; in January 1918, for example, the Food Administration's chief official in Indiana asked that state's citizens "to go on a strictly wheatless diet until after the next harvest," and in April 1918 Indiana retailers were enjoined to sell no more than two pounds of sugar to "town customers" and no more than five pounds to "country customers." *Indiana Bulletin*, April 5, 1918, 3, and June 28, 1918, 5. Price regulation of sugar remained in effect until 1920. McHenry, "Price Stabilization Attempts in the Grocery Trade in California," 124, asserted that Food Administration regulations replaced the demand for resale price maintenance during 1917 and 1918, but this connection seems weak, given that the regulations were not imposed until the waning days of the war.
34. Sears, Roebuck, then strictly a mail-order house with no branches, was the largest retailer in the United States, and probably in the world, for the second decade of the twentieth century. However, Sears's sales began to slump in 1920 as the company headed into a financial crisis. Information about individual retailers' sales in this period is fragmentary and, in the case of certain companies, subject to frequent revision. The following ranking of the world's largest retailers in 1920 was compiled from published sources:

Company	*Sales ($m)*	*Company*	*Sales ($m)*
Great Atlantic & Pacific	$235	Gimbel Brothers	$66
Sears, Roebuck	$234	Marshall Field	$65
F. W. Woolworth	$141	John Wanamaker	$65
Montgomery Ward	$102	R. H. Macy	$45
United Cigar Stores	$80	Le Bon Marché (France)	$40
May Stores	$68	Selfridges (U.K.)	$30

Sources: Newspaper reports; *Printers' Ink*, October 12, 1922, 85. Figure for Marshall Field excludes wholesale business.

8: THE CHAIN-STORE PROBLEM

1. Barbara McLean Ward, "Crossroads of a Neighborhood in Change: The Abbotts' Corner Store," in Ward, *Produce and Conserve*.
2. Shideler, "Chain Store" (Ph.D. diss.), chap. 4, 20. At the time, Chicago had a population of 2.7 million and an average of 4.34 people per household, yielding 622,120 households. U.S. Department of Commerce, *Census of Distribution: Atlanta, Georgia*, mimeo, October 16, 1927.
3. Writing in 1931, Carl W. Dipman described an ideal grocery store as being 40 feet deep and 18 to 30 feet wide, or 720–1,200 square feet; *Modern Grocery Store*, 23. Of the 585,980 food stores in the United States in 1929, including 104,089 general stores selling food, 58 percent were leased. For grocery stores, the average rent was $708 per year. General stores showed a different pattern, presumably because of the low cost of property in rural locations; 70 percent of them were in premises owned by the proprietor, and those in leased premises paid an average rent of only $471 per year; *1930 Retail Census*, 49. A 1924 Harvard Business School survey revealed an average annual rent of $948, or $79 per month, but this survey undersampled the retailers with the lowest turnover, who likely also paid the lowest rent. See Bureau of Business Research, Harvard University Graduate School of Business Administration, *Operating Expenses in Retail Grocery Stores in 1924*, 37. See the description and photograph of Sun Grocery, which opened in Tulsa, in 1926, in Wilson, *Cart That Changed the World*, 34–35.
4. Jerry Litvin, interview by Jessica Kaz, box 2, JHSGW; Claude Jinkerson, Maurice Hartshorn, et al., "Grocery Clerks' Local 648 in San Francisco," interview by David F. Selvin and Corinne L. Gilb, November 18, 1957, Institute of Industrial Relations Oral History Project, University of California at Berkeley.
5. *1930 Retail Census*, 53, 45.
6. Deutsch, *Building a Housewife's Paradise*, 34; Bureau of Business Research, Harvard University Graduate School of Business Administration, *Operating Expenses in Retail Grocery Stores in 1923*, 30.
7. *Operating Expenses in Retail Grocery Stores in 1923*, 11, reports that 61 percent of sales at stores surveyed were made on credit. *1930 Retail Census*, 70; Pearl Cohen interview, box 2, JHSGW; Finlay, *Paul Finlay's Book for Grocers*, 91.
8. On product selection, see Finlay, *Paul Finlay's Book for Grocers*, 92. Sugar accounted for 7.4 percent of grocery-store sales in 1929; *1930 Retail Census*, 159. In 1917–19, the average after-tax income of urban wage-earning families was $1,505, of which an average of $549 was spent on food. With the 1967 level set equal to 100, food consumption per capita in 1920 was 82.6; not until 1940 did the index reach 90. U.S. Bureau of the Census, *Historical Statistics of the United States*, 321, 328.
9. Harold Katzman, "Pop's Grocery Store," *Record*, August 1989, 31, JHSGW. Rockmoor Grocery was the first store in what later became the Winn-Dixie chain. The anecdote about hamburger appears in the privately published recollections of one of that company's founders, J. E. Davis, *Don't Make A&P Mad*, 45.
10. Memoir of Edward L. Snyder, box 2, JHSGW.
11. Cohen, *Making a New Deal*, 110. In the early twentieth century, so few African-American grocers were able to achieve even modest prosperity that successful grocers became symbols of racial achievement; see the numerous profiles of grocers in Richings, *Evidences of Progress Among Colored People*.

12. A 1920 study found that while Chicago families would buy clothing and other dry goods downtown, they bought 95 percent of their meat and 81 percent of their groceries in their immediate neighborhoods. See Shideler, "Chain Store," chap. 3, 14. Expenditures per store calculated from *1930 Retail Census*, 49.
13. The annual pay for the average full-time employee in food retailing was $1,243 in 1929; *1930 Retail Census*, 45. Reports of sales and profitability in food retailing based on voluntary surveys were extremely problematic because samples were biased toward stores whose managers were more competent and successful and therefore more likely to respond to surveys. The earliest known survey, in 1918, found the "average" profit among 1,076 grocers to be 2.3 percent of sales, but the word "average" appears to be used in the sense of "modal"; see Bureau of Business Research, Harvard University Graduate School of Business Administration, *Management Problems in Retail Grocery Stores*, 9. A corresponding 1919 study of only 263 stores reported average net profit of 2 percent, with a range from an improbably high 19.8 percent to a loss of 10.3 percent of sales; Bureau of Business Research, Harvard University Graduate School of Business Administration, *Operating Expenses in Retail Grocery Stores in 1919*, 10. The 1923 study of 471 non-chain grocers found the modal profit to be $1,170 on annual sales of $65,000, or 1.8 percent; *Operating Expenses in Retail Grocery Stores in 1923*, 8. The 1924 study found modal sales of $73,000 and net profit equaling 1.8 percent of sales, but reported profitability was only 1 percent for stores with less than $30,000 of annual sales and 1.4 percent for stores with sales of $30,000–$50,000; Bureau of Business Research, Harvard University Graduate School of Business Administration, *Operating Expenses in Retail Grocery Stores in 1924*, 55. All of these studies, by their authors' own admission, are based on nonrepresentative samples; the typical store covered in the 1924 study, for example, had six employees, including partners and proprietors, at a time when the average grocery store had a single paid employee other than the owners.
14. Furst, "Relationships Between the Numbers of Chain and Individually Owned Grocery Stores in Fort Wayne," 340; Boer, "Mortality Costs," 54; McGarry, *Mortality in Retail Trade*, and McGarry, "Mortality of Independent Grocery Stores in Buffalo and Pittsburgh"; Vivien Marie Palmer, "History of the Communities," vol. 1, "Documentary History of the Rogers Park Community, Chicago" (Chicago, 1925), doc. 31.
15. U.S. Bureau of the Census, *Fifteenth Census: Census of Distribution. Wholesale Distribution (Trade Series). Groceries and Food Specialties*, 16, 38, 45; Still, "Mortality of Seattle Grocery Wholesalers," 162.
16. *Corbin's Weekly Salesman*, February 23, 1923, CHS; Finlay, *Paul Finlay's Book for Grocers*, 14–19.
17. U.S. Department of Commerce, *Census of Distribution: Chicago, Illinois*, mimeo, December 2, 1927.
18. U.S. Congress, Joint Commission on Agricultural Inquiry, *Marketing and Distribution*, 108; Nourse, *Chicago Produce Market*, 102; Wilson, *Cart That Changed the World*, 28.
19. FTC, *Wholesale Marketing of Food*, 160.
20. U.S. Bureau of the Census, *Fourteenth Census of the United States*, vol. 8, *Manufactures, 1919: General Report and Analytical Tables*, 17; Koch, *Financing of Large*

Corporations, 113; Moses, "G. Harold Powell and the Corporate Consolidation of the Modern Citrus Enterprise."

21. Duddy and Revzan, "Transportation and Marketing Facilities for Fresh Fruits and Vegetables in Chicago," 282–84; U.S. Congress, Joint Commission on Agricultural Inquiry, *Marketing and Distribution*, 105. South Water Street, later renamed West Wacker Drive, was one block from the Loop in downtown Chicago.
22. According to R. L. Polk, a market-research firm, about 50,000 of the estimated 337,665 grocery stores and meat markets operating in 1923 were chain owned, although many of the chains were extremely small; Shideler, "Chain Store," chap. 4, 18. Great Atlantic & Pacific reported inventory worth $23.8 million on February 28, 1920; *WSJ*, April 24, 1920. Sales for the full year were $235 million, meaning that inventories equaled 10 percent of annual sales. The national average of seven turns appears in U.S. Congress, Joint Commission on Agricultural Inquiry, *Marketing and Distribution*, 163; although its precision is open to question, this average was based on a sample that included large chains, so the average for the smallest grocers may well have been less.
23. Estimated net profit for food retailers averaged 4.2 percent from 1913 to 1919 (excluding 1914 and 1915, for which data are unavailable), but fell to 2.5 percent in both 1920 and 1921. Wholesale grocers' profits averaged 1.5 percent of sales from 1913 to 1919, excluding 1914 and 1915, but averaged -0.81 percent in 1920 and 1921. U.S. Congress, Joint Commission on Agricultural Inquiry, *Marketing and Distribution*, 158, 173. There were sporadic anti-chain efforts during the war, such as an organization of twenty-five hundred retail grocers and twenty-four jobbers formed in Philadelphia in 1917 to mount a publicity campaign against the newly formed American Stores Company; see Shideler, "Chain Store," chap. 6, 16. On A&P's expenses, see "Charts, Presidents' Meeting, October 28th and 29th, 1925," box 57, Gx. On the National Association of Retail Grocers' debate, see Tedlow, *New and Improved*, 218. On the Missouri group, see Shideler, "Chain Store," chap. 6, 17.

9: WRONG TURNS

1. "Josephine Burnet Hartford," *Montclair Times*, May 11, 1944; Montclair Horse Show Inc. Collection, box 1728, MPL; "A&P Goes to the Wars," *Fortune*, April 1938, 96. Hartford relatives were prominent at the Montclair Horse Show; at least five family members took boxes at the 1937 show. "Horse Show Opened by Montclair Club," *NYT*, October 2, 1937.
2. Avis H. Anderson, *A&P*, 56–57; Ruth Reynolds, "Spotlight Hits Shrinking Hartfords," *New York Sunday News*, January 9, 1938; "Wife Asks Alimony of $50,000 a Year from President Hartford of A. and P. Stores," *NYT*, July 19, 1924.
3. Pauline Hartford passport application, January 9, 1917; John Augustine Hartford passport application, September 18, 1924; "John A. Hartford and Former Wife Rewed," *NYT*, May 5, 1925; Avis H. Anderson, *A&P*, 56, 58.
4. "Died," *NYT*, June 30, 1922. The information about the family's belief that Edward refused to seek medical care for religious reasons was provided by Avis Anderson of the Hartford Family Foundation.
5. Nourse, *Chicago Produce Market*, 95n.

6. William G. Wrightson was the husband of Josephine Clews, daughter of George H. Hartford's daughter Minnie. The ad was reprinted in A&P, "Guard Our Good Name," n.d. [c. 1970]. On average, grocery wholesalers turned their stock of non-perishables 5.5 times per year in the 1913–21 period, implying inventory equal to 9.45 weeks of sales. Average retail stock turns for the 1913–21 period were 7.7, or 6.8 weeks of sales. On average, then, the period between wholesalers' receipt of goods and retailers' final sale was more than 16 weeks. In both cases, no figures are available for 1914 and 1915. U.S. Congress, Joint Commission on Agricultural Inquiry, *Marketing and Distribution*, 157, 163. This interpretation is consistent with the view of Alfred Chandler, *The Visible Hand* (Cambridge, Mass., 1977), 236, that for chain retailers, "economies of scale and distribution were not those of size but of speed. They did not come from building larger stores; they came from increasing stock-turn." However, it is important to emphasize, as Chandler did not, that in food retailing, unlike general-merchandise retailing, distribution economies depend heavily on *local* scale because of the need for frequent replenishment of stores.
7. John Hartford quotation is from "Red Circle and Gold Leaf," *Time*, November 13, 1950. On scientific retailing, see Hess, "Selling Distribution and Its New Economics," *Annals of the American Academy of Political and Social Science* 115 (1924). The entire issue of that prestigious publication was devoted to "scientific distribution."
8. "A&P Premium Booklet—1923, Lewiston, Pa., Store," folder 150, HFF.
9. On the meat packers, see "Losses of Packers in 1921," *Barron's*, February 3, 1922, 10. Tr 20429. In 1920, A&P owned eight manufacturing plants, including three coffee plants, two bakeries, a cheese warehouse, and two canneries. FTC, *Chain Store Manufacturing*, Senate doc. 13, 73rd Cong., 1st sess., April 5, 1933. In 1913, retailers and bakeries had earned roughly equal amounts of profit on every loaf of bread. By the end of World War I, bakeries were capturing a much larger slice, and retailers' share had shrunk. The same trend held for products such as cornflakes and oatmeal. U.S. Congress, Joint Commission on Agricultural Inquiry, *Marketing and Distribution*, 209–16.
10. Avis H. Anderson, *A&P*, 63–67.
11. "A&P National Dairy Division, July 24, 1975," binder 8B, HFF; bill of sale, HFF.
12. "Wartime Building," *NYT*, May 10, 1918; "Bread 2 Cents in Chicago," *NYT*, February 6, 1923; "Great Atlantic & Pacific Tea Co.," *WSJ*, October 25, 1923; "A&P Cuts Bread Prices," *WSJ*, February 7, 1927; Rentz, "Death of Grandma," MS, 51–52; FTC, *Chain Store Manufacturing*.
13. U.S. Department of Commerce, Bureau of Fisheries, *Report of the United States Commissioner of Fisheries, 1923*, 64–65; *1924*, 90; *1926*, 282–86.
14. Avis H. Anderson, *A&P*, 90–91.
15. Ibid., 84–85; Great Atlantic & Pacific Tea Co., *Three Score Years and Ten*, 37; "A&P Cuts Bread Prices."
16. Avis H. Anderson, *A&P*, 32; "Employees to Share Chain Store Profit," *NYT*, June 5, 1925; "Dividends Declared," *NYT*, May 15, 1924; "Eight Companies Declare Dividends," *NYT*, May 15, 1925.
17. "Charts, Presidents' Meeting, October 28th and 29th 1925," box 67, Dx 212.

18. Baxter, *Chain Store Distribution and Management*, 181; "Grocers Thrive in Philadelphia," *WSJ*, September 12, 1925. Factory profits are in Adelman, *A&P*, 254. For physical volume and selling expenses, see Adelman, *A&P*, 434, 436. Adelman, *A&P*, 438, constructed estimates of the company's equity investment, including retained surplus. His calculations show that return on equity in 1924 was 7.1 percent, the lowest of any year during the decade. Adelman, *A&P*, 445, estimates that cash flow was negative in 1923, 1924, and 1925.

10: THE PROFIT MACHINE

1. Herbert Hoover, "The Problem of Distribution," delivered before the National Distribution Conference, January 14, 1925.
2. Woolworth's sales came to $216 million in 1924, and those of Sears, Roebuck, the third-largest retailer, were $206 million. The companies' fiscal years were not identical. John Hartford quotation is at Tr 20436. Adelman, *A&P*, 29, emphasizes the lack of strategic planning.
3. John A. Hartford to Mr. Friele (title unknown), February 23, 1924, file 157, HFF.
4. Hartford to John B. Edsall (manager), telegram, Newburgh, N.Y., February 11, 1924, file 157, "Correspondence from John A. Hartford," HFF; Merle Crowell, "You Don't Have to Be Brilliant," *American Magazine*, February 1931, 21. Some of the reporting forms are in folder 150, HFF.
5. U.S. Congress, Joint Commission on Agricultural Inquiry, *Marketing and Distribution*, 206. Operating expenses are given in Adelman, *A&P*, 436. A three-minute call from New York to Chicago could take hours to set up and cost $4.65; U.S. Bureau of the Census, *Historical Statistics of the United States*, 784, ser. R 14. Store clerks' pay varied considerably by location. In San Francisco, where wages were probably well above the national average, clerks earned $30–$36 for a six-day, fifty-four-hour week, or $5–$6 per day; see David F. Selvin, *Union Profile: The Fifty Years of Grocery Clerks Union, Local 648* (San Francisco, 1960), 18; *Fortune*, July 1930.
6. Comments of S. M. Flickinger in Russell, Lyons, and Flickinger, "Social and Economic Aspects of Chain Stores," 35; Crowell, "You Don't Have to Be Brilliant," 21; "National Tea Stock Listed," *NYT*, April 13, 1924. In November 1925, 1,657 stores owned by three companies were combined into the publicly traded First National Stores, and the following year 784 stores controlled by the Skaggs family were assembled into Safeway Stores; "1,657 Stores in Merger," *NYT*, November 26, 1925; "Safeway Stores Offered," *NYT*, November 24, 1926. Kroger Grocery and Baking Company, the second-largest food chain, would have a public issue in 1927; "To Float Big Block of Kroger Shares," *NYT*, December 7, 1927.
7. "Big Warehouses Sold," *NYT*, January 23, 1925.
8. "Great Atl. & Pac. Forms New Company," *WSJ*, June 4, 1925; Gx 103 and "Brief for the United States," 225, Danville trial.
9. "Employees to Share Chain Store Profit," *NYT*, June 5, 1925; "Great Atl. & Pac. Forms New Company"; "Increased Dividend and Extras Voted," *NYT*, August 17, 1928; Great Atlantic & Pacific Tea Co. Certificate Book, HFF.

   In February 1926, the U.S. Department of Justice brought an antitrust suit against National Food Products Corporation, claiming that it was attempting to set up a "food trust" by acquiring control of numerous grocery retailers and manufacturers, including Great Atlantic & Pacific. The suit implied that the purpose of A&P's stock issuance was to enable it to participate in the trust. The allegations were rather far-fetched. National Food Products was an investment company, similar to a closed-end mutual fund, intending to invest in the food industry, in which many companies were issuing shares for the first time. As of the date of the lawsuit it had raised $1.8 million through stock sales, not enough to control any major grocery chain, much less the largest retailer in the world, which by its own estimate was worth $58 million at the time (Adelman, *A&P*, 438). It is improbable that the Hartford brothers would have been interested in joining in the sort of trust described by the government, as this would have required them to surrender absolute control of their company. John Hartford denied that A&P was controlled by National Food Products and emphasized that the only reason for issuing stock was to provide shares for employees. See "Government Sues to Stop $160,000,000 Food Store 'Trust,'" *NYT*, February 14, 1926; "Lawyer Ridicules Suit on 'Food Trust,'" *NYT*, February 15, 1926; "Halsey Quits Board of New Food Trust," *NYT*, February 16, 1926.

10. Gx 103. A&P's annual data books, containing a standard set of tables and charts, are in RG 60, General Records of the U.S. Department of Justice, Antitrust Division, Litigation Case Files, Enclosures to Classified Subject Files, 1930–87, boxes 36 and 37, NARA-CP. Other data were distributed at the meetings of division presidents without inclusion in the annual book.
11. Charts for Division Presidents' Meetings, January 27–28, 1927, February 9, 1928, and February 20, 1929, box 67, Danville trial enclosures; Gx 103 and Dx 212. The most common measure of corporate profitability, return on equity, is not relevant for A&P during this period, as the company had no publicly traded stock and its privately held shares had only the nominal value assigned when they were issued. Adelman, *A&P*, 438, constructed estimates of the company's equity investment, including retained surplus. His calculations show that return on equity in 1924 was 7.1 percent, the lowest of any year during the decade. The company's stated investment was $25.3 million in the year ending February 1921; $62.6 million in the year ending February 1926; and $118.8 million in the year ending February 1930; see "A&P Growth Is Told at Hearing," *WSJ*, October 25, 1930. However, these figures are not consistent with those reported by Adelman. On the meager return in 1925, see Green, "Vertical Integration" (B.A. thesis), 22.
12. "Atlantic & Pacific Tea Sales About $450,000,000," *NYT*, January 1, 1926.
13. Hartford quotation, from the minutes of the division presidents' meeting of February 3 and 4, 1926, is in Gx 105. Adelman, *A&P*, 445, estimates that cash flow was negative in 1923, 1924, and 1925.
14. Dx 213, "Charts, Presidents' Meeting, February 3rd and 4th, 1926," box 67; "Brief for the United States," 13, Danville trial.
15. Adelman, *A&P*, 32, 257; "Brief for the United States," 13, 74, 153, 317, Danville trial; Great Atlantic & Pacific Tea Co., *Three Score Years and Ten*, 18.
16. Adelman, *A&P*, 112, 120, 225.
17. FTC, *Chain Stores: Final Report on the Chain-Store Investigation* (Washington, D.C., 1935), 90; Adelman, *A&P*, 237.

18. "A&P Tea Co. Plans Increase in Advertising," *Hartford Courant*, July 2, 1926; Crowell, "You Don't Have to Be Brilliant," 112.
19. Gx 107 and 404; Green, "Vertical Integration," 17. Alfred Chandler was bewildered by the apparently informal coordination between A&P's central staff and its operating divisions, suggesting that it "may pose problems in maintaining effective central control." He thought the Hartfords might have modeled their organization's structure on that of Swift & Company, the largest meat packer, which published detailed information about its corporate structure in the 1920s and 1930s. See his "Management Decentralization," 163–64.
20. Adelman, *A&P*, 112.
21. Baum, "Chain Store Methods," 282; Adelman, *A&P*, 468; Avis H. Anderson, *A&P*, 85.
22. Between 1914 and 1930, A&P acquired only 300 stores, representing 1.5 percent of the total number of stores it opened during that period. It closed 4,896 stores over the same period; FTC, *Chain Stores: Growth and Development of Chain Stores*, 36, 77; "A&P Price Action Credited in Growth," *NYT*, August 10, 1930; "St. Louis A&P Building," *NYT*, September 17, 1928; "Bond Flotations," *NYT*, May 9, 1929; "Bond Flotation," *NYT*, August 21, 1929; J. C. Furnas, "Mr. George & Mr. John," *Saturday Evening Post*, December 31, 1938, 55.
23. Charts, Division Presidents' Meetings, January 27–28, 1927, February 9, 1928, and February 20, 1929, boxes 35 and 67, Danville trial.
24. Gx 107.
25. "A&P Cuts Bread Prices," *WSJ*, February 7, 1927; "Great A&P Sales Up $100,000,000," *WSJ*, January 7, 1928; "Cigarette Prices Are Slashed Here," *NYT*, April 24, 1928; "Cut $4,000,000 Off United Cigar Net," *NYT*, January 10, 1930; "Schulte Demands Cigarette War End," *NYT*, April 17, 1929; "Retailers Aroused by Cigarette War," *NYT*, May 21, 1929; "Schulte Minority Hits Management," *NYT*, April 22, 1930.
26. In February 1927, A&P's balance sheet showed $15.6 million of cash and securities against $179,000 of debts; by February 1931, cash reached $41 million, and debts were only $458,000. Over the same period, even after generous dividend payouts, retained earnings climbed from $9 million to $57 million. Five years of balance-sheet data are shown in William Henry Smith, "A Billion-Dollar Cash Business," *Barron's*, November 25, 1929, 12. "A&P Expands in Houston," *WSJ*, October 28, 1927; "'A&P' in Canada," *WSJ*, June 27, 1927; "Atlantic & Pacific," *WSJ*, May 8, 1930; "A&P Decides to Sell as Well as Buy in Northwest," *Business Week*, April 8, 1931, 11.
27. FTC, *Chain Stores: Sources of Chain-Store Merchandise*, 23–24, 29; Great Atlantic & Pacific Tea Co., *Three Score Years and Ten*, 37.
28. Among the critics was Fiorello La Guardia, then a congressman and soon to become New York City's mayor, who warned in a March 1930 radio talk that shoppers needed to patronize independent stores to avoid "a gigantic food trust in this country." See box 37(A), WPP. FTC, *Chain Store Manufacturing*, Senate doc. 13, 73rd Cong., 1st sess., April 5, 1933, 30; "Puts U.S. Meat Bill at $5,000,000,000 Yearly," *WSJ*, November 8, 1930; "A&P Price Action Credited in Growth," Adelman, *A&P*, 265; "Postum Company, Inc.," *Barron's*, August 13, 1928, 10; Rentz, "Death of Grandma," MS, 54; William Henry Smith, "A Billion from 'Cash and Carry,'" *Barron's*, January 19, 1931, 22; A&P, "A&P, an Organization and Its Work-

ers" (1930), 22, 29. The 1930 census counted 29.9 million "family households." The number of nonfamily households was not reported, but the 1940 figure of 3.5 million suggests that the 1930 figure would have been between 2.5 and 3 million, yielding a total of approximately 32 million households.

29. Rentz, "'Death of Grandma,'" 9; "A&P Construction Plan Gets Underway," *WSJ*, June 9, 1930; A&P, "A&P, an Organization and Its Workers," 5.
30. "Gives Outing to 200 at Mountain Retreat," *NYT*, September 29, 1929; "Capital Rise Voted by New Haven Road," *NYT*, April 17, 1930. John Hartford was elected a director of National Bank of Commerce on July 25, 1928. Board minutes give no indication that A&P did business with the bank prior to his election to replace a director who retired due to ill health. See National Bank of Commerce, Board of Directors minutes, 1927 and 1928, JPMC. When that institution merged with the larger and more prestigious Guaranty Trust Company in 1929, Hartford joined the merged institution's board, serving alongside such notables as John T. Dorrance, head of Campbell Soup Company, an A&P supplier; the retailer Marshall Field; the 1924 presidential candidate John W. Davis; Richard B. Mellon, brother of Treasury Secretary Andrew Mellon and president of Mellon Bank; the investment banker W. Averell Harriman, who controlled a major stake in the Union Pacific Railroad; and several members of one of Guaranty Trust's founding families, the Whitneys; *Guaranty News*, February 1929 and March 1929, JPMC.

11: MINUTE MEN AND TAX MEN

1. Evans Clark, "Big Business Now Sweeps Retail Trade," *NYT*, July 8, 1928. According to the article, the next seven chain operators, F. W. Woolworth, Kroger, J. C. Penney, S. S. Kresge, Gimbel Brothers, American Stores, and May Department Stores, had a combined 8,803 stores. A&P alone was said to have 17,500, although company records show a shorter number. The article estimated A&P's annual sales to be $750 million, and those of Kroger, the next-largest grocer, to be $161 million. A&P's reported sales were $761 million in the year ending February 1928.
2. U.S. Bureau of the Census, *Fifteenth Census of the United States: 1930 Retail Distribution: Summary for the United States* (Washington, D.C., 1933), 45.
3. *City of Danville v. Quaker Maid Inc.*, 211 Ky. 677. The Danville ordinance divided grocery stores, meat markets, and fish markets into three classes. "Regular service" establishments were to pay $12 per year plus $5 for each employee over two. "Cash and carry" grocers without self-service stores were to pay $50 per year plus $25 for each employee over two, while self-service grocers operating on a cash-and-carry basis were to pay $40 per year plus $30 for each employee over two. The Kentucky Court of Appeals ruled that the way a store did business was not a reasonable distinction for purposes of taxation.
4. Lebhar, *Chain Stores in America*, 153; F. J. Harper, "'A New Battle on Evolution': The Anti–Chain Store Trade-at-Home Agitation of 1929–1930," *Journal of American Studies* 16 (1982), 412; Alfred G. Buehler, "Anti-Chain-Store Taxation," 350. A&P's average profit per store was $947 in the year ending February 1927, and $1,208 the following year. On the Pennsylvania law, see Richard C. Schragger, "The Anti–Chain Store Movement, Localist Ideology, and the Remnants of the Progressive Constitution, 1920–1940," 1036.

5. "A&P Attacked," *Time*, April 23, 1928; Senate resolution 224, 70th Cong., 1st sess.; "Chain Head Can See No Basis for Probe," *NYT*, May 13, 1928.
6. "Chain Stores and the Groceryman," *Review of Reviews* 78 (1928), 109; Dx 998, 999, 1000.
7. James L. Palmer, "Economic and Social Aspects of Chain Stores," 277; President's Research Committee on Social Trends, *Recent Social Trends in the United States* (New York, 1933); Shideler, "Chain Store" (Ph.D. diss.), chap. 1, 9; W. A. Masters, "The Chain Store, the Catalog House, and the Tax Payer" (St. Joseph, Mo., 1928), 11, Mms 159, LSUS.
8. Lebhar, *Chain Stores in America*, 154; FTC, *Chain Stores: Scope of the Chain-Store Inquiry*, 10; FTC, *Chain Stores: Cooperative Grocery Chains*, xvi.
9. O'Pry, *Chronicles of Shreveport and Caddo Parish*, 355.
10. Ibid.; U.S. Department of Commerce, Bureau of Navigation, "Radio Service Bulletin," June 1, 1922. Dates of licensing were obtained from a helpful article, "Shreveport Radio Stations of the 1920s," jeff560.tripod.com/am14.html, accessed September 15, 2009.
11. U.S. Department of Commerce, "Radio Service Bulletin," September 1, 1925, 7; January 31, 1928, 20; February 28, 1929, 12; June 29, 1929, 17; Derek Vaillant, "Bare-Knuckled Broadcasting," 196; Harper, "'New Battle on Evolution,'" 413.
12. Doerksen, *American Babel*, chap. 5.
13. Philip Lieber, "The Menace of the Chain Store System" (1929), Mms 159, LSUS; Harry W. Schachter, "War on the Chain Store," *Nation*, May 7, 1930, 544.
14. Schachter, "War on the Chain Store," 544; *Printers' Ink*, February 20, 1930, 4.
15. Harper, "'New Battle on Evolution,'" 414; Charlie C. McCall, "Live and Let Live," Mms 159, LSUS; R. K. Calloway, "The Handicappers or the Chain Store Menace," Mms 159, LSUS.
16. Vaillant, "Bare-Knuckled Broadcasting," 199; Harper, "'New Battle on Evolution,'" 417, 423; Lebhar, *Chain Stores in America*, 158. Pay for grocery clerks was commonly in the range of \$15–\$30; see Edward G. Ernst and Emil M. Hartl, "Chain Management and Labor," *Nation*, November 26, 1930, 574.
17. Duncan was convicted in 1930 of indecency for uttering the phrase "By God" on the air, and the Federal Radio Commission revoked his station's license. Flowers, *Japanese Conquest of American Opinion*, 265; Flowers, *America Chained*, 57.
18. On Coughlin, see Brinkley, *Voices of Protest*. Brinkley makes no mention of the chain-store issue or the anti-chain broadcasters. W. K. Henderson, "On Chain Store Monopoly and Packers Consent Decree" (n.d., 1930), PSOC 5/31, Notre Dame University Archives, South Bend, Ind.
19. Lebhar, *Chain Stores in America*, 160–61.
20. Ibid., 163.
21. Ibid., 164; Alfred G. Buehler, "Anti-Chain-Store Taxation," 350; Ingram and Rao, "Store Wars," 31; Hardy, "Taxation of Chain Retailers in the United States," 258; Lee, "Recent Trends in Chain-Store Tax Legislation," 267; Schachter, "War on the Chain Store," 545.
22. The first FTC report, *Chain-Store System of Marketing and Distribution*, was released as Senate doc. 146, 71st Cong., 2nd sess., May 12, 1930. Four further reports on chain stores had followed by the end of 1931, and many more throughout the

decade. Numerous issue guides for debaters were published during these years, several of them with the assistance of the National Chain Store Association; see, for example, Ezra Buehler, *Chain Store Debate Manual*, and Somerville, *Chain Store Debate Manual*. Oliver Clinton Carpenter, *Debate Outlines on Public Questions* (New York, 1932), 88–102, addressed the chain-store question in more balanced fashion. James L. Palmer, *What About Chain Stores?* (New York, 1929); Russell, Lyons, and Flickinger, "Social and Economic Aspects of Chain Stores," 27–36; Edward G. Ernst and Emil M. Hartl, "Chains Versus Independents," *Nation*, November 12–December 3, 1930; John T. Flynn, "Chain Stores: Menace or Promise?" *New Republic*, April 15–29, 1931; Arthur Capper, "The Chain Store Problem," address over WJSV, March 21, 1930, collection 12, box 38, KSHS.

23. *Jackson v. State Board of Tax Commissioners of Indiana*, 38 F.2d 652 (1930); *State Board of Tax Commissioners v. Jackson*, 283 U.S. 527 (1931); *Great Atlantic & Pacific Tea Co. v. Maxwell*, 284 U.S. 575 (1931).
24. Lebhar, *Chain Stores in America*, 129, 168.
25. Minutes of the meeting of division presidents, November 10–11, 1927, vi, xiv, in box 35, Danville trial exhibits; Tedlow, *New and Improved*, 195; Lebhar, *Chain Stores in America*, 169; A&P, "A&P, an Organization and Its Workers" (1930); Dx 124, box 66.
26. Gx 114; "A&P Price Action Credited in Growth," *NYT*, August 10, 1930.

12: THE SUPERMARKET

1. "Financial Notes," *NYT*, July 26, 1928. The depreciated value of A&P's real-estate holdings fell 13 percent from 1926 to 1930 as the company shed property. Total assets nearly doubled over the same period, so land and buildings declined from 8 percent of the company's assets to only 3.6 percent, insulating the company against loss in the event the value of real estate needed to be written down; William Henry Smith, "A Billion from 'Cash and Carry,'" *Barron's*, January 19, 1931.
2. Ward, *Produce and Conserve*, 230; Davis, *Don't Make A&P Mad*, 45. Census product-line data are not available prior to 1929, but studies such as Croxton's *Study of Housewives' Buying Habits in Columbus, Ohio, 1924* suggest that the vast majority of housewives purchased meat at meat markets and milk at dairy stores, rather than at grocery chains. The first census survey of 1929 found that meat accounted for 17 percent of sales at combination stores. U.S. Bureau of the Census, *Fifteenth Census of the United States: 1930 Retail Distribution: Summary for the United States* (Washington, D.C., 1933), 159; U.S. Bureau of the Census, *Historical Statistics of the United States*, 695.
3. Clarke, "Consumer Negotiations," 109; Roger Horowitz, *Putting Meat on the American Table*, 138–39; Rentz, "'Death of Grandma,'" MS, 54; Dx 438, box 66.
4. Shideler, "Chain Store" (Ph.D. diss.), chap. 2, 6, pointed out that one effect of the automobile and improved mass transit was to encourage mobility within the city. "With the shifting of families about the city, standardized stores . . . have a distinct advantage because it in effect removes the strangeness of the new environment for the incoming family."
5. Dipman, *Modern Grocery Store*, 4, 8, 13, 23, 27; Davis, *Don't Make A&P Mad*, 44. Average sales at traditional stores were around $18,000 per year, at combination stores $33,000; U.S. Bureau of the Census, *1930 Retail Distribution*, 45.

6. Baxter, *Chain Store Distribution and Management*, 179; "A&P from A to Z," *Business Week*, September 30, 1932; Dx 401, box 67. A store that opened in Philadelphia in 1929 covered twenty thousand square feet, making it the largest unit in the entire chain; see "A&P Leases Philadelphia Store," *NYT*, December 11, 1929.
7. "Charts, Presidents' Meeting, August 16, 1928," box 67, Danville trial; "Brief for the United States," 156, Danville trial.
8. Appel, "Supermarket," 41–43; Mayo, *American Grocery Store*, 138; Phillips, "Supermarket," 193. See also Goldman, "Stages in the Development of the Supermarket."
9. Tedlow, *New and Improved*, 226–29. Cullen's letter appears in M. M. Zimmerman, *The Super Market: A Revolution in Distribution*, 32–35, and is reprinted in substantial part in Tedlow, *New and Improved*, 381–84. Data on combination store sales and operating costs are from U.S. Bureau of the Census, *Census of Distribution, Retail Chains* (Washington, D.C., 1933), 36–37.
10. *Business Week*, February 8, 1933; Appel, "Supermarket," 44; Mayo, *American Grocery Store*, 145.
11. For example, the San Francisco wholesaler Wellman, Peck & Company formed Neighborhood Stores Inc., a voluntary chain with three thousand member stores. Wellman, Peck & Co., *Our First 100 Years* (San Francisco, 1949).
12. M. M. Zimmerman and F. R. Grant, "Warning: Here Comes the Super-Market!" *Nation's Business*, March 1937, 21; Phillips, "Supermarket," 190.
13. Adelman, *A&P*, 41–42; Gx 134.
14. Minutes of Central Western Division, January 13, 1933, Gx 146.
15. A&P's gross profit on coffee was 45 percent in 1920 and 1921, implying an 82 percent markup; after dipping as low as 20 percent in 1928, it settled in the 30 percent range for several years; see "Charts, Presidents' Meetings, year ending March 1, 1941," 162, box 36, Danville trial exhibits.
16. Minutes of division presidents meeting, June 25, 1931, box 67, Danville trial exhibits.
17. Dx 420; Tr 20438; Phillips, "Supermarket," 195; "The Consumer Accepts the Supermarket," *Super Market Merchandising*, November 1936, 15. Retail food sales were $10.8 billion in 1929, but due to deflation fell to $8.4 billion in 1935.
18. "Grocers Call A&P a Monopoly; Put Up the Money to Prove It," *Business Week*, June 22, 1932, 8. According to Dipman, *Modern Grocery Store*, 4, the average margin in food retailing fell from 25 percent around 1920 to 20 percent or less by 1931.
19. See, for example, "People," *Time*, September 21, 1931; "$100,000, Please, for Charm and Poise," *Xenia* (Ohio) *Evening Gazette*, September 19, 1931; "Highlights of Broadway," *Albuquerque Journal*, November 19, 1931; "Mystery Romance of the Chain Store Heir," *Hamilton* (Ohio) *Daily News*, November 28, 1931; "Josephine Hartford Bryce," *NYT*, June 10, 1992.
20. "Private Lives," *Life*, January 25, 1937, 58; "Spotlight Hits Shrinking Hartfords," *New York Sunday News*, January 9, 1938; "Huntington Hartford, A&P Heir Adept at Losing Millions, Dies at 97," *NYT*, May 20, 2008.
21. For contemporaneous discussion of the social factors behind the anti-chain movement, see James L. Palmer, "Economic and Social Aspects of Chain Stores." On the anti-chain movement in Chicago, see Deutsch, *Building a Housewife's Paradise*, 78–80.

22. The 1939 *Census of Business*, vol. 1, *Retail Trade*, pt. 1, 170, shows that 119,024 independent grocery stores then in operation were established from 1930 to 1937; typical mortality estimates imply that the number surviving in 1939 was less than half the total number established in 1930 to 1937. The number of proprietors rose from 284,277 in 1929 to 318,736 six years later and reached 351,981 by 1939; ibid., 57; Adelman, *A&P*, 430.
23. Baxter, *Chain Store Distribution and Management*, 17; FTC, *Final Report on the Chain-Store Investigation*, vol. 5, 38; FTC, *Chain Store Inquiry*, vol. 3, *Chain Stores: Chain-Store Leaders and Loss Leaders*, Senate doc. 51, 72nd Cong., 1st sess. (1932), xi.

13: FRANKLIN ROOSEVELT

1. Alter, *Defining Moment*, 77.
2. Seamans to Roosevelt, January 19, 1933; Rund to Roosevelt, February 18, 1933; McKay to Roosevelt, April 13, 1933; Applegate to Roosevelt, n.d., all in OF 288, Chain Stores, 1933–34, FDR.
3. The foundational texts of 1920s consumerism were Chase, *Tragedy of Waste*, one of the first books to explore the manipulation of consumer preferences by advertising, and Chase and Schlink, *Your Money's Worth*, which became a bestseller. Chase and Schlink were the co-founders of Consumers' Research. Means, "The Consumer and the New Deal," 7.
4. U.S. Bureau of the Census, *Historical Statistics of the United States*, 319; Bolin, "Economics of Middle-Class Family Life."
5. Perhaps the earliest articulation of the consumerist view was Orleck, "'We Are That Mythical Thing Called the Public.'" See also Orleck, *Common Sense and a Little Fire*, 235–39. Alan Brinkley goes even further, contending, "The 'New Dealer' antimonopolists were worried principally about protecting consumers"; *End of Reform*, 64. Subsequent assertions of consumers' preeminence can be found in Lizabeth Cohen, *A Consumers' Republic*, 24; Donohue, *Freedom from Want*, 171–82; McGovern, *Sold American*, 135; Deutsch, "From 'Wild Animal Stores' to Women's Sphere." Jacobs, *Pocketbook Politics*, 95–135, provides a more balanced exploration of the tension between the New Deal's producerist and consumerist inclinations. The quotation is from Donohue, *Freedom from Want*, 228.
6. Brinkley, *End of Reform*, 59.
7. Federal Reserve Bank of Boston, "Closed for the Holiday: The Bank Holiday of 1933," n.d.; Huff, *Chain Store Tyranny and the Independent Grocers' Dilemma*.
8. Donovan, a Wall Street lawyer, was among a small number of guests at Roosevelt's birthday party in Warm Springs, Georgia, in 1933. Roosevelt subsequently named him head of the new U.S. intelligence agency, the Office of Strategic Services, during World War II. "Report $99,460 Spent on Donovan Campaign," *NYT*, November 19, 1932; "Ford Paid $25,000 Radio Bill," *NYT*, January 7, 1933.
9. 48 Stat. 31, sec. 8; 48 Stat. 195, sec. 3.
10. National Association of Chain Stores, *The Chain Store Industry Under the National Industrial Recovery Act* (New York, 1934), 41, 53.
11. Dx 144, box 66.
12. National Association of Chain Stores, *Chain Store Industry*, 65–67.

13. Dameron, "Retailing Under the N.R.A., I," 1.
14. Hawley, *New Deal and the Problem of Monopoly.*
15. Alexander, "N.R.A. and Distribution," 197.
16. M. L. Toulme (secretary, National-American Wholesale Grocers' Association) to McIntyre, November 4, 1933; NAWGA, "News About Codes," November 3, 1933; NAWGA, "A Special Petition to President Roosevelt," November 3, 1933, all in PPF 2538, FDR. NRA Consumer Advisory Board, "The Purpose of the N.R.A. as Seen by the Consumers' Advisory Board," Gardiner Means Papers, box 2, FDR. On the use of meat as a loss leader due to its exclusion from the food retail code, see Emanuel Celler to Hugh Johnson (administrator, NRA), August 24, 1934, in Leon Henderson Papers, box 11, FDR.
17. In 1933, 3.1 percent of A&P's stores were unprofitable, but 84 percent of the unprofitable stores had been open for three or more years, meaning that at most seventy-five of the hundreds of stores in operation for less than three years lost money; see data in Adelman, *A&P*, 450. Pelz, "Developments Under the N.R.A. and A.A.A.," 21–22; Dameron, "Retailing Under the N.R.A., I," 20. For discussion of various proposals, see *Retail Clerks International Advocate*, September–October 1933, 12, and January–February 1934, 14. As Charles F. Phillips points out, grocers conventionally took low markups on staples such as lard and sugar and higher markups on slow-moving items; attempts by chains to standardize markups during the 1920s proved "disastrous" and drove away business. See Phillips, "Price Policies of Food Chains," 379.
18. Dameron, "Retailing Under the N.R.A., II," 201; Records Related to the Roberts Committee Investigation, box 2, Records of the Compliance Division, Records of the National Recovery Administration, RG 9, NARA-CP; "Complaints Docketed by NRA State Offices," Office Files of Enid Baird, box 3, Records of the Trade Practice Studies Section, Records of Division of Review, Records of the National Recovery Administration, RG 9, NARA-CP; NRA, "Retail and Wholesale Distribution Project of the Division of Research and Planning," Leon Henderson Papers, box 4, FDR; Dx 419, box 66.
19. "State Chain Store Taxes (as of May 15, 1937)," Office of Tax Policy, Subject Files, box 13, RG 56, General Records of the Department of the Treasury, NARA-CP; Davis, *Don't Make A&P Mad*, 93.
20. *Tide: Of Advertising and Marketing*, February 1935, 13.
21. Alfred G. Buehler, "Chain Store Taxes," 180; Morris, "Economics of the Special Taxation" (Ph.D. diss.), 36; John P. Nichols, *Chain Store Manual* (New York, 1936), 74. A&P's financial reports did not distinguish chain-store taxes from sales taxes, which came into use during this period but were low and frequently exempted food; see Dx 499.
22. Ross, "Store Wars," 131; Morris, "Economics of the Special Taxation," 36.
23. "Food Trade Heads Aid Farm Revival," *NYT*, July 10, 1933; "Support Pledged for Blanket Code," *NYT*, July 22, 1933.
24. Brinkley, *End of Reform*, 61; Committee on Unfair Trade Practices, "Code-Making and Code-Enforcement," March 21, 1935, RG 40, Department of Commerce, Office of the Secretary, Business Advisory Committee Records, 1933–38, box 2, NARA-CP. "Five Picked to Pass on Industry Loans," *NYT*, July 4, 1934; Robert H. Jackson, "The Big Corporations Rule," *New Republic*, September 4, 1935, 99–101;

Gx 156, box 68; "A Vote on the NRA," *Barron's*, July 2, 1934, 5. In 1937, after he had become assistant attorney general for antitrust, Robert H. Jackson told lawyers that only when all laws "are brought to exert their pressures toward the encouragement of small business rather than toward its destruction, can we say that we have a national policy against monopoly." "The Struggle Against Monopoly," speech to Georgia Bar Association, May 28, 1937.

25. "NRA and Business Profits," *Barron's*, July 2, 1934, 6; Dx 506, box 66; Adelman, *A&P*, 51, 430, 434, 438; "Brief for the United States," 166, Danville trial.
26. *Schechter Poultry Company v. United States*, 295 U.S. 532, 537 (1935).
27. F. M. Massman (president, Food and Grocery Chain Stores of America Inc.) to members, telegram, May 27, 1935, OF 288, FDR; A. T. Martin (executive secretary) to W. P. Robert (chairman, Committee to Report on Changes in Labor and Trade Practice Standards), memo, August 24, 1935; Edward D. McLaughlin (state NRA director, Arkansas) to Major General Amos A. Fries, memo, August 1, 1935; W. H. Loughry (executive secretary, Food and Grocery Bureau of Southern California) to G. F. Ashley (NRA, San Francisco), July 2, 1935; all in box 5; J. E. Wrenn (state NRA officer, Kansas) to Fries, July 15, 1935, box 6, Records Related to the Roberts Committee Investigation; Report by Wesley O. Ash, NRA office, San Francisco, Miscellaneous Records of Legal, Compliance, and Other Divisions, box 77, Records of the National Recovery Administration, RG 9, NARA-CP; Food & Grocery Distributors Code Authority, District No. 2, California, Miscellaneous Records of Legal, Compliance, and Other Divisions, box 76. On the repeated attempts to restore NRA-like price regulations in California, see McHenry, "Price Stabilization Attempts in the Grocery Trade in California."
28. "Departures from Code Standards of Hours and Wages by Chain and Independent Grocers in the Retail Food and Grocery Trade," Records Related to the Roberts Committee Investigation, box 5; Adelman, *A&P*, 434, 438.
29. Hawley, *New Deal and the Problem of Monopoly*, 40, 255–56.

14: WRIGHT PATMAN

1. On Jacobs, see George Purl (Texas state senator) to R. W. Lyons (national chain-store lobbyist), March 2, 1935, in "Special Investigation Concerning Chain Store Bill," September 30–October 2, 1935, Governor James Allred Files, box 2000/188, 17, TSL; "Carry Chain Store Fight to Capital," *Chicago Journal of Commerce*, February 16, 1935.
2. Nancy Beck Young, *Wright Patman*, 11–22. Young notes that in 1965, five of the thirty committee chairmen in the U.S. House of Representatives were Cumberland graduates. Boxes 77(B) and 81(C), WPP; David A. Horowitz, *Beyond Left and Right*, 103.
3. Watkins, *Hungry Years*, 132–36.
4. Nancy Beck Young, *Wright Patman*, 31, 56, 63; box 76(A), WPP; "Statement of Receipts and Disbursements on Books and Folders," May 7, 1935, box 127(C), WPP.
5. Ickes, *Secret Diary of Harold L. Ickes*, 356; "Merchants of the Nation Organize to Act as Unit on Economic Issues," *NYT*, April 17, 1935; House resolution 203, 74th Cong., 1st sess., April 24, 1935; "Representative Cochran Ill," *NYT*, May 4, 1935; Cochran to Patman, n.d. [June 1935], box 37(C), WPP.

6. Patman to John J. O'Connor (chairman, House Rules Committee), May 31, 1935, box 37(C), WPP.
7. J. F. Carroll (president, General Marketing Counselors Inc.) to Patman, May 29, 1935, box 37(C), WPP; *Retail Ledger*, Report No. 98, July 5, 1935.
8. Everett MacIntyre (Special Investigating Committee staff) to Harry L. Underwood (Office of the U.S. District Attorney), Washington, D.C., June 14, 1935, box 37(C), WPP; deposition of John E. Barr, June 10, 1935, box 90(B), WPP; *Retail Ledger*, Report No. 98, July 5, 1935. Logan's connection with Barr had an even stranger aspect: Logan testified that Barr had told him that the National Anti–Chain Store League was secretly accepting money from German sources to establish a journal, to be distributed through small merchants, that would be used as a vehicle for Nazi propaganda. Logan to Patman, July 25, 1935, box 37(C), WPP.
9. Logan to Patman, July 25, 1935, box 37(C), WPP.
10. The original version of the bill, labeled "Drafted by the General Counsel of the United States Wholesale Grocers' Association Inc.," is in box 37(C), WPP; *Congressional Record* 79 (June 11, 1935), 9077, 9318, 9423; J. H. McLaurin (president, United States Wholesale Grocers) to members, July 22, 1935, box 37(B), WPP. Hawley, *New Deal and the Problem of Monopoly*, 250, ties the bill directly to the demise of the NRA. On the dinner, see J. H. McLaurin to Hatton W. Sumners, June 18, 1935, in Judiciary Committee, U.S. House of Representatives, Papers Accompanying Specific Bills and Resolutions, 74th Cong., RG 233, HR 74A-D21, box 186, NARA-LA.
11. Total sales at food stores of all types, from candy stands to fish markets, were $8.36 billion in 1935. A&P's sales were $872 million, or about one-ninth of total food-store sales. Sales at grocery stores were $6.3 billion, giving A&P a 14 percent market share. Aggregate sales figures are from U.S. Bureau of the Census, *Census of Business*, vol. 1, *Retail Trade: 1939, Part 1* (Washington, D.C., 1941), 57; *Report by the Special Investigating Committee on that Part of House Resolution 203 Relating to the Organization and Lobbying Activities of the American Retail Federation*, vol. 1, 430, 460–61; Daughters, *Wells of Discontent*, 175.
12. *Report by the Special Investigating Committee*, vol. 1, 448–67; *Retail Ledger*, Report No. 99, July 10, 1935.
13. *Report by the Special Investigating Committee*, vol. 3, 90; vol. 4, 1–12; Wolff, "Patman Tax Bill on Chain Stores."
14. *Report by the Special Investigating Committee*, vol. 2, 16; *Congressional Record* 79 (June 11, 1935), 9077.
15. For Allred's message to the legislature of February 25, 1935, see "Special Investigation Concerning Chain Store Bill," box 2000/188, 37, TSL. The letters are in Allred Files, box 1985/024-42, TSL; "Texas: Bluebonnet Boldness," *Time*, June 8, 1936.
16. James V. Allred, *Legislative Messages of Hon. James V. Allred, Governor of Texas, 1935–1939* (Austin, 1939), 83; "Special Investigation Concerning Chain Store Bill," box 2000/188, 3–15, TSL.
17. Provisions of tax laws are compiled in Morris, "Economics of the Special Taxation," 266–69.
18. Elmore Whitehurst, "Hatton W. Sumners: His Life and Public Service," www.hattonsumners.org/library/public_service.pdf, accessed October 5, 2009.

19. Roosevelt to the 1934 Boston Conference on Distribution, PPF 1802, FDR; comments to press are cited in OF 288, Chain Stores, 1935–36. See also Emanuel Celler, "Statement in Opposition to Patman Bill H.R. 8442," Judiciary Committee, U.S. House of Representatives, 74th Cong., RG 233, HR 74A-D21, box 186, NARA-LA.
20. Stevens, "Comparison of Special Discounts and Allowances"; United States Wholesale Grocers' Association, *Bulletin*, no. 67, July 3, 1935, and E. S. Briggs (general manager, American Fruit and Vegetable Shippers Association) to Sumners, July 8, 1935, both in Judiciary Committee, U.S. House of Representatives, 74th Cong., RG 233, HR 74A-D21, box 187, NARA-LA; testimony of Horace Herr, *Hearings Before the Committee on the Judiciary on H.R. 4995 and H.R. 5062*, 74th Cong., 1st sess. (1935), 7.
21. *Hearings Before the Committee on the Judiciary on H.R. 4995 and H.R. 5062*, 30–31; W. W. Schneider (Monsanto) to Sumners, telegram, July 10, 1935, box 186; Sydney Anderson (vice president, General Mills) to Sumners, February 20, 1936, box 187; Hausler-Kilian Cigar Company, San Antonio, to Sumners, telegram, April 28, 1936, box 187; O. V. Snyder (president, Pacific Match Company) to United States Wholesale Grocers' Association, July 12, 1935, box 187; all in Judiciary Committee, U.S. House of Representatives, 74th Cong., RG 233, HR 74A-D21, NARA-LA.
22. *Hearings Before the Committee on the Judiciary on H.R. 4995 and H.R. 5062*, 366; Morris, "Economics of the Special Taxation," 126.
23. McIntyre to Patman, November 27, 1935; Patman to McIntyre, November 30, 1935; Patman to Roosevelt, January 13, 1936; all in box 37(B), WPP; McIntyre to Roosevelt, memo, December 13, 1935, OF 288, FDR; McIntyre to Patman, telegram, December 21, 1935, PPF 3982, FDR.
24. Statement of women's groups, Judiciary Committee, U.S. House of Representatives, 74th Cong., RG 233, HR 74A-D21, box 187, NARA-LA; *Hardware Trade Journal*, April 1936, 21. The petitions are filed in RG 233, Committee Papers, House Committee on Interstate and Foreign Commerce, 74th Cong., HR74A-H6.7, box 407, NARA-LA. Druggists' letters are in RG 233, HR 74A-D21, box 187, NARA-LA.
25. Charles M. Marsh (chairman, Federal Trade Commission) to Hubert Utterback, March 4, 1935, Judiciary Committee, U.S. House of Representatives, 74th Cong., RG 233, HR 74A-D21, box 186, NARA-LA; most food-trade associations agreed in late 1935 to support a grocery price-fixing plan that would be administered by the FTC, but the plan was so extreme that the agency would not endorse it; "For FTC Control," *Business Week*, January 4, 1936, 4. U.S. Department of Commerce, Business Advisory Council, "Report of the Committee on Distribution Problems," 1936, RG 40, Department of Commerce, Office of the Secretary, Business Advisory Council, Records, 1933–38, box 2, NARA-CP; Filene to Roosevelt, April 1, 1936, and Wood to McIntyre, February 21 and June 5, 1936, OF 288, FDR; "Odds on Price-Control Law," *Business Week*, March 7, 1936, 9.
26. Sumners to Adolf Mayer, Dallas, Texas, March 26, 1936, Judiciary Committee, U.S. House of Representatives, 74th Cong., RG 233, HR 74A-D21, box 187. Kurtz, Vorhies, and Ozment, "Robinson Patman Act Revisited."
27. Nancy Beck Young, *Wright Patman*, 81; *Congressional Record* vol. 80 (1936), 8102.

28. Ross, "Winners and Losers Under the Robinson-Patman Act"; Adelman, *A&P*, 430.
29. R. J. Coar (United States Recording Company) to Patman, June 10, 1936, box 76(C), WPP; J. A. R. Moseley Jr. to Patman, May 20, 1936, and Patman to Moseley, May 25, 1936, box 77(B), WPP; "Itinerary," box 77(B), WPP; Patman to Roosevelt, October 6, 1936, PPF 3982, FDR.
30. C. F. Hughes, "The Merchant's Point of View," *NYT*, January 5, 1936; Thomas F. Conroy, "Threat to Jobbers Seen in Chain Plan," *NYT*, January 12, 1936; "A&P Is Ready to Fight," *Business Week*, January 11, 1936.

15: THE FIXER

1. Among the critics is Mayo, *American Grocery Store*, 146–47.
2. Tr 438–39.
3. Deutsch, "From 'Wild Animal Stores' to Women's Sphere," 147; Phillips, "Supermarket," 199.
4. "Brief for the United States," 657–58, Danville trial; Adelman, *A&P*, 65–69, 436; "A&P Help Yourself Store," *WSJ*, September 9, 1936.
5. Gx 188; Tr 818.
6. Dx 511, 512, box 66; Dx 388, box 67; Gx 221; Tr 983.
7. E. G. Yonker (Sanitary Grocery Company, Washington) to L. A. Warren (Safeway Stores, Oakland), February 3, 1937, RG 60, General Records of the Department of Justice, Antitrust Division, Enclosures to Classified Subject Files, 1930–87, Class 60 enclosures, box 71, NARA-CP.
8. Gx 194; Tr 849. Wilson, *Cart That Changed the World*, 88–93, credits the Oklahoma grocer Sylvan Goldman with the invention of the wheeled shopping cart, but did not search for antecedents or competing claimants. Catherine Grandclément, "Wheeling One's Groceries Around the Store: The Invention of the Shopping Cart, 1936–1953," in Warren Belasco and Roger Horowitz, eds., *Food Chains*, 233–51, provides a more thorough and balanced discussion of the development of the modern shopping cart. Both authors agree that the wheeled cart was important in the rapid growth of self-service food retailing.
9. In 1937, the peak year, A&P paid $2.4 million in chain-store taxes, equivalent to 26 percent of its after-tax profits. Such tax payments fell to $2.1 million in 1938, the year following the first large-scale store closings and supermarket openings. Adelman, *A&P*, 54.
10. Patman to Sam Rayburn, August 1, 1938, box 129(A), WPP; *Congressional Record*, 76th Cong., 1st sess., January 24, 1939, 9.
11. Patman to McIntyre, PPF 3982, FDR; "Coster-Musica Funeral Is Held," Associated Press, December 19, 1938; "End M'Gloon's Examination in Fraud Case," *Bridgeport* (Conn.) *Times-Star*, April 19, 1940; "Head of Old Drug Firm Commits Suicide After Fantastic 15-Year Hoax," *Life*, December 26, 1938, 18–19. See also the April 1940 correspondence between Patman and Robert R. McCormick, publisher of the *Chicago Tribune*, box 37(B), WPP.
12. "Hughes Springs, Texas," Handbook of Texas Online, www.tshaonline.org/handbook/online/articles/HH/hjh14.html, accessed December 2, 2009; *Congressional Record*, 75th Cong., 1st sess., 5936, June 17, 1937; Patman, "Absentee Own-

ership," *Vital Speeches of the Day*, November 15, 1938, 71; "Fortune Survey," *Fortune*, January 1937, 154.

13. Patman to "Dear Friend," June 23, 1936, box 90(A), WPP; "Manufacturers Likely to Get Early Benefits Under Chain Store Law," *WSJ*, July 2, 1936; "New Patman Bill Aimed Directly at Chain Stores," *WSJ*, October 5, 1936.
14. Tr 18050; "Great A&P Tea Co.," *WSJ*, January 1, 1936. On Ewing's long and colorful career, see "Caruthers Ewing Dies at 75," *Memphis Press-Scimitar*, August 20, 1947. On his predecessor, see the obituary "Charles H. O'Connor, Ex-Counsel to A&P," *NYT*, January 21, 1946. John had begun to speak of working with grocery manufacturers to fight chain-store taxes as early as March 1935, but had taken no action; Gx 162; Tr 738.
15. Fulda, "Food Distribution," 1092–1100; "Forcing Price Law Issue," *Business Week*, September 5, 1936.
16. "First Price Probe Started by FTC," *WSJ*, August 8, 1936; "A&P 'Within Law,'" *WSJ*, August 28, 1936; "This Is Business!" *Time*, April 12, 1937; "New Buying Policy Adopted by A&P Following Patman Act," *WSJ*, March 30, 1937; "Robinson-Patman Act Unlawful Says A&P," *WSJ*, February 9, 1937; "Brief for the United States," 245, Danville trial.
17. See W. A. Ayres (chairman, Federal Trade Commission) to Roosevelt, April 14, 1937, and Roosevelt to Vice President John Nance Garner, April 24, 1937, *Congressional Record*, 75th Cong., 1st sess., 7490, July 23, 1937; *Congressional Record*, 75th Cong., 1st sess., 5911–14, 5936; Rayburn to Walter D. Adams (editor, *Texas Druggist*), June 22, 1937, box 3R275, SRP.
18. Lebhar, *Chain Stores in America*, 223.
19. Helen Woodward, "How to Swing an Election," *Nation*, December 11, 1937, 638–40; Lebhar, *Chain Stores in America*, 224–33; T. Eugene Beatty, "Public Relations and the Chains," *Journal of Marketing* 7 (1943), 250; California Chain Stores Association, *Fifty Thousand Percent Chain Store Tax*, 11, 26.
20. "'Loss Leader' Lost," *Business Week*, February 29, 1936, 14; "Kroger Grocery, Great A&P Hit by New Kentucky Tax," *WSJ*, May 11, 1936; "New Chain Store Tax Proposed," *WSJ*, October 3, 1936; *Sphere* 19 (March 1937), in box 37(B), WPP; "State Chain Store Taxes," RG 56, General Records of the Department of the Treasury, Office of Tax Policy, Division of Research and Statistics, Subject Files, box 13, NARA-CP; "4 More States Consider Taxing Chain Stores," *WSJ*, June 5, 1937; "A&P Sues to Test Minnesota Price Law for 10% Mark-Ups," *WSJ*, September 2, 1937; "Anti–Chain Store Bill," *WSJ*, May 7, 1937.
21. "Chainsters' Tussle," *Time*, June 14, 1937; "State Drops Milk Action Against Atlantic & Pacific," *WSJ*, June 25, 1936; "N.Y. Chain-Store Tax Proposal," *WSJ*, January 7, 1938; Tr 17407-2, Dx 499.
22. "A&P Goes to the Wars," *Fortune*, April 1938, 134; Tr 19746. Later that year, Catchings was to make John Hartford one of the first U.S. subscribers to a service that pumped music into customers' homes, marketed under the name "Muzak." See "Muzak Music," *Time*, November 1, 1937.
23. "Carl Byoir Dead; Publicist Was 68," *NYT*, February 4, 1957; "Cultivating Cuba," *Time*, June 2, 1930.
24. Byoir to Marvin McIntyre, October 2, 1934, PPF 3982, FDR; "To War," *Time*, March 7, 1932.

25. Joseph L. Cohn to uncertain recipient, May 29, 1933, PPF 3982, FDR; "Doherty Week," *Time*, January 16, 1933; Gould, *Summer Plague*, 60; "FDR: Day by Day," FDR.
26. Byoir's relationship with Roosevelt was sufficiently jovial that the president bet a necktie that the 1935 ball would raise less than raised in 1934. Roosevelt lost. "President Gets Birthday Ball Funds Report," *Washington Post*, November 20, 1935; PPF 2176, FDR. Byoir to McIntyre, October 2, 1934; Early to Byoir, October 5, 1934, PPF 3982, FDR; "Party at Hotel Opens Its Season at Coral Gables," *Washington Post*, December 6, 1936; McIntyre to E. M. Watson, memo, November 6, 1935; Watson to McIntyre explaining why such a promotion was impossible, memo, November 9, 1935, PPF 2176, FDR; Early to Byoir, January 14, 1938, Stephen T. Early Files, box 1, FDR. Byoir's White House visits, with the exception of the one on inauguration eve 1937, are in Pare Lorentz Chronology, FDR; "President Is Host to Campaign Aides," *NYT*, January 20, 1937.
27. Tr 19752.
28. Tr 19755.
29. Tr 19763; "Campaign Planned to Fight Chain Tax," *NYT*, March 1, 1938; "Chain Tax Fought by Trade Groups," *NYT*, March 2, 1938; "Chain Tax Measure Argued at Albany," *NYT*, March 3, 1938. On the Buffalo dairy situation, see "Report on Progress of Food Chain Investigation, March 30, 1942," RG 122, Records of the Federal Trade Commission, Bureau of Economics, Records of Roy A. Prewitt, box 6, NARA-CP.

16: FRIENDS

1. Wright Patman, "Happy New Year for Chain Stores?" *Barron's*, December 27, 1937, 3; Patman to "Dear Colleague," January 15, 1938, box 37(B), WPP; FTC, "In the Matter of the Great Atlantic & Pacific Tea Company," Docket No. 3031, "Finding as to the Facts and Conclusion," January 25, 1938, and press release, January 26, 1938. Patman also asked the FTC to probe the Hartfords' newest venture, *Woman's Day*, a glossy magazine started in 1937 that sold for two cents per copy only at A&P. Patman fumed that the magazine was an attempt to skirt the Robinson-Patman provision requiring that advertising allowances be paid proportionately to all retailers: instead of granting allowances, he thought, manufacturers might pay off A&P by purchasing ads. The FTC took no action.
2. The original text proposed by Patman to his co-sponsors is in box 37(C), WPP; *Congressional Record*, 75th Cong., 3rd sess., February 14, 1938.
3. "Patman to Reintroduce Chain Store Tax Bill," *WSJ*, June 21, 1938. Estimated costs of the tax in 1938 appear in Lebhar, *Chain Stores in America*, 241. Due both to the impending tax bill and to the shift to supermarkets, most chain grocers' store counts fell sharply during 1938; A&P, for example, had 13,268 stores in February 1938, including a couple hundred in Canada, but only 10,835 stores one year later. Chain-store interests estimated later in 1938 that the legislation would cost A&P $472 million a year and twenty-three other chains a collective $385 million. Sears, Roebuck, the second-largest U.S. retailer, was not on the list, but it estimated that the Patman bill would cost it $20 million a year; "1937 Was Best Year for Sears, Roebuck," *NYT*, March 23, 1938.

4. "Patman Offers Bill to Tax Chain Stores," *WSJ*, February 15, 1938; Patman comment of February 18, 1938, in Ways and Means Committee, Committee Papers, Records of the U.S. House of Representatives, 75th Cong., RG 233, box 329, NARA-LA; Franklin D. Roosevelt, "Annual Message to Congress," January 3, 1938.
5. Bernard Kilgore, "Crackdown on the Chains," *WSJ*, February 23, 1938.
6. "Chain Tax Fought by Trade Groups," *NYT*, March 2, 1938; *Congressional Record*, 75th Cong., 3rd sess., app., 893; Patman speech to National Retail Lumber Dealers Association, Washington, D.C., May 10, 1938, box 37(B), WPP. A variety of speeches and materials from 1938 anti-chain efforts are in boxes 37(A), (B), and (C), WPP. In one tiny example of the conflict between individuals' interests as consumers and as producers, the April 1, 1938, issue of *The Farmers' Friend*, the Louisiana Farmers' Protective Union newspaper, criticized A&P for selling two pints of strawberries for twenty-five cents, barely above cost, even as it ran an A&P advertisement touting five pounds of sugar for twenty-five cents at the stores in Ponchatoula and Hammond; OF 288, FDR. See also Hass, "Social and Economic Aspects of the Chain Store Movement" (Ph.D. diss.), 166.
7. Patman to Roosevelt and to Robert H. Jackson (assistant attorney general for antitrust), April 24, 1938, box 37(B), WPP; Roosevelt, "Message to Congress on Curbing Monopolies," April 29, 1938, John T. Woolley and Gerhard Peters, American Presidency Project, www.presidency.ucsb.edu/ws/?pid=15637, accessed December 24, 2009; Public resolution 113, 75th Cong.; Harold E. Hufford and Watson G. Caudill, *Preliminary Checklist of the Records of the Temporary National Economic Committee* (Washington, D.C., 1944), iii–vi.
8. Legislative Reference Service to Patman, March 24, 1938, box 37(C), WPP; "A&P Goes to the Wars," *Fortune*, April 1938, 96.
9. Tr 19763.
10. See testimony of Raymond C. Baker, Tr 14182; "Brief for the United States," 1046, Danville trial; "Victor Schiff, 53, a Publicist Here," *NYT*, December 17, 1959.
11. OF 172, box 5, FDR.
12. The Patman appointment in Roosevelt's office is noted in the Pare Lorentz Chronology, FDR.
13. Silverman, "Hours of Work in Retail Trade" (master's thesis), 19; "In New Jersey," *NYT*, January 7, 1916; "Grocery Clerks Out, Ask Shorter Hours," *NYT*, September 7, 1916; Brody, *Butcher Workmen*, 130; Great Atlantic & Pacific Tea Co., *Three Score Years and Ten*, 47; *Retail Clerks International Advocate*, September–October 1932, 2. Nationwide membership in the Retail Clerks International Protective Association, which represented principally grocery-store clerks, fell from 21,200 in 1921 to 10,300 in 1923, and was so low by the end of the decade that the union canceled its national convention; Silverman, "Hours of Work in Retail Trade," 45.
14. *Retail Clerks International Advocate*, July–August 1932, 12.
15. "Labor Moves on the Chains," *Business Week*, November 3, 1934; "A&P Exodus," *Time*, November 5, 1934; "Atlantic & Pacific Brothers," *Time*, November 12, 1934; John Hartford to "Dear Friend," November 10, 1934, HFF; "'Out of Cleveland' Says A&P Head," *NYT*, October 30, 1934; "A&P Reopens Cleveland Stores," *Retail Clerks International Advocate*, November–December, 1934, 1.
16. Brody, *Butcher Workmen*, 137; John A. Hartford to Mr. Connors (unidentified), August 11, 1937, file 157, HFF.

17. John A. Hartford to Charles Roppelt (store manager, New York), December 31, 1936, file 157, HFF.
18. Chester Wright's role was revealed publicly by David A. Munro, publisher of an advertising newsletter called *Space and Time*, in the issue of February 5, 1940, box 37A, WPP; Tr 1,331.
19. Brody, *Butcher Workmen*, 142; United Grocery Worker "Strike Bulletin," May 4, 1937, and United Warehouse Workers Union Local 205 National Tea Organization Committee, March 22, 1937, both in Sidney Lens Papers, box 49, CHS. Another CIO union later charged that A&P supervisors were forcing workers to sign cards pledging that they would not join a CIO union; "The Union Organizer," 1941, United Grocery and Produce Employees Union, Local 329, CIO, in Sidney Lens Papers, box 50, CHS.
20. Tr 1290; Brody, *Butcher Workmen*, 138–39; "Brief for the United States," 1056, Danville trial; W. C. Gilbert (acting director, Legislative Reference Service) to Patman, October 28, 1938, box 37(C), WPP; American Federation of Labor, *Report of the Fifty-eighth Annual Convention*, 424, 570; "A&P Signs with Five A.F. of L. Unions in Washington, Chicago," *WSJ*, November 16, 1938; Roat, "Current Trends in Public Relations," 515; "A&P and the Unions," *Space and Time*, box 37(A), WPP; *Retail Clerks International Advocate*, November–December 1938, 10. Among A&P's opponents were the construction unions, which objected to A&P's use of non-union construction labor. See *Bricklayer, Mason, and Plasterer*, December 1938, 70.
21. Tr 14229; "A&P Backs Fight on 'Hidden Taxes,'" *NYT*, August 12, 1936; "A&P Gives $2,000 to Aid Study of Living Costs," *WSJ*, August 12, 1938.
22. Tr 19768; Temporary National Economic Committee, "Problems of the Consumer," pt. 8 of *Investigation of Concentration of Economic Power*, 3393; Gx 4406, Tr 14763.
23. "The NCTC News," November 1938, Dx 859, box 66; Temporary National Economic Committee, *Investigation of Concentration of Economic Power*, 3391. For examples of the National Consumers Tax Commission's self-promotion, see "Magnate Pays Way for Women to Dig into Civic Tax Spending," *St. Petersburg* (Fla.) *Evening Independent*, March 29, 1940; "Mrs. S. C. Scott Leads New Unit to Study Taxes," *Tulia* (Tex.) *Herald*, February 16, 1939; Phillips, "Chain, Voluntary Chain, and Independent Grocery Store Prices, 1938," 24–29.
24. "A&P Opens Fight on Chain Tax Bill," *NYT*, September 15, 1938; "Wide Praise Won by A&P Campaign," *NYT*, September 18, 1938. According to Byoir, the statement was drafted by himself after fifteen or sixteen meetings with both Hartford brothers, with another five or six meetings to revise the draft statement before its release; Tr 19776.

17: DEFYING DEATH

1. Patman to Roosevelt, telegram, July 15, 1938; Patman to McIntyre, July 16, 1938; McIntyre to Patman, July 16, 1938; press release, July 16, 1938, all box 77(C), WPP.
2. Patman to Rayburn, telegram, July 28, 1938; Rayburn to Patman, July 30, 1938; Patman to Martin Dies, August 1, 1938; Ewing Thomason to Patman, August 23, 1938; Patman to Thomason, August 31, 1938; Patman to Ed Gossett, August

31, 1938; Patman to Sam Hanna, October 3, 1938; Patman to Rayburn, October 21, 1938; Patman to J. E. Josey, *Houston Post*, October 22, 1938; Patman to Hanna, October 28, 1938; Bankhead and Rayburn to Patman, January 2, 1939, all box 129(A), WPP; Patman to Frank E. Mortenson (California Retail Druggists' Association), September 11, 1938, box 37(B), WPP.

3. "Dies Opens War on Propagandists," *NYT*, August 4, 1938.
4. South Trimble (clerk of the House) to Patman, July 29, 1938, box 37(C), WPP; Patman to Walter Rice (attorney, antitrust division), September 29, 1938, and Patman to Roosevelt, November 25, 1938, box 37(B), WPP; Roosevelt to Patman, November 30, 1938, OF 288, FDR; "Colorado No," *Time*, November 21, 1938.
5. Patman to "Dear Colleague," n.d., box 37(B), WPP.
6. "Charges Half-Truths Used by Proponents of Chain Store Taxes," *WSJ*, December 31, 1938; "A&P Head Says Chain Stores Face Crossroads in History," *WSJ*, January 3, 1939; Geo. M. Roberts (superintendent of weights and measures, District of Columbia) to Patman, November 2, 1938, box 37(C), WPP.
7. Frank Parker Stockbridge, "Battle of the Chains," *Barron's*, February 27, 1939; "Brief for the United States," 1057, 1060, Danville trial; Mark Levy, *Chain Stores: Helpful and Practical Information for a Real Estate Broker* (Chicago, 1940), 62.
8. Dx 860, box 66; Minsky, "Propaganda Bureaus as 'News Services,'" 679; "Boomerang," *Time*, January 30, 1939; "Oppose Patman Chain Store Bill," *WSJ*, February 4, 1939; Byoir to Early, January 10, 1939, and Early to Byoir, January 13, 1939, Stephen T. Early Papers, box 1, FDR; "Chains Agree to Fight 'Anti' Laws Collectively," *WSJ*, October 17, 1938. The offer to Farley was reported in Ray Tucker's "National Whirligig" column on April 6, 1939.
9. "Elliott Roosevelt Got $200,000 from Head of A&P, Lawyer Says, Repaid $4,000," *NYT*, June 13, 1945.
10. "Reporting the Matter of the Loan of John A. Hartford to Elliott Roosevelt," House of Representatives Report No. 1033, 79th Cong., 1st, sess., October 1, 1945, 8; "Gen. Roosevelt Borrowed $600,000," *NYT*, September 16, 1945. Elliott Roosevelt claimed that his father "never promoted or assisted my personal business affairs"; "Elliott Roosevelt Brands as a Lie Tale That Father Helped in Loans," *NYT*, August 1, 1945, but he did not deny that President Roosevelt spoke with Hartford about the loan.
11. "A Loan from the Grocer," *Time*, June 25, 1945; Jesse Jones, *Fifty Billion Dollars: My Thirteen Years with the RFC* (New York, 1951).
12. "Scandal or Slander?" *Washington Post*, June 15, 1945; Westbrook Pegler to Patman, August 7, 1945, and Patman to Pegler, August 9, 1945, box 119(A), WPP; Patman to Robert L. Doughton (chairman, Ways and Means Committee), September 29, 1945, box 102(A), WPP.
13. "Patman Chain Tax Said to Have Only Slight Chance," *Progressive Grocer*, February 1939, 163; Gerrit Vander Hooning (president, National Association of Retail Grocers) to Roosevelt, February 11, 1939; Early to Vander Hooning, February 17, 1939, PPF 2538, FDR; Patman to Roosevelt, May 11, 1939, box 37(B), WPP; May 22, 1939, address to American Retail Federation, in John T. Woolley and Gerhard Peters, American Presidency Project, www.presidency.ucsb.edu/ws/?pid=15763, accessed December 20, 2009; Patman to George Schulte, October 17, 1939, box 37(C), WPP.

14. "Plan New Anti-chain Campaign," *Business Week*, July 8, 1939, 30; "Chain-Tax Proposals Killed in 26 States This Year; Levies in 3 Others Were Voided," *NYT*, July 7, 1939; Lee, "Recent Trends in Chain-Store Tax Legislation"; *Great Atlantic & Pacific v. F.T.C.*, 10 F.2d 673 (3rd Cir., September 22, 1939).
15. Patman statement, June 7, 1939, box 37(C), WPP; unidentified writer to Mr. Kile, memo, July 16, 1939, Records of the U.S. House of Representatives, 76th Cong., Papers Accompanying Specific Bills and Resolutions, RG 233, HR76A-D39, box 395, NARA; Freedom of Opportunity Foundation, "Bulletin," August 21, 1939, box 37(B), WPP. Ingram and Rao, "Store Wars," 457–59, point to the diffuse interests of anti-chain campaigners as a source of political weakness.
16. Patman to "Dear Colleague," September 15, 1939, box 37(C), WPP; Patman to Schulte, October 17, 1939, box 37(C), WPP; Capper to Stratton Shartel, July 26, 1939, KSHS; Roosevelt to Doughton, memo, November 14, 1939, and Doughton to Roosevelt, November 17, 1939, OF 288, FDR. "I am merely passing this along to you," Roosevelt wrote to Doughton, marking his thoughts "personal." "I regret that Mr. Patman thought it was necessary to call the matter of a hearing on his bill to your attention," Doughton responded.
17. Feldman, "Legislative Opposition," 339.
18. *WSJ*, March 5, 1940; House Committee on Ways and Means, 76th Cong., 3rd sess. , *Excise Tax on Retail Stores: Hearings Before Subcommittee on H.R. 1, March 17 through May 16, 1940* (Washington, D.C., 1940), 775, 1053, 1060, 1107, 1122, 1127, 1362–68; Ryant, "The South and the Movement Against Chain Stores," 216–17. See also Caroline F. Ware Papers, box 45, FDR.
19. Wallace to Doughton, April 2, 1940; Noble to Doughton, May 16, 1940; Ewin L. Davis (chairman, Federal Trade Commission) to Doughton, March 26, 1940, RG 233, Records of the U.S. House of Representatives, 76th Cong., box 395, NARA-LA; RG 40, General Records of the Department of Commerce, Records of the Office of the Secretary, Subject Files of Undersecretary of Commerce Edward J. Noble, box 5, NARA-CP; typescript, April 3, 1940, by Weaver Myers, attorney, Joint Committee on Internal Revenue Taxation, RG 56, General Records of the Department of Treasury, Office of Tax Policy, Subject Files, box 13, NARA-CP. The meeting with Arnold is in Patman's appointment book for 1940, box 1705, WPP; letters to Rayburn, box 3R284, SRP; Brandeis to Patman, April 14, 1940, box 37(B), WPP.
20. Patman's addresses on CBS are in box 37(B), WPP; the May 18, 1940, address on NBC Blue is in box 37(A), WPP.
21. Byoir, a lieutenant colonel in the Army Reserve, was so upset by Patman's statements that he wrote to Roosevelt about it; Byoir to Roosevelt, PPF 2176, FDR. "Dies Group Offers to Hear Byoir Reply," *NYT*, June 4, 1940; McCormack statement in box 37(B), WPP.
22. U.S. Bureau of the Census, *Fifteenth Census of the United States: 1930 Retail Distribution: Summary for the United States* (Washington, D.C., 1933), 28; U.S. Bureau of the Census, *Census of Business, Retail Trade*, vol. 1, pt. 1 (Washington, D.C., 1941), 57; Albright, "Changes in Wholesaling," 31.
23. Bruce M. Fowler and William H. Shaw, "Distributive Costs of Consumption Commodities," *Survey of Current Business*, July 1942, 16.

18: THE FOURTH REVOLUTION

1. Dx 92, box 68; Dx 135, box 68; Gx 359, Tr 1441. On A&P's violation in Ohio, see H. L. English (secretary, Ohio Fair Trade Committee, Columbus) to S. H. Tenover (Kroger Grocery and Baking Company, Cincinnati), February 4, 1941, RG 60, General Records of the Department of Justice, Antitrust Division, Enclosures to Classified Subject Files, 1930–87, Class 60 enclosures, box 72, NARA-CP.
2. "Brass Tacks for the Investor," *Barron's*, January 2, 1939, 20; "Income Reported by Corporations," *NYT*, June 2, 1937.
3. Adelman, *A&P*, 453; "A&P Goes to the Wars," *Fortune*, April 1938, 138.
4. Mark Levy, *Chain Stores: Helpful and Practical Information for a Real Estate Broker* (Chicago, 1940); Dx 383, box 67; Deutsch, "From 'Wild Animal Stores' to 'Women's Sphere,'" 149; Dx 384, box 67. At the end of 1940, A&P had 1,396 supermarkets, and its total sales at supermarkets in that year were $593.5 million. This yields average annual sales per store of $425,143, or $8,176 per week. However, as 277, or 20 percent, of the stores counted at year-end had been open for less than a full year, average weekly sales were probably considerably higher than these figures suggest. According to figures in Adelman, *A&P*, 447–48, only 72 of the 923 A&P supermarkets functioning in the September–November 1939 period had weekly sales below $5,000, but a majority had sales between $5,000 and $9,999.
5. Gx 317.
6. Dx 577a.
7. "Memorandum of Interviews with Members of United Fresh Fruit & Vegetable Association, Chicago, Illinois, January 22 to 25, 1945," box 66, Danville trial records; Gx 2319, box 66; Dx 612, box 67.
8. Rentz, "Death of 'Grandma,'" MS, 60–65; Adelman, *A&P*, 468.
9. Gx 209; Tr 898.
10. U.S. Bureau of the Census, *Census of Business*, vol. 1, *Retail Trade*, pt. 1, 817. A&P had 851 self-service stores with sales exceeding $5,000 per week, or $260,000 per year. Adelman, *A&P*, 448–49.
11. Dx 504, box 66.
12. Gx 2656, Tr 9556; Gx 3031, Tr 10555; Dx 87, box 68.
13. Several examples of John Hartford's correspondence with store managers are in file 157, HFF.
14. Comment of Central Division president C. A. Brooks, August 25, 1935, Dx 252, box 66; Dx 268, box 66; "Red Circle and Gold Leaf," *Time*, November 13, 1950.
15. "Charts, Presidents' Meeting, February 9, 1928," box 67, Danville trial files; Dx 283, box 66.
16. Dx 507, box 66; Rentz, "Death of Grandma," 47.
17. Dx 433, box 66; Dx 504, box 66; Gx 162, Tr 738; Dx 450, box 66.
18. Dx 254, box 66; Dx 517, box 66; Dx 259, box 66.
19. Much Safeway correspondence of this sort is in RG 60, General Records of the Department of Justice, Antitrust Division, Enclosures to Classified Subject Files, 1930–87, Class 60 enclosures, box 72, NARA-CP.
20. Gx 2683, Tr 9654; Dx 683, box 66; Gx 2754, Tr 9894; Dx 341, Tr 16393; Tr 20451. In January 1937, John demanded the immediate firing of an assistant superintendent after learning that a store in Buffalo had sold "18 or 20 items" below cost; see Dx 1017, box 66.

21. Dx 286, 287, 289, 290, 291, 293, 294, 296, 298, 299, 301, box 66.
22. Dx 302, box 66.
23. On the disregard of return on investment as a performance measure, see the testimony of A. G. Hoadley, president of the Middle Western Division, at Tr 15136. See also Gx 218, Tr 965. John's appeal failed; at the end of fiscal year 1940, A&P showed earnings of $7.92 per share.
24. Adelman, *A&P*, 454; "Chain-Store Gains Laid to Attacks," *NYT*, January 2, 1940.

19: THE TRUSTBUSTER

1. Patman to Flynn, May 15, 1941, box 82(c), WPP; Caro, *Years of Lyndon Johnson*, 675–740.
2. Gressley, *Voltaire and the Cowboy*, 19.
3. Brinkley, "Antimonopoly Ideal and the Liberal State," 559; Gressley, *Voltaire and the Cowboy*, 269.
4. Arnold, *Folklore of Capitalism*, 212; Miscamble, "Thurman Arnold Goes to Washington," 5–8. For critiques of Arnold's realism, see Kesselman, "Frontier Thesis and the Great Depression," 266, and Gressley, "Colonialism," 72.
5. There is an ample literature on the Roosevelt administration's antitrust policies in the late 1930s. See, among many other sources, Hawley, *New Deal and the Problem of Monopoly*; Hofstadter, *Age of Reform*, 314–22; Leuchtenberg, *Franklin Roosevelt and the New Deal*, 148–50; Gressley, "Thurman Arnold, Antitrust, and the New Deal," 230–31; Edwards, "Thurman Arnold and the Antitrust Laws"; Waller, "Antitrust Legacy of Thurman Arnold."
6. "Memorandum for Assistant Attorney General Antitrust Division: General Outlines of the Food Investigation," June 13, 1940, reprinted in Arnold, *Bottlenecks of Business*, 225. Arnold's comment is at 239.
7. Copies of the pamphlets are in RG 56, General Records of the Department of the Treasury, Central Files of the Office of the Secretary, box 134, NARA-CP. "Byoir 'Exoneration' Is Hit as Too Hasty," *NYT*, July 22, 1940; "Byoir, Publicity Man, Called Nazi Agent, Assails Patman," *Washington Post*, August 30, 1930; Patman's appointment books are in WPP, box 1705.
8. On the Connecticut case, see "Grocers Indicted as Price Fixers," *NYT*, May 24, 1941. The cheese indictment, *U.S. v. Great Atlantic & Pacific Tea Co. et al.*, Criminal 11-345, Southern District of New York, September 25, 1941, is in box 66, Danville trial files; see also "Price-Fixing of State's Cheese Laid to 2 Big Concerns, 90 Others," *NYT*, September 26, 1941. On the bread case, *U.S. v. Great Atlantic & Pacific*, U.S. District Court for the District of Columbia, Criminal 67845, see Tr 85.
9. "Memorandum for the Federal Bureau of Investigation," December 4, 1941, RG 122, Records of the Federal Trade Commission, Bureau of Economics, Office File of Roy A. Prewitt, box 6, NARA-CP; "Food Groups Fined in Connecticut Case," *NYT*, November 4, 1941; "Fines Are Assessed in 2 Cheese Cases," *NYT*, September 7, 1944; "Acquitted in Bread Price Suit," *NYT*, March 20, 1942; "Food Monopolies Held to Be Waning," *NYT*, September 16, 1941. This evidence of Thurman Arnold's ambivalence about antitrust enforcement, as demonstrated by his division's simultaneous attacks on price-fixing and price competition, is at odds

with the widely held view that he had a "comprehensive antitrust program," as asserted by Miscamble, "Thurman Arnold Goes to Washington," 14. Corwin Edwards, Arnold's chief economist, went so far as to assert in 1943 that the antitrust division had become the "special custodian of the interests of consumers, small businessmen, and other victims of monopoly and restraint of trade," without acknowledging that the interests of consumers and small businessmen were often at odds; see "Thurman Arnold and the Antitrust Laws," 354. On commodity agreements, see Wells, *Antitrust and the Formation of the Postwar World*, 69.

10. "A&P Gives Part Pay to Its Service Men," *NYT*, December 31, 1940; "Need for Reducing Cost of Distribution Greater Because of War, Says Hartford," *NYT*, January 2, 1941; "A&P Pays More to Produce Trades," *NYT*, March 18, 1941.
11. "A&P Gives 5-Day Week," *NYT*, April 29, 1941; "A&P Sales at Top; Profit Rate Drops," *NYT*, June 27, 1941; "A&P Pays Men in Service," *NYT*, November 25, 1941; "Bonuses Announced," *NYT*, December 5, 1941; "A&P Backs Curbs on Price of Food," *NYT*, December 31, 1941.
12. William R. Watkins (special assistant to the attorney general) to Food Chain Staff, memo, February 6, 1942, RG 122, Records of the Federal Trade Commission, Bureau of Economics, Office File of Roy A. Prewitt, 1939–60, box 6, NARA-CP. A&P estimated the government took 100,962 documents from its files, whereas the government's count was 87,577; see Affidavit of Alma Hawkes, secretary to Caruthers Ewing, in RG 21, Records of the U.S. District Courts, Records of the U.S. District Court, Eastern District of Illinois, Danville Division, Criminal Records, Criminal Case Files, box 149, NARA-C. Patman's lunch with Arnold appears on Patman's calendar; see box 1705, WPP.
13. "Report of Progress of Food Chain Investigation, March 30, 1942," 1/9, 2/1, 3/3, 2/10, 2/11, 1/4. Collection of thirty thousand to fifty thousand documents was cited in *U.S. v. New York Great Atlantic & Pacific Tea Co.*, 52 F. Supp. 683 (N.D. Texas).
14. Wells, *Antitrust and the Formation of the Postwar World*, 80–81; Brinkley, "Antimonopoly Ideal and the Liberal State," 577.
15. Dx 991; Dx 993. The Federal Trade Commission, which had legal authority separate from that of the antitrust division, proposed in 1942 to punish A&P for unfair treatment of Washington state apple growers, but it rescinded the order after acknowledging that A&P was entitled to the lowest prices for paying cash. Arnold's lawyers were unmoved. FTC docket 3344.
16. Indictment, *U.S. v. New York Great Atlantic & Pacific Tea Company*, case 10512 (Criminal), N.D. Texas, November 25, 1942; *U.S. v. New York Great Atlantic & Pacific Tea Co.*, case 10603, 137 F.2d 459 (5th Cir., July 30, 1943), rehearing denied September 1, 1943. On the local A&P, see "New A&P Super-store Opens Here," *Danville Commercial-News*, September 22, 1938.
17. "U.S. vs. A&P Company," *Danville Commercial-News*, April 28, 1945; Report of Pretrial Conference, box 149, Danville trial, NARA-C; "86 Days of A&P Anti-trust Trial Cost Estimates $2,000,000—and That's Not All!" *Danville Commercial-News*, October 21, 1945. The Justice Department subsequently filed antitrust suits against Safeway and Kroger as well, but these were much smaller in scope and far less complex to try.
18. Tr 20432; "Exhibits Pile Up in A&P Trial; May Pass 4,000," *Chicago Tribune*, July 1, 1945; "Crowd Fills Court to See John Hartford," *Chicago Tribune*, October 24, 1945; "Lindley Denies Motion to Rule Out 250,000 Documents in A&P Case,"

Danville Commercial-News, April 16, 1945; "A&P Anti-trust Trial to Resume in Federal Court," *Sunday Commercial-News*, September 16, 1945; "A&P Defense Rests Case as Hartford Defines Profit," *Danville Commercial-News*, October 24, 1945.

19. Gressley, *Voltaire and the Cowboy*, 54.
20. For an overview of thinking about vertical integration in the 1940s, see G. E. Hale, "Vertical Integration: Impact of the Antitrust Laws upon Combinations of Successive Stages of Production and Distribution," *Columbia Law Review* 49 (1949), 921–54.
21. Tr 2798; Tr 5725–33; Dx 706.
22. "Brief for the United States," 854, Danville trial; Tr 20618.
23. Dx 577; 67 F. Supp. 655, 657.
24. Tr 20825.
25. Tr 20825; Gx 314; Adelman, *A&P*, 138; Tr 17202–4.
26. 67 F. Supp. 636, 641; Final order, September 27, 1946, Danville trial.
27. *U.S. v. New York Great Atlantic & Pacific Tea Co.*, 7th Cir., case 9221, February 24, 1949, 173 F. 2d 88.
28. L. A. Warren (president, Safeway) to Lawrence Giles (Safeway's attorney with Chadbourne, Hunt, Jaeckel & Brown, New York), March 15, 1937, and L. Giles, "Memorandum Regarding Safeway Stores, Incorporated," April 7, 1937, both in RG 60, General Records of the Department of Justice, Antitrust Division, Enclosures to Classified Subject Files, 1930–87, Class 60 enclosures, box 71, NARA-CP.
29. M. A. Adelman, "The A&P Case: A Study in Applied Economic Theory." The dissertation was later published in revised form as *A&P: A Study in Price-Cost Behavior and Public Policy.* Joel B. Dirlam and Alfred E. Kahn, "Antitrust Law and the Big Buyer: Another Look at the A&P Case"; M. A. Adelman, "Dirlam and Kahn on the A&P Case"; Fulda, "Food Distribution."
30. The antitrust division's budget increased from $432,000 in 1938, the year Arnold took over, to $2.3 million in 1942. "Appropriation Figures for the Antitrust Division," www.justice.gov/atr/public/10804a.htm, accessed March 24, 2010.
31. Harry Truman, "Annual Message to the Congress on the State of the Union," January 6, 1947; Truman, "Annual Budget Message to the Congress, Fiscal Year 1948," January 10, 1947; H. Graham Morison, interview by Jerry N. Hess, August 4 and 10, 1972, 293, Harry S. Truman Library and Museum, www.trumanlibrary.org/oralhist/morison2.htm and morison3.htm, accessed March 24, 2010.

20: MOM AND POP'S LAST STAND

1. On the labor shortage, see Minutes, meeting of division managers and division meat merchandisers, Kroger Grocery and Baking Company, June 26–27, 1941, in RG 60, General Records of the Department of Justice, Antitrust Division, Enclosures to Classified Subject Files, 1930–87, Class 60 enclosures, box 75, NARA-CP. On relative chain-store performance, see Reba L. Osborne, "Retail Sales of Chain and Mail-Order Firms," *Survey of Current Business*, February 1944, 12–20; Genevieve B. Wimsatt, "Business Discontinuances, 1940–42," *Survey of Current Business*, November 1943, 18. Byoir comment is in Gx 234.
2. Jacobs, "'How About Some Meat?'" 916.

3. Galbraith to Henderson, memo, December 8, 1942, Leon Henderson Papers, box 29, FDR.
4. Pettengill, "Comparative Retail Grocery Ceiling Prices in Los Angeles," 149; Galbraith to Henderson, memo, October 6, 1942, and "Retail Price Plan," December 5, 1942, Leon Henderson Papers, box 29, FDR.
5. "Won't Go Hungry, Says A&P Head," *NYT*, January 3, 1943; Clement Winston and Reba L. Osborne, "The Pattern of Chain Store Sales in Retail Distribution," *Survey of Current Business*, July 1947, 12.
6. Peter M. Tamburo (chief regional investigator, Office of Price Administration [OPA], Dallas) to Edward Crane (regional attorney, OPA), memo, July 27, 1942; Geoffrey Baker (associate price executive, food and food products branch, OPA) to M. B. Schilling (A&P), August 26, 1942; Byron Jay (A&P) to Henry Curran (OPA), June 1, 1943; R. B. Sharbrough (department of research and statistics, A&P) to W. A. Neilander (OPA), December 15, 1941; Sharbrough to Galbraith, April 4, 1942; W. A. Donahoe (sales manager, A&P, Scranton, Pa.) to Wm. P. Farrell (acting price executive, OPA, Scranton), September 13, 1943; T. A. Connors (A&P, Chicago) to Victor Lea (fats and oil division, OPA), telegram, April 1, 1942; all in RG 188, Office of Price Administration, Price Records, National Office, Food Price Division Central Files, Non-governmental Correspondence, 1941–43, box 3132, NARA-CP. Newspaper articles attributed supermarkets' poor financial performance during the war to lack of inventory, but this does not appear to be accurate in the case of A&P, whose inventory-to-sales ratios in February 1943 and February 1944 were higher than before the war.
7. Patzig, "Effect of the War on Retail Food Outlets," 111.
8. "A&P Sales Rise to $1,471,177,992," *NYT*, July 27, 1943; "Food Chains Lose Under War Curbs," *NYT*, August 15, 1945; Clement Winston and Reba L. Osborne, "Postwar Patterns of Chain and Independent Store Sales," *Survey of Current Business*, January 1949, 10; Office of Price Administration, Office of Temporary Controls, "Survey of Chain Grocery Stores and Wholesale Grocers: Summary of Operating Data for Various Periods, 1936 Through 1945," May 1947.
9. AG, February 13, 1946, 44, 54–57; Winston and Osborne, "Pattern of Chain Store Sales," 13; Merrill Lynch, Pierce, Fenner & Beane, *Chain Stores: Investigate Then Invest* (New York, 1948), 15.
10. U.S. Bureau of the Census, *Statistical Abstract, 1952* (Washington, D.C., 1952), 726; *Progressive Grocer*, September 1947, 86. The number of supermarkets in 1941 is necessarily an approximation, as there is no precise definition of "supermarket." One of the suburban communities with robust population growth was Orange, New Jersey, where the large home George H. Hartford had built in the late 1860s was torn down in 1948, to be replaced by an apartment complex; see "Geo. Hartford, Head of A&P, Dies at Age 92," *Montclair* (N.J.) *Times*, September 26, 1957.
11. Applebaum, "Adjustment of Retailing to 1941 Conditions," 440; *Progressive Grocer*, March 1945, 169, 162; September 1945, 96; March 1949, 57.
12. Moss, "Constructing the Supermarket," typescript; Deutsch, "From 'Wild Animal Stores' to Women's Sphere"; Progressive Grocer, *Self-Service Food Stores* (New York, 1946), 17; Paul Levasseur and Carrol Waldeck, "Consider These Points if You're Making Plans to Modernize," *Progressive Grocer*, October 1948, 65; Charles

W. Hauch, "Prepacking of Fruits & Vegetables Reduces Waste, Saves Labor," *Progressive Grocer,* March 1946, 62.

13. *Progressive Grocer,* September 1946, 85, and October 1946, 194; Rentz, "Death of 'Grandma,'" MS, 64; A&P, "The Feeders Primer" (New York, 1937), HFF; Arnold Nicholson, "More White Meat for You," *Saturday Evening Post,* August 9, 1947, 12; Bugos, "Intellectual Property Protection in the American Chicken-Breeding Industry," 139; "Adequate '47 Food Supply Is Forecast by Hartford," *NYT,* December 26, 1946; "Economy, Service Held Grocers' Aim," *NYT,* December 24, 1947; "A&P President Says Grocers' Inventories Are Healthiest in Years," *WSJ,* December 24, 1947; Shane Hamilton, "The Economies and Conveniences of Modern-Day Living: Frozen Foods and Mass Marketing, 1945–1965," *Business History Review* 77 (2003), 36–37; *Progressive Grocer,* October 1952, 115.
14. Patman's speeches bore titles such as "How A&P Beat the Chain-Store Tax Bill—Now It Can Be Told," *Congressional Record,* September 19, 1945, H.R. 4200, 79th Cong., introduced September 27, 1945. Critical letters from the Commerce and Treasury departments are in RG 56, General Records of the Department of the Treasury, Central Files of the Office of the Secretary of the Treasury, 1933–56, box 134, NARA-CP; Robert L. Doughton (chairman, Ways and Means Committee) to Patman, June 21, 1949, box 847A, WPP; Richard R. Haas to Patman, memo, September 30, 1949, box 102(A), WPP; Suzanne Manfull to Patman, October 10, 1949, box 102(A), WPP; J. R. Alexander to Patman, September 17, 1949, box 37(C), WPP.
15. Robert K. Walsh, "Uncle Sam, A&P, and John Q. Public," *Washington, D.C., Sunday Star,* December 4, 1949; "Democrats Happy over Minton's Rise," *NYT,* September 16, 1949.
16. "Anti-trust Suit Asks A&P Be Split," *WSJ,* September 16, 1949; Walsh, "Uncle Sam"; Cabell Phillips, "U.S. Versus the A&P: The Two Arguments," *NYT,* December 11, 1949. For a legal analysis in support of the government's position, see Hirsch and Votaw, "Giant Grocery Retailing and the Antitrust Laws."
17. Douglas Larsen, "Vast Propaganda War Spurred by A&P Suit," *New York World-Telegram,* November 9, 1949; "McGrath Defends Anti-trust Actions in Food Industry," *WSJ,* March 14, 1950; Bergson, "The Antitrust Laws and the A&P Case," speech to Operation Incorporated, October 19, 1949, Chicago, and "Statement by Assistant Attorney General Herbert A. Bergson," October 12, 1949, both in RG 60, General Records of the Department of Justice, Antitrust Division, Enclosures to Classified Subject Files, 1930–87, Class 60 enclosures, box 23; "U.S. Aim Cited in A&P Suit," *NYT,* October 21, 1949; *Collier's,* November 26, 1949.
18. "The A&P Case—and the Trade's Reaction," *Progressive Grocer,* October 1949, 54; *Washington News,* October 31, 1949; Larsen, "Vast Propaganda War"; *World Telegram,* October 28, 1949; James A. Williams, "Economy Is Sound, Sales Group Told," *NYT,* December 4, 1949. Among Patman's speeches are "A&P Falsehoods Blanket the Nation," *Congressional Record,* October 26, 1949; and "A&P's Nation-Wide Propaganda Campaign," *Congressional Record,* March 20, 1950.
19. Walsh, "Uncle Sam"; Harry Borton to J. Howard McGrath, October 10, 1949, and Edmund A. Nelson to McGrath, October 14, 1949, RG 60, General Records of the Department of Justice, Antitrust Division, Enclosures to Classified Subject Files, 1930–87, Class 60 enclosures, box 23; "Senate Quiz Told A&P Gets Rebates,"

NYT, December 14, 1949; "Voters Side with A&P in U.S. Suit," *World-Telegram*, November 21, 1949.

20. "A&P Files Reply, Denying Monopoly," *NYT*, April 11, 1950. See, for example, *Chicago Tribune*, May 12, 1950; Mrs. Otis Cutler to McGrath, May 2, 1950, and Nathan Helms to Truman, May 2, 1950, both in RG 60, General Records of the Department of Justice, Antitrust Division, Enclosures to Classified Subject Files, 1930–87, Class 60 enclosures, box 79; E. C. Cornelius (McKinney, Texas) to Rayburn, June 8, 1950, and Raymond Graves (Melissa, Texas) to Rayburn, May 17, 1950, both box 3R369, SRP; H. D. Jackson to Patman, n.d., and Patman to Jackson, May 25, 1950, both box 37(C), WPP.
21. "Bergson Resigns as 'Trust Buster,'" *NYT*, September 15, 1950.
22. "Red Circle and Gold Leaf," *Time*, November 13, 1950; "Letter from the Editor," *Time*, May 5, 1954; "Hartford Predicts Ample Food Supply," *NYT*, December 29, 1950; Toney Terry Hatfield, "Boss Hartford of the A&P," *Coronet*, May 1951, 94.
23. "Attacks on Bigness Declared Unwise," *NYT*, January 15, 1951; *Schwegmann Brothers v. Calvert Distillers*, 341 U.S. 384, May 21, 1951; Jaffe, "The Supreme Court, 1950 Term."

21: THE FALL

1. "John A. Hartford Dies in Elevator," *NYT*, September 21, 1951; "O.W.S. Biography—Notes from 1951 Through 1960," HFF; "400 Attend Funeral of John A. Hartford," *NYT*, September 25, 1951; "Mrs. John A. Hartford," *NYT*, September 6, 1948; "$55,605,290 Estate to Pay Small Tax," *NYT*, June 30, 1954.
2. "D. T. Bofinger Promoted," *NYT*, February 7, 1949; "Bofinger Spurred on Coffee Data," *NYT*, December 8, 1949; "David T. Bofinger, President of A&P," *NYT*, December 20, 1949.
3. "Who's News," *NYT*, June 13, 1950; Robert E. Bedingfield, "Personality: Wary Empire Builder at A&P," *NYT*, January 11, 1959; testimony of Charles W. Parr, head of A&P field buying offices, at Danville trial, Tr 199.
4. "Fair Trade Called Price Fixing Cloak," *NYT*, February 14, 1952; "President Accepts Resignations of Two," *NYT*, June 26, 1952; *U.S. v. New York Great Atlantic & Pacific Tea Co.*, Civil Action 52-139 (S.D. N.Y., January 19, 1954), 1954 U.S. Dist. Lexis 3678; "Food Chain Offers Consent Decree in Anti-trust Suit," *WSJ*, April 6, 1953; "U.S. and A&P Settle Anti-trust Suit," *WSJ*, January 20, 1954.
5. Market-share estimates are from *Progressive Grocer*, July 1952, 134.
6. George Melloan, "Supermarket Surge: Bigger, Frillier Stores Rise Across Land in Record Building Boom," *WSJ*, October 19, 1953. The 1954 tax law allowed extremely rapid depreciation of commercial buildings, providing developers with large amounts of tax-free income for the first ten to fifteen years of a building's life; see Thomas W. Hanchett, "U.S. Tax Policy and the Shopping-Center Boom of the 1950s and 1960s," *American Historical Review* 101 (1996), 1082–1110. The queen visited the Giant supermarket in Hyattsville, Maryland, on October 19, 1957. On evening hours, see *Progressive Grocer*, April 1952, 114.
7. U.S. Bureau of the Census, *1958 Census of Business*, vol. 1, *Retail Trade—Summary Statistics* (Washington, D.C., 1961), 2-4, 2-17, 3-4. In 1958, 80 percent of all food stores, excluding seasonal farm stands, had three or fewer paid employees. On store owners' income, see *Progressive Grocer*, November 1954, 43, 54.

8. As late as 1959, Burger defended the decision not to expand in the West and the Southwest with the comment, "It's silly to Pioneer too much. Once you get out of Chicago, people have to drive for miles and miles to get to densely populated areas as we know them here." See Bedingfield, "Wary Empire Builder at A&P."
9. In 1953, the average supermarket lease at a shopping center lasted 10 years, with two five-year renewal options, and fixed the rent at 1 percent of sales. Stores at non-shopping-center locations typically had 10-year leases and fixed-dollar rents. By 1959, the vast majority of new supermarkets had leases of 15 years or more. A&P's average during this period is unknown, but in 1971 its average lease commitment was 5.8 years, far less than its competitors'. *Progressive Grocer,* January 1954, 83, and March 1960, 130; "A&P—1972," Harvard Business School Case 9-27-114, 1972.
10. Melloan, "Supermarket Surge"; *Progressive Grocer,* February 1952, 70; October 1952, 116; November 1951, 14; May 1954, 144; and April 1960, F3.
11. *Progressive Grocer,* July 1953, 105, and September 1953, 38; Charles E. Egan, "Brownell Scores 'Fair Trade' Laws," *NYT,* April 2, 1955; "Discount Houses Strengthen Grip," *NYT,* January 3, 1956; *Cox v. General Electric,* Supreme Court of Georgia, January 10, 1955, 222 Ga. 286; *Union Carbide and Carbon Corp. v. White River Distributors,* Supreme Court of Arkansas, February 7, 1955, 224 Ark. 558; *McGraw Electric v. Lewis & Smith Drug Co.,* Supreme Court of Nebraska, February 11, 1955, 159 Neb. 703.
12. "George Hartford of A&P Dies at 92," *NYT,* September 25, 1957; "Geo. Hartford, Head of A&P, Dies at Age 92," *Montclair* (N.J.) *Times,* September 26, 1957.
13. "Hermit Kingdom: The Isolated A&P Eases Its Border Guard After a Subtle Struggle," *WSJ,* December 12, 1958.
14. "A&P Proposes to Revise Set-Up," *NYT,* November 7, 1958; "Evolution at A&P," *NYT,* November 8, 1958; "Big Public Offering of Stock in A&P Set by Hartfords," *NYT,* March 5, 1959; "Two A&P Holders to Sell 1,800,000 Shares to Public," *WSJ,* March 5, 1959; "A&P 1,800,000-Share Secondary Offering on Market Priced at $44.50," *WSJ,* March 25, 1959.
15. "Hermit Kingdom."
16. "How Goliath Grew: A&P's Saga Includes a Pagoda, Price Wars, and Buying Brigades," *WSJ,* December 19, 1958; "Votes at A&P," *Time,* December 22, 1958; Bedingfield, "Wary Empire Builder at A&P."
17. Gross profit figures through 1943 were revealed in the Danville trial exhibits and reported in Adelman, *A&P,* 436. Gross profit figures for 1962–70 are in "A&P—1972." "A&P Ends Ban on Trading Stamps," *WSJ,* January 27, 1960; "A&P to Start Issuing Trading Stamps in More of Its Grocery Stores," *WSJ,* January 30, 1962; *Progressive Grocer,* December 1963, 52, and April 1963, 6.
18. Tedlow, *New and Improved,* 250; Progressive Grocer, *Facts in Grocery Distribution* (1962), 13; *Progressive Grocer,* February 1962, 102, and April 1962, 56; James J. Nagle, "Most Food Chains Limit Side Lines," *NYT,* March 6, 1960; James J. Nagle, "Food Chains Turn to Discount Field," *NYT,* September 3, 1961; "A&P Called Interested in Food Concession of a Proposed Discount Store in Illinois," *WSJ,* August 30, 1961; "California Firm Says It Is Discussing Drug Units at Some A&P Stores," *WSJ,* October 18, 1961; "A&P Plans General Store Next to a Supermarket," *WSJ,* March 15, 1962; "A&P Closes Test Store Retailing Nonfood Items," *WSJ,* April 1, 1964.

19. "Public Holders Attend A&P Annual Meeting for 1st Time, Told Dividend May Be Raised," *WSJ*, June 5, 1959; "A&P Says It Won't Increase Prices to Get Higher Profits; 1st Fiscal Period Net Fell," *WSJ*, June 22, 1960.
20. *Progressive Grocer*, April 1960, F13; October 1961, 42; October 1965, K12, K32.
21. "John D. Ehrgott Elected A&P President Despite Protest by All 6 Outside Directors," *WSJ*, January 25, 1963; "Revolt Against Age," *Time*, February 1, 1963.
22. Robert E. Bedingfield, "Hartford Will Sell A&P Shares," *NYT*, June 8, 1966.
23. Vartanig G. Vartan, "Quiet Evolution Noted at A&P," *NYT*, June 28, 1964; "A&P Sales Drop 2.6% in Quarter," *NYT*, July 10, 1964; Dan Dorfman, "Heard on the Street," *WSJ*, August 22, 1968; "Foundation Rejects Data Processing Bid," *WSJ*, December 11, 1968; Ernest Holsendolph, "Gulf & Western Bids for A&P Stock," *NYT*, February 2, 1973; Ernest Holsendolph, "Gulf & Western Draws New Rebuff on A&P Bid," *NYT*, March 13, 1973.
24. Fred M. Hechinger, "U.S. Foundations Worth 11 Billion," *NYT*, July 11, 1960; Leonard Sloane, "Crucial Year for Chain," *NYT*, February 5, 1973; Jacobson, *Greatest Good*, 3, 235; "Hartford Foundation Asks A&P to Plan a Stock Sale," *NYT*, May 1, 1976; "Market Place," *NYT*, July 6, 1976.
25. "Tengelmann Pursuing Mergers," *NYT*, January 20, 1979; "Tengelmann Unit Buys A&P Shares," *NYT*, February 22, 1979.

22: THE LEGACY

1. A&P filed for protection under chapter 11 of the U.S. Bankruptcy Code on December 12, 2010.
2. On consolidation in the manufacturing sector, see Naomi R. Lamoreaux, *The Great Merger Movement in American Business, 1895–1904*.
3. McGrath's speech to the United States Wholesale Grocers' Association, quoted in *Progressive Grocer*, April 1950, 162.
4. For an attempt to analyze the economic benefits of entrepreneurship in a rigorous fashion, see William J. Baumol, *The Microtheory of Innovative Entrepreneurship*.
5. 57 F. Supp. 635, 664.
6. James W. Gruebele, Sheldon W. Williams, and Richard F. Fallert, "Impact of Food Chain Procurement Policies on the Fluid Milk Processing Industry," *American Journal of Agricultural Economics* 52 (1970), 395–402, found, for example, that vertical integration in milk processing resulted in fewer but larger dairy plants. The economics of vertical integration subsequently changed in ways disadvantageous to A&P. In 1965, the company opened the world's largest food-processing plant in Horseheads, New York. The Horseheads plant, with 1.5 million square feet under a single roof, was A&P's first large investment in food manufacturing in decades. It made 550 different products, from canned soup to mayonnaise, all for sale under the trusted Ann Page name. But the rise of television advertising in the 1950s had given a boost to brand-name foods and dulled the appeal of store brands such as Ann Page. As A&P responded to declining sales by closing stores, the Horseheads plant was badly underutilized. It was finally abandoned in 1983. In a neat historical irony, part of its site was later occupied by a retailer that decided not to integrate vertically into manufacturing: Walmart. "Wal-Mart to Hold Grand Opening," *Corning (N.Y.) Leader*, February 28, 2008, www.the-leader.com/news/business/x2052202396, accessed June 10, 2010.

7. On the Illinois banking laws, see www.obre.state.il.us/cbt/STATS/br-hist.htm, accessed June 30, 2010; Tara Rice and Erin Davis, "The Branch Banking Boom in Illinois: A Byproduct of Restrictive Branching Laws," *Chicago Fed Letter,* May 1, 2007. Colorado's motor vehicle dealer statute, Colorado Statutes 12-6-120.5, is one of many that bar manufacturers from selling cars to the public. "Liquor Initiatives Stir Up Old Dispute," *Seattle Times,* August 21, 2010. Alabama's ban on self-distribution by brewers can be found in Title 28, Chap. 9 of the state code. On professional licensing, see Stephanie Simon, "A License to Shampoo," *WSJ*, February 7, 2011.
8. There is an extensive literature on the industrialization of food, explored most eloquently in Michael Pollan, *The Omnivore's Dilemma* (New York, 2006).
9. Among the studies comparing chain and independent grocery prices, see FTC, *Chain Store Inquiry: Prices and Margins of Chain and Independent Distributors, Vol. 4* (Washington, D.C., 1933 and 1934); Paul D. Converse, "Prices and Services of Chain and Independent Stores in Champaign-Urbana, Illinois," *NATMA Bulletin*, October 1931; James L. Palmer, "Economic and Social Aspects of Chain Stores"; Phillips, "Chain, Voluntary Chain, and Independent Grocery Store Prices, 1930 and 1934"; Taylor, "Prices in Chain and Independent Grocery Stores in Durham, North Carolina," 413.
10. Data in U.S. Bureau of the Census, *Historical Statistics of the United States*, 324, show that food spending in 1934–35 came to one-third or more of income for households with annual incomes below $1,500, a definition that took in sixteen million households. Per capita consumption and nutrition are in ibid., 328. On inner-city grocery prices, see Donald E. Sexton Jr., "Comparing the Cost of Food to Blacks and to Whites—a Survey," *Journal of Marketing* 35 (July 1971), 45.
11. Numerous books explore such claims against Walmart; see, for example, Charles Fishman, *The Wal-Mart Effect*; Nelson Lichtenstein, *The Retail Revolution: How Wal-Mart Created a Brave New World of Business*; Nelson Lichtenstein, ed., *Wal-Mart: The Face of Twenty-First-Century Capitalism*; and Ellen Ruppel Shell, *Cheap: The High Cost of Discount Culture.*

BIBLIOGRAPHY

BOOKS

Adelman, M. A. *A&P: A Study in Price-Cost Behavior and Public Policy*. Cambridge, Mass.: Harvard University Press, 1966.

Albion, Robert Greenhalgh. *The Rise of New York Port, 1815–1860*. New York: Charles Scribner's Sons, 1939.

Alter, Jonathan. *The Defining Moment: FDR's Hundred Days and the Triumph of Hope*. New York: Simon & Schuster, 2006.

Anderson, Avis H. *A&P: The Story of the Great Atlantic & Pacific Tea Company*. Charleston, S.C.: Arcadia, 2002.

Anderson, Oscar E. *The Health of a Nation: Harvey W. Wiley and the Fight for Pure Food*. Chicago: University of Chicago Press, 1958.

Arnold, Thurman W. *The Bottlenecks of Business*. Washington, D.C.: Reynal and Hitchcock, 1940.

———. *The Folklore of Capitalism*. New Haven, Conn.: Yale University Press, 1937.

Bacon, Albion Fellows. *Beauty for Ashes*. New York: Dodd, Mead, 1914.

Barger, Harold. *Distribution's Place in the American Economy Since 1869*. Princeton, N.J.: Princeton University Press, 1955.

Baumol, William J. *The Microtheory of Innovative Entrepreneurship*. Princeton, N.J.: Princeton University Press, 2010.

Baxter, William. *Chain Store Distribution and Management*. New York: Harper & Brothers, 1928.

Beckert, Sven. *The Monied Metropolis: New York City and the Consolidation of the American Bourgeoisie*. Cambridge: Cambridge University Press, 1993.

Belasco, Warren, and Roger Horowitz, eds. *Food Chains: From Farmyard to Shopping Cart*. Philadelphia: University of Pennsylvania Press, 2008.

Brinkley, Alan. *The End of Reform*. New York: Random House, 1995.

———. *Voices of Protest: Huey Long, Father Coughlin, and the Great Depression*. New York: Vintage Books, 1982.

Brody, David. *The Butcher Workmen: A Study of Unionization*. Cambridge, Mass.: Harvard University Press, 1964.

Brown, Stephen A. *Revolution at the Checkout Counter*. Cambridge, Mass.: Harvard University Press, 1997.

Buehler, Ezra. *Chain Store Debate Manual*. New York: National Chain Store Association, 1931.

Caro, Robert. *The Years of Lyndon Johnson: The Path to Power.* New York: Knopf, 1982.

Chase, Stuart. *The Tragedy of Waste.* New York: Macmillan, 1925.

Chase, Stuart, and Frederick John Schlink. *Your Money's Worth: A Study in the Waste of the Consumer's Dollar.* New York: Macmillan, 1927.

Clark, Eleanor Sterling. *Orange, New Jersey, 1806–1956.* Orange, N.J.: Orange Public Library, 1956.

Cohen, Lizabeth. *A Consumer's Republic: The Politics of Mass Consumption in Postwar America.* New York: Knopf, 2003.

——. *Making a New Deal: Industrial Workers in Chicago, 1919–1939.* Cambridge: Cambridge University Press, 1990.

Croxton, Frederick E. *A Study of Housewives' Buying Habits in Columbus, Ohio, 1924.* Columbus: Bureau of Business Research, Ohio State University, 1926.

Dallas, Helen. *Chain Stores Pro and Con.* New York: Institute of Consumer Education, 1940.

Darby, William. *The Story of the Chain Store: A Study of Chain Store Policies and Methods.* New York: Dry Goods Economist, 1928.

Daughters, Charles G. *Wells of Discontent: A Study of the Economic, Social, and Political Aspects of the Chain Store.* New York: Newson, 1937.

Davis, J. E. *Don't Make A&P Mad.* Privately published, 1990.

Deutsch, Tracey. *Building a Housewife's Paradise: Gender, Politics, and the American Grocery Store in the Twentieth Century.* Chapel Hill: University of North Carolina Press, 2010.

Dipman, Carl W., ed. *The Modern Grocery Store.* New York: Progressive Grocer, 1931.

Doerksen, Clifford J. *American Babel: Rogue Radio Broadcasters of the Jazz Age.* Philadelphia: University of Pennsylvania Press, 2005.

Donohue, Kathleen G. *Freedom from Want: American Liberalism and the Idea of the Consumer.* Baltimore: Johns Hopkins University Press, 2006.

Finlay, Paul. *Paul Finlay's Book for Grocers.* San Francisco: Honig-Cooper, 1924.

Fishman, Charles. *The Wal-Mart Effect.* New York: Penguin Press, 2006.

Flowers, Montaville. *America Chained: A Discussion of "What's Wrong with the Chain Store."* Pasadena, Calif.: Montaville Flowers Publicists, 1931.

——. *The Japanese Conquest of American Opinion.* New York: George H. Doran, 1917.

Gould, Tony. *A Summer Plague: Polio and Its Survivors.* New Haven, Conn.: Yale University Press, 1995.

Gressley, Gene M., ed. *Voltaire and the Cowboy: The Letters of Thurman Arnold.* Boulder: Colorado Associated University Press, 1977.

Hawley, Ellis W. *The New Deal and the Problem of Monopoly.* Princeton, N.J.: Princeton University Press, 1966.

Hofstadter, Richard. *The Age of Reform: From Bryan to FDR.* New York: Knopf, 1955.

Horowitz, David A. *Beyond Left and Right: Insurgency and the Establishment.* Champaign: University of Illinois Press, 1996.

Horowitz, Roger. *Putting Meat on the American Table: Taste, Technology, Transformation.* Baltimore: Johns Hopkins University Press, 2006.

Huff, Sidney H. *Chain Store Tyranny and the Independent Grocers' Dilemma.* Pittsfield, Mass.: Sidney H. Huff, 1934.

Ickes, Harold L. *The Secret Diary of Harold L. Ickes: The First Thousand Days, 1933–1936*. New York: Simon & Schuster, 1954.

Jacobs, Meg. *Pocketbook Politics: Economic Citizenship in Twentieth-Century America*. Princeton, N.J.: Princeton University Press, 2005.

Jacobson, Judith S. *The Greatest Good: A History of the John A. Hartford Foundation*. New York: John A. Hartford Foundation, 1984.

Jones, Geoffrey, and Nicholas J. Morgan, eds. *Adding Value: Brands and Marketing in Food and Drink*. London: Routledge, 1994.

Kanigel, Robert. *The One Best Way: Frederick Winslow Taylor and the Enigma of Efficiency*. New York: Little, Brown, 1997.

Kennedy, David M. *Over Here: The First World War and American Society*. New York: Oxford University Press, 1982.

Kirstein, George. *Stores and Unions*. New York: Fairchild, 1950.

Koch, Albert Ralph. *The Financing of Large Corporations, 1921–1939*. New York: National Bureau of Economic Research, 1943.

Koehn, Nancy F. *Brand New: How Entrepreneurs Earned Consumers' Trust from Wedgwood to Dell*. Boston: Harvard Business School Press, 2001.

Laird, Pamela Walker. *Advertising Progress: American Business and the Rise of Consumer Marketing*. Baltimore: Johns Hopkins University Press, 1998.

Lamoreaux, Naomi R. *The Great Merger Movement in American Business*. New York: Oxford University Press, 1985.

Lebhar, Godfrey M. *Chain Stores in America*. New York: Chain Store, 1952.

Leuchtenberg, William. *Franklin D. Roosevelt and the New Deal, 1932–1940*. New York: Harper & Row, 1963.

Levenstein, Harvey. *Revolution at the Table: The Transformation of the American Diet*. New York: Oxford University Press, 1998.

Lichtenstein, Nelson. *The Retail Revolution: How Wal-Mart Created a Brave New World of Business*. New York: Metropolitan Books, 2009.

——, ed. *Wal-Mart: The Face of Twenty-First-Century Capitalism*. New York: New Press, 2006.

Mayo, James M. *The American Grocery Store: The Business Evolution of an Architectural Space*. Westport, Conn.: Greenwood Press, 1993.

McCraw, Thomas K. *Prophets of Regulation: Charles Francis Adams, Louis D. Brandeis, James M. Landis, Alfred E. Kahn*. Cambridge, Mass.: Harvard University Press, 1984.

McGarry, Edmund D. *Mortality in Retail Trade*. Buffalo: Bureau of Business and Social Research, 1930.

McGovern, Charles P. *Sold American: Consumption and Citizenship, 1890–1945*. Chapel Hill: University of North Carolina Press, 2006.

McKay, Ernest A. *The Civil War and New York City*. Syracuse, N.Y.: Syracuse University Press, 1990.

Nasaw, David. *Andrew Carnegie*. New York: Penguin Press, 2006.

Norcross, Frank W. *A History of the New York Swamp*. New York: Chiswick Press, 1901.

Nourse, Edwin Griswold. *The Chicago Produce Market*. Boston: Houghton Mifflin, 1918.

Nystrom, Paul. *Chain Stores*. Washington, D.C.: Chamber of Commerce of the United States, 1930.

O'Pry, Maude Hearn. *Chronicles of Shreveport and Caddo Parish*. Shreveport, La.: Journal Printing Co., 1928.

Orleck, Annelise. *Common Sense and a Little Fire: Women and Working-Class Politics in the United States, 1900–1965*. Chapel Hill: University of North Carolina Press, 1995.

Palamountain, Joseph C., Jr. *The Politics of Distribution*. Cambridge, Mass.: Harvard University Press, 1955.

Perlow, Austin. *A Union Which Is Concerned: The Story of Amalgamated Meat-Cutters and Retail Food Store Employees Union, Local 342, AMC & BW of NA-AFL-CIO*. Jamaica, N.Y.: The Local [196?].

Pierson, David Lawrence. *A History of the Oranges to 1921*. New York: Lewis Historical Publishing Co., 1922.

Richings, G. F. *Evidences of Progress Among Colored People*. Philadelphia: Geo. S. Ferguson, 1905.

Schumpeter, Joseph. *Capitalism, Socialism, and Democracy*. 3rd ed. New York: Harper & Row, 1950.

Scoville, Joseph Alfred. *The Old Merchants of New York City*. New York: Carleton, 1863.

Shell, Ellen Ruppel. *Cheap: The High Cost of Discount Culture*. New York: Penguin Press, 2010.

Smith, H. Allen. *Robert Gair: A Study*. New York: Dial Press, 1939.

Somerville, John. *Chain Store Debate Manual*. New York: N.p., 1930.

Stanwood, Edward. *American Tariff Controversies in the Nineteenth Century*. New York: Russell and Russell, 1903.

Taussig, F. W. *The Tariff History of the United States*. 6th ed. New York: G. P. Putnam's Sons, 1914.

Tedlow, Richard. *New and Improved: The Story of Mass Marketing in America*. New York: Basic Books, 1990.

Wakeman, Abram. *History and Reminiscences of Lower Wall Street and Vicinity*. New York: Spice Mill, 1914.

Walsh, William I. *The Rise and Decline of the Great Atlantic & Pacific Tea Company*. Secaucus, N.J.: Lyle Stuart, 1986.

Ward, Barbara McLean, ed. *Produce and Conserve, Share and Play Square: The Grocer and the Consumer on the Home-Front Battlefield During World War II*. Portsmouth, N.H.: Strawbery Banke Museum, 1994.

Watkins, T. H. *The Hungry Years: A Narrative History of the Great Depression*. New York: Henry Holt, 1999.

Wells, Wyatt. *Antitrust and the Formation of the Postwar World*. New York: Columbia University Press, 2002.

Whittemore, Henry. *Founders and Builders of the Oranges*. Newark, N.J.: L. J. Hardham, 1896.

Wilentz, Sean. *Chants Democratic: New York City and the Rise of the American Working Class, 1788–1850*. New York: Oxford University Press, 1984.

Wilson, Terry. *The Cart That Changed the World: The Career of Sylvan N. Goldman*. Norman: University of Oklahoma Press, 1978.

Young, James Harvey. *Pure Food: Securing the Federal Food and Drugs Act of 1906*. Princeton, N.J.: Princeton University Press, 1989.

Young, Nancy Beck. *Wright Patman: Populism, Liberalism, and the American Dream.* Dallas: Southern Methodist University Press, 2000.

Zimmerman, M. M. *The Super Market: A Revolution in Distribution.* New York: McGraw-Hill, 1955.

PAMPHLETS

Bureau of Business Research, Harvard University Graduate School of Business Administration. *Management Problems in Retail Grocery Stores. Bulletin,* no. 13 (1919).

Bureau of Business Research, Harvard University Graduate School of Business Administration. *Operating Expenses in Retail Grocery Stores* (1919–30).

California Chain Stores Association. *The Fifty Thousand Percent Chain Store Tax.* Sacramento, Calif., 1936.

Great Atlantic & Pacific Tea Co. *Three Score Years and Ten.* New York: Great Atlantic & Pacific Tea Co., 1929.

——. *You . . . and Your Company.* N.p.: Great Atlantic & Pacific Tea Co., 1944.

Retail Clerks International Protective Association. *Proceedings.*

ARTICLES

"A&P Century of Progress." *Central Manufacturing District Magazine* 43 (June 1959), 6–13.

Abbott, John C. "Food Marketing in Western Europe Today." *Journal of Marketing* 27 (1963), 17–22.

Adelman, M. A. "The A&P Case: A Study in Applied Economic Theory. *Quarterly Journal of Economics* 53 (1949), 238–57.

——. "Dirlam and Kahn on the A&P Case." *Journal of Political Economy* 61 (1953), 436–44.

Albright, John. "Changes in Wholesaling, 1929–1939." *Journal of Marketing* 6 (1941), 31–37.

Alexander, Ralph S. "The N.R.A. and Distribution—a Friendly Criticism." *American Marketing Journal* 1 (1934), 197–205.

Anderson, Oscar E., Jr. "The Pure-Food Issue: A Republican Dilemma, 1906–1912." *American Historical Review* 61 (1956), 530–73.

Appel, David. "The Supermarket: Early Development of an Institutional Innovation." *Journal of Retailing* 48 (1972), 39–53.

Applebaum, William. "Adjustment of Retailing to 1941 Conditions." *Journal of Marketing* 5 (1941), 438–42.

Applebaum, William, and David Carson. "Supermarkets Face the Future." *Harvard Business Review* 35 (1957), 123–35.

Baum, H. A. "Chain Store Methods of Buying Fresh Fruits and Vegetables." *Journal of Farm Economics* 12 (1930), 280–82.

Beattie, T. Eugene. "Public Relations and the Chains." *Journal of Marketing* 7 (1943), 245–55.

Bell, Richard. "Food Retailing in the British Isles." *European Retail Digest* 28 (December 2000), 22–28.

Bliss, Perry. "Schumpeter, the 'Big' Disturbance, and Retailing." *Social Forces* 39 (October 1960–May 1961), 72–76.

Boer, A. E. "Mortality Costs in Retail Trades." *Journal of Marketing* 2 (1937), 52–60.

Bolin, Winifred D. Wandersee. "The Economics of Middle-Income Family Life: Working Women During the Great Depression." *Journal of American History* 65 (1978), 60–74.

Bostwick, Frank A. "Why Jewel Sparkles." *Central Manufacturing District Magazine* 33 (December 1949), 23–27.

Brinkley, Alan. "The Antimonopoly Ideal and the Liberal State: The Case of Thurman Arnold." *Journal of American History* 80 (1993), 557–79.

Brown, Martin, and Peter Philips. "Craft Labor and Mechanization in Nineteenth-Century American Canning." *Journal of Economic History* 46 (1986), 743–56.

Buehler, Alfred G. "Anti-Chain-Store Taxation." *Journal of Business of the University of Chicago* 4 (1931), 346–69.

———. "Chain Store Taxes." *Journal of Marketing* 1 (January 1937), 177–88.

Bugos, Glenn E. "Intellectual Property Protection in the American Chicken-Breeding Industry." *Business History Review* 66 (1992), 127–68.

Bullock, Roy J. "The Early History of the Great Atlantic & Pacific Tea Company." *Harvard Business Review* 11 (1933), 289–98.

———. "A History of the Great Atlantic & Pacific Tea Company Since 1878." *Harvard Business Review* 12 (1933), 59–69.

Carhart, E. R. "The New York Produce Exchange." *Annals of the American Academy of Political and Social Science* 38 (1911), 206–21.

Carlson, Albert S., and John Weston. "The Sweet Corn Industry of Maine." *Economic Geography* 10 (1934), 382–94.

Cassady, Ralph, Jr. "The Los Angeles Wholesale Grocery Structure, 1920–1946." *Journal of Marketing* 14 (1949), 169–77.

Chandler, Alfred D., Jr. "Management Decentralization: An Historical Analysis." *Business History Review* 30 (1956), 111–74.

Clarke, Sally. "Consumer Negotiations." *Business and Economic History* 25 (1997), 101–22.

Converse, Paul D. "Employment, Wages, and Labor Relations in Marketing." *Annals of the American Academy of Political and Social Science* 209 (1940), 149–57.

———. "Twenty-five Years of Wholesaling: A Revolution in Food Wholesaling." *Journal of Marketing* 22 (1957), 40–53.

Coppin, Clayton. "James Wilson and Harvey Wiley: The Dilemma of Bureaucratic Entrepreneurship." *Agricultural History* 2 (1990), 167–81.

Cuff, Robert D. "Creating Central Control Systems: Edwin F. Gay and the Central Bureau of Planning and Statistics, 1917–1919." *Business History Review* 63 (1989), 588–613.

Dameron, Kenneth. "Retailing Under the N.R.A., I." *Journal of Business of the University of Chicago* 8 (1935), 1–26.

———. "Retailing under the N.R.A., II." *Journal of Business of the University of Chicago* 8 (1935), 188–212.

Dawson, John A., Anne M. Findlay, and Leigh Sparks. "The Impact of Scanning on Employment in UK Food Stores: A Preliminary Analysis." *Journal of Marketing Management* 2 (1967), 285–300.

Deutsch, Tracey. "From 'Wild Animal Stores' to Women's Sphere: Supermarkets and the Politics of Mass Consumption, 1930–1950." *Business and Economic History* 28 (1999), 143–53.

De Vyver, Frank T. "The Present Status of Labor Unions in the South: 1948." *Southern Economic Journal* 16 (1949), 1–22.

Dirlam, Joel B., and Alfred E. Kahn. "Antitrust Law and the Big Buyer: Another Look at the A&P Case." *Journal of Political Economy* 60 (1952), 118–32.

Dodge, John F., Jr. "Labor Law: Objects of Union Action: Organization of Managers of Retail Chain Stores as Proper Object." *Michigan Law Review* 53 (1954), 298–300.

Duddy, E. A., and D. A. Revzan. "Transportation and Marketing Facilities for Fresh Fruits and Vegetables in Chicago." *Journal of Business of the University of Chicago* 12 (1939), 280–97.

Edwards, Corwin. "Thurman Arnold and the Antitrust Laws." *Political Science Quarterly* 58 (1943), 338–55.

Estey, Marten S. "Patterns of Union Membership in the Retail Trades." *Industrial and Labor Relations Review* 8 (1955), 557–64.

———. "The Strategic Alliance as a Factor in Union Growth." *Industrial and Labor Relations Review* 9 (1955), 41–53.

Faville, David E. "Comparison of Chain and Independent Grocery Stores in the San Francisco Area." *Journal of Marketing* 1 (1936), 87–90.

Feldman, George J. "Legislative Opposition to Chain Stores and Its Minimization." *Law and Contemporary Problems* 8 (1941), 334–47.

François, Pierre, and Joseph Leunis. "Public Policy and the Establishment of Large Stores in Belgium." *International Review of Retail, Distribution, and Consumer Research* 1 (1991), 469–86.

Frank, Ronald E., Paul E. Green, and Harry F. Sieber Jr. "Household Correlates of Purchase Price for Grocery Products." *Journal of Marketing Research* 4 (1967), 54–58.

Fulda, Carl H. "Food Distribution in the United States: The Struggle Between Independents and Chains." *University of Pennsylvania Law Review* 99 (1951), 1051–1162.

Furst, Russell L. "Relationships Between the Numbers of Chain and Individually Owned Grocery Stores in Fort Wayne." *Journal of Business of the University of Chicago* 5 (1932), 335–45.

Gilchrist, Franklin W. "Self-Service Retailing of Meat." *Journal of Marketing* 13 (1949), 295–304.

Gilligan, C. T., P. M. Rainford, and A. R. Thorne. "The Impact of Out-of-Town Shopping." *European Journal of Marketing* 8 (1974), 42–46.

Goldman, Arieh. "Stages in the Development of the Supermarket." *Journal of Retailing* 51 (1975–76), 49–64.

Green, Robert T., Eric Langeard, and Alice C. Favell. "Innovation in the Service Sector: Some Empirical Findings." *Journal of Marketing Research* 11 (1974), 323–26.

Gressley, Gene M. "Colonialism: The Perpetual Pendulum." *Montana: The Magazine of Western History* 38 (1988), 69–73.

———. "Thurman Arnold, Antitrust, and the New Deal." *Business History Review* 38 (1964), 214–31.

Grether, E. T. "Geographical Price Policies in the Grocery Trade, 1941: A Note." *Journal of Marketing* 8 (1944), 417–22.

Gruebelle, James W., Sheldon W. Williams, and Richard F. Fallert. "Impact of Food Chain Procurement Policies on the Fluid Milk Processing Industry." *American Journal of Agricultural Economics* 52 (1970), 395–402.

Hall, Joseph B. "Barney Builds a Business." *Bulletin of the Cincinnati Historical Society* 26 (1968), 290–316.

Hanchett, Thomas W. "U.S. Tax Policy and the Shopping-Center Boom of the 1950s and 1960s." *American Historical Review* 101 (1996), 1082–1110.

Hannan, Michael T., and John Freeman. "The Ecology of Organizational Mortality: American Labor Unions, 1836–1985." *American Journal of Sociology* 94 (1988), 25–52.

Hardy, Frederick K. "Taxation of Chain Retailers in the United States." *Journal of Comparative Legislation and International Law,* 3rd ser., 18 (1936), 257–61.

Harper, J. F. "'A New Battle on Evolution': The Anti-Chain-Store Trade-at-Home Agitation of 1929–1930." *Journal of American Studies* 16 (1982), 407–26.

Hess, Herbert W. "Selling Distribution and Its New Economics." *Annals of the American Academy of Political and Social Science* 115 (1924), 1–7.

Hirsch, Werner Z. "Grocery Chain Store Prices: A Case Study." *Journal of Marketing* 21 (1956), 9–23.

Hirsch, Werner Z., and Dow Votaw. "Giant Grocery Retailing and the Antitrust Laws." *Journal of Business of the University of Chicago* 25 (1952), 1–17.

Ho, Suk-ching, and Ho-fuk Lau. "Development of Supermarket Technology: The Incomplete Transfer Phenomenon." *International Marketing Review* 5 (Spring 1988), 20–30.

Ingram, Paul, and Hayagreeva Rao. "Store Wars: The Enactment and Repeal of Anti-Chain-Store Legislation in America." *American Journal of Sociology* 110 (2004), 446–87.

Jacobs, Meg. "'How About Some Meat?': The Office of Price Administration, Consumption Politics, and State Building from the Bottom Up, 1941–1946." *Journal of American History* 84 (1997), 910–41.

Jaffe, Louis L. "The Supreme Court, 1950 Term." *Harvard Law Review* 65 (1951), 118–21.

Kebker, V. W. "Operation of the Unfair Trade Practices Act in the Large Cities of Kansas." *Journal of Marketing* 7 (July 1942), 22–31.

Kesselman, Steven. "The Frontier Thesis and the Great Depression." *Journal of the History of Ideas* 29 (1968), 253–68.

King, Clyde Lyndon. "Can the Cost of Distributing Food Products Be Reduced?" *Annals of the American Academy of Political and Social Science* 48 (1913), 199–224.

Koehn, Nancy F. "Henry Heinz and Brand Creation in the Late Nineteenth Century: Making Markets for Processed Food." *Business History Review* 73 (1999), 349–93.

Krislov, Joseph. "Raiding Among the 'Legitimate' Unions." *Industrial and Labor Relations Review* 8 (October 1954), 19–29.

Kurtz, David L., Douglas W. Vorhies, and John Ozment. "The Robinson Patman Act Revisited: A Review of Senator Robinson's Papers." In *Contemporary Marketing*

History: Proceedings of the Sixth Conference on Historical Research in Marketing and Marketing Thought*, 153–60. East Lansing: Michigan State University Press, 1994.

Langeard, Eric, and Robert A. Peterson. "Diffusion of Large-Scale Food Retailing in France: Supermarché and Hypermarché." *Journal of Retailing* 51 (Fall 1975), 43–63.

Langrehr, Frederick W., and Richard K. Robinson. "Shoppers' Reactions to Supermarket Price Scanning and Shopper Price Marking." *Journal of Consumer Affairs* 13 (1979), 370–79.

Law, Marc T. "The Origins of State Pure Food Regulation." *Journal of Economic History* 63 (2003), 1103–30.

Lee, Maurice. "Recent Trends in Chain-Store Tax Legislation." *Journal of Business of the University of Chicago* 13 (1940), 253–74.

Levin, Sharon G., Stanford L. Levin, and John B. Meisel. "Intermarket Differences in the Early Diffusion of an Innovation." *Southern Economic Journal* 51 (1985), 672–80.

Levy, Daniel, Mark Bergen, Shantanu Dutta, and Robert Venable. "The Magnitude of Menu Costs: Direct Evidence from Large U.S. Supermarket Chains." *Quarterly Journal of Economics* 112 (1997), 791–825.

MacLachlan, Douglas L., and Homer Spence. "Public Trust in Retailing: Some Research Findings." *Journal of Retailing* 52 (Spring 1976), 3–8.

Marion, Bruce W., Willard F. Mueller, Ronald W. Cotterill, Frederick E. Geithman, and John R. Schmelzer. "The Price and Profit Performance of Leading Food Chains." *American Journal of Agricultural Economics* 61 (August 1979), 420–33.

McClelland, W. G. "Sales per Person and Size in Retailing: Some Fallacies." *Journal of Industrial Economics* 6 (1958), 221–29.

McEnroe, P. V., H. T. Huth, E. A. Moore, and W. W. Morris III. "Overview of the Supermarket System and the Retail Store System." *IBM Systems Journal* 14 (1975), 3–15.

McGarry, Edmund D. "The Mortality of Independent Grocery Stores in Buffalo and Pittsburgh, 1919–1941." *Journal of Marketing* 12 (July 1947), 14–24.

McHenry, Lorenzo Alva. "Price Stabilization Attempts in the Grocery Trade in California." *Journal of Marketing* 2 (1937), 121–28.

Means, Gardiner C. "The Consumer and the New Deal." *Annals of the American Academy of Political and Social Science* 173 (1934), 7–17.

Minichiello, Robert J. "The Real Challenge of Food Discounters." *Journal of Marketing* 31 (April 1967), 37–42.

Minsky, Louis. "Propaganda Bureaus as 'News Services.'" *Public Opinion Quarterly* 2 (1938), 677–79.

Miscamble, Wilson D. "Thurman Arnold Goes to Washington: A Look at Antitrust Policy in the Later New Deal." *Business History Review* 56 (1982), 1–15.

Moore, Geoff, and Andy Robson. "The UK Supermarket Industry: An Analysis of Corporate Social and Financial Performance." *Business Ethics: A European Review* 11 (2002), 25–39.

Moore, John R. "The Effect of the Financial Arrangements of Shopping Centers on Concentration in Food Retailing." *Journal of Farm Economics* 44 (1962), 178–82.

Moses, H. Vincent. "G. Harold Powell and the Corporate Consolidation of the Modern Citrus Enterprise, 1904–1922." *Business History Review* 69 (1995), 119–55.

Moyer, M. S. "The Roots of Large Scale Retailing." *Journal of Marketing* 26 (October 1962), 55–59.

Mueller, Robert W. "Movements in the Retail Distribution of Food in the U.S." *Journal of Farm Economics* 38 (May 1956), 336–47.

Naden, Kenneth D., and George A. Jackson Jr. "Prices as Indicative of Competition Among Retail Food Stores." *Journal of Farm Economics* 35 (1953), 236–48.

Nakamura, Leonard I. "The Measurement of Retail Output and the Retail Revolution." *Canadian Journal of Economics* 32 (1999), 408–25.

Newcomer, Mabel, and Margaret Perkins. "Price Variations Among Poughkeepsie Grocers." *Journal of Marketing* 4 (1939), 39–44.

Oakes, Ralph H. "Price Differences for Identical Items in Chain, Voluntary Group, and Independent Grocery Stores." *Journal of Marketing* 14 (1949), 434–36.

Oi, Walter Y. "The Supermarket: An Institutional Innovation." *Australian Economic Review* 37 (2004), 337–42.

Orleck, Annelise. "'We Are That Mythical Thing Called the Public': Militant Housewives During the Great Depression." *Feminist Studies* 19 (1993), 147–72.

Palmer, James L. "Economic and Social Aspects of Chain Stores." *Journal of Business of the University of Chicago* 2 (1929), 272–90.

Patzig, R. E. "The Effect of the War on Retail Food Outlets." *Journal of Marketing* 9 (1944), 109–13.

Pelz, V. H. "Developments Under the N.R.A. and A.A.A. That May Affect the Marketing of Food Products." *American Marketing Journal* 1 (1934), 19–23.

Pennington, M. E. "Relation of Cold Storage to the Food Supply and the Consumer." *Annals of the American Academy of Political and Social Science* 48 (1913), 154–63.

Pettengill, Robert B. "Comparative Retail Grocery Ceiling Prices in Los Angeles." *Journal of Marketing* 8 (1943), 145–49.

Phillips, Charles F. "Chain, Voluntary Chain, and Independent Grocery Store Prices, 1930 and 1934." *Journal of Business of the University of Chicago* 8 (April 1935), 143–49.

———. "Chain, Voluntary Chain, and Independent Grocery Store Prices, 1938." *Journal of Business of the University of Chicago* 12 (1939), 24–29.

———. "An Economic Analysis of the Supreme Court's Decisions on Chain-Store Taxation." *Journal of Business of the University of Chicago* 11 (1938), 51–69.

———. "An Evaluation of Large-Scale Retailing with Emphasis on the Chain Store." *Law and Contemporary Problems* 8 (1941), 348–58.

———. "Price Policies of Food Chains." *Harvard Business Review* 19 (1941), 377–87.

———. "The Supermarket." *Harvard Business Review* 16 (1938), 188–200.

Powers, Elizabeth T., and Nicholas J. Powers. "The Size and Frequency of Price Changes: Evidence from Grocery Stores." *Review of Industrial Organization* 18 (2001), 397–416.

Roat, Evelyn C. "Current Trends in Public Relations." *Public Opinion Quarterly* 3 (1939), 507–15.

Ross, Thomas W. "Store Wars: The Chain Tax Movement." *Journal of Law and Economics* 29 (1986), 125–37.

———. "Winners and Losers Under the Robinson-Patman Act." *Journal of Law and Economics* 27 (1984), 243–71.

Russell, Fred A., R. W. Lyons, and S. M. Flickinger. "The Social and Economic Aspects of Chain Stores." *American Economic Review* 21 (March 1931), 27–36.

Ryant, Carl G. "The South and the Movement Against Chain Stores." *Journal of Southern History* 39 (May 1973), 207–22.

Salmon, Walter J., Robert D. Buzzell, and Stanton G. Cort. "Today the Shopping Center, Tomorrow the Superstore." *Harvard Business Review* 52 (January–February 1974), 89–98.

Sato, Yoshinobu. "Characteristics of the Japanese Supermarket and the Learning Process of Foreign-Affiliated Large Store Retailers." *Japanese Economy* 32 (Fall 2004), 76–91.

Saunders, C. T., and R. E. Crum. "International Comparisons of Productivity Growth in the 1950's." *Journal of the Royal Statistical Society, Series A (General)* 126 (1963), 227–36.

Savir, D., and G. J. Laurer. "The Characteristics and Decidability of the Universal Product Code Symbol." *IBM Systems Journal* 14 (1975), 16–33.

Schapker, Ben L. "Behavior Patterns of Supermarket Shoppers." *Journal of Marketing* 30 (October 1966), 46–49.

Schragger, Richard C. "The Anti-Chain Store Movement, Localist Ideology, and the Remnants of the Progressive Constitution, 1920–1940." *Iowa Law Review* 90 (2005), 101–84.

Shaw, Gareth, Louise Curth, and Andrew Alexander. "Selling Self-Service and the Supermarket: The Americanisation of Food Retailing in Britain, 1945–60." *Business History* 46 (2004), 568–82.

Simms, E. W. "Again, Chain Stores and the Courts." *Virginia Law Review* 26 (1939), 151–67.

Slichter, Sumner H. "The Cream of Wheat Case." *Political Science Quarterly* 31 (1916), 392–412.

Solomon, Benjamin. "Dimensions of Union Growth, 1900–1950." *Industrial and Labor Relations Review* 9 (1956), 544–61.

Stevens, W.H.S. "A Comparison of Special Discounts and Allowances in the Grocery, Drug, and Tobacco Trades." *Journal of Business of the University of Chicago* 7 (1934), 95–105.

Still, Richard R. "Mortality of Seattle Grocery Wholesalers." *Journal of Marketing* 18 (1953), 160–65.

Stout, Donald E. "Research and Control in a Modern Supermarket." *Journal of Industrial Economics* 3 (1954), 60–71.

Tallman, Gerald B. "Retail Innovations Challenge Manufacturers." *Harvard Business Review* 40 (September–October 1962), 130–41.

Taylor, Malcolm D. "Prices in Chain and Independent Grocery Stores in Durham, North Carolina." *Harvard Business Review* 8 (1930), 413–24.

Teitelman, Sam. "Self-Service Meat Retailing in 1950." *Journal of Marketing* 15 (1951), 307–18.

Tomlins, Christopher L. "AFL Unions in the 1930s: Their Performance in Historical Perspective." *Journal of American History* 65 (1979), 1021–42.

Tousley, Rayburn D. "Reducing Distribution Costs in the Grocery Field: A Case Study." *Journal of Marketing* 12 (1948), 455–61.

Troy, Leo. "Trade Union Membership, 1897–1962." *Review of Economics and Statistics* 47 (1965), 93–113.

Vaillant, Derek. "Bare-Knuckled Broadcasting." *Radio Journal: International Studies in Broadcast and Audio Media* 1 (2004), 193–211.

Veit, Helen Zoe. "'We Were a Soft People': Asceticism, Self-Discipline, and American Food Conservation in the First World War." *Food, Culture & Society* 10 (2007), 167–90.

Waller, Spencer Weber. "The Antitrust Legacy of Thurman Arnold." *St. John's Law Review* 78 (2004), 569–613.

Wolff, Reinhold. "The Patman Tax Bill on Chain Stores." *Trade Regulation Review* 2 (1938), 9.

Wood, Donna J. "The Strategic Use of Public Policy: Business Support for the 1906 Food and Drug Act." *Business History Review* 59 (1985), 403–32.

Zundel, Raulston G. "Conflict and Co-operation Among Retail Unions." *Journal of Business* 27 (1954), 301–11.

MANUSCRIPT

Rentz, John A. "The Death of 'Grandma': The Hartfords' Great Atlantic and Pacific Tea Company, A&P" (1983).

DISSERTATIONS AND WORKING PAPERS

"A&P—1972." Harvard Business School Case 9-274-114, 1972.

Bullock, Roy Johnson. "A History of the Chain Grocery Store in the United States." Ph.D. diss., Johns Hopkins University, 1933.

Ellsworth, Lucius F. "Craft to National Industry in the Nineteenth Century." Ph.D. diss., University of Delaware, 1971.

Green, Sedgwick William. "Vertical Integration and the Anti-trust Laws, with Special Reference to the Great Atlantic & Pacific Tea Company." B.A. thesis, Harvard University, 1950.

Hass, Harold M. "Social and Economic Aspects of the Chain Store Movement." Ph.D. diss., University of Minnesota, 1939. Repr., New York: Arno Press, 1979.

Mack, Adam. "Constructing the Supermarket: Grocers, Senses, and the Rise of Modern Food Shopping." Typescript, 2009.

Morelli, Carlo. "The Development of Chain Store Retailing in the US and Britain, 1850–1950." Dundee Discussion Papers in Economics 148, University of Dundee, September 2003.

Morris, Bruce Robert. "The Economics of the Special Taxation of Chain Stores." Ph.D. diss., University of Illinois, 1937. Repr., New York: Arno Press, 1979.

Palmer, Vivien Marie. "History of the Communities." Chicago: University of Chicago, Local Community Research Committee, 1925–30.

Ruenheck, Wilbert Henry. "Business History of the Robert Gair Company, 1864 to 1927." Ph.D. diss., New York University, 1951.

Shideler, Ernest Hugh. "The Chain Store: A Study of the Ecological Organization of a Modern City." Ph.D. diss., University of Chicago, 1927.

Silverman, Roselyn. "Hours of Work in Retail Trade, 1880–1920." Master's thesis, Columbia University, 1950.

GOVERNMENT DOCUMENTS

Hunt, Arthur L. *Fruits and Vegetables, Fish, and Oysters, Canning and Preserving.* Washington, D.C.: Census Bureau, 1902.

Temporary National Economic Committee. *Investigation of Concentration of Economic Power.* Washington, D.C.: U.S. Government Printing Office, 1939.

U.S. Bureau of Labor Statistics. *Retail Prices, 1913 to December 1920.* Washington, D.C.: U.S. Government Printing Office, 1922.

U.S. Bureau of the Census. *Fifteenth Census of the United States, 1930.* Washington, D.C.: U.S. Government Printing Office, 1933.

——. *Fourteenth Census of the United States, 1920.* Washington, D.C.: U.S. Government Printing Office, 1923.

——. *Historical Statistics of the United States, Centennial Edition.* Washington, D.C.: U.S. Government Printing Office, 1976.

U.S. Congress. Joint Commission on Agricultural Inquiry. *Marketing and Distribution.* Washington, D.C.: U.S. Government Printing Office, 1922.

U.S. Department of Commerce. *Census of Distribution.* Mimeo, 1927.

U.S. Federal Trade Commission. *Chain Stores: Cooperative Grocery Chains.* Senate doc. 12, 72nd Cong., 1st sess., 1931.

——. *Chain Stores: Final Report on the Chain-Store Investigation.* Washington, D.C.: U.S. Government Printing Office, 1935.

——. *Chain Stores: Growth and Development of Chain Stores.* Senate doc. 100, 72nd Cong., 1st sess., 1932.

——. *Chain Stores: Scope of the Chain-Store Inquiry.* Senate doc. 31, 72nd Cong., 1st sess., 1931.

——. *Chain Stores: Sources of Chain-Store Merchandise.* Senate doc. 30, 72nd Cong., 1st sess., 1931.

——. *Chain-Store System of Marketing and Distribution.* Senate doc. 146, 71st Cong., 2nd sess., 1930.

——. *Resale Price Maintenance.* House of Representatives doc. 1480, 65th Cong., 3rd sess., December 3, 1918.

——. *A System of Accounts for Retail Merchants.* House of Representatives doc. 1355, 64th Cong., 1st sess., July 15, 1916.

——. *Wholesale Business of Retail Chains.* Senate doc. 29, 72nd Cong., 1st sess., 1931.

——. *Wholesale Marketing of Food.* Washington, D.C.: U.S. Government Printing Office, 1920.

ACKNOWLEDGMENTS

Historical research is not a solitary process. Many people aided my research for *The Great A&P and the Struggle for Small Business in America.* Some were enthusiastic when they heard about the chain-store wars and learned that the old A&P they remembered from childhood was once part of the largest retail enterprise in the world. Others were bemused that anyone would care about grocery stores. All deserve my thanks.

The far-flung repositories of the National Archives and Records Administration were indispensible in researching this book. The details at the heart of *The Great A&P* come from the extensive legal record created in the course of the criminal antitrust trial in *U.S. v. New York Great Atlantic & Pacific.* Those who think the U.S. government is overzealous about sealing public records will not be surprised to learn that the entire case file, including the trial transcript and the thousands of exhibits originally produced in open court in 1945, was considered classified as late as 2009, and was released to me only upon the filing of requests under the Freedom of Information Act. These records are now available for public use, albeit in extremely dirty cartons, at the National Archives in College Park, Maryland, and I thank James R. Mathis and Heather MacRae for arranging their release. Duplicates of some of the trial materials are also available at the National Archives and Records Administration's Great Lakes Region archives in Chicago, where Scott M. Forsythe and Donald W. Jackanicz assisted me; for reasons known only to the muses, those materials were never classified.

At the National Archives' Center for Legislative Archives in Washington, D.C., Rodney A. Ross helped me locate congressional documents related to the chain-store controversies. The staff of the National Archives' New York branch found Civil War–era records concerning both George H. Hartford and George F. Gilman; and Georgia Higley, head of the newspaper section at the Library of Congress, gave me access to periodicals that are critical to understanding commodity markets in the Civil War era. Archivists at the Franklin D. Roosevelt Presidential Library in Hyde Park, especially Virginia Lewick, guided me through a mass of relevant records. Wright Patman's papers are at the Lyndon B. Johnson Presidential Library in Austin, Texas, where Bob Tissing was my navigator.

In New Jersey, Avis Anderson went out of her way to help me with materials from the Hartford Family Foundation's collection. George H. Hartford is all but forgotten in Orange, but Doris Walker, former director of the Orange Public Library, came up with microfilms of local newspapers and historical materials. Bob Leach of the Jersey City Public Library provided materials about A&P's headquarters complex there. Father Augustine Curley, O.S.B., of St. Benedict's Preparatory School in Newark, located early yearbooks mentioning George L. Hartford. In New York, the staffs of the New-York Historical Society and the New York Public Library's manuscripts division helped me delve into the tea and leather trades in the 1850s. Mary Witkowski of the Bridgeport Public Library sent me articles about George F. Gilman, and even found photos of him. My thanks also to Kathy Maher of the Barnum Museum in Bridgeport—although my hunch that Gilman and P. T. Barnum knew each other personally remains only a hunch.

Claire Uziel of the Jewish Historical Society of Greater Washington helped me with that organization's collection of oral histories related to Jewish grocers. Debbie Vaughan, archivist at the Chicago History Museum, led me to a wealth of information on the food trade. David Kessler of the Bancroft Library at the University of California at Berkeley came up with oral histories and other documents related to the grocery business in the early decades of the twentieth century. Sarah Ticer, an intern at the Dolph Briscoe Center for American History at the University of Texas, arranged for me to use Sam Rayburn's papers. In the midst of major renovation, the staff of the Texas State Library and Archives located documents related to that state's chain-store debates in the 1930s.

Domenica Carriere of the Archives and Special Collections Department, Noel Memorial Library, at Louisiana State University in Shreveport, W. K. Henderson's hometown, sent me transcripts of anti-chain broadcasts on KWKH. Sharon Sumpter, an archivist at the University of Notre Dame in South Bend, Indiana, furnished a copy of one of Henderson's broadcasts. I also wish to record my thanks to Jocelyn K. Wilk of the Columbia University Archives; Debbie Greeson of the Kansas Historical Society; Edwin Frank and Chris Ratliff of the Special Collections Department at the University of Memphis library; and Marcia Stentz of the Hudson's Bay Company Archives. Barry Herbert, deputy librarian of the Seventh Circuit Court of Appeals in Chicago, sought out pictures of Judge Walter Lindley, and Becky Woodrum of the U.S. bankruptcy court in Danville, Illinois, gave me a tour of the building where the 1945 antitrust trial was held.

I received suggestions and helpful leads from Tracey Deutsch, Hasia Diner, Joshua Freeman, Thomas Kessner, Nelson Lichtenstein, Terri Lonier, David Nasaw, and Helen Veit, and from participants at meetings of the American Historical Society and the Business History Conference. The guidance of my agent, Ted Weinstein, and of Thomas LeBien, my editor at Farrar, Straus and Giroux, was vital. I owe a special debt to Margaret Cannella for getting me interested in the grocery trade in the first place.

This book is dedicated to my father, Harry Levinson, who long ago wrote an article for executives titled "Don't Choose Your Own Successor." Unfortunately, his advice came too late for the Hartfords.

INDEX